The Cornish in the Caribbean

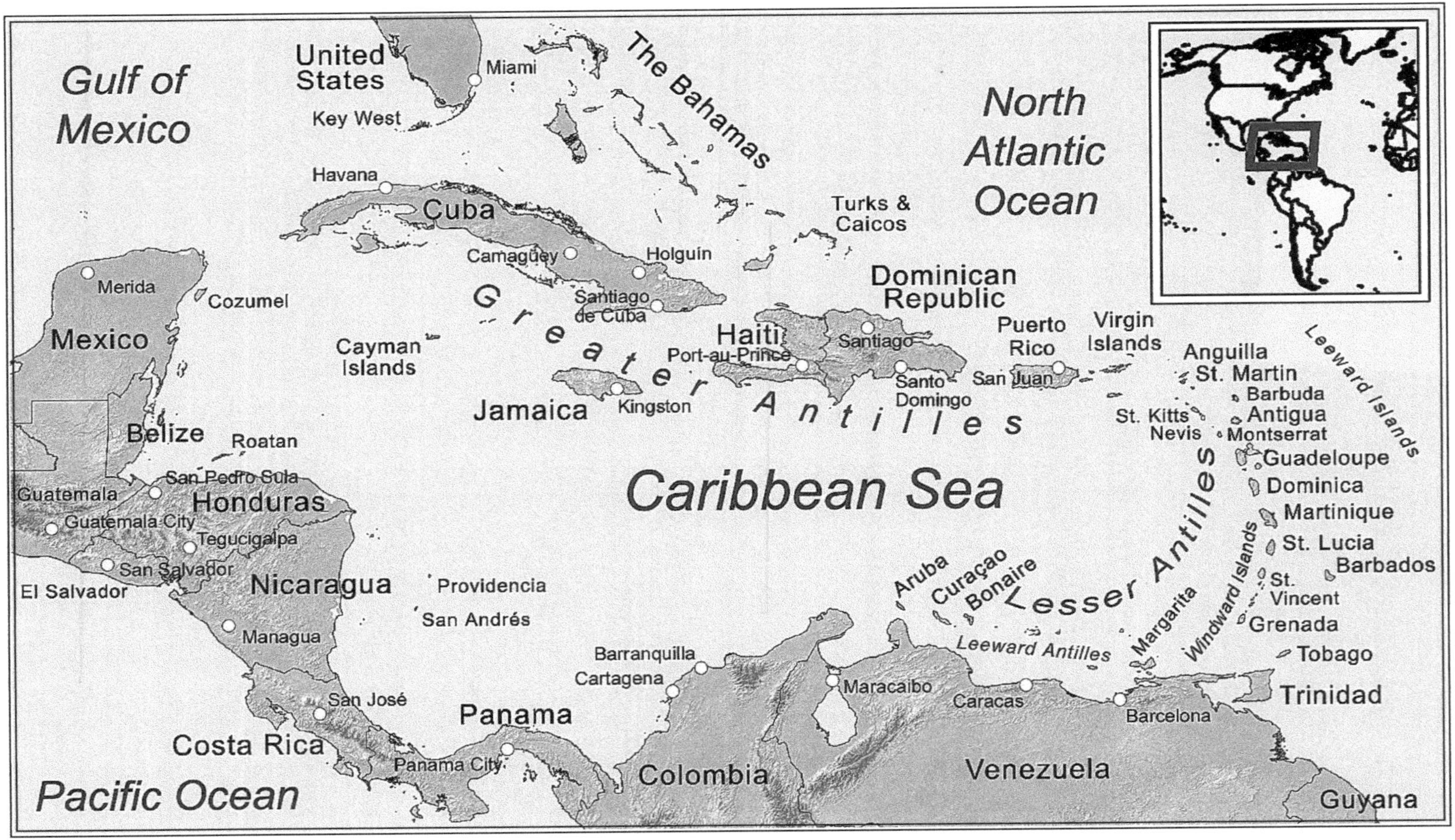
Gulf of Mexico
United States
Miami
Key West
The Bahamas
North Atlantic Ocean
Havana
Cuba
Turks & Caicos
Camagüey
Holguín
Merida
Cozumel
Santiago de Cuba
Dominican Republic
Greater Antilles
Mexico
Cayman Islands
Haiti
Port-au-Prince
Santiago
Santo Domingo
Puerto Rico
San Juan
Virgin Islands
Anguilla
St. Martin
Barbuda
Antigua
St. Kitts
Nevis
Montserrat
Leeward Islands
Guadeloupe
Dominica
Martinique
St. Lucia
Barbados
St. Vincent
Grenada
Tobago
Trinidad
Windward Islands
Jamaica
Kingston
Belize
Roatan
San Pedro Sula
Guatemala
Honduras
Guatemala City
Tegucigalpa
San Salvador
El Salvador
Nicaragua
Providencia
San Andrés
Managua
Caribbean Sea
Aruba
Curaçao
Bonaire
Lesser Antilles
Leeward Antilles
Margarita
Barranquilla
Cartagena
Maracaibo
Caracas
Barcelona
San José
Panama
Costa Rica
Panama City
Colombia
Venezuela
Guyana
Pacific Ocean

The CORNISH *in the* CARIBBEAN

From the 17th to the 19th Centuries

Sue Appleby

Copyright © 2023 Sue Appleby
Reprinted with minor revisions from the 2019 hardback edition

The moral right of the author has been asserted.

Apart from any fair dealing for the purposes of research or private study, or criticism or review, as permitted under the Copyright, Designs and Patents Act 1988, this publication may only be reproduced, stored or transmitted, in any form or by any means, with the prior permission in writing of the publishers, or in the case of reprographic reproduction in accordance with the terms of licences issued by the Copyright Licensing Agency. Enquiries concerning reproduction outside those terms should be sent to the publishers.

All images used are from Wikimedia Commons and, unless otherwise noted, are in the Public Domain

Matador
9 Priory Business Park,
Wistow Road, Kibworth Beauchamp,
Leicestershire. LE8 0RX
Tel: 0116 279 2299
Email: books@troubador.co.uk
Web: www.troubador.co.uk/matador
Twitter: @matadorbooks

ISBN 9781803137308

British Library Cataloguing in Publication Data.
A catalogue record for this book is available from the British Library.

Printed and bound by CPI Group (UK) Ltd, Croydon, CR0 4YY
Typeset in 12pt Adobe Jenson Pro by Troubador Publishing Ltd, Leicester, UK

Matador is an imprint of Troubador Publishing Ltd

For my brother,
John Appleby (1928–2017),
with love and respect.

Contents

Foreword ix

Acknowledgements xii

Introduction xv

1. The British Leeward Islands — 1
2. Jamaica and the Cayman Islands — 33
3. In Defence of the Empire — 69
4. The Falmouth Packet Service — 103
5. Barbados, the British Windward Islands and Trinidad — 127
6. Gold and Diamonds: the Mines of British Guiana and Aruba — 156
7. Men of God: Methodist Missionaries — 184
8. Gold and Copper: The Mines of Cuba and the Dominican Republic — 205
9. Copper and Guano: The Mines of Virgin Gorda and Sombrero — 233

Appendix 1	BACKGROUND HISTORY OF THE BRITISH LEEWARD ISLANDS	259
Appendix 2	INDENTURED CORNISHMEN WHO SAILED FROM PLYMOUTH TO ST. CHRISTOPHER IN 1634	264
Appendix 3	BACKGROUND HISTORY OF JAMAICA AND THE CAYMAN ISLANDS	266
Appendix 4	MAJOR MILITARY CONFLICTS THAT IMPACTED THE CARIBBEAN DURING THE 18TH AND 19TH CENTURIES	270
Appendix 5	BACKGROUND HISTORY OF BARBADOS, THE WINDWARD ISLANDS AND TRINIDAD	274
Appendix 6	BACKGROUND HISTORY OF BRITISH GUIANA AND ARUBA	278
Appendix 7	THE EARLY HISTORY OF METHODISM AND THE DEVELOPMENT OF ITS POPULARITY IN CORNWALL	285
Appendix 8	BACKGROUND HISTORY OF CUBA AND THE DOMINICAN REPUBLIC	289
Appendix 9	BACKGROUND HISTORY OF VIRGIN GORDA	297
Bibliography		301
Index		335

Foreword

Cornwall, at the southwestern end of Britain, is not just another English county. With only one land border, the River Tamar which divides it from Devon, it is, as Sue Appleby writes, almost an island with its three sea coasts. There always was, and still is, a distinct Cornish 'ethnic' identity, forged through its unique history, its language, and its Celtic culture. Indeed, in 2014 the Cornish people were recognized under EU law as a distinct, minority ethnic group. Cornish, a Celtic language with similarities to Breton, Welsh and Gaelic, was a living language up to the late 1700s. As a result of efforts to revive it, an estimated 300 people now speak it fluently, and it was recognized as a minority language of the UK in 2002. Anglo-Cornish was a distinct variant of English at least up to the early 1900s. Cornwall's economy was traditionally based on mining (tin and copper), fishing, sea-faring, smuggling and wrecking—activities which have entered into British popular culture through the novels by Daphne du Maurier (and the movies made of them) and the TV series *Poldark*, based on the twelve books by Winston Graham.

Historians of the Caribbean have long been aware of the important role played in the British islands by another, even more distinctive ethnic group, the Scots. After the Act of Union in 1707, the inhabitants of the small and impoverished former kingdom grasped the opportunities offered by the expanding empire, especially the West Indian islands. The eminent historian Richard Sheridan published a pioneering article on 'the role of the Scots in the economy and society of the West Indies' in 1977, and full-length books followed, like A. Karras, *Sojourners in the Sun: Scottish Migrants in Jamaica and the Chesapeake, 1740–1800* (1992), T. M. Devine, *Scotland's Empire: The Origins of the Global Diaspora* (2004), and Douglas Hamilton, *Scotland, the Caribbean and the Atlantic World, 1750–1820* (2005). Scottish surnames and place names are all over the English-speaking Caribbean.

But, though there is considerable literature on the Cornish Diaspora, the Caribbean has been largely omitted from it. This is the gap filled by Sue Appleby's meticulously researched and very readable book. It tells the stories of the many, and very diverse, Cornish men and women who went to the Caribbean, and worked, exploited and fought (and sometimes died) there, over a span of nearly three centuries starting in the 1630s.

Some were wealthy plantation owners who made fortunes out of the labour of enslaved Africans who they owned. In Jamaica, Britain's biggest West Indian colony and the most profitable until after 1807, the Price dynasty belonged to the elite of planters and slave-owners. Rose Price, who died in 1834 just as slavery was abolished, combined his Jamaican plantation business with an active involvement in the public and economic life of Cornwall. (When Jamaica was divided into three counties in 1758, one was called Cornwall, with its chief town named for the Cornish port of Falmouth.) Another such Cornish planter and slave-owning dynasty was the Mathew family, which owned estates in several islands in the 1700s, including Antigua and Tobago. At the other end of the social scale, many Cornish men and women came to the early English colonies like St Kitts and Barbados as indentured servants in the 1600s, shipping from the West Country port of Bristol to lives little better than those of the enslaved Africans.

Cornish men were active in the armed services, taking part in the innumerable sea and land battles through which the Western European powers vied for supremacy in the Caribbean and the Atlantic. Others were missionaries, especially Methodist clergy coming to evangelise the enslaved people from the late 1700s—Methodism was especially strong in Cornwall, particularly among mining families. They worked in many of the islands, British, Danish, Swedish and Dutch.

Appleby shows how the heritage and occupational skills traditional in Cornwall were applied to the West Indies. For instance, a lively trade developed between Penzance and Jamaica in the 1770s with the main commodity being salted Cornish pilchards. Sea-faring had always been crucial to the Cornish economy, and many younger sons of the gentry in the 1700s and 1800s joined the Royal Navy as officers, seeing action in the

Caribbean in the protracted conflicts with Holland, Spain and France. The Pellews were the outstanding Cornish naval dynasty of the period. Others worked in the merchant marine, like the 'Packet Captains' who commanded the sailing ships of the Falmouth packet service which took the mail to and from the Caribbean in the 1700s and up to 1823. It ran two services, one to Jamaica, and one to Barbados and the Leeward Islands.

But the most striking transfer of Cornish skills to the Caribbean was to be found in mining. As the Cornish tin and copper mines declined, and often closed, in the middle decades of the nineteenth century, the 'Great Emigration' of miners and their families got underway. They went all over the world, often to work in the very overseas mines which had put them out of employment at home, mines that could produce metals more cheaply than the older Cornish ones that had been worked for centuries. Appleby follows Cornish mining engineers, foremen and labourers to mines in Jamaica in the 1840s/50s, to guano mining on Sombrero Island near Anguilla in the 1860s to 1880s, to copper mines on Virgin Gorda in the British Virgin Islands in the mid-nineteenth century, to gold and diamond mining in British Guiana in the 1880s, 1890s and early 1900s, to gold mining on Dutch Aruba in the late 1800s, and to Cuba for copper mining around the same period. These men, often accompanied by women and children, were highly mobile, as they had to be, for many of these Caribbean mining ventures lasted only a few years. Though the underground workers, and the engineers and 'mine captains', were all men, some women did work at surface jobs in these West Indian mining operations. Besides the expertise and personnel, much of the equipment and machinery also came from Cornwall.

This book makes an original and valuable contribution to the literature on the Cornish Diaspora, and to the historiography of the Caribbean. And its focus on the many human stories of Cornish people in the islands makes it a readable and engaging study.

Bridget Brereton
University of the West Indies, St Augustine
Trinidad & Tobago
August 2018

Acknowledgements

Researching and writing about the Cornish in the Caribbean has taken me on a long journey. In the literal sense, I travelled from Antigua to Cornwall, and also from Antigua to the British Virgin Islands, Barbados, Jamaica, St. Kitts and Nevis, and Trinidad and Tobago. The journey in search of the information I needed was also long. I used a wide range of sources: 19th-century British colonial records, the development plans of environmental non-government organisations, maritime history, social histories of the Caribbean, investment company archives, the diary of a Cornish miner in Cuba, family histories, mining company information on mineral deposits, newspaper archives, and information gleaned from conversations with experts in various fields. For helping me complete my journey, I have many to thank.

At home in Antigua, Michelle Henry, Chris Waters, and the library staff at the Museum of Antigua and Barbuda provided useful references; author Joanne Hillhouse helped me to tighten up my story, while Susan Lowes, professor at Teachers College, Columbia University, and a researcher into the history of the Eastern Caribbean, gave me guidance on the chapter titled 'The British Leeward Islands', and encouraged me to persevere with rewrites.

In Cornwall, I found a wealth of information thanks to Angela Broome at the Courtney Library, Claire Morgan at the Cornish Studies Centre, the volunteers at the Cornwall Family History Society, the staff at the Cornwall Record Office and the volunteers at the Bartlett Library, National Maritime Museum Cornwall, and the Morrab Library. Roy Bluett added to my information about the Price family of Penzance and Jamaica. A special thank you is due to Tony Pawlyn, head of research at the Bartlett Library, for reading the chapters 'The Falmouth Packet

Service' and 'In Defence of the Empire' and for his valuable insights and comments. Polly Attwood at the Hypatia Trust put me in contact with Tehmina Goskar, consultant curator and heritage interpreter, who in turn put me in contact with Leslie Trotter, then a PhD student at the University of Exeter Institute of Cornish Studies, and with Chris Evans, professor of history at the University of South Wales, both of whom generously shared their research with me. I also much appreciate Chris taking the time to read, and comment on, 'Gold and Copper: The Mines of Cuba and the Dominican Republic' and 'Copper and Guano: The Mines of Virgin Gorda and Sombrero'. As in earlier visits to Cornwall, Mike and Averil Inglefield provided me with both useful information and hospitality.

In London, Paula Togher from the Baring Archive was very cooperative in scanning and emailing me information.

During the time I spent on Tortola and Virgin Gorda in the British Virgin Islands, the assistance of Deirdre Potter, National Parks Trust, Jennifer Flemming-Henry, National Archives and Records Management Unit, and the staff at the Library Services Department, Caribbean Studies Unit, was much appreciated. It was good to spend time with Bernadine Louis and Peter Moll, colleagues from library days and both useful sources of information. To Peter I owe special thanks for accompanying me to the Copper Mine on Virgin Gorda and for completing some research for me at the National Archives.

In Barbados, Karen Proverbs at the Department of Archives and Harriet Pierce at the Shilstone Memorial Library, Barbados Museum & Historical Society, provided me with useful documents and guidance, as did Victoria O'Flaherty at the National Archives in St Kitts and Sarita Francis at the Montserrat National Trust.

On Nevis, Gennifer Broadbelt at the Nevis Historical and Conservation Society, Adella Meade at the Nevis Public Library, and Lashawn Liburd and Richard Lupinacci at the Hermitage went out of their way to provide me with information and contacts.

In Trinidad, the staff at the Heritage Library, National Library and Information System Authority gave me access to a wide range of regional resources, while the research staff at the National Library of Jamaica provided me with useful information that I would not otherwise have sourced. Gabrielle Fernandes at the Susan Craig-James Heritage Library in Tobago helped me to find information about Cornish planters on Tobago, and was a pleasure to work with.

Cordel Matthews, Archivist at the National Public Library, Archives and Documentation Services in St Vincent and the Grenadines sent me links to information that I would otherwise have missed.

The Rev. Dr John C. Neal and Cedric Appleby – as far as I know, not a relation of mine – both helped me find hard-to-source information on some of the Cornish Methodist missionaries who worked in the Caribbean.

Flynn Warmington, George Waterman, Wesley Johnston, David Gaunt, Kate Crombie, Heather Wilkie and Cherryl Head all generously shared information from their family tree research.

Caroline Petherick did an excellent job of copy editing, adding in some local Cornish information that was new to me as she went through my manuscript while the expert team at Troubador Publishing / Matador guided me smoothly through the publication process.

In conclusion, a huge thank you to Bridget Brereton, Professor Emerita of History at the St Augustine Campus of the University of the West Indies, Trinidad, who read through each chapter as I completed the first draft and made valuable comments concerning the accuracy of the information I researched.

Sue Appleby
Antigua, 2018

Introduction

My interest in writing about the connection between Cornish men and women and the Caribbean developed while I was researching and writing about my mother's family. During the 19th century, as part of Cornwall's 'Great Emigration,' they dispersed from Towan Farm near Porthpean, on the south Cornish coast, to as far away as Tasmania and South Africa and to as near as Hackney, London.[1] During my visits to Cornwall, historians, librarians and researchers remarked to me that while much had been written about the Cornish diaspora in most parts of the world, the Caribbean had mostly been left out; as I was in some small part Cornish and had spent my adult life in the Caribbean, why didn't I write something? I decided to take up the challenge. Philip Payton's *The Cornish Overseas: a History of Cornwall's 'Great Emigration'* (2005) gave me an excellent general introduction to the 19th century emigration of Cornish miners, while Sharron P. Schwartz's *The Cornish in Latin America: 'Cousin Jack' and the New World* (2016) provided a detailed account of the Cornish contribution to the 19th century development of Latin American mining resources, including those of Cuba and Virgin Gorda.

Britain's Caribbean colonies were, and often still are, referred to as 'The West Indies', but as I have also written about the one-time Spanish possessions of Cuba and the Dominican Republic and, to an extent, the once-French colony of Haiti, I have throughout used the more inclusive term 'Caribbean'.

While I researched 19th-century Cornish miners as they travelled to all parts of the Caribbean mining world in search of employment, I broadened my scope to include the early days of European settlement, when Cornish men and women were among those who came to the

---

1   Now available in a new edition: Appleby, Sue. *The Hammers of Towan: A Nineteenth-Century Cornish Family.* 2nd ed. Kibworth Beauchamp: Troubador, 2021.

Caribbean. One of the earliest known to me is the Puritan Reverend Nicholas Leverton, who left St Endellion near Padstow for Barbados in 1634. For a time he lived on the island of Providence, where the goal of the Providence Island Company was to establish its colony as the leading Puritan settlement in the New World. Another early settler, Abednego Mathew, was a Royalist in the days of Cromwell's Commonwealth, and may well have chosen to leave England for a distant Caribbean shore; in Mathew's case his destination was St Christopher, one of the Leeward Islands. Some of the Monmouth Rebellion's Cornish supporters also left for the Caribbean after their defeat in 1685; a few of those came by choice while the less fortunate were made prisoners of war and shipped out to the colonies as indentured labourers, where few of them survived for long.

Some Cornishmen supported the Parliamentarians and, under orders from Cromwell to take the island of Hispaniola from Spain, sailed to the Caribbean with Admiral Penn and General Venables. However, the English invading force failed in its objective and its commanders, unwilling to return home and face Cromwell after defeat, turned their attention towards the poorly defended Spanish island of Jamaica. The English fleet succeeded in taking Jamaica, and some members of the invasion force, including Cornishman Francis Price, decided to stay on. Many of these early Caribbean settlers became successful sugar planters and, like Abednego Mathew's family (at first on St Christopher, but later purchasing additional estates in Antigua and Tobago), expanded their property by acquiring estates on other British-owned islands.

As the wealthy planters increasingly left their plantations in the care of managers and returned to the 'Mother Country', few whose origins lay in Cornwall chose to settle back in their home county. Instead, they much preferred to purchase their new country estates within easy reach of London, where they could exercise their influence on political developments and help to ensure that events favoured the interests of the plantocracy. The Bristol area was another popular choice, as many of the planters had business interests relating to the trade in sugar and slaves based in Bristol, a port city with the added attraction of being conveniently near to the sophisticated entertainments of Bath.

Britain had to defend its Caribbean colonies from rival European powers, including Spain, France and the Dutch Republic, and Cornishmen such as the admirals Edward Boscawen, Christopher Cole and Charles Penrose, who had grown up near to the sea and had learnt sailing skills at an early age, made a notable contribution to the Royal Navy's manpower on the Jamaica and Leeward Island Stations. Royal Navy ships often anchored in the Cornish deep-water harbour of Falmouth where, in the days of sail, the port's far-westerly position gave them clear access to the open sea and the Trade Winds, which would carry them to the Caribbean. The Falmouth packet service was stationed at Falmouth for the same reason, and was the chief means of communication between Britain and her colonial possessions in the Caribbean.

In the early 19th century, John Wesley's Methodist form of Christianity became increasingly popular in Cornwall: his local preachers spread the simple message that redemption was available to all, and that living standards could be improved through self-help. The Methodists' missionary spirit naturally led to the development of overseas missions, and under the influence of Dr Thomas Coke the Caribbean was one of the first regions to receive missionaries. As Methodism was so widespread in Cornwall, many of the missionaries were from that area, and their experience of working with Cornish communities of miners, fishermen and agricultural labourers, many of whom felt marginalised by society, gave those missionaries a special understanding of the skills needed to minister to the slaves and free coloured people of the Caribbean.

From about the middle of the 19th century, Cornish miners began to travel out to the Caribbean, especially to the copper mines of Cuba and Virgin Gorda, but also to what was then British Guiana, to Jamaica, Aruba, to the Dominican Republic, and to islets such as Sombrero. Economic factors were the driving force behind this migration, as the mining industry in Cornwall was by this time in decline. Cornish mineral reserves were beginning to run out and the price of copper crashed, while there was increased competition from overseas mining developments. New resources of gold, silver and copper were being discovered, and new mines were opening from Australia to South Africa, from the United

States to Bolivia, and from Mexico to the Caribbean. Paradoxically, as international competition caused unemployment in Cornish mines, the overseas mines provided new employment opportunities, as Cornish miners, whose hard-rock mining skills were much sought after by overseas mining companies, found new work overseas. The new companies were willing to offer better pay than the local mines, and employed agents to recruit men from Cornwall. One such recruit was Alfred Jenkin, based in Redruth, who was employed for several years by one of the El Cobre mines in Cuba.

Miners often travelled alone to their new place of employment, either because they were single or because they preferred to leave their family in Cornwall and remit part of their wages back home. Some miners sent for their family once they were settled, while others married into the local community. Virgin Gorda was an exception, as some of the miners from St Austell brought their spouses with them when they first came to the island. Here the wives were employed, as they had been in Cornwall, as surface workers or 'bal maidens' (from the Cornish word 'bal' meaning a mine and the English word 'maiden' meaning a young or unmarried woman), a term that disguises the grindingly hard work they did. At the end of their contract, or if the mining enterprise failed, the miners usually returned to Cornwall, although their stay was often temporary. Many, like Mine Captain Frederick Gribble, who had worked in the United States, Australia and Venezuela before going out to British Guiana, or Mine Captain Benjamin Rule, who had worked in Mexico and the United States before being employed on Aruba, went back and forth between Cornwall and whichever overseas mine needed their expertise.

As my research progressed, I was increasingly struck by certain similarities between Cornwall and many of the islands of the Caribbean. Surrounded on three sides by the sea, and on the fourth side by the River Tamar, Cornwall is almost an island: Cornish people still talk about going 'over to England', or 'up-country', as if theirs is somehow a place apart, and many Cornish people, like island people, grow up familiar with the ways of the sea, often earning their living from fishing or in the marine trades.

In the days of the Great Emigration, Cornish women were often left behind by their departing men. The women had to be independent, look after the family and fend for themselves – just like Caribbean women, who also saw their men leave home to make a living: Jamaican men for example went to dig the Panama Canal and to build the railway that runs from the coast up into the Andes in Ecuador. And just as some Caribbean women joined their men at their various places of employment, so did some Cornish women. When Cornishman John Holman began work at the El Cobre mines in Cuba, he was accompanied by his wife Amelia. She had already lived with him in South America, where she had given birth to a daughter, and in Jamaica, where she had another daughter, before adding a third daughter and a son to the family during her stay in Cuba. Somehow, Amelia managed to bring up a family of four children in a variety of communities and in far from ideal conditions. A strong woman.

For readers who are interested in the history of the Caribbean, the major military conflicts that impacted the Caribbean during the 18th and 19th centuries, and the early history of Methodism and the development of its popularity in Cornwall, I have written about these in the appendices that you will find at the end of this book.

The research I have undertaken for this project has been wide-ranging and has produced many files of information and references that would benefit from further study. but rather than attempting to be comprehensive in my approach, to bring the Cornish in the Caribbean to life, I have opted to focus on people and events that have a story to tell. Please enjoy the story.

Sue Appleby
Antigua, 2018

1

The British Leeward Islands[1]

The voyage across the Atlantic from Plymouth had been long and uncomfortable, and when the Cornishmen aboard the *Robert Bonaventure* came ashore on the Caribbean island of St Christopher in 1634 there was little to remind them of home. All twenty-one were husbandmen or agricultural labourers used to working the land, but none had any experience of growing the crops on which the economy of St Christopher depended: tobacco, sea island cotton, spices, indigo and arrowroot – crops that needed a regular supply of labour if they were to be grown profitably. All the men had sailed as indentured labourers, recruited by individual merchants or ships' masters. Back in England, there had been no shortage of those willing to provide their labour and give up their freedom for a period of between three and ten years to work for a settler in one of the colonies. In exchange for the labourers' work, the settler had agreed to pay their passage, maintain them for the duration of their contract and, if they completed their contract, supply them with £10 in cash or with land or tobacco worth an equivalent amount. As sugar became a major crop, it was also used as a means of payment.[2]

The men on the *Robert Bonaventure* came from all over Cornwall, many of them in their twenties, and had set sail in February 1634. Two of the men, Rawleigh Edye from Bodmin and Anthony Pearse from St Breock, were only fifteen years old. Another two, Christopher Carter,

---

1 See Appendix 1 for a background history of the British Leeward Islands.
2 Button, Andrea. *The trade in white labour in 17th century Bristol*. Accessed 10 October 2015, http:humanities,uwe.ac.uk/bhr/Main/white_labour/servants.htm

probably from St Giles on the Heath, and Nicholas Dabbin from St Stephens, were mature men, in their forties.[3] Later the same year, another twenty Cornishmen, again mostly husbandmen, embarked for St Christopher, this time on the *Margaret*.[4] Many of these men were also in their twenties, although one, Samuell Purfroy from St Ives, was only thirteen.[5] No women are listed, even though women are estimated to have made up about 25 per cent of the migrants.[6]

Setting out with high hopes of making a good life for themselves in a new colony, the migrants often worked under deplorable conditions:[7] the work was hard and the food poor, and most worked as field hands under the control of an overseer who beat them as he saw fit. They encountered diseases such as yellow fever, malaria and dysentery which were easily caught and usually fatal. In addition, they could be bought and sold, and were not allowed to marry without the permission of their owner, so some tried to escape, only to be hunted down and brought before the courts.[8] Research into primary and secondary sources has so far not found any further reference to any of the men listed. Did Thomas Pollard and Martin Rooby – both aged twenty-three and from Gwinear, so most likely friends – manage to make a better life for themselves? What happened to Anthony Pearse and Samuell Purfroy, who had set out on a new adventure at such a young age? Were Francis and Robert Pedlar, both from St Breock, brothers? If so, did they manage to complete their indentures and return home? How did the middle-aged Christopher Carter and Nicholas Dabbin adapt to the demands of labouring in a heat to which they were certainly not accustomed? Perhaps the records

---

3   Cooper, Cliff. 'Barbados connection.' *Cornwall Family History Society Journal*, p.7. (No.79, March 1996).
4   Ibid., p.7.
5   See Appendix 2 for a full listing of indentured Cornishmen sent to St Christopher in 1634.
6   Button, Andrea. *The trade in white labour in 17th century Bristol*. Accessed 10 October 2015, http:humanities,uwe.ac.uk/bhr/Main/white_labour/servants.htm
7   Conditions were similar throughout the Caribbean. See Beckles, Hilary McD. *White servitude and black slavery in Barbados 1627–1715*. Knoxville: University of Tennessee Press, 1989, for an in-depth study of the conditions of both indentured labourers and slaves.
8   Schwartz, Sharron P. *The Cornish in Latin America: 'Cousin Jack' and the New World*. Wicklow: The Cornubian Press, 2016, p.274.

were incomplete, or were lost, or perhaps none out of the forty-one men and boys from those two ships survived. Although many, as the lists of Cornishmen sent to St Christopher show, were indentured in the prime of life, the survival rates were low and an estimated 50 to 75 per cent of indentured labourers died before their indenture was completed.[9]

The indentured labourers who survived and had opted to be paid in land seldom succeeded in making their smallholdings pay. The piece of land was too small, and they did not possess the means to hire the labour they needed to develop their property, especially when sugar, whose cultivation needed substantial investment in both land and labour, began to replace the sea island cotton, spices, indigo and arrowroot which had first been grown. So the survivors of contract labour usually either continued as labourers, worked as overseers or became artisans.[10]

Some of the labourers, especially vagrants, criminals, and prisoners of war, had been indentured against their will. During the English Civil Wars (1642–1651) Oliver Cromwell's forces took many Royalist prisoners, who were sent off to the Leeward Islands. Then, after the failure of the 1685 Monmouth Rebellion, supporters of the Duke of Monmouth were added to their number. Monmouth had many Cornish supporters – the rebellion was also known as the 'Revolt of the West' or the 'West Country Rebellion' – and some of the rebels were among those indentured.[11]

One Cornishman who left home around the middle of the 17th century was Abednego Mathew (about 1633–1681). He, however, was no indentured labourer but a member of a well-established Cornish family,

---

9   Button, Andrea. *The trade in white labour in 17th century Bristol.* Accessed 10 October 2015, http:humanities,uwe.ac.uk/bhr/Main/white_labour/servants.htm
10 Ibid.
11 The Monmouth Rebellion was an attempt to overthrow James II, who had become King of England, Scotland and Ireland upon the death of his elder brother, Charles II, on 6 February 1685. James was a Roman Catholic, and the many Protestants under his rule opposed his succession. James Scott, 1st Duke of Monmouth, the eldest of Charles II's many illegitimate sons, claimed that he was the rightful heir to the throne and attempted to overthrow James.

and could trace his roots back to the Glamorganshire earls of Llandaff.[12] Born at Pennytenny, St Kew, on the north coast of Cornwall, he joined the army at an early age, rising to the rank of colonel. Probably a Royalist, at some time in his early adult life he thought it wise to leave Cornwall and set sail for the Leewards, where he obtained grants of land on Antigua and St Christopher. A newcomer to the islands, he increased his standing in the local community when he married Susannah Sparrow, a wealthy heiress from St Christopher. As colonel of the local militia, and captain of a company of the king's troops, he was in part responsible for maintaining order and defending the island, and by 1671 he had been made Deputy Governor of St Christopher, an influential post. A certain Mrs Lanaghan, always a reliable reporter of the inside story or contemporary gossip, thought Mathew had been appointed to the position 'through the interest (it is supposed) of his second cousin, George, Duke of Albemarle... which situation he honourably filled until his death, 18 April, 1681.'[13] This is quite possible, as Mathew may well have known the Duke of Albemarle, who was both a West Country man and a Royalist. Albemarle would later play an important part in the restoration of the monarchy.

By the time Abednego Mathew died in 1681, sugar production was largely replacing all the other crops in the Leeward Islands, and the supply of indentured labour could no longer meet the demand for production. So the labourers were gradually replaced by slaves from Africa, who had been traded into the Caribbean by the Dutch since the early part of the 17th century.

Abednego Mathew's son William Mathew I (1665–1705), the first of several members of the family so named,[14] was born on St. Christopher. As a young man he moved to England where he joined the Coldstream

---

12   Much of the information on the Mathew family was sourced from: Oliver, Vere Langford. *The history of the island of Antigua: one of the Leeward Caribees in the West Indies, from the first settlement in 1635 to the present time.* Vol.2. London: Mitchell and Hughes, 1896, pp.252–258.
13   *Antigua and the Antiguans: a full account of the Colony and its inhabitants from the time of the Caribs to the present day interspersed with anecdotes and legends.* Vol.2. St John's: Antiguan Publishing Trust, 1980, p.337. Work attributed to a Mrs. Flannigan or Lanaghan, first published in 1844.
14   The various William Mathews are identified by naming them I, II and III. Later in the chapter, the same is done for the Daniel Mathews and for the Parsons family of Montserrat.

Guards and rose to the rank of colonel. He married well, to the wealthy Katherine Remee, Baroness van Lamput, and for a time the couple lived on St Christopher, where Katherine gave birth to a daughter, Louisa, and a son, William (William II). In 1702, William I, back in England, was made Brigadier-General of Her Majesty's Guards, and two years later he was appointed Captain-General and Governor-in-Chief of the Leeward Islands. Accompanied by his wife, he set sail for Antigua, but he was not long in office, for he died on 4 December in the following year.

William Mathew I's son, William Mathew II (1684–1752) spent his youth on St Christopher. Like his father he left for England as a young man and, continuing the family tradition, joined the Coldstream Guards, where he superseded his father's achievement by attaining the rank of general. In about 1710 he married Anne Hill, the daughter of General Thomas Hill, who had been Deputy Governor of St Kitts. Anne died soon after their marriage, and William then married Anne Smith, daughter of the Hon. Daniel Smith, President of the Nevis Council, and Deputy Governor of Nevis from 1712 to 1722. On her father's death, Anne inherited valuable estates in St Christopher, Nevis and Antigua, so once again the Mathew family increased their wealth and standing in the local community through marriage. Anne gave birth to five children,[15] and after her death in 1730 William married a third time, to Margaret Garnier, with whom he had one son.[16]

For most of his adult life William Mathew II was involved in the administration of the Leeward Islands. In 1714 he acted as Governor of the Leeward Islands for a year, and in 1715 he became Lieutenant-Governor of St Christopher. During his tenure he was given the task, along with the other appointed commissioners, of disposing of the lands on the French-owned part of St Christopher which had been given to Britain by the 1713 Treaty of Utrecht. Under the treaty it had been agreed that these French lands, totalling about 16,000 acres: 'shall be sold at the best advantage'.[17]

---

15   Ibid., p.338.
16   Archives Wales. *Glamorgan Archives Mathew family of St Kew, Cornwall, and the Caribbean islands papers*. Accessed 12 October 2015, http://www.archiveswales.org.uk/anw/get_collection.php?inst_id=33&coll_id=2289&expand=
17   Email from Victoria O'Flaherty, Archivist, National Archives, St Kitts, 26 January 2016.

William Mathew II had a difficult time managing his responsibilities as Lieutenant-Governor of St Christopher. This was in part due to his apparent lack of administrative and diplomatic skills, but was also the outcome of his never-ending efforts to promote the interests of his brother-in-law, William Pym Burt, a planter and member of the Council of Nevis, who was married to William's sister, Louisa. On William's recommendation, Burt, having moved to St Christopher, joined the St Christopher Council. William also recommended Burt for the position of judge on St Christopher, but as Burt was now a member of the St Christopher Council, members of that council objected to the recommendation, reasoning that holding both positions might result in a conflict of interest.

William's reputation was not improved by his frequent replacement of government officials without providing sufficient proof of his actions either to the local colonists or to his superiors in London, the Lords of Trade and Plantations. In 1726 he dismissed one of the St Christopher judges because he was 'disordered in his senses'.[18] A year later he dismissed the Chief Justice of St Christopher, John Greatheed, and replaced him with Jeremiah Browne, 'a gentleman vastly superior to the former in knowledge of the law, of a most plentyfull fortune (the former was most indigent) and whose integrity and candour is unspotted.'[19]

In spite of his unpopularity, in 1729 William became Governor of the Leeward Islands, and moved to Antigua to take up his post where, as on St Christopher, he soon upset the local colonists. The position of governor, although influential, was often difficult to manage effectively. The British government firmly believed that it had charge of colonial government, and only valued its colonial possessions if they made a profit through trade. This view was, understandably, not shared by the colonists. The elected Houses of Assembly and appointed Legislative Councils, established by Britain in the hope that they would help attract colonists who would support government views, instead became the focus for expressing local discontent. To deal with this unwelcome situation, the British government depended on the governor to smooth relations between island representatives and

---

18   Birch, Chris. *The milk jug was a goat: two families, two Caribbean islands 1635–1987*. Cambridge: Pegasus Publishers, 2008, p.58.
19   Ibid., p.58.

itself.[20] But rather than acting as a mediator, Mathew seemed determined to exasperate both parties. To aggravate matters further he continued to correspond with their Lordships on Burt's behalf when his brother-in-law was dismissed from the Council of St Christopher:

> *My brother Colonel Burt being removed by their Lordships from the Board, I shall not presume to place him there again. He has been pretty much mortified at being under their Lordships' displeasure, who have thought fitt to turn him out of the Council of an Island he has been wholly settled in these six years, and yet continue him in the Council of Nevis, where he does not go for above a week in a year.*[21]

In 1730, the Council of St Christopher advised that the chief justice, Jeremiah Browne, should be replaced because of 'breaches of duty'.[22] Still promoting the interests of his brother-in-law, William recommended Burt for the position. But the arrangement was short-lived, as within the year King George II signed a warrant for Browne's reinstatement. William, meanwhile, continued to dismiss and appoint government officials as he saw fit. In 1735, he dismissed the Chief Justice of St Christopher, James Gordon, while he was on leave in England. He then suspended the Judge of the Vice-Admiralty Court in Antigua, Benjamin King for, as he put it:

> *direct disobedience to his [the Leeward Islands Governor's] commands [and for treating] him in his character of Chief Governor as well as personally with great indecency.*[23]

A few years later, the Chief Justice of Nevis, Joseph Herbert, was impeached for: 'high crimes and misdemeanors [and for] entertaining wicked and corrupt designs and views.'[24] Colonel Edward Jessup, a member

---

20 Metcalf, George, for the Royal Commonwealth Society. *Royal government and political conflict in Jamaica, 1729–1783*. London: Longmans, 1965, p.1.
21 Birch, Chris. *The milk jug was a goat: two families, two Caribbean islands 1635–1987*. Cambridge: Pegasus Publishers, 2008, p.58.
22 Ibid., p.59.
23 Ibid., p.60.
24 Ibid., p.60.

of the Council of Montserrat, was dismissed on suspicion of being a Roman Catholic, to be replaced by William Mathew Burt – who was, not unexpectedly, William Pym Burt's son and William's nephew. The Lords of Trade and Plantations wrote to their governor in no uncertain terms:

> Your irregular method of suspending the members of His Majesty's Council and neglecting to send over the necessary proofs of your charge against them has already been the occasion of much difficulty and delay, and as we had so lately reproved you for the little regard you have paid to His Majesties [sic] instructions in this particular, in Col Jessup's case, we did not expect to find so much cause to complain of it a second time.[25]

In 1750, Governor Mathew, suffering from gout and far from well, went to London on leave. Summoned to appear before the Lords of Trade and Plantations, he wrote: 'I grow very old and sickly. I hope your Lordships will not be too exact with me,'[26] adding that 'the gout has so weak'n me I can never clamber up that long Stair Case but must some how get carryd up.'[27] No doubt, having given the lords plenty of cause for concern over the years, he was not eager to face them in person. But having duly reported to his superiors, he sailed back to Antigua, where his health continued to deteriorate and where he died two years later.

William Mathew II's will shows the extent of his properties and the considerable number of slaves he had owned, not only on Antigua and St Christopher but also on Tortola. His son, William Mathew III, had died young, so it was his grandson, William Mathew IV, who inherited much of his property:

> My grandson William Mathew [William Mathew IV] ... is entitled to the plantation of Drew's Hill, in St. John's Parish, Antigua, of 277 acres, also land in the parish of St. Thomas, Middle Island, St. Christopher's, of 137 acres ... To my son Isaac, all my land in Tortola ... My house

---

25 Ibid., p.62.
26 Ibid., p.63.
27 Ibid., p.63.

and lots of land on Brimstone Hill fortification in St. Christopher's to go to the possessor of Penitenny and Cupid's Garden and Middle Island. All my houses and lots of land on Monk's Hill fortification, Antigua, to go to my son Daniel's plantation called Constitution Hill and Drew's Hill ... Whereas I own the 5 rocks called the 5 Islands close by Antigua and Crabb Island and the 2 little islands near by, called Great and Little Passage I give the 5 Islands to go with Drew's Hill and the others to go with Penitenny and Cupid's Garden ... Schedule of negroes on Drew's Hill: 97 men, 17 boys, 75 women, 6 girls, 32 infants, total 227; and on Penitenny: 8 French negroes [part of St Kitts was still owned by France, and these slaves might shave been purchased from a French planter], 39 men, 49 women, 12 boys, 10 girls, 33 infants, total 146.[28]

The Penitenny Plantation on St Christopher was named for his grandfather's place of origin, and although it seems unusual to pair two tiny islets in Antigua with plantations in St Christopher, as they were of little commercial value perhaps he was not much concerned as to who would inherit them.

Wealthy planter families often intermarried, and the next generation of the Mathew family were no exception: for example, William Mathew II's second son, Daniel Mathew I (1716–1777), born in Antigua, first married Penelope Smith, the niece of his father's second wife, Anne Smith. (But in about 1744 Daniel divorced Penelope because of her adultery with the St Christopher planter William Buckley.[29] A few years later, in 1750, Daniel married Mary Byam, daughter of the Antiguan planter George Byam.)

Like many of his fellow planters, Daniel Mathew I, although he owned substantial properties in the Caribbean, preferred to live in England and to leave his estates to be run by an attorney or manager. He had a London residence in Cavendish Square, and a country estate – not in Cornwall but in Kelvedon, Essex. Many absentee planters owned a London town

---

28 Oliver, Vere Langford. *The history of the island of Antigua: one of the Leeward Caribees in the West Indies, from the first settlement in 1635 to the present time*. Vol.2. London: Mitchell and Hughes, 1896, p.254.
29 Who she later married.

house and a country residence in the home counties, locations near the seat of government, so that they could better influence the colonial trade policies on which their fortunes depended. The West Indian planters were a social and political force to be reckoned with. As Natalie Zacek writes:

> *they appeared on the metropolitan social scene as 'the most conspicuous rich men of their time.' Whether in London's Portman Square, on estates in the English countryside ... West Indian planters 'formed a social circle of their own and were bound together by intermarriages, common interest, and firm and lasting friendships.' A circle from which the majority of Britons, even those of the greatest wealth and social status, felt themselves alienated. Even George III professed himself surprised by the 'Extravagence and Luxury ... and a certain Species of Vanity' that he considered characteristic of the West Indian planters and was wary of the political and economic power wielded by the West India Lobby.*[30]

To advertise his status, Daniel Mathew I had himself and his family painted, complete with marble statuary, by the fashionable German portrait painter Johann Zoffany: Daniel is standing on the right-hand side, casting a benevolent eye over his wife Mary, seated at the far left, and over his children.

Daniel Mathew I's will of 1777 shows that by the time of his death the Mathew properties had extended as far south as Tobago. He left the St Christopher estates and the property in England to his elder son, Daniel Mathew II, while his younger son, George Mathew, was initially willed the estates in Tobago and Antigua. This legacy was later changed: the estates were sold, and George instead received £10,000 and the money to purchase a lieutenancy in the army.

Daniel Mathew I's younger brother, Abednego Mathew (1724–1795), was born on the Mathew family plantation in the Parish of St Mary Cayon on St Christopher, and following family tradition went to England to join the Coldstream Guards. In 1752 he married Jennett

---

30 Zacek, Natalie A. *Settler Society in the English Leeward Islands, 1670–1776.* Cambridge: Cambridge University Press, 2015.

The Mathew Family at Felix Hall, Kelvedon, Essex.
Painter: Johann Zoffany. Date: between 1763 and 1764.
Courtesy of the Athenaeum, http://www.the-athenaeum.org/art/detail.
php?ID=195932.

Buckley, only surviving child and heir of the wealthy St Christopher planter William Buckley. On her father's death in 1754, Jennett inherited Buckley's Estate, which lies on the western outskirts of Basseterre, the capital of St Christopher. Through gaining ownership of his wife's properties, Abednego became one of the wealthiest planters on the island – but his marriage, like that of his brother, Daniel Mathew I, was not to last. Jennett and Abednego separated, their ongoing bitter disagreements concerning ownership of the Mathew estates leading to ongoing conflict within the family. Abednego remained at Buckley's, and was said to be one of the few planters who encouraged his slaves to attend church and become baptised. There is a part of Buckley's Estate that is known as Negro Church Field, and services were probably held for the slaves somewhere in the area.[31]

---

31 *Historic Basseterre: Buckley's Estate.* Accessed 12 October 2015, http://www.historicbasseterre.com/hs_summation.asp?HSID=19

Like Daniel Mathew I, Abednego was an absentee planter. He owned an estate at Sixpenny Handley in Dorset, and became Member of Parliament for the village of Corfe Castle, which lies about 30 miles from Handley. There he died in 1795.

Daniel Mathew I's youngest brother, Edward Mathew (1729–1805), was born in Antigua and then, like the other members of his family, went to England as a young man, where he became equerry to George III, and fought in the American Revolutionary Wars. He married Lady Jane Bertie, daughter of the third Duke of Ancaster, and served as governor of the island of Grenada between 1784 and 1789.[32] He was made a general in 1797, and died in England on Christmas Day in 1805.

In 1806, the Leeward Islands Caribee government was divided into two administrative units, with Antigua, Barbuda, Redonda and Montserrat in one group, and St Christopher, Nevis, Anguilla and the British Virgin Islands in the other. This grouping dissolved in 1816, leaving the islands with a greater degree of autonomy. In 1833, the Leewards were brought back under one governor, and Dominica was added to the group; but it was not until 1871 that the British government was able to legislate the formation of a federation of the islands through the Leeward Islands Act, and the Federal Colony of the Leeward Islands was established.

By the 1850s the Mathew estates in St Christopher, including Buckley's, Dewar, Mathews and Olivees (or Olivers), belonged to George Benvenuto Buckley Mathew (1807–1897).[33] Grandson of Daniel Mathew, he married three times and was a man of many parts. He followed family tradition by joining the Coldstream Guards, where he rose to the rank of captain, and was Member of Parliament for both Athlone in Ireland and Shaftesbury in Dorset. From 1844 to 1849 he was in the Caribbean, serving as Governor of the Bahamas, and from 1850 to 1853 he served as British Consul in Charleston, South Carolina. From 1853 to 1856 he was British Consul in Philadelphia – a post

---

32 For more on Edward Mathew, see Chapter 5: Barbados, the Windward Islands and Trinidad.

33 *Historic Basseterre: Buckley's Estate*. Accessed 12 October 2015, http://www.historicbasseterre.com/hs_summation.asp?HSID=19

from which, at the request of the United States government, he resigned after he had attempted to recruit Americans to fight in the 1853–1856 Crimean War, a conflict in which the United States was not involved.[34] He was later Minister Plenipotentiary to both Argentina and Brazil. He died in London in October 1879, but was buried, as he had requested, in the churchyard of St Kew in Cornwall, near to Pennytenny, 'where his ancestors had originally lived'[35] – one member of the Mathew family who had returned to his Cornish roots.

While the Mathew family were establishing themselves as wealthy planters and important members of the local and Leeward Islands administration on the islands of St Christopher, Antigua and Tortola,

The parishes of the islands of St Christopher and Nevis.

---

34 *Buckley-Mathew, George Benvenuto*. Buckley-Mathew collection. Accessed 13 October 2015, http://library.missouri.edu/specialcollections/buckley-mathew-george-benvenuto-buckley-mathew-collection/
35 *Sir George Buckley Mathew*. Accessed 12 October 2015, http://www.findagrave.com/cgi-bin/fg.cgi?page=gr&GRid=134230305&ref=acom

the Webbe family, originally from the area around Falmouth in Cornwall, followed a similar path on the neighbouring island of Nevis. As on St Christopher, indentured labour from England was initially used to plant and harvest the local crops grown for export to England: tobacco, indigo, and spices such as ginger. At least one Cornishman, William Perryman, was among the labourers, indentured in September 1664 to serve on Nevis for nine years.[36] But, as elsewhere in the Caribbean, when sugar came to replace the earlier crops and became the dominant industry, slaves replaced indentured labour, and men such as Perryman were no longer required.[37]

The Webbe family owned several sugar plantations, including Stony Hill (also spelt Stoney Hill) in the parish of St George's Gingerland – the parish named after the ginger crop that was once grown there. Stony Hill is situated up in the foothills of Nevis Peak, at an altitude that provides some relief from the heat of the coast, especially at night. It is also on the windward side of the island, so that it receives the full benefit of the trade winds. From the plantation house, the Webbes could look down to New River Plantation on the coast, once a Webbe property, and feel relieved that they didn't have to live there, especially during the hottest months of the year.[38] New River had been established in the early 1720s by the planter William Earle, and was later bought by Josiah Webbe who owned it until his death in about 1765. It was then bought by William Maynard and Walter Nisbet, but Webbe family interest in the estate was still maintained as Walter Nisbet's father was married to Josiah Webbe's daughter.

In January, 1753, the Webbes, such well-respected planters of the Nevis community, found themselves involved in a murder case. Doctor James Webbe owned Bridgewater Estate and was in debt to Matthew Mills, a rich planter on St Christopher. By order of the court, Bridgewater Estate was disposed of by public sale on 7 November 1752, and to pay off his debt Dr Webbe was to give the proceeds from the sale to Matthew

---

36 *Virtual Jamestown: registers of servants sent to foreign plantations; Bristol Registers 1654–1686.* Accessed May 2015, http://www.virtualjamestown.org/indentures/about_indentures.html#Bristol
37 Gordon, Joyce. *Nevis: Queen of the Caribees.* 5th ed. Oxford: Macmillan Education, 2005, pp.1–3.
38 Observations made by the author during a visit to Stony Hill in October 2015.

Mills. Both Matthew Mills and the lawyer James Barbot, a good friend of Webbe, were present at the sale:

> *the former [Mr Mills] to push on the sale, in order to recover what was due to him, and the latter [Mr Barbot] to prevent its taking effect, or to become the purchaser for his friend Dr. Webbe, who had very ill will to have his estate sold to a stranger, because he had a rich uncle upon the island [George Webbe the Elder], on whom he hoped to prevail to pay his debts and preserve the estate, which he has since done.*[39]

Mr Mills and Mr Barbot quarrelled about the sale of Bridgewater, and on 19 November 1752, Matthew Mills was found murdered on the shore at Frigate Bay, St Christopher, which lies just across the narrow channel between Nevis and St Christopher. Matthew Mills' slave, Coomy, claimed that he had seen Mills and Barbot fighting at Frigate Bay and that Barbot had killed Mills. Peter, a slave belonging to a Mr Halburd, stated that he had rowed Barbot from Frigate Bay to Nevis after the murder. But the law forbade slaves from testifying against free persons, so Coomy and Peter were unable to testify. Coomy's statement was made on his behalf by John McKenley, the overseer of Spooner's Plantation, to whom Coomy had run for help when he saw Mills and Barbot fighting. Peter's statement was made by John Cribbe, the owner of the small boat that Peter had used to row Barbot back to Nevis.[40] James Barbot was arrested for the murder; he acted in his own defence and was convicted of the murder. He was executed by hanging at Basseterre on 20 January 1753.

The Webbes, in common with the Mathews of St Christopher and other members of the Caribbean plantocracy, intermarried with other members of their circle. They not only married into local families, including the Nesbits, the Daniells, the Maynards and the Tobins,

---

39 Oliver, Vere Langford. *Caribbeana : being miscellaneous papers relating to the history, genealogy, topography, and antiquities of the British West Indies*. London: Mitchell, Hughes and Clarke, 1910, Vol.6, p.34.
40 Zacek, Natalie A. *Settler Society in the English Leeward Islands, 1670–1776*. Cambridge: Cambridge University Press, 2015, pp.260–261.

but into planter families from other islands, including the Woodleys, who owned plantations on St Christopher, and the Parsons, who owned plantations on both St Christopher and Montserrat. These intermarriages caused financial complications after Emancipation in 1834, when slave owners received compensation for the value of the slaves on their property. Members of the same family, and members of families related by marriage, made competing claims and counter-claims to secure the compensation. Claims were further complicated because many planters had mortgaged their property and were in debt to the supplier of the mortgage, who could also stake a claim in payment of an outstanding mortgage.

The case of Stony Hill provides an example. Compensation for the estate's 126 slaves was registered on 31 October 1836 at £2,214 13s 10d. A claim was made by George Webbe the Younger, who had mortgaged Stony Hill to Charles Pinney and his business partner Robert Case but was still running the property. Pinney and Case, as mortgagees in possession of the property, made a counter-claim. The wealthy Pinney family had plantations on Nevis, and were also Bristol-based sugar agents and ship owners – but their wealth came primarily from mortgages offered to fellow planters, successful counter-claims to slave compensation, and the interest on loans made to fellow planters, who were preferably owners of large plantations:

> *The Pinneys, especially Charles, often said that they would rather lend to great planters than to small, for a great estate or group of estates could be made to pay its way when a small one could not.*[41]

As the two families had been friends for several generations, George Webbe the Younger was on good terms with John Pinney, but George was not an easy man to get along with:

> *John Pinney showed to George Webbe as much consideration and delicacy as his exact and ungracious nature allowed him to feel.*

---

41 Pares, Richard. *A West-India fortune*. London: Longmans, Green and Co., 1950, p.239.

> Webbe's 'warm and animated language' moved him [John Pinney] so much that he lent £5,000 at an anxious time (July 1800) ... He got a mortgage for this debt but refrained, presumably for the sake of Webbe's credit in Nevis, from sending it out to be registered, thereby depriving himself of a security upon which he invariably insisted at other times. ... George Webbe repaid these unique little gestures of propitiation by persistent cantankerousness.[42]

A counter-claim for compensation for the loss of the labour of the Stony Hill slaves was made by George Webbe Parson. His mother, Frances Webbe, daughter of George Webbe the Younger, married into the Parsons family, which had plantations on both St Christopher and Montserrat. Another counter-claim was made by Royal Navy Lieutenant Charles Webbe, a packet ship commander living in Flushing, near Falmouth. Charles was George Webbe the Younger's son by Phyllis Symonds. Charles states in his will that should his half-brother George Cavell Webbe die without issue, his executors:

> shall and will take possession of the ... freehold Estates, plantations, sugar lands, buildings and habitations situate on the Isle of Nevis ... as bequeathed to me by the last will and testament dated 14 October 1826 of the late George Webbe Esq. of Nevis.[43]

Basing his suit on his father's declaration, Charles Webbe believed he had the right to file a counter-claim for compensation. But Charles was unfortunately lost at sea with all his crew on a packet ship voyage in 1839,[44] and Charles Cavelle Webbe died unmarried and without children. Compensation for the loss of the labour of the Stony Hill slaves was eventually awarded to Charles Pinney and Robert Case, and

---

42 Ibid., pp.253–254.
43 *Charles Webbe*. Kew: National Archives, nd. Prerogative Court of Canterbury and Related Probate Jurisdictions: Will Registers; Class: PROB 11; Piece: 1916.
44 Cornwall Online Parish Clerks. *Mylor: some memorial inscriptions*. Accessed 7 December 2015, http://www.cornwall-opc.org/Par_new/l_m/pdfs/mylor_mis.pdf Transcribed from LDS Film 476219 by Shirley Cattermole.

also to George Webbe Parson: £100 went to Parson and £2,114 13s 10d to Pinney and Case: they had certainly been repaid for their mortgage loan.[45] The 126 slaves of course received no compensation of any kind.

Not all members of the Webbe family were slave owners. Although his parents, James and Elizabeth (née Webbe) Tobin owned the 175 slaves at Stoney Grove Estate on Nevis, James Webbe Tobin (1767–1814), the grandson of George Webbe the Elder, was an abolitionist. He visited Nevis from time to time, but lived in Bristol, where he became friends with the Cornish scientist Humphrey Davy and participated in some of his experiments. James was also a poet, and knew Samuel Taylor Coleridge, William Wordsworth and Robert Southey, contributing five poems to the second volume of Southey's *Annual Anthology*. When in his mid-thirties James began to lose his eyesight, he returned to Nevis, where he campaigned until his death against the treatment of the island's slaves.[46]

Several members of later generations of the Webbe family held positions in the colonial administration of Nevis: Josiah Webbe Maynard was President of the Nevis Council from 1841 to 1842 and George Cavell Webbe from 1860 to 1864, but it was the Hon. George Webbe (about 1795–1871), who is best remembered for his public service. Like many of his relatives, he had been born in the Falmouth area of Cornwall, and went to Nevis as a young man to assist in running the family plantations. In 1829 he was appointed Chief Justice of Nevis, a position he held until 1855. He was also Colonial Treasurer and Judge of the Court of Complaints for Nevis, serving in these positions until his retirement from public office in 1862. During his years of service, he was responsible for the administration of the island on three occasions.

He was a devout Methodist, and following Emancipation he built for his workers a Sunday school and a chapel, both of which were run by Methodist missionaries. The Rev. John Bell was the first missionary to arrive, and took up his duties early in 1839. He was unfortunately dead from yellow fever in less than a year, leaving a young wife and baby son.

---

45 Legacies of British slave ownership. Nevis 38 (Stoney Hill) Claim Details & Associated Individuals. Accessed 8 December 2015, https://www.ucl.ac.uk/lbs/
46 Romantic Circles. *James Webbe Tobin (1767–1814)*. Accessed 9 December 2015, https://www.rc.umd.edu/node/59426

His successor, the Cornish Rev. Benjamin Tregaskis,[47] fell ill with the same disease soon after he arrived from the island of Tortola – but he survived, largely as a result of the care he received from George Webbe and his wife Sarah. In October 1839 the Rev. Tregaskis wrote of his treatment in glowing terms to his Mission House in England:

> *As soon as His Honour was made acquainted with the fact of my illness he came to the Mission House and proposed that I should be removed to his residence ... [and] in the cool of the second day of my illness, His Honour came with his easy English-built carriage ... both the Judge and His Lady watched over me with all possible solicitude, securing to me the most minute attendance and ministering their own hands to alleviate my condition. My convalescence also, when it began was not at all retarded by the highly interesting and comprehensive conversation with which I was privileged.*[48]

His Honour and his lady showed the same care and attention when John Bell's wife Mary and baby son were preparing to return to England, and Tregaskis further enthused:

> *You have doubtless heard of the kindness shown to our dear sister Bell also, since the removal of her affectionate husband. I have seen the Judge here working with his own hands, arranging her boxes and otherwise assisting in her behalf. The dear infant is doing well through the kind attention of Mrs. Webbe and the blessing of God.*[49]

The Hon. George Webbe also had a lifelong interest in scientific development, especially in the field of astronomy, and was a Fellow of the Royal Astronomical Society and of the Scientific Association of Trinidad. He contributed scientific papers to both organisations on

---

47 For more information on Benjamin Tregaskis, and other Cornish Methodist missionaries in the Caribbean, see Chapter 7: Men of God: Methodist Missionaries.
48 Uppingham Methodist Church. *Mary Drake and the missionary*. Uppingham: Uppingham Methodist Church, nd, np.
49 Ibid.

topics such as 'Estimated position of the great comet of 1844–5 made at Nevis in the West Indies', which appeared in the *Monthly Notices of the Royal Astronomical Society* in 1846[50].

When members of the Webbe family were living at Stony Hill Plantation on Nevis, they had a good view from their house of the neighbouring island of Montserrat, where the Parsons, another planter family with Cornish connections, had property. The two families were related by marriage, as Frances, daughter of George Webbe the Elder, had married Edward Parson III, who had been born in Constantine, near Falmouth, on the south coast of Cornwall. The first Edward Parson (?–about 1729) arrived in Montserrat in around 1680, and is recorded as buying property in the parish of St Anthony in 1681. In 1712, along with fellow planter George Wyke, he successfully led the island's militia in its defence against a French attack, after which he was appointed Commissioner in Chief of Montserrat. When Edward Parson I died, he left his widow, Grace, and four children, of whom Edward Parson II was the only surviving son.

In 1738, Edward Parson II married Mary Woodley, daughter of William Woodley, the owner of Profit Plantation in St John Capisterre, in the north of St Christopher. (The Parsons and the Woodleys, like the Mathews and the Webbes, intermarried with other planter families, including the Dasents and the Millses. Bridget Woodley was the sister-in-law of Matthew Mills, the St Christopher planter who was murdered in November 1752.) At the time of their marriage, Edward Parson II was forty-two and Mary Woodley only nineteen. The Woodley plantations were larger and more prosperous than the Parson properties, and Edward was planning to invest in buying an estate in England, factors which may have influenced his decision to marry the young and wealthy Mary.[51]

Edward Parson II and his family left for England in 1740, accompanied by Mary's mother, Bridget, and the slaves John Lewis Woodley and Hester Woodley with her young daughter, Jane Woodley. Edward bought property in Little Parndon in Essex, and built a large

---

50   Webbe, George. 'Estimated position of the great comet of 1844–5.' *Monthly Notices of the Royal Astronomical Society*, (Vol. 6, p.206). Accessed 9 December 2015, http://articles.adsabs.harvard.edu/full/seri/MNRAS/0006//0000206.000.html
51   Lake, Hazel. *Sugar planters in Little Parndon*. Harlow: Lake, 2002, pp.6–7.

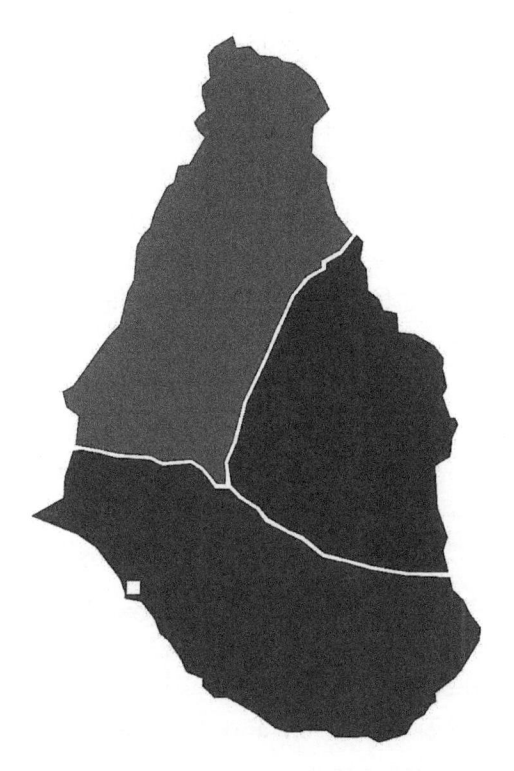

The parishes of the island of Montserrat: Saint Peter is shown to the north, Saint Georges to the east and Saint Anthony to the south. The capital, Plymouth, is marked with a square.

and elegant residence there. Hester remained a slave until her death, her ownership having passed on Bridget's death to her daughter, Mary Parson. Hester was buried in St Mary's Parish Church, Little Parndon.[52] Edward Parson II died in February 1780, and his eldest son, Edward Parson III, inherited the Little Parndon, Montserrat and St Christopher properties. This Edward married Frances Webbe in 1766, and the couple raised a family at Little Parndon.

The ongoing conflict between the British and the French, as they fought for supremacy in the Caribbean during the American Revolutionary War, caused destabilisation in many of the islands, both because the islands changed hands between the warring European powers so frequently, and

---

52 Tam, Laird. *Hester the slave*. np: Tam, 1 December 2010. Accessed 10 December 2015, https://www.youtube.com/watch?v=htplEYHtXMc

because the Caribbean planters could no longer depend on trading with the mainland American colonies. When the 1783 Treaty of Paris brought peace and France relinquished all claims on St Christopher, Nevis and Montserrat, some stability returned to the Leeward Islands. Edward Parson III and his family then returned to St Christopher, where he bought a plantation at Dieppe Bay in the north of the island, a property near to the Profit Estate, belonging to the Woodley family.[53]

After Emancipation, the Parson family sought payment of compensation for the loss of their slaves on their plantations on Montserrat and St Christopher. Various family members made claims, and as they had mortgaged some of their properties counter-claims were made by the mortgage suppliers. Compensation for the 165 slaves on Parson's estate in the south of Montserrat was contested by George Webbe Parson, the Rev. William Woodley Parson, John Frederick Pinney – who was mortgagee in possession of the property – and by three other claimants. The award of £2,451 10s 9d was split between Pinney, Webbe Parson and Woodley Parson: six-sevenths of the compensation went to Pinney and one-seventh went jointly to Webbe Parson and Woodley Parson.[54] Once again the Pinney family had profited handsomely from a mortgage agreement.

On the neighbouring island of Antigua, without having to do legal battle with any opposing claimants, Sir Christopher Bethell Codrington (1764–1843) managed to acquire compensation for the loss of his slaves both on his numerous Antiguan properties and on his Barbuda estate. The first member of his family to come to the Caribbean, Christopher Codrington (?–1656), had settled on Barbados in 1649, and his son and grandson, both named Christopher, were each in turn appointed as Governor of the Leeward Islands. The Codrington estates in Antigua included Clare Hall, near to the capital of St John's, and the properties at New Work, Cotton, Betty's Hope and Garden, all in the parish of St Peter's. From about 1685, the family also leased the island of Barbuda from the English government.

---

53 Lake, Hazel. *Sugar planters in Little Parndon*. Harlow: Lake, 2002, p.35.
54 *Legacies of British slave ownership*. Accessed throughout 2015, https://www.ucl.ac.uk/lbs/

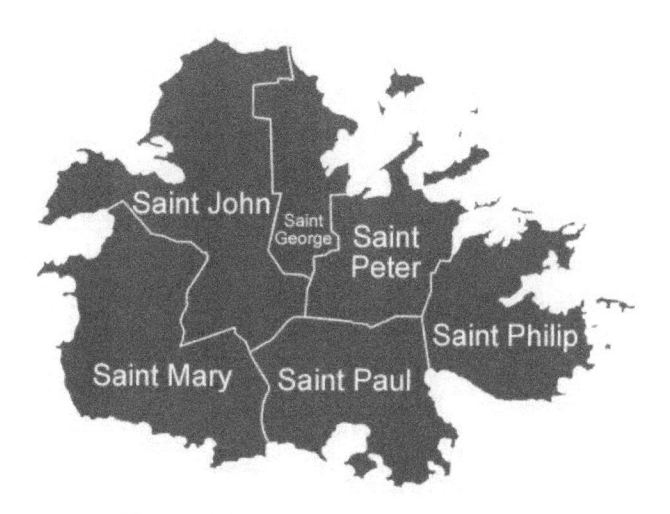

The parishes of the island of Antigua.

Sir Christopher was an absentee landlord, and while he lived at Dodington Park, the family estate in Gloucestershire, England, he employed attorneys[55] to run his Caribbean business affairs. With their employers far away, these managers sometimes gave in to temptation and profited from dishonest business practices. Such was the case with Codrington's attorney for Betty's Hope and Barbuda; he was discovered selling Barbuda produce for his own profit. He was dismissed in 1801, but it was not until 1804 that a suitable replacement was found: the Cornishman John James. James must have been highly recommended: to retain his services Sir Christopher offered him an annual salary of £200, twice the amount earned by his predecessor.[56] James was also to be paid a 5 per cent commission on the profit from sales, later raised to 7 per cent, a perk that Sir Christopher no doubt hoped would prevent James from selling produce independently and encourage him to increase the overall profit made from the estate.[57]

---

55 In the Caribbean context, an 'attorney' was a plantation manager working under the authority of letters of attorney from an absentee estate owner.
56 Murray, Roy James. '"The man that says slaves be quite happy in slavery … is either ignorant or a lying person": An account of slavery in the marginal colonies of the British West Indies.' PhD diss., University of Glasgow, 2001, pp.72–73.
57 Tweedy, Margaret T. 'A history of Barbuda under the Codringtons 1738–1833.' PhD diss., University of Birmingham, 1981, p.70.

John James had been born in Marazion, near Penzance on the south coast of Cornwall, in February 1772. His father, also John James, was captain of the *Marazion*, a merchant ship and privateer authorised by the British government to capture French enemy vessels.[58] In February 1798 John James the Younger married Elizabeth Wingfield, who came from a well-respected local family with connections to the St Aubyn family, whose family seat, the small island of St Michael's Mount, lies just offshore from Marazion. John and Elizabeth had three children, all born before their father left Marazion to take up his post as Christopher Codrington's attorney. James sailed first to Antigua, where he familiarised himself with operations at Betty's Hope Estate, and then sailed on to the island of Barbuda.[59]

Barbuda lies about 39 miles (63 km) north of Antigua. With poor soil, and low and unreliable rainfall, the island never produced commercial crops on a large scale. So it was first developed by the Codrington family as a stock-rearing facility to supply their Antigua sugar estates with meat and draught animals.[60] The range of products later diversified to include a wider range of items including hides, corn, wood, charcoal, lime (used in the production of sugar) and turtles (both the meat and the shell), and fish. These were sent to the Codrington estates on Antigua, to the British naval base at English Harbour on the south coast of Antigua, to neighbouring islands and, in the case of turtle shell, occasionally to England.[61]

As Henry Nelson Coleridge noted when he visited in 1825, Barbuda is low-lying and surrounded by reefs:

> *It is so low and level that I at least could not distinctly make it out, till we were within four miles of it. The coast is beset with shoals and reefs*

---

58 The National Archives of the UK. Public Record Office. *High Court of Admiralty: Prize Court: Registers of Declarations for Letters of Marque*. HCA 26/6/123.
59 *Cornwall OPC Database*. Accessed throughout 2015, http://www.cornwall-opc-database.org/
60 Tweedy, Margaret T. 'A history of Barbuda under the Codringtons 1738–1833.' PhD diss., University of Birmingham, 1981, p.i.
61 Watters, David R. 'Observations on the historic sites and archaeology of Barbuda.' *Journal of Archaeology and Anthropology*, pp.125–156 (Vol 3, No.2, 1980).

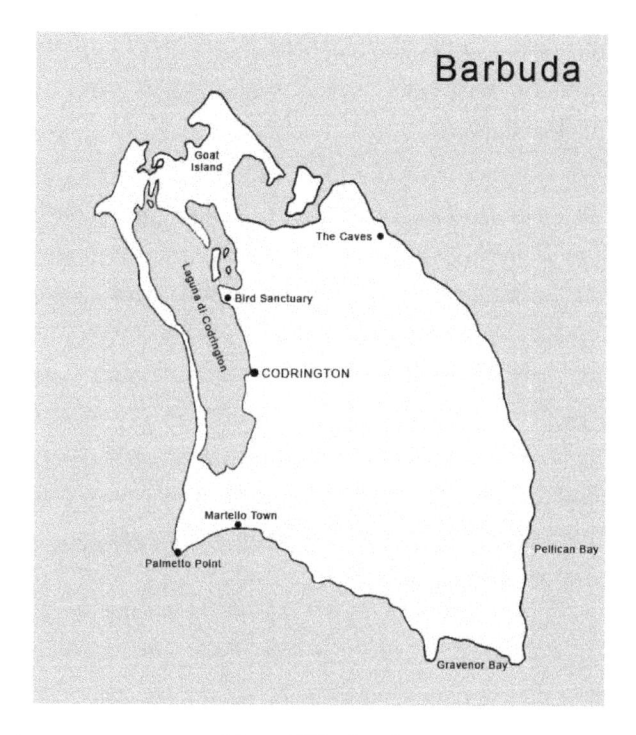

Map of Barbuda.

under water, and it was a matter of some anxiety to see how the vessel insinuated itself, as it were, between these rocks, a man standing on the bowsprit and giving his directions every minute to the helm.[62]

Vessels ran aground or were wrecked around the coast of Barbuda on a regular basis, and the money made from salvaging the contents of these vessels added considerably to the Codrington wealth. Sir Christopher was no doubt aware that John James had the skills to manage any salvage opportunities that came his way: he came from a Cornish seafaring family, where the rocky coastline and strong onshore winds caused many vessels to founder, and Cornish men and women were accustomed to supplementing their income from the profit to be made from salvage.[63]

---

62 Coleridge, Henry Nelson. *Six months in the West Indies in 1825*. London: John Murray, 1826, p.274.
63 Within maritime law, the law of salvage states that a person who recovers another person's ship or cargo after peril or loss at sea is entitled to a reward commensurate with the value of the property so saved.

When John James arrived on Barbuda and had familiarised himself with the estate, he wrote to Sir Christopher to give him his first impressions of the island:

> *From the observations I have been able to make I find in the first place a very valuable stock of Negroes, amounting in all to three hundred and fourteen including children, many of them very able tradesmen of every description ... The island ... at this time has a very favourable appearance, there having been a great plenty of rain, consequently great plenty of feed for the stock, but I am informed that one part of the year during the dry months, the island is very much distressed; when they are obliged to feed the cattle on bush, at which time great numbers of the old ones die; there is some hay made every year, but not nearly enough to serve them in the very dry season, it is therefore kept for the horses as they will not like the cattle and sheep eat the bush; it would therefore be a great object to raise something that might supply the place of grass during the dry weather ... There are spots of very good ground on the island, where ploughs may be used to great advantage, both in raising corn, and also some sort of food for the cattle, but of what kind I am as yet at a loss to say, but that great benefit would arise from the use of the plough I have not the least doubt of, especially as there is such a number of young Oxen on the place and now perfectly idle ... As to the accounts they are all kept at Antigua, and we know nothing of them here neither of the disposal of the stock we sent off ... There was a Vessel wracked [sic] on the island on the night of the 7th inst. But very little of the cargo has been saved. I shall be very much obliged to you for the permission to have the use of a horse.*[64]

James had a businesslike approach to the development of the Barbuda estate, and by the following August he was ready to suggest improvements which would increase the quantity and quality of the island's produce. In a letter penned to Sir Christopher from Antigua on 2 August 1805, he writes:

---

64 *The Letters of John James Esq.: a collection of letters written by the estate manager of Barbuda and Clare Hall, Antigua 1804–1826.* Accessed January 2016, http://johnjamesesq.blogspot.ca/

I do not hesitate to say that I think the produce of Barbuda may be improved in most respects ... The methods which you propose respecting the sheep I think highly advisable to try ... as they have been degenerating some time, and do not now sell for near what they did three or four years since ... I will not attempt to say how far sheep dogs may be useful, but at present a couple of Bull dogs would be much more acceptable to us, at this time we are in the realist want of them having but one on the Island ... cattle without doubt is the greatest object on the place and attended with as little trouble as anything, there is a constant demand for fat ones to a greater amount than Barbuda can supply ... We are now preparing for corn which does by the present method take up a very great proportion of our time, and at present there is a vast deal of work to be done, which I shall be able to state much better in a future letter.[65]

Despite James' efforts to manage the property efficiently, by January 1809 Sir Christopher was complaining that the profits were no higher than before, and that his investments in Barbuda were not bringing an adequate return. He writes to James:

When I reflect upon the Size of Barbuda 39000 Acres cover'd with stock of all kinds, with upwards of 250 Negroes upon it, and then look at the Returns from such Possessions, I feel that some great Errors must have pervaded the plans hitherto pursued.[66]

Like many absentee planters, Sir Christopher tended to blame the inactivity of local managers for any shortfall in profit, and failed to acknowledge the difficulties of working with Barbuda's poor soil and frequent droughts – ongoing challenges which in fact had a much greater impact on profit margins than the perceived poor performance of management staff.[67] There was also the problem of maintaining regular

---

65   Ibid.
66   Tweedy, Margaret T. 'A history of Barbuda under the Codringtons 1738–1833.' PhD diss., University of Birmingham, 1981, p.70.
67   Ibid., p.79.

communication between employer and employees, as Barbuda was less accessible than the other Leeward Islands: once letters from England had arrived in Antigua, they then had to be transhipped to Barbuda.

Notwithstanding Sir Christopher's complaints, John James continued to implement his plans for improving sheep and wool production and to take advantage of any salvaging opportunities that presented themselves. At the end of 1817 he writes to his employer that he is:

> *happy to find the Wool sold to your satisfaction, I shall do every thing in my power to increase the flock of woolly sheep, in my next I will endeavour to form some idea of the number of sheep we shall be enabled to keep ... My business in this Island has been to settle the salvage of a small Schooner which was wrecked on the North side of Barbuda, on the night of the 20th of last month; she was last from Philadelphia, and had a valuable Cargo on board, consisting of Brandy, Wine, Soap, Lard &c, she sank about 2 O:Clock in the morning; three miles from the shore, and before day light was entirely in pieces, therefore nothing was saved but what drifted to the shore, & was sold in this Island for about £700 Currency; the Crew who saved themselves in their Boat had secured the whole before I got to the beach, the vessel having gone to pieces before day light the wreck was discovered by the person I had sent round the Bays. As we did not assist in saving the Cargo the Magistrates have only awarded us the trouble of transporting the Articles to this Island [Antigua], for which they have given £100 Currency ... Since my last we have had an abundance of rain in fact rather too much, when I left Barbuda the low lands were entirely under water, so much so that Cart could not get from the Castle to the Fort.*[68]

When on Barbuda, James resided at Codrington Castle, which had been built to defend the land and sea approaches to Codrington Village, standing midway on the east shore of the large lagoon that lies on the west coast of the island. That settlement was – and indeed still is – the only

---

68 *The Letters of John James Esq.: a collection of letters written by the estate manager of Barbuda and Clare Hall, Antigua 1804–1826.* Accessed January 2016, http://johnjamesesq.blogspot.ca/

centre of population on Barbuda. Here was the estate's administrative centre, where all the slaves, overseers and managers lived, and where facilities such as the tannery were located.[69]

In early September 1818, James writes to Sir Christopher concerning the building of a boat that would allow sugar to be conveniently shipped to Antigua. John James the Elder, as a ship's captain, would most likely have handed down to his son a knowledge of what it took to build a strong, seaworthy vessel, and the letter shows a practical approach to boat building:

> *In a letter of 9th July of last year, I informed you of the necessity there was of building a vessel for the use of this Island, and your Antigua Estates; I am now happy to say that it is in a great state of forwardness, and could be launched in a very short time ... she is built of the very best materials, and I trust will be a fine vessel, of about sixty tons and will carry thirty two Hhds [Hogsheads] of Sugar. I have, from Bolts obtained from Wrecks, then enable entirely to Copper fasten her; the Deck as well as Bottom, & Bands. I therefore trust you will have no objection to have her bottom Coppered as far as her light watermark ... The vessel now in use is very old, and must soon be condemned; I have been patching her ever since I have been on the Island.[70]*

In the same letter, he expresses his concern about providing the slaves with new clothing:

> *The list of the things for the Island is absolutely necessary the Negroes having had no clothing since 1815 the date of the last Invoice.[71]*

---

69 Watters, David R. 'Historical documentation and archaeological investigation of Codrington Castle, Barbuda, West Indies.' *Annals of Carnegie Museum*, pp.229–288 (Vol.66, No.3, August 1977), p.232.
70 *The Letters of John James Esq.: a collection of letters written by the estate manager of Barbuda and Clare Hall, Antigua 1804–1826.* Accessed January 2016, http://johnjamesesq.blogspot.ca/
71 Ibid.

Plantations were expected to provide their slaves with new clothing annually, but Sir Christopher was apparently unwilling to meet his obligations in this respect, as no clothing provision had been made for three years. Sir Christopher was known to be an opponent of the Abolitionist movement: in 1832, quoting from a letter he had received from John James back in 1825, he wrote in the *Anti-Slavery Reporter*:

> Mr. James, in 1825, states the negroes to be happy and contented although under the greatest subordination; and, in proof, he mentions his having frequently slept in the woods (pirates frequently landing); by the side of his horse surrounded by 100 to 150 of them.[72]

Despite the supposed happiness of Codrington's slaves, there were several instances of slave resistance and rebellion on Barbuda. The most frequent cause was various plans to transfer slaves from Barbuda either to the Codrington estates on Antigua, or to estates in the Leeward and Windward Islands, or to plantations in the southern colonies of the newly independent United States of America.

During a visit to England in 1815, James asked Sir Christopher to allow his wife and children to accompany him back to Antigua. Sir Christopher gave his permission and the family settled on Barbuda, but in 1822 they moved to the Codrington estate at Clare Hall on Antigua. Here they lived extravagantly and entertained lavishly. As Sir Christopher was financially responsible for the whole family he was, understandably, most displeased. John James, now spending most of his time at Clare Hall with his family and drinking heavily, gave far less attention to his Barbuda responsibilities than previously, and only occasionally visited the island.[73] The James family now fits the sharp-penned Mrs Lanaghan's description of an attorney. 'Before emancipation,' she writes:

---

72 'Correspondence between Sir C.B. Codrington and T.F. Buxton Esq. on the subject of slavery.' *The Anti-Slavery Reporter*, pp.301–302. (Vol.5, no.2, Nov.15, 1832).
73 Tweedy, Margaret T. 'A history of Barbuda under the Codringtons 1738–1833.' PhD diss., University of Birmingham, 1981, pp.58–59.

the attorney ... employed as many of the slaves as suited them, in the capacity of domestic servants, which slaves were of course fed from the estate provision; then the attorney has one or two horses allowed him, and if he purchases any more from his private funds, the estate finds them in corn and grass; he keeps a flock of sheep, for which the property also stands caterer; and now and then his employer may forward him a hogshead [63 gallons] of porter, or a pipe [126 gallons] of Madeira ... Thus, in the end, his pomp and grandeur is kept up at a very moderate charge to his own pocket ... [and while] they are travelling the high-road to preferment and honour, their wives are proceeding with railway speed in the paths of affectation and conceit.[74]

Although the relationship between Sir Christopher and James continued to deteriorate, the attorney continued to look after the affairs of the Codrington estates until his death. He died in Antigua in July 1826 and was buried in the churchyard of the Anglican cathedral in the city of St John, Antigua's capital.[75]

Soon after John James died there was a change in the membership of the Leeward Islands: in 1833 the island of Dominica was added to the group, and was administered by a lieutenant-governor who reported to the Antigua-based Governor of the Leeward Islands. In 1861, Thomas Price (1817–1864) was appointed Lieutenant-Governor of Dominica. The youngest son of Cornishman, Sir Rose Price, a wealthy sugar planter in Jamaica and 1st Baronet of Trengwainton, Thomas had been born at the family estate, Trengwainton Manor, which lies on the edge of the small village of Madron, near Penzance. In May 1845 he married Anna Macnamarra, a London stockbroker's daughter, and by 1852 they had four children.[76] After a brief visit to the family estates in Jamaica, Thomas

---

74 *Antigua and the Antiguans: a full account of the Colony and its inhabitants from the time of the Caribs to the present day interspersed with anecdotes and legends.* Vol.2. St John's: Antiguan Publishing Trust, 1980, pp.198–199. Work attributed to a Mrs. Flannigan or Lanaghan, first published in 1844.
75 Oliver, Vere Langford. *The history of the island of Antigua: one of the Leeward Caribees in the West Indies, from the first settlement in 1635 to the present time.* Vol.3. London: Mitchell and Hughes, 1899, p.376.
76 Blewett, Roy. *The Price and Rose Price family tree.* Penzance: Blewett, January 2013.

Price returned to England and for a time found employment as a bank manager.[77] Appointed as Colonial Treasurer of Antigua, he returned to the Caribbean in late 1852.[78] As he tried to administer the colony's finances, liabilities were always more in evidence than assets, yet Antigua always seemed to manage to maintain a measure of financial stability, causing Price to remark: 'Antigua is like a cat with nine lives; she's somehow always light upon her legs.'[79]

In 1857, Thomas was made president of the British possessions in the Virgin Islands and moved to Tortola with his family, where his wife Anne died in 1858. During his presidency he oversaw the activities of the Virgin Gorda Mine Adventure,[80] a copper mining concern on the neighbouring island of Virgin Gorda which was worked by a number of miners from his native Cornwall. While employed as president, he was also sent briefly to act as a temporary administrator for the government of St Christopher and was acting superintendent in Honduras before being transferred to Dominica in October 1861.[81] He remained as Lieutenant-Governor of Dominica until, while on a visit to Antigua, he was taken ill and died in October 1864. He was perhaps the only person of Cornish heritage to hold a government position in Dominica.

---

77 The National Archives of the UK. Public Record Office. *Census Returns for 1851.* HO/107/169/7.
78 Great Britain. Colonial Office. *The Colonial Office list 1862.* London: Edward Stanford, 1862, p.143.
79 Price, Thomas. *On the Finances of the Island of Antigua.* St John's: Price, 1854. Pamphlet with no pagination.
80 For more about Thomas Price, see Chapter 2: Jamaica, and Chapter 9: Copper and Guano: the Virgin Gorda and Sombrero Mines.
81 Great Britain. Colonial Office. *The Colonial Office list 1862.* London: Edward Stanford, 1862, p.143.

2

Jamaica and the Cayman Islands[1]

Francis Price was a man of vision. In 1655, he sailed under the command of General Robert Venables and Admiral William Penn when they took Jamaica from Spain. Probably of Welsh heritage, Price may have joined Cromwell's army as a soldier of fortune before it left England, but he could have been recruited from Barbados or one of the Leeward Islands; either way, at the taking of Jamaica he was a lieutenant.[2] Jamaica was largely undeveloped, but Price saw opportunities for the acquisition of land on a large scale, which would establish him as a man of substance in the colony.

In 1665, he received two grants of land: one of 150 acres at Flamingo Savannah, the other of 175 acres at Guanaboa Vale; these properties were both in the parish of St Catherine and to the west of the town of St Jago de la Vega, renamed Spanish Town by the English. In 1670, he was granted a further 840 acres at Luidas Vale, also in St Catherine's Parish. This latest acquisition, then thick forest and uncultivated savannah and connected to the rest of the parish only by an unpaved track, he named Worthy Park.[3] His new grant was far from being the cultivated and cared-for property that the word 'park' implies, but Price saw its potential and for the remainder of his life focused on making a profit from the sugar grown at Guanaboa, so that he could afford to develop Worthy Park. Through careful purchases of surrounding land, he managed to double

---

1   See Appendix 3 for a background history of Jamaica and the Cayman Islands.
2   Craton, Michael and James Walvin. *A Jamaican Plantation: The History of Worthy Park, 1670–1970.* Toronto: University of Toronto Press, 1970, p.29.
3   Ibid., p.27.

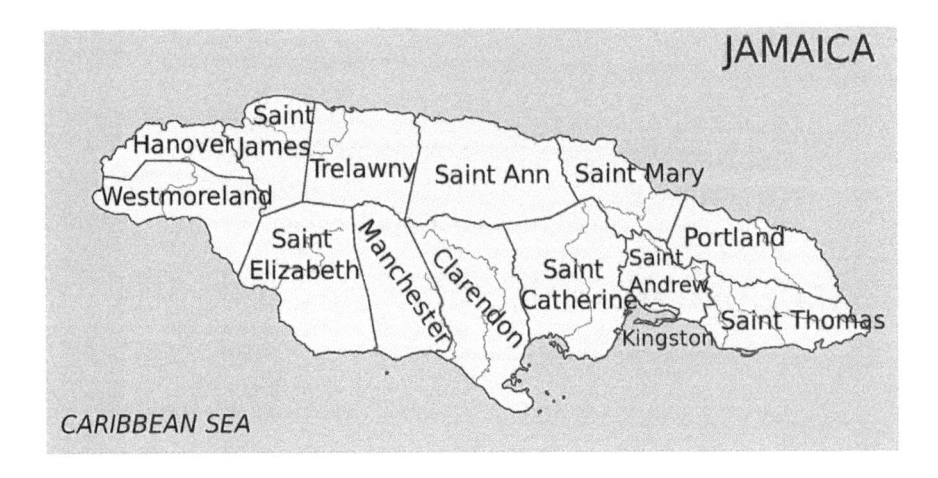

The parishes of the island of Jamaica.

the size of Worthy Park, and built the first Great House on the property, where he lived with his wife Elizabeth and their family.[4]

In the early days of colonisation, as in Barbados and the Leeward Islands, many of the labourers hired to develop the newly established farms and estates were supplied through the system of indenture, and some of them came from Cornwall;[5] in 1685, Christopher Tayler from Falmouth was indentured for four years and shipped from Bristol to Jamaica on the *Dragon*, and in the same year Richard Mitchell from Lanivet, also indentured for four years, shipped from Bristol on the *Providence*.[6]

Two of Francis Price's sons, Francis and Thomas, died young, and it fell to the remaining son, Charles Price I – the first of several so named in the Price family – to continue to develop and expand the family holdings. Rose Hall Estate came into the family by the marriage of Charles' sister Elizabeth into the Rose family. In about 1703, Charles married Sarah Edmunds, and had a large family of seven daughters and six sons,[7] although many died

---

4   Ibid., pp.40–41.
5   Schwartz, Sharron P. *The Cornish in Latin America: 'Cousin Jack' and the New World*. Wicklow: The Cornubian Press, 2016, p.52.
6   *Virtual Jamestown: registers of servants sent to foreign plantations; Bristol Registers 1654–1686*. Accessed May 2015, http://www.virtualjamestown.org/indentures/about_indentures.html#Bristol
7   Blewett, Roy. *The Price and Rose Price family tree*. Penzance: Blewett, January 2013.

at a young age. Charles never left Jamaica,[8] although he left provision in his will for the education of his remaining children in England and for the purchase of property there.[9] Thanks to his shrewd business management, Worthy Park became an established and profitable sugar estate, and he became a pillar of local society, serving in the St John's Militia where he eventually became colonel, and on the parish bench as a justice of the peace. He was also a member of the Jamaica Assembly, but contributed little to its deliberations and in 1725 was expelled because of his failure to attend their meetings. By the end of his life, Colonel Charles had the means to build a house in Spanish Town, and died a well-loved member of his community. A memorial from his son, Charles Price II, describes him as:

> *Just, Charitable, Courteous, Affable to his Inferiors, patient of Injuries and Slow to wrath. A Man of Integrity, & so firm to his word, that he inviolably preserv'd the same even to the strictest Nicety of Honour, meek he was but truly brave.*[10]

Charles Price II and his brothers, Thomas Rose and John, all made use of the funds provided by their father for their education. Charles went to Trinity College, Oxford, where his tutor was Dr Frank Nicolls from Penzance in Cornwall. He was a well-respected physician, who later became Court Physician to King George II [11] and when John, a student at Winchester College, became ill Charles sought the advice of Dr Nicholls. The doctor recommended the mild climate and coastal breezes of his native Penzance, and arranged for him to stay there with the Badcock family, who lived in Chapel Street. Here John recovered his health, and in 1736 married his host's daughter, Margery. [12]

---

8   As the Price family named a son Charles over several generations, they are differentiated by labelling them Charles Price I, II, etc.
9   Sparrow, Elizabeth. *The Prices of Penzance: the influence of 18th century Jamaican sugar plantation owners on West Cornwall*. Penzance: Penzance Library, 1985, p.2.
10 Craton, Michael and James Walvin. *A Jamaican Plantation: The History of Worthy Park, 1670–1970*. Toronto: University of Toronto Press, 1970, p.64.
11 *Trereife Manor House*. Accessed 21 January 2016, http://trereifepark.co.uk/the-house/
12 Sparrow, Elizabeth. *The Prices of Penzance: the influence of 18th century Jamaican sugar owners on West Cornwall*. Penzance: Penzance Library, 1985, p.3.

At the time of his marriage, John's annual income from the Price family estates in Jamaica was about £2,000, so he could well afford the large house which he built at the top of Chapel Street. Here, in 1738, Margery gave him a son, who was also named John. When his son was about a year old, his father decided to return to Jamaica. He planned to assess the management skills of his brothers, Charles II and Thomas Rose, who were managing the family estates, but John died in early 1739, a few months after reaching Jamaica. Thomas Rose died a few years later, leaving Charles II in control of the family properties. Like Charles Price I, Charles II had joined the Jamaica Assembly but, unlike his father, he took an active part in its proceedings and by 1739 was one of its most prominent members. In the following years he gained effective control of the Assembly by means of an alliance with Jamaica's governor, Cornishman Edward Trelawny.

Trelawny had been born in 1699 at Trelawne Manor, near the south coast village of Looe in Cornwall. He was the son of Sir Jonathan Trelawny,[13] 3rd Baronet of Trelawne and Bishop of Exeter, in Devon. Educated at Westminster School in London and Christ Church College, Oxford, he was eager to join the military, but his father thought otherwise, and as Sir Jonathan was not a man to be crossed Edward turned his interest to politics. The Trelawnys were one of the oldest parliamentary families in Cornwall, and thanks partly to his father's influence he became, in 1723, one of the Members of Parliament for West Looe, one of Cornwall's rotten boroughs,[14] continuing to represent the small community until 1732.[15] His early career was spent as a commissioner for victualling the armed forces and as a commissioner of customs in Edinburgh, Scotland.[16]

---

13 Sir Jonathan was well known for having once been imprisoned in the Tower of London by King James II for signing a petition against the 1687 Declaration of Indulgences, and is thought to be the hero of the rousing Cornish anthem called *The Song of the Western Men*, better known as *Trelawny*.
14 A rotten borough was a community which had decreased too much in size and population to justify separate representation but was nevertheless still entitled to elect and send one or more members of parliament: West Looe, at that time with a population of probably less than 1,000, was entitled to two MPs until the Reform Act of 1845.
15 Metcalf, George, for the Royal Commonwealth Society. *Royal government and political conflict in Jamaica, 1729–1783*. London: Longmans, 1965, p.58.
16 Morgan, Claire. *Governors of Jamaica: Edward and William Trelawny*. Redruth: Cornish Studies Library, nd, p.1.

In 1736, he was offered the position of Governor of Jamaica, which he took up in 1738. Soon after his arrival he negotiated a peaceful settlement with the Maroons, the runaway slaves who continued to threaten Britain's interests on the island. He governed Jamaica during a time of conflict between the European powers in the region and, perhaps because he had been prevented by his father from following a military career, he now took every opportunity to fight in defence of Britain's interests. During the War of Austrian Succession he raised a regiment in Jamaica, and was at Britain's defeat at Cartagena de las Indias in 1741. He later became captain of a regiment of foot soldiers, known as Colonel Edward Trelawny's, and in 1748 fought at the Battle of Port Louis, when Admiral Charles Knowles attacked and destroyed the large French fort on the coast of the French colony of Saint-Domingue.[17]

The alliance between Charles Price II and Edward Trelawny helped both men. Price's influence as a wealthy planter helped Trelawny manage the Assembly and the Council, while Trelawny's support helped elevate Price to the position of Speaker of the Assembly, a position which gave him influence with the Jamaican government and enabled him to obtain Crown land when and where he wanted it. He managed to secure grants of huge tracts of land, and to buy up neighbouring properties whenever they became available. As the Price sugar estates continued to grow, more labour was needed to develop and work the land at a profit, and Charles II became one of the largest slaveholders on the island.[18]

Edward Trelawny continued as governor until in 1751 he was allowed to resign on grounds of ill health. His successful relationship with the Assembly was perhaps his greatest achievement, as he:

came to identify with local interests so completely that factions could no longer form for and against the Governor as a function of the rift between Imperial and colonial interests. In his last Assembly, Trelawny signed many controversial Acts without a murmur [perhaps knowing

---

17 Salusbury-Trelawny of Trelawne, John Barry. *The Trelawny family*. Hythe: Trelawny, nd, p.47.
18 Craton, Michael and James Walvin. *A Jamaican Plantation: The History of Worthy Park, 1670–1970*. Toronto: University of Toronto Press, 1970, pp.76–82.

full well that they would be revoked once forwarded to London] ... and at his departure he received a vote of thanks of almost unprecedented fulsomeness.[19]

Relieved of his responsibilities, he boarded the man of war *Assurance* with his wife for a voyage back to England, where he hoped to spend a well-earned and pleasant retirement. The ship had almost reached port when it was shipwrecked off the Needles, the distinctive stacks of chalk that rise out of the sea on the western end of the Isle of Wight. After he and his wife had been rescued and taken ashore, the governor, who was already in poor health:

immediately and without refreshing himself – notwithstanding the Badness of the Weather ... set about preserving the People on board this Wreck, for which end he hired two Sloops, and waited on shore himself to see them taken care of at their landing.[20]

This activity left the governor in a worsening state of health and with a bad cold. When Admiral Charles Knowles, the new Governor of Jamaica, asked after his well-being, Francis Gashry, who had been Trelawny's personal agent during his time as Governor of Jamaica,[21] wrote:

'Mr. Trelawny is at Bath he has been very much out of order for want of perspiration tho he is growing somewhat better yet I fear this climate will not agree with him.'[22]

Gashry proved to be correct, for while Edward Trelawny recovered from his cold, his health continued to deteriorate during the following months. He died in January 1754, while staying at Hungerford Park in Berkshire.

---

19 Ibid., p.77.
20 British Library. *Trelawny letters*. Western Flying Post 7.5.1753 p.1. col.3. Typescript from National Library of Jamaica file on Edward Trelawny.
21 Metcalf, George for the Royal Commonwealth Society. *Royal government and political conflict in Jamaica, 1729–1783*. London: Longmans, 1965, p.59.
22 British Library. *Trelawny letters*. Add 19038 ff 50. Typescript from National Library of Jamaica file on Edward Trelawny.

In 1758, the British government gathered the existing Jamaican parishes into the three counties of Cornwall, Middlesex and Surrey, enabling court sessions to be held along the lines of the British county court system. The reasoning behind the choice of names is uncertain, but 'Cornwall' was perhaps chosen as the name of the county to the west of Jamaica because it was the county to the west of England.

With the diplomatically skilled Edward Trelawny gone, the Jamaica Assembly was eager to strengthen its position as the voice of the local plantocracy, and to present a united front to Edward Trelawny's successor, Admiral Charles Knowles. The leading Jamaican politicians therefore met at Charles Price II's house in Spanish Town to form a coalition: The Jamaica Association. The members had powerful connections with the government in London, and Governor Knowles, having failed to manage this newly belligerent Assembly, was soon recalled to London.[23]

In 1763, Charles Price II, now aged 55, pleaded ill health and retired from the Assembly, but he missed being at the centre of the island's political life, and two years later returned to serve another term. He also became Custos (keeper of the parish records) for St Mary's Parish, Judge of the Supreme Court and a major-general in the Jamaica Militia. In 1768 he was nominated for the council by another Trelawny: Captain Sir William Trelawny, Royal Navy, a cousin of Edward Trelawny, now Governor of Jamaica; and in the same year, he was made a baronet by George III. He was now Sir Charles Price, 1st Baronet of Rose Hall,[24] a most gratifying end to his career.

Unlike Cousin Edward, William Trelawny had not been discouraged from making a career in the armed forces and he had joined the Royal Navy, where he was quickly promoted through the ranks. His early political career was, like Edward's, based on Trelawny family influence in the Cornish rotten borough of West Looe, where he was elected Member of Parliament in 1756. In 1757, he was promoted to captain of the 70-gun frigate *Lyon*, and sailed to the Caribbean to join the squadron of Commodore Robert Hughes where he took part in the invasion of the

---

23 Craton, Michael, and James Walvin. *A Jamaican Plantation: The History of Worthy Park, 1670–1970.* Toronto: University of Toronto Press, 1970, p.77–78.
24 Ibid., p.79.

French island of Guadeloupe. William's ship was badly damaged in the battle and he was wounded and sent back to England. It was not until 1766 that, following the recall of Governor Lyttelton, he was selected to return to the Caribbean as Governor of Jamaica.[25]

When William arrived on the island to take up his post in September 1768, one of the first issues he had to deal with was a demand from the eastern part of the Parish of St James for the creation of a separate parish for their area. Since the early 18th century the parishioners had lobbied the Assembly, complaining that their parish capital of Montego Bay was too far away, making it difficult for them to travel there to conduct business. Their wishes were granted in 1770 when, with the support of the governor, a new parish was formed by an Act of the Assembly. William Trelawny signed the Act into being and in gratitude the parishioners named the new parish Trelawny. Now not only did Trelawny parishioners have a shorter journey to make when they went to town, but they also had their

Cornwall Street, Falmouth, Jamaica, from Adolphe Duperly's
Daguerian Excursions in Jamaica, 1840
Courtesy of the British Library Online Gallery.

---

25 Metcalf, George, for the Royal Commonwealth Society. *Royal government and political conflict in Jamaica, 1729–1783.* London: Longmans, 1965, pp.172–173.

own representation in the Assembly, increasing their political influence within the colony.[26] The name chosen for the capital of the new Parish was Falmouth, named after the Cornish port of the same name, and one of its streets was known as Cornwall Street.

William Trelawny thus gained the respect of the local plantocracy – no easy accomplishment for a representative of the British government – and he looked forward to a successful administration. Regrettably, this was not to be, as his life was cut short when he died from yellow fever in late 1772. As a mark of appreciation:

> *the house of assembly ... on receiving the information of the melancholy event, voted a magnificent funeral to his excellency's remains, at the public expense, in order, as expressed in the vote, 'to testify the grateful respect which the house entertain of his excellency's merit, the sense they have of the great and universal satisfaction which his mild and equitable administration gave to all ranks of people, and the real regret they feel at his loss.' Accordingly on Sunday evening, the 13th instant, the body lay in state in the council-chamber, which was hung with black, and illuminated with large tapers of wax; and to their great honour, the members of the legislature, the officers of the navy, army and militia, the magistrates, and all ranks of people, seemed to vie with each other in showing the most grateful testimony of respect and regard to the governor's memory.*[27]

After a solemn procession through the town, followed by a moving funeral service when notwithstanding 'the prodigious concourse of all ranks of people to view the ceremony the most profound silence was observed,'[28] William Trelawny was buried in the church at Spanish Town. His wife, Laetitia, returned to England, accompanied by the family doctor, one Dr John Wolcot.

Wolcot was a man of many parts. Born in Devon in May 1738, on the death of his father he went, aged 13, to live with his uncle in Fowey on the

---

26 Pickersgill, Fay. *Jamaica's fascinating Falmouth*. Kingston: Pickersgill, 2013, p.2.
27 '[William Trelawny] Kingston in Jamaica, Dec. 19.' *The Monthly Chronologer*, np. (May 1773).
28 Ibid.

south coast of Cornwall. Although from an early age he enjoyed music, was good at drawing and wrote poetry, he decided to qualify as a doctor. He was distantly related to the Trelawny family through marriage, and this was the most likely reason for his subsequent selection as physician to William Trelawny and his family during his Jamaica governorship. Not long after Wolcot's arrival in Jamaica, a cleric in the Parish of St Ann, the largest parish on the island, became seriously ill, and as the position looked as if it might soon become available Wolcot promptly returned to England where he set about joining the priesthood and:

availing himself of the lax discipline of the time, was admitted to Holy Orders as a Deacon, by Terrick, Bishop of London, on the 24th June, 1769, and on the day following was ordained a priest by the same prelate, signed his Declaration of Conformity, and received his license as a Priest in Jamaica.[29]

Speedily returning to Jamaica after this rapid ordination, he was disappointed to learn that the resident cleric had survived. He was offered another, minor, clerical appointment, but as he had also been given the opportunity to become physician general to the Horse and Foot Militia of the island he decided to revert to his lay profession. But the death of William Trelawny put an end to any hopes Wolcot had of promotion within the colonial service, and having returned to London with Lady Trelawny he established himself as a doctor in Truro. Here he met the Cornish artist John Opie and, recognising talent when he saw it, became his first patron and agent. While practising medicine in Cornwall he began to write satire under the pseudonym Peter Pindar and then in later life moved to London where his writing became popular, enabling him to change profession once again, and make his living as a satirist.

Charles Price II died in the same year as his friend William Trelawny, having spent much of his later life energetically building and furnishing splendid houses on his estates. Charles' grandfather, Francis Price, would

---

29 Rogers, John Jope. *Opie and his Works: being a catalogue of 760 pictures by John Opie, R.A. preceded by a biographical sketch.* London: Paul and Dominic Colnaghi, 1878, p.8.

have been pleased to see the fruition of his vision of establishing the family as an important part of Jamaica's plantocracy. In 1760, Charles built an imposing dwelling on the Rose Hall Estate.[30] This was the house that would later become the focus of the legend of Annie Palmer, the so-called 'white witch of Rose Hall', whose supposedly cruel and murderous activities, although they have long been disproven, continue even now to be part of local folklore.[31] Charles also enlarged his father's Spanish Town house, and in about 1765 built a magnificent house at Decoy Estate, his favourite property, up in the hills of St Mary's Parish. He was so attached to the Decoy that he left instructions for his body to be buried in the grounds of the house. The hospitality offered to visitors by Charles and his wife was memorable: the Great House was;

> *the abode of cheerfulness and hospitality: to these, the delightful air breathed here, and the amiable qualities of the owner of this paradise, mutually contributed. This, which I may justly call the temple of social enjoyments, was constantly open to the reception of worthy men, whether of the island or strangers: and few gentlemen of rank, whether of the Army or Navy, on service here, quitted the island without having passed some of their time at the Decoy.*[32]

This glowing description was written by Edward Long, whose Cornish family had established connections with Jamaica in the mid-17th century, when Edward's grandfather, Samuel, had been Speaker of the Assembly. Edward's father, also Samuel, owned Tredudwell Manor near Fowey, but had been born in Jamaica. He was a member of the Council and owner of Lucky Valley Estate in Clarendon Parish, which lies in the south of the island. Edward had been born in August 1734 at Roselyon Manor in St Blazey, not far from the Tredudwell family property.

---

30 Parker, Matthew. *The Sugar Barons*. London: Windmill Books, 2012, p.285.
31 Yates, Geoffrey S. *Rose Hall: death of a legend*. Accessed 21 January 2016, http://www.jamaicanfamilysearch.com/Samples2/mpalmer.htm
32 Long, Edward. *The History of Jamaica: Or, General Survey of the Ancient and Modern State of that Island, with Reflections on Its Situation, Settlements, Inhabitants, Climate, Products, Commerce, Laws, and Government*. Cambridge: Cambridge University Press, 2010, pp.76–77.

He studied law, but on his father's death in 1757 left for Jamaica to manage Lucky Valley Estate. He became a judge at the Vice-Admiralty Court, and in August 1758 married Mary Ballard, a wealthy sugar heiress. Elected to the Assembly for the Parish of St Ann, he briefly became Speaker of the Assembly before returning to England because of ill health. He later spent many years as a member of the powerful London Society of West India Planters and Merchants.[33] Perhaps best remembered for his *History of Jamaica*, from which the quotation above about the hospitality at the Decoy is taken, he was not only strongly in favour of slavery, but considered enslaved Africans to be a different and inferior species.[34]

Another of Charles Price II's Cornish visitors was one of Admiral Edward Boscawen's sons, William Glanville Boscawen (1749–1769), who was serving on the Jamaica Station. He unfortunately drowned while bathing in a canal on the property, and Long writes of the strong emotional impact the young man's death had on his host.[35]

This sad accident was inexpressibly afflicting to Sir Charles, and left so strong an impression on his mind that, before his own decease, he gave particular directions to inter his body close by his friend.[36]

Dr Wolcot was moved to write an elegy on William Boscawen's death, which was published in 1779. This was read by Admiral Boscawen's widow, who then wrote to Wolcot thanking him for his heartfelt lines.

---

33 The London Society of West India Planters and Merchants was established to represent the views of the British West Indian plantocracy and played a major role in resisting the abolition of the slave trade and slavery. The society was formed in 1780 and brought together three different groups: British sugar merchants, absentee planters and colonial agents. It started with a predominantly Jamaican leadership, but as Emancipation approached in the 1830s the leadership came to include a broader range of planter interests from across the British Caribbean. The society evolved into the West India Committee.
34 Morgan, Kenneth. *Materials on the history of Jamaica in the Edward Long papers held at the British Library.* London: Brunel University, 2006, pp.1–2.
35 Rogers, John Jope. *Opie and his works: being a catalogue of 760 pictures by John Opie, R.A. preceded by a biographical sketch.* London: Paul and Dominic Colnaghi, 1878, p.10.
36 Long, Edward. *The History of Jamaica: Or, General Survey of the Ancient and Modern State of that Island, with Reflections on Its Situation, Settlements, Inhabitants, Climate, Products, Commerce, Laws, and Government.* Cambridge: Cambridge University Press, 2010, p.77.

The letter in turn led to Wolcot making Mrs Boscawen's acquaintance and to her subsequent patronage of John Opie.[37]

When Charles Price II died he possessed 26,000 acres, spread throughout eleven parishes, perhaps the largest acreage ever owned by an individual in Jamaica. But in his frenzy to acquire land, he had overstretched his resources and, like many of his fellow planters, was sometimes forced to mortgage his land to pay for the management of his estates. The beginning of the American Revolutionary War, which disrupted trade between the Caribbean and American colonies, saw the further collapse of the Price estates.

Charles Price II's second son, Charles Price III, inherited his father's property after the death of first-born son, Rose Price, in 1765; Charles Price III became 2nd Baronet of Rose Hall. For several years he struggled to cope with his father's debt, and in 1775 went to England to try and come to an arrangement with the family's major creditors, the London sugar agents Serocold and Jackson. He failed; and in the same year, nine of the Price estates, including Rose Hall and Worthy Park, were conveyed to the firm until the outstanding debt could be paid. Charles returned to Jamaica in 1779 and was able to continue borrowing to keep the remaining property functioning, but by the time the American Revolutionary War ended and the market for sugar began to improve, it was too late to rescue most of the estates. He was unable to pay the debt owed to his creditors and, one after the other, most of the remaining properties were sold: Rose Hall for £18,000 in 1788 and his father's beloved Decoy the following year for only £2,500.[38]

Worn out by the efforts he had made to improve the Price family finances, Charles left Jamaica and moved to an elegant house in Grosvenor Square, London: he finally became an absentee planter. Before he left he gave his attorney, Malcolm Laing, £7,000 to cover immediate expenses, instructing him to keep the Worthy Park accounts more systematically and to send them each year to his cousin, John Price II, in Penzance. Charles

---

37 Rogers, John Jope. *Opie and his works: being a catalogue of 760 pictures by John Opie, R.A. preceded by a biographical sketch.* London: Paul and Dominic Colnaghi, 1878, p.10.
38 Craton, Michael and James Walvin. *A Jamaican Plantation: The History of Worthy Park, 1670–1970.* Toronto: University of Toronto Press, 1970, pp.163–164.

III had no children to carry on the responsibility of managing whatever remained of the family inheritance, and before his death in 1789, when the baronetcy of Rose Hall came to an end, he confirmed the arrangement his father, Charles Price II, had made in his will, which stated that Worthy Park was to be kept within the family. He also managed to pass his share of Worthy Park on to his cousin John Price, almost free of debt.[39]

After his father's death at Worthy Park when he was only one year old, John Price grew up in Penzance and, as a young man went out to Worthy Park with his mother, Margery. The pair stayed in Jamaica for about eight years, during which time John met and married Elizabeth Williams Brammer, the daughter of Dr John Brammer, Worthy Park's physician. Their first child, Charles Godolphin, was born at Worthy Park in 1765. Plans were already under way for John and his family to return to Penzance when his mother died in 1766. Rather than sailing on one of the regular Falmouth packets for Cornwall, they left on a ship bound for London, perhaps to meet with Mr Serocold and Mr Jackson to try and come to an arrangement about the looming debts of the Price estates. After docking in London, the family, complete with Margery in her coffin, eventually reached Penzance and Margery was buried in the family vault next to her husband John who, after his death at Worthy Park, was brought back to Penzance for burial.[40]

From their well-appointed house in Chapel Street, John Price II and his wife now set about living up to the image of the wealthy and cultured absentee planter. John bought up land in the area and, north of the fishing port of Newlyn, built himself a small country retreat at Chywoone Grove. He began to take part in the public life of Penzance, joining the town council, becoming a magistrate and going on to be elected mayor.[41] He took up the study of history and archaeology, writing a history of St Michael's Mount, the home of the St Aubyn family, and he discovered several ancient artefacts on his own property. He knew Dr Wolcot and was a patron of the good doctor's protégé, John Opie.

---

39   Ibid., p.164.
40   Sparrow, Elizabeth. *The Prices of Penzance: the influence of 18th century Jamaican sugar plantation owners on West Cornwall*. Penzance: Penzance Library, 1985, p.6.
41   Ibid., pp.7–8.

In November 1768 John and Elizabeth had a second son. They named him Rose, after John's eldest cousin Rose, who had died in Jamaica in 1765. In 1774 John became High Sheriff of Cornwall,[42] but while his public life was reassuringly successful it left him little time to pay attention to his wife. Elizabeth became involved in a project to set up an infirmary, assisted by the young vicar of the neighbouring village of Gulval, the Rev. John Penneck. It was said that even for a doctor's daughter she spent more time working closely with Penneck than was necessary to ensure the success of her project. While the infirmary was being built her marriage crumbled, and John became estranged from his wife.

By the late 1770s, John had built up a small but significant trading business between Penzance and Jamaica, supplying salt pilchards, which became a local staple. Salt fish, usually cod supplied from the American colonies, was in short supply during the American Revolutionary War, so Cornish pilchards were a welcome addition to the Jamaican diet, where they were an important part of a slave's food. The trade continued as an annual shipment of a variety of cargo came back to Cornwall. In April 1787, for example, the brig *Nancy* arrived in Kingston, Jamaica, from Penzance under the command of local seaman, Captain William Treluddra, carrying 642 barrels of salt pilchards and 5 tons of potatoes. On the return journey she carried 126 hogsheads of sugar, 25 puncheons of rum, a quantity of old copper, 8 planks of mahogany wood and 6 kegs of tamarind fruit.[43]

John Price II was not the only local trader with business in Jamaica. Abraham Hart (about 1710–1784) was another. His family had come to Penzance from Weinheim, a town in the south of Germany,[44] and became part of the small Jewish communities which were established in Penzance and Falmouth in the early 18th century, when both towns were thriving commercial centres. The members of the Jewish communities provided

---

42 Craton, Michael and James Walvin. *A Jamaican Plantation: The History of Worthy Park, 1670–1970*. Toronto: University of Toronto Press, 1970, pp.164–165.
43 Sparrow, Elizabeth. *The Prices of Penzance: the influence of 18th century Jamaican sugar plantation owners on West Cornwall*. Penzance: Penzance Library, 1985, pp.13–14.
44 *Rabbi Abraham Hart*. Accessed 10 September 2016, http://www.farhi.org/wc117/wc117_320.htm

services needed by the two port towns, setting themselves up as retailers, tailors, jewellers, silversmiths, clockmakers, pawnbrokers, and wine and spirit merchants. Abraham Hart became a rabbi and a well-known scholar in the area,[45] and a leading member of the Penzance community which in 1740 leased land for a cemetery and by 1768 had built a synagogue in New Street. Abraham Hart established himself as a retailer and jeweller and as an importer of wines and spirits, specialising in rum. The rum he sourced mostly from Jamaica, and he is believed to have spent time on the island during the 1750s, where he familiarised himself with the origins of the various available rums and began to develop business partnerships with the local agents.[46] In his search for high quality rum, maybe he met with John Price, a fellow townsman with an in-depth knowledge of Jamaican plantations and the rum they produced. Hart imported his wines and spirits into Newlyn and, by the time of his death, had established a company with an excellent reputation.

Abraham Hart's son, Ezekiel Lazarus Hart (about 1739–1803),[47] inherited the business on his father's death and in 1790 Ezekiel's son, Lemon Hart, took charge. Lemon Hart (1771–1845), whose Hebrew name was Asher Laman ben Eleazer,[48] was determined to expand the business to include the production of blended rum. He built a distillery at the top of Jennings Street in Penzance[49] and, like his grandfather, travelled to the Caribbean to select the best rums, importing not only from Jamaica but from the colony of Demerara, on the north-east coast of South America.[50]

Like his grandfather, Lemon Hart was a leading figure in the local community. He was *parnassa*, or warden, of the synagogue, a member of

---

45 Rubinstein, William D., Michael Jolles and Hilary L. Rubinstein. *The Palgrave dictionary of Anglo-Jewish history*. Basingstoke: Palgrave Macmillan, 2011, p.403.
46 *Lemon Hart: a real rum story*. Accessed 11 September 2016, http://thedabbler.co.uk/2011/02/lemon-hart-a-real-rum-story/
47 Rubinstein, William D., Michael Jolles and Hilary L. Rubinstein. *The Palgrave dictionary of Anglo-Jewish history*. Basingstoke: Palgrave Macmillan, 2011, p.403.
48 Ibid., p.403.
49 Smelt, Maurice. *101 Cornish lives*. Penzance: Alison Hodge, 2006, p.116.
50 *Destiny: Hart of heritage*. Accessed 11 September 2016, http://www.lemonhartrum.com/pathway.html

both the Masonic and the Druids' lodges in the nearby town of Redruth,[51] and served as an officer in one of the local militias during the Napoleonic Wars.[52] Like the Price family, he lived in a large house on Chapel Street, and in 1804 he established the Lemon Hart Company, producing his blend of Demerara rums under the name Lemon Hart Rum, a brand you can still buy.

At about this time, Lemon Hart was appointed as the official supplier of rum to the Royal Navy. Rum had been recognised as an official daily ration by the navy since the mid-17th century and was sourced from several spirit merchants and traders at various ports, but in the late 18th century the Admiralty made the decision to appoint an official supplier of rum. Hart succeeded in obtaining the contract, under the terms of which he was to supply 100,000 gallons of rum annually. He held the contract for many years,[53] expanding his business to London and moving his rum stocks to the newly opened West India Docks.[54] After his move to London, he continued to support the Penzance Jewish community, buying the freehold of both the synagogue and the cemetery, and donating items for the use of the synagogue. He died in Brighton in October 1845, and his son, David, then took over the business, now trading as Lemon Hart & Son. In 1892 the company joined rum importers Portal Dingwall & Norris, to form a powerful London-based alliance which remained intact for half a century.

While Lemon Hart was taking over the family business from his father, at the Price residence on Chapel Street John and Elizabeth's elder son, Charles Godolphin, had died, leaving Rose Price their only child. Rose went to the local Latin School in Penzance and then to Magdalen College, Oxford, where his tutor was John Vinicombe, who came from

---

51 Rubinstein, William D., Michael Jolles and Hilary L. Rubinstein. *The Palgrave dictionary of Anglo-Jewish history*. Basingstoke: Palgrave Macmillan, 2011, p.403.
52 *Lemon Hart: a real rum story*. Accessed 11 September 2016, http://thedabbler.co.uk/2011/02/lemon-hart-a-real-rum-story/
53 The British Library Board. 'The government contract for 100,000 gallons of rum for the navy.' *Morning Post*, p.4 (21 December 1849). British Newspaper Archive, accessed 11 September 2016,. http://www.britishnewspaperarchive.co.uk/
54 For more information on the West India Docks facility, see Chapter 5: Barbados, the British Windward Islands and Trinidad.

Madron, a village near Penzance. Soon after his matriculation in 1787, Rose, accompanied by Vinicombe, set off on a Grand Tour of Europe. While the two were travelling, Charles Price III died in London, leaving John Price in control of the family's business affairs as well as the annual accounts of Worthy Park, sent to Penzance by the attorney Mr Laing, which were giving cause for alarm.[55] When Rose returned from his extended journey in 1791, having travelled through France at the height of the revolution, he and John Vinicombe were promptly sent out to Jamaica to investigate the Price properties.

When Rose Price and John Vinicombe inspected the accounts, they were appalled at what they found. Not only had Malcolm Laing, the attorney, kept the accounts badly, but he had deposited the £7,000 left by Charles III for management of the estate into his own account. He and the overseer were summarily dismissed. Rose took over the management of Worthy Park and invested heavily in his efforts to turn the estate into a viable business. His first task was to increase sugar production. The acreage under cultivation was extended, and mechanisation of the sugar mills, based on machinery used in Cornish mines, was introduced. To cope with the increased production, the slave labour force was increased, and the number of slaves rose from 338 to 528. He collected statistics concerning their health, he improved their diet, and he built new lodgings and a slave hospital.[56] Slaves that were more humanely treated and better fed worked harder, and the healthier the slaves born on the estate, the fewer new slaves would have to be bought each year.[57] His motive was not humanitarian. It was to increase the efficiency of sugar production.

Rose also rationalised the estate's sugar and rum exports. At one time most of Worthy Park's rum and some of its sugar was sold on the local market, but now almost everything was shipped to Britain, to the London merchant Thomas Smith.[58] There were many mechanical, civil engineering and clerical improvements to be made, including: an ambitious

---

55 Craton, Michael and James Walvin. *A Jamaican Plantation: The History of Worthy Park, 1670–1970*. Toronto: University of Toronto Press, 1970, p.166.
56 Ibid., p.172.
57 Ibid., p.173.
58 Ibid., p.115.

road construction project designed to ease the challenge of transporting sugar from the estate to the harbour for shipment; better management of the milling process; and the improvement of the accounting system. Rose brought over several Cornishmen from the Penzance area to help with the work, including Robert Richards, a chief clerk from a solicitor's office, the miller, William Pengelly, Robert Ellis, a book-keeper, and Charles Dale, a blacksmith.[59]

Soon after his arrival a young enslave girl by the name of Lizette caught Rose's attention. Her mother was the enslaved woman Eleanor Price, perhaps the child of an earlier member of the Price family, and her father was probably a Worthy Park book-keeper called Nash. Lizette was manumitted by Rose and bore him two children, Elizabeth and John. Before he left Jamaica, he arranged with one Peter Douglas, the owner of neighbouring Point Hill Estate, to later send the children to England for education. Elizabeth married a Scottish clergyman, settled in Scotland and never returned to Jamaica, while John studied engineering and returned to Jamaica in 1823 to live with his mother, Lizette, and her family.[60]

Rose Price made significant changes to the running of Worthy Park, and before he returned to Penzance in September 1795 he advised his attorney and overseer to continue implementing the accounting system he had put in place. 'There are always', he wrote:

> *five separate books to be kept on Worthy Park viz: a great Plantation Book, a store book, a Boiling House book, a still House Book, and a Daily labour Book. I have left five compleat Books on the Estate & I request that when they are filled with writing that five more be purchased or written home for, and that the old ones may be carefully laid up, as the Books of the Estates are the only Records by which future generations can inform themselves of the management of the Plantations.*[61]

---

59 Sparrow, Elizabeth. *The Prices of Penzance: the influence of 18th century Jamaican sugar plantation owners on West Cornwall.* Penzance: Penzance Library, 1985, p.15.
60 Smith, Raymond T. *The matrifocal family: power, pluralism and politics.* New York: Routledge, 2014, pp.90–91.
61 Craton, Michael and James Walvin. *A Jamaican Plantation: The History of Worthy Park, 1670–1970.* Toronto: University of Toronto Press, 1970, p.viii.

In the hope that a significant increase in his attorney's salary would prevent the man from lining his own pockets at the estate's expense, Rose offered him an additional £100 over the £200 he had previously been paid.[62]

The substantial sums Rose spent on the Jamaica estates plunged the family into debt, and his father had to borrow heavily from the Prices' sugar agent, Thomas Smith, to enable the estates to function at all. In return for the loan, Worthy Park and its related properties were placed in trust to Thomas Smith for ninety-nine years, during which time the entire production was to be consigned to Smith until the loan was paid off.[63]

In 1797, John Price died at his retreat at Chywoone, and Rose Price, now twenty-nine, inherited both the Jamaica plantations and many of his father's local responsibilities. He became a magistrate and, as the war with France continued, raised two companies of infantry, many of whose soldiers were miners from the area. Later he would become President of the Penzance Public Library – now the Morrab Library,[64] the West Penwith Savings Bank, and the local branch of the Society for the Promotion of Christian Knowledge.[65] A year after his father's death he married Elizabeth Lambart, a young woman from County Meath, Ireland, with valuable connections to the upper echelons of British society.[66] For the first years of married life, thanks to the conditions laid down by his uncle, Charles Price III, he enjoyed a large income. But his father's house on Chapel Street no longer met his social aspirations, nor indeed the growing size of his family. He needed a larger and more imposing residence, and made plans to build a house near Chywoone, first building a windbreak so large that locals referred to it as 'Price's Folly'; but his wife persuaded him against the idea, and he instead bought Kenegie Manor in Guval. In 1814 Rose Price, like his father before him, became High Sheriff of Cornwall and, in the same year, bought Trengwainton Manor near the village of Madron. In 1815, most likely due to the influence of his wife's

---

62 Ibid., p.175.
63 Ibid., p.178.
64 Smelt, Maurice. *101 Cornish lives*. Penzance: Alison Hodge, 2006, p.193.
65 Craton, Michael and James Walvin. *A Jamaican Plantation: The History of Worthy Park, 1670–1970*. Toronto: University of Toronto Press, 1970, p.185.
66 Ibid., p.179.

relations, he was made 1st Baronet of Trengwainton. The family moved into Trengwainton in 1817, following the completion of alterations to the house and the establishment of a walled garden built to the dimensions of Noah's Ark as described in the Bible, and here he lived in style, and wore a coach attended with four postillions: enslaved people brought from Jamaica who were dressed in rich livery, and wore powdered wigs.[67]

Many of his children married well, but in the face of declining sugar profits the expense of keeping them all in the manner to which they had become accustomed became increasingly difficult. Sir Rose encouraged his wife's wealthy relations to invest in his estates, but the debt on Worthy Park continued to increase, and the arrangements with creditors became ever more complicated. Like his uncle Charles Price III, he underestimated how far the sugar market would decline below a certain level, and overestimated the worth of his land and slaves.

In his last years, as the Abolitionist movement grew and it became clear that the end of slavery was inevitable, Rose Price wrote a pamphlet in which, although he presents himself as a radical reformer, he clearly speaks to the views of the plantocracy. Entitled, rather obscurely, *Pledges on Colonial Slavery, to Candidates for Seats in Parliament, Rightly Considered*, it set out to prove three principal points: that while slavery was abhorrent it was much better than the life of a free labourer in England; that slavery under the English was much preferable to slavery under any other nation; and that black people, although they alone were suited to labour in the tropics, would only work if forced to do so. Members of Parliament were therefore encouraged to continue slavery, but if this was not to be, to put legislation in place that would force the emancipated slaves to continue working on the plantation and ensure that the slave owners were properly compensated for the loss of their slave labour.[68] Emancipation came in 1834, but Rose Price did not live long enough to see its effects: he died in late September 1834, two months after the Emancipation Act had come into force.[69]

---

67 Sparrow, Elizabeth. *The Prices of Penzance: the influence of 18th century Jamaican sugar plantation owners on West Cornwall*. Penzance: Penzance Library, 1985, p.27.
68 Craton, Michael and James Walvin. *A Jamaican plantation: the history of Worthy Park, 1760–1970*. Toronto: University of Toronto Press, 1970, pp.191–192.
69 Ibid., p.203.

At his death most of his sons and daughters had already received their share of the settlement from the Price estates, and the most valuable legacies were made to his wife Elizabeth's relations: her brother, the Earl of Talbot, Talbot's sons, and her uncle, Lord Shelburne. While Rose Price's direct family were no doubt disappointed that they did not receive more, they must also have been relieved that they were not made responsible for managing the declining Price estates. As Craton and Walvin observe:

> *Rose Price's favours were double-edged, since his noble relatives were also appointed trustees. Conveniently provided with instructions to sell whatever was necessary to fulfill the financial bequests, they found themselves responsible for an estate that proved to be unsaleable, whose creditors now numbered over twenty and whose encumbering debts, constantly increasing, would take a further thirty years to determine.*[70]

As Rose Price's eldest son, Rose Lambart, had predeceased his father, the baronetcy passed to the next son, Charles Dutton Price who had apparently behaved in such a way that he was disinherited: his father left him nothing but the proverbial shilling, considering even that to be:

> *more than his base and unnatural conduct to me and my family deserves but I will and I hope that though he may for a time persist in the career of vice and infamy which now mark his conduct he may die a penitent sinner in the strict sense of our Blessed Saviour.*[71]

Charles Dutton died unmarried and without issue in 1872, when the baronetcy passed to the descendents of Rose Price's next eldest son, Francis, a captain in the 19th Regiment of Foot and 78th Highlanders, who died in 1839. Among Rose Price's other sons, it was his second-youngest son, George who took up the challenge of managing what remained of the Pirce estates in Jamaica, while John (John Price III)

---

70 Ibid., pp.187–188.
71 Ibid., p.203.

became a lawyer and, like his youngest brother Thomas, spent his career in the colonial service.[72]

In 1838 the British government, recognising that the post-Emancipation attempt to implement the apprenticeship of the recently enslaved in its Caribbean colonies was not succeeding, replaced it with a free wage labour system. The change-over caused confusion in the labour management of many plantations, including the Price properties. Many newly-freed men and women left the estates to work for themselves, and estates such as Worthy Park were left without enough labour to produce their sugar. In an effort to find an approach to managing the situation, Thomas Price was sent out to Jamaica in early 1841 – but he was unable to make any progress and after only four months returned to Penzance. Two years later George Price took up the challenge. Perhaps he had better management skills than Thomas, but he also had a financial advantage: he had married Emily Plunkett, daughter of the wealthy 14th Baron of Dunsany, and so had the financial backing of his father-in-law, which gave him access to the funds that enabled him to continue efforts to save the affairs of the Price estates.

George understood what his brother Thomas had not: that the supposed unreliability of the now free labour force was not because the work force was by its very nature unreliable, but was in fact the result of the irregular work offered by the sugar plantations. The busy planting and harvesting seasons of the year were interspersed with months when no work was available, and no wages earned. Workers therefore found other ways to earn their living, often growing provision crops for sale in the local market. They were, unsurprisingly, not willing to give up the regular income this provided and go back to the backbreaking work of planting and cutting cane and boiling sugar.

Mechanisation seemed a way of cutting back on the dependence on casual labour; mechanisation would provide a means of raising the profitability of the Price sugar estates, so they could compete with the cheaper production prices achieved by countries such as Brazil and

---

72   Craton, Michael and James Walvin. *A Jamaican plantation: The history of Worthy Park, 1670–1970*. Toronto: University of Toronto Press, 1970, pp.203–204.

the Spanish colonies of Cuba and Puerto Rico, where slave labour was still in use. George Price ordered an increasing amount of machinery, including boilers and clarifiers and a steam engine that operated on the same principle as the engines used to pump water out of mines all over Cornwall. He built the first estate railway in Jamaica, which had a main line, several movable branch lines to lead into each cane field, and a branch line to carry the cane trash from the sugar factory. Unfortunately, he had not thought through his mechanisation project sufficiently thoroughly: he failed to check that the machines he ordered were suitable for the local tropical climate or to consider that they might be damaged during transport and need repair on arrival. Nor did he ensure that those who operated the machines would receive solid training in their correct use and maintenance. As a result, the machinery was often of little use, and sugar production fell yet further.

In late 1847, George Price was recalled to England by one of his father's trustees, Viscount Ingres, to explain his extravagant use of funds and poor results. In Jamaica, George's place was taken by the attorney Gilbert Shaw, and George remained in England to try and save his reputation. Both George and his brother Thomas claimed that it was the longstanding debt that was preventing the development of the Price estates and that given time and higher sugar prices, conditions would improve. George's father-in-law believed that the brothers were correct, and on condition that George returned to Jamaica advanced the sum of £5,000 to pay off the most pressing debts. The majority of the trustees and creditors were, however, more interested in disposing of the estates than helping them to prosper, and when the Encumbered Estate Act came into force in 1854 it was only a matter of time before the estates were sold. This Act established the principle that creditors be paid in proportion to their debt; it set up a Court of Commissioners to ascertain the authenticity of debts and to organise the sale of property; and legislated that the proportional settlements be accepted by the creditors.[73] The Act was signed into Jamaican law in 1861, and was of mixed blessing:

---

73   Ibid., pp.234–236.

> *Without the Act, encumbered estates could not have been sold; yet sale itself spelt defeat, prices were derisory and, as with the compensations of 1834 [paid to slave owners for the loss of their slave labour after Emancipation], it was found that the chief beneficiaries were not the planters [and certainly not the ex-slaves] but the merchants [such as the Price's sugar agent Thomas Smith] and mortgage-holders [such as the Pinneys of Nevis] who had always been their creditors.*[74]

Worthy Park was sold at auction in June 1863 for £8,500 exclusive of stock. The price paid amounted to little more than an eighth of Worthy Park's debts and was handed over to the trustees for distribution to the creditors according to their share. The Price family, for better or worse, now finally parted company with Worthy Park.[75]

After the sale of Worthy Park, George Price moved to Spanish Town, where he played an increasing part in local Jamaican affairs. His liberal views were almost unique among white politicians of his day, as he held respect for the free black majority. In 1864, in protest against the autocratic and oppressive administration of Governor Eyre, he resigned his positions as Custos of St Catherine's Parish and Justice of the Peace. Conditions for black Jamaicans continued to get worse: the economy continued to deteriorate, the unemployment rate grew, and the price of imported food or clothing continued to rise. Violence against the white elite began to flare up, culminating in the town of Morant Bay, the capital of St Thomas Parish in the south-east of the island. In October 1865, black labourers surrounded the town's courthouse, which was filled with sugar planters and members of the court. A black labourer was on trial, charged with trespassing on an abandoned plantation, and his fellow workers, led by Paul Bogle,[76] were incensed that a man should be brought

---

74   Ibid., p.234.
75   Ibid., p.238.
76   Paul Bogle had been born a free man in about 1822. He became a Baptist deacon in Stony Gut, a village located a few miles north of Morant Bay, and a firm political supporter of George William Gordon. Gordon was a wealthy mulatto businessman, magistrate and politician, one of two representatives to the Assembly from the Parish of St Thomas, and a leading critic of the policies of Governor Eyre. For his part in the Morant Bay Rebellion, Bogle was captured, and hanged on 24 October 1865. He was named a National Hero of Jamaica in 1969.

to court for such an offence. They set the courthouse on fire, and anyone trying to escape was killed. In all, twenty-five people died and thirty-one were injured, and Governor Eyre's reaction was swift and brutal: labourers were rounded up and 439 were either hung or shot by firing squads. Hundreds more had their homes burnt down.[77]

Following the events at Morant Bay and their aftermath, George Price decided he could no longer live in Jamaica and, accompanied by his servant Charles Colbrook, returned to England.

Charles Colbrook.
Courtesy of the Morrab Library, Penzance, Cornwall.

---

77   Cavanaugh, Jake. *The cause of the Morant Bay Rebellion: 1865*. Accessed 26 January 2016, http://scholar.library.miami.edu/emancipation/jamaica4.htm

He went not to Penzance but to the Isle of Wight, off the south coast of England. Here he continued to campaign against Governor Eyre, and wrote *Jamaica and the Colonial Office: who caused the crisis?* In this book, so unlike his father's earlier pamphlet, he argued that the problems in Jamaica were caused not by the intransigence and idleness of the black population, but because of poor economic conditions. This, he wrote, was because most of the investors of capital and the skilled white workers had left the island, and because the British government appeared unconcerned about Jamaica's future development. George Price believed that black Jamaicans, if given education and guidance, would 'ultimately be able to assist materially in their own government',[78] a view surely almost unique for a sugar planter to hold in the later 19th century, and a view he held until his death in 1890.

Charles Price in about 1880.
Courtesy of the Morrab Library, Penzance, Cornwall.

---

78   Ibid., p.230.

Sugar was Jamaica's main product, the means of wealth for the Price family and other members of the plantocracy, and while there was some evidence of mineral resources, especially copper, on the island, nothing was done to exploit it after the early Spanish attempts at mining. When sugar was doing well, planters saw no point in investing in an alternative industry, even though they imported considerable quantities of copper for use in their sugar factories: the large round 'coppers' used to boil the sugar cane were an essential part of the production process. As the wealthy planter Mr Beckford remarked, pointing to his cane fields: 'with such a mine of wealth on the surface, it would be idle to search for one beneath it.'[79]

In 1720, Colonel Charles Long made the first large-scale attempt to exploit Jamaica's mineral resources. Like his relation Edward Long – he who had penned the enthusiastic description of the Decoy Estate belonging to Charles Price II – Colonel Long had Cornish roots. Without any proof of the existence of a workable lode of copper or silver on the island, he secured a Royal Patent from King George I, which gave him and his fellow investors the right to mine all the gold and silver resources on Jamaica. The Royal Mines Company was established, and had no difficulty selling its shares in both England and Jamaica, quickly raising £150,000. Colonel Long assumed the position of treasurer, and also took on the responsibility of supervising the selection of miners and their transportation, along with their tools and equipment, to Jamaica. It is likely, given the Long family connection with Cornwall, that many of the miners were Cornishmen, but there is no record of their names. Administrative staff were also employed, and engineers were belatedly sent to survey the island for workable gold and silver resources.

They reported that they had found none. As the mining project was a lost cause, Colonel Long looked for an alternative investment for the Royal Mines Company funds. He chose the South Sea Company, a British joint-stock company which, with the support of the British government, had been created in 1711 to help consolidate and reduce the national debt. As the company's shares rose in value, Colonel Long was

---

79 Gardner, William James. *A history of Jamaica from its discovery by Christopher Columbus to the present time; including an account of its trade and agriculture* … London: Elliot Stock, 1873, p.162.

one of many who invested in it, but after expanding its operations and producing ever higher dividends for its investors, the company suddenly failed. The collapse of the South Sea Bubble, as it came to be called, put Colonel Long in court, and his assets, including 14,000 acres of land and six estates in Jamaica, were seized. Colonel Long did not survive the humiliation, and died in May 1723 at the age of 44.[80]

Apart from brief attempts at mining copper and silver in the Healthshire Hills, and lead on the Hope Estate in the parish of St Andrew, interest in exploiting Jamaica's mineral resources did not revive until the mid-19th century, when similar projects were under way on the islands of Cuba, Virgin Gorda and Aruba.

In 1840, a Cornish miner discovered copper deposits in the Port Royal Mountains, which lie about 10 miles from Kingston, in St Andrew's Parish. A company was formed, and a shaft sunk which yielded a rich ore, containing 55 per cent copper. Apparently as a result of lack of capital investment, the enterprise closed down in December 1846, but in 1853 a new company was established: the Port Royal and St Andrew's Copper Mining Company, with a capital of £25,000.[81] The mining area was at a relatively high elevation, and believed to be free from yellow fever.[82] Cornishman Captain Clemes was employed as the mine captain and he, along with sixteen Cornish miners, a smith and Mr Hocking, a carpenter, set sail for Jamaica in July of 1853.[83] Henry Lowry, from Truro in Cornwall, was employed as chief officer and given the task of reporting on the potential of the mine. Soon after his arrival, Lowry wrote to his sister, Hespie, telling her something of his daily life at Silver Hill Estate where he was living. 'I am up every day at 6,' he writes:

---

80 Vendryes, Harry E. *An old Jamaican mining venture.* Transcript of broadcast made over Radio ZQ1 in Jamaica on 1 May 1946.
81 British Library Board. 'Mining intelligence.' *Royal Cornwall Gazette*, p.7 (14 January 1853). British Newspaper Archive, accessed 9 September 2016. http://www.britishnewspaperarchive.co.uk/
82 British Library Board. 'Foreign Intelligence.' *Norfolk News*, p.2 (30 July 1853). British Newspaper Archive, accessed 10 October 2014. http://www.britishnewspaperarchive.co.uk/
83 Schwartz, Sharron P. *The Cornish in Latin America: 'Cousin Jack' and the New World.* Wicklow: The Cornubian Press, 2016, p.153.

What with mining, and writing and riding from one part of the country to another, my hands overflow with work. The Fever has been very prevalent in the Island, and a great many English people have recently died – some of the Cornish Miners who came out in the same ship with me for another Company, died a week or two ago. One only of our men has died: Hocking the Carpenter ... With you at home it is now dull, dreary, foggy November, but here with us it is hotter than the hottest Summer's day in England. From my windows I have such a beautiful prospect. A tributary of the Yellow River flows just below them, and as it winds its silvery way among the rocks and through the thickets of Bamboo and Cedar Trees, it forms a sweet stanza in the poetry of nature.[84]

As might be surmised from Lowry's description of the view from his windows, he was something of a poet, but some of his observations are more down to earth. Continuing his letter to his sister, he writes:

There are many inconveniences, the heat is very intense. You cannot walk out in the day for ten minutes without being just as wet with perspiration as if you had been in a shower of rain. My hands and arms are every now and then covered with little sores arising from ants and mosquito bites. As for the rats, I am obliged to keep a whip behind my pillow to drive them off the bed.[85]

Although the initial belief that there was no yellow fever in the mining area had proved to be false, when Lowry returned to England in 1855, he reported that the operation at the Silver Hill section of the mine looked promising:

Labour is generally abundant, and the natives are likely soon to become tolerably efficient workmen. It is my decided conviction that the operation, at Silver Hill in particular, will result favourably; the lode is the only quartz lode (I have brought specimens for your inspection)

---

84 Henry Lowry. Accessed 18 July 2016, http://www.haine.org.uk/haine-web/mariamartin.htm
85 Ibid.

which I have seen in Jamaica, and is in every respect promising as could be desired. I believe nothing but a little perseverance will be requisite to make Silver Hill an important and profitable mine. As the operations have proceeded, nothing has occurred to alter my convictions ... I think any company would be warranted in spending a much larger amount of capital than has already been spent in the operations here, if it should be required, and I have no hesitation in recommending you to the effectual and complete development of the mineral ground.[86]

By 1856, the potential of making a profit from the Silver Hill Mine looked less certain and at the annual meeting of the company held in February 1856, the chairman reported that the 'expectations of the operations at Silver Hill had not yet been realised'.[87] Lowry believed that with further investment the mine could be successful, while Clemes, having submitted accounts that clearly showed the mine was operating at a loss, believed that it was time to call a halt to the mining operations.[88] The company was subsequently dissolved.

In 1841, copper was also discovered at Mount Vernon in St Thomas Parish, and the Jamaica Copper Mining Company was set up with a small capital of £11,600. The proprietors sought advice on how best to develop the mine from one Señor Don Renaldo, the captain of the successful El Cobre mine in Cuba. In June of 1841, they requested his assistance in a letter sent via the Jamaica Packet, and the gentleman 'was daily expected,'[89] although why El Cobre mine would be willing to advise a rival company is unclear.

Progress was slow, but the company resolved to issue new shares and raise more capital. Development continued, and a 30-foot water wheel with wood frames was ordered from West & Sons, an engineering firm

---

86 *A Cornish mine agent in 1850s Jamaica.* Accessed 20 July 2016, https://gwinowan.wordpress.com/2015/03/21/a-cornish-mine-agent-in-1850s-jamaica/
87 British Library Board. 'Port Royal and St Andrew's Copper Mining Company.' *London Daily News*, p.3 (28 February 1856). British Newspaper Archive, accessed 20 July 2016. http://www.britishnewspaperarchive.co.uk/
88 Ibid.
89 'Copper mining in Jamaica.' *The Civil Engineer and Architect's Journal.* (June 1841).

in St Blazey, Cornwall.[90] Between 1854 and 1857, 207 tons of ore were shipped to Liverpool, but the mine ultimately failed after there was insufficient capital available to purchase the pump engines needed to keep the mine in operation.[91]

In 1853, copper was found in the north-east of Jamaica, in what was then Metcalf Parish but would, in 1866, become part of St Mary's Parish.[92] Several mines were opened in the area, including Job's Hill and Pembroke. Cornwall again provided the mining expertise: six Cornish miners were sent out to Job's Hill where, along with local labourers, they drove adits[93] into the conical-shaped hill. All reports on the copper ore were optimistic, and it was thought that the mine would prove profitable.

The Job's Hill and Pembroke copper mines.
From an 1870 woodcut engraving in the author's collection.

---

90 Copy of scale drawing of the water wheel sourced from the Cornwall Records Office.
91 'Jamaica's mineral deposits.' *Sunday Gleaner*, p.16. (25 October 1973).
92 In 1839 Sir Charles Metcalfe became Governor of Jamaica. Just before he left office in 1842, Metcalfe Parish was created from parts of the parishes of St George and St Mary. In 1866 Metcalf Parish was incorporated into St Mary's Parish.
93 An adit (from Latin *aditus*, entrance) is an entrance to an underground mine which is horizontal or nearly so.

In the same year, the copper deposits of the Sue River in Metcalf Parish were thought to be promising, and the Sue River Copper and General Mining Company was established with a capital of £40,000. One of the first Cornish miners to go and work the Sue River lode was William Lawrence from Nancledra, near Penzance. Having made the journey and started work in the mine, by June 1854 he was dead. He died from cholera which, like yellow fever and malaria, caused the death of many of the miners who sailed out to the Caribbean.[94] In 1854 more Cornish miners, led by mine captain Richard Hollow, went out to the Sue river. They included the carpenter, Thomas Burrell, the smith, James Nankervis, and the miners, William P. Berryman, James Christopher, John Kemp, John Martin, Thomas Nicholls and William Truscott.[95]

All these Jamaican mining ventures failed, from either lack of capital, poor management, a drop in the quality of the ore, or the fall in the international price of copper. The views expressed by one Mr Hoyte, a shareholder in the Port Royal and St Andrew's Copper Mining Company, and reported in the *London Daily News* of 13 March 1855, provide a good summary of the challenges of establishing a profitable copper mine in mid-19th-century Jamaica:

> *There were plenty of mineral indications in every part of the island, but the question was whether mining could be carried out at a profit. He [Mr Hoyte] had the utmost confidence in the board of directors, and he perfectly exonerated them from attempting to lead the shareholders astray. He believed that every hill-side would produce valuable ore, but he doubted whether it could ever be worked at a remunerative profit.*[96]

---

94   Courtney Library. *Cornish people overseas from 1840: index compiled from local newspapers.* Truro: Courtney Library, nd.
95   Schwartz, Sharron P. *The Cornish in Latin America: 'Cousin Jack' and the New World.* Wicklow: The Cornubian Press, 2016, p.153.
96   British Library Board. 'Port Royal and St Andrew's Copper Mining Company.' *London Daily News*, p.7 (13 March 1855). British Newspaper Archive, accessed 20 July 2016. http://www.britishnewspaperarchive.co.uk/

It was not until the discovery of bauxite in the 20th century that Jamaica's mining industry began to make a significant contribution to the local economy.

When Francis Price, the patriarch of the Price family, came to Jamaica in 1655, he was not the only Cornishman to make the decision to settle in Jamaica. A fellow soldier, named Bawden or Bodden, also remained in Jamaica, but by 1658 he had moved on to the nearby Cayman Islands, where he was one of the earliest settlers.[97]

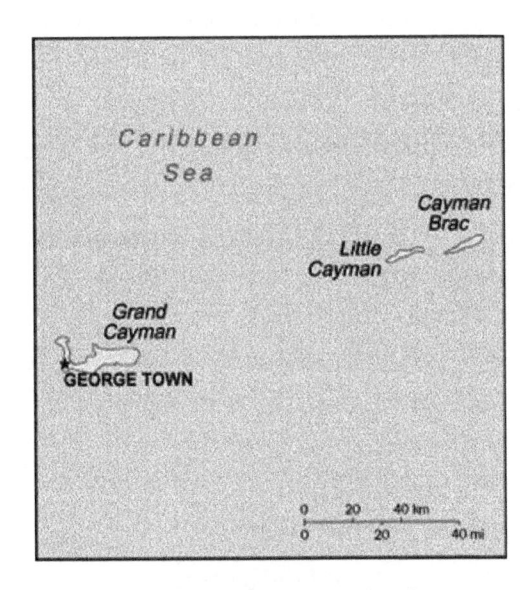

Map of the Cayman Islands.

The first recorded settlements in the Cayman Islands were located on Little Cayman and Cayman Brac, and were established between 1661 and 1671 when Sir Thomas Modyford was Governor of Jamaica. Spain had recognised British possession of the Cayman Islands in the 1670 Treaty of Madrid, but because of continual attacks by Spanish privateers on the settlers, Modyford's successor called them back to Jamaica. By 1700, settlers began to return, including Bodden's grandson Isaac Bodden, who was listed as Grand Cayman's first official inhabitant.

---

97 'Cayman Islands search for relatives of their Cornish forefathers.' *Daily Telegraph* (6 April 2017). Accessed 9 May 2017, http://www.telegraph.co.uk/news/2017/04/06/cayman-islands-search-relatives-cornish-forefathers/

During the 18th century, the Cayman Islands were well known to the pirates that roamed the area, including Cornishman, Thomas Anstis who, along with fellow Cornishman, Richard Harris, served under the Welsh pirates, Captain Howell Davis and Captain Bartholomew Roberts. Anstis was put in command of one of Robert's ships, the brigantine *Good Fortune*, but when in mid-April 1721 Roberts' ships headed for Africa, Anstis decided to stay in the Caribbean, and the *Good Fortune* slipped away from the convoy in the night. Sailing north, Anstis managed to capture the *Morning Star*, which was subsequently armed with thirty-two guns. Anstis now had two ships, but because of her superior speed and manoeuvrability he chose to continue as commander of the *Good Fortune*.

Perhaps because his crews were making less money from their plundering than they had expected, fighting broke out between those who had chosen piracy as a career and those who had been forced into service. Those who claimed that Roberts and Anstis had employed them against their will decided to petition the British king, George I, for a pardon.[98] But in August 1722, after waiting nine months for a reply, they heard that far from agreeing to pardon them King George was sending Admiral Sir John Flowers, in command of HMS *Hector* and HMS *Adventure*, to put an end to their piracy. The pirates sailed south for the Cayman Islands, where the *Morning Star* ran aground off Grand Cayman. As her crew were being rescued by the *Good Fortune*, the pirates were sighted by Flowers. Anstis managed to escape on the *Good Fortune*, but over forty of his men were captured by a boarding party from the Royal Navy ships. Anstis sailed for the Bay of Honduras, taking at least three prizes during the voyage before bringing their crews on board to augment his remaining crew. After sinking the captured ships, he sailed for the Bahamas, taking both the sloop *Antelope* and another ship as prizes on the way. In April 1723, Anstis sailed south, landing on Tobago to careen the ships he had just taken. Here they were discovered by the HMS *Winchelsea*, which

---

98 Johnson, Charles. 'Of Captain Anstis, and his crew,' in *A General History of the Pyrates: from their first rise and settlement in the island of Providence to the present time*. London: T. Warner, at the Black-Boy in Pater-Noster-Row, 1724. Amazon Kindle edition – no pagination. Charles Johnson is thought to be a pseudonym of either the author Daniel Defoe, or the printer and journalist Nathaniel Mist.

was on a routine visit to the island. Anstis's crew burnt their two new ships and fled into Tobago's interior, but many were captured by the *Winchelsea*'s marines. Anstis and his remaining crew escaped aboard the *Good Fortune*, but some on board, unsettled by recent events, mutinied, and shot and killed Anstis as he slept in his hammock. The mutineers then imprisoned the crew members still loyal to their murdered captain and sailed south to Curaçao, where they surrendered to the Dutch authorities. The mutineers received amnesty, and their prisoners – those who had supported Anstis – were hanged.[99]

The Bodden family remained on the Cayman Islands and became an important local family: Bodden Town on Grand Cayman is named for them. Though the Cayman Islands were always regarded as a dependency of Jamaica, it was not until 1863 that an Act of the British Parliament formalised the relationship. But in 1962, when Jamaica became independent, the islands opted to remain under the British Crown. They are now a British Overseas Territory, with an economy based on tourism and financial services.

---

99 Ibid.

3

In Defence of the Empire

Throughout the 18th century and into the 19th the defence of Britain's Caribbean interests largely depended on the presence of its naval and military forces in the region.[1] Cornwall, while having few titled aristocrats, was rich in landed gentry,[2] and the armed forces promised a career to many of their younger sons, who knew that the family home and estate would be the inheritance of the eldest son. In Cornwall, the sea is never far away, and sailing and navigation skills were learnt at an early age. Many joined the Royal Navy, often going to sea as young boys and as they gained experience began to look for postings that would bring them promotion to a higher rank. For some, a spell on the Jamaica Station or the Leeward Islands Station seemed an excellent opportunity, but service in the Caribbean was a double-edged sword: while the high mortality rate from tropical diseases increased the likelihood of early promotion, there was every chance of catching a tropical disease oneself and dying at a young age.[3]

Not long after Jamaica had been ceded to England by the 1670 Treaty of Madrid, Cornishman Stephen Hutchens (about 1669–1709) joined the Jamaica Station. He had been born in the village of Paul, near the fishing village of Newlyn in the far west of Cornwall. He joined the Royal Navy as a young man and in 1695, aged 26, was assigned to the newly built

---

1 See Appendix 4 for background information on the major conflicts that impacted the Caribbean during the 18th and 19th centuries.
2 Gill, Crispin. *The great Cornish families: a history of the people and their houses*. Tiverton: Cornwall Books, 1995, p.i.
3 Wareham, Thomas. *The frigate captains of the Royal Navy, 1793–1815*. PhD thesis, University of Exeter, May 1999, pp.102–103.

HMS *Scarborough* sailing from Plymouth. In 1697, the *Scarborough* went first to Barbados, and then patrolled the seas around Anguilla, Puerto Rico, Jamaica and Cartagena de Indias, now part of Colombia. Hutchens was promoted to lieutenant, and in 1701 sailed on the *Scarborough* under the command of Captain Thomas Hudson to join the Jamaica Station, where he was promoted to commander of the *Scarborough* in 1702. He was made her captain in 1704, and under the command of Commodore Charles Wager patrolled the coasts of Germany and Norway towards the north coast of Russia before returning to the Jamaica Station via Barbados and Montserrat in June 1707. Hutchens remained captain of the *Scarborough* until he was given command of HMS *Portland* in July 1708.[4]

From his base on the Jamaica Station, Hutchens had great success in capturing enemy ships. In January 1709, he accompanied a convoy of merchant ships bound for England, and on his return to the Jamaica Station he captured a French ship off Cap St Nicolas on the north-west coast of Hispaniola. His prize was worth £6,000. In April 1709, he received information that four large enemy ships laden with valuable cargo and bullion were anchored off the small island of Bastimentos, a Spanish possession off the north coast of what is now Panama. He set out from Jamaica, determined to take them as prizes. Two of the ships managed to sail away, leaving Hutchens to fight the *Coventry*, a ship captured from the English fleet, and the *Mignon*, a French ship recently arrived from Guinea. After a hard battle, Hutchens succeeded in recapturing the *Coventry*. The *Mignon* got away, but only after she transferred her cargo of treasure and bullion onto the *Coventry*. Hutchens' capture of the *Coventry* earned him a considerable prize: the bullion alone was worth 20,000 Spanish dollars.[5] After these successes he returned to Port Royal, where he became unwell and, 'being sick and weak in body, but of sound and perfect mind and memory,'[6] wrote his will. He left £600 to build almshouses 'for the being

---

4   *The life, times and influences of Captain Stephen Hutchens of Paul, near Penzance, Cornwall.* Accessed 21 July 2016, http://freepages.family.rootsweb.ancestry.com/~treevecwll/hutchens.htm
5   Ibid.
6   Ibid.

maintenance and provision of 6 of the poorest men and 6 of the poorest women who are or shall be born in the said Parish of Paul for ever;'[7] £100 for the 'repairing amending and beautifying'[8] of the Paul Parish Church, and £20 to the Minister of Paul Church 'to buy him a suit of Mourning to wear in memory of me.'[9] The Hutchens Trust, set up by his executors, is still active, and his gift that established the almshouses continues to benefit the local community. Hutchens died on 24 August 1709, eight days after completing his will. He was 40 years old.

Another young Cornishman who served on the Jamaica Station early in his career was Edward Boscawen (1711–1761).[10] He had been born at Tregothnan House near Truro, the home of the Boscawen family since the 14th century. Edward's father, Hugh Boscawen, made his money from the copper mines at Chacewater and Gwennap, had a successful career as a Whig[11] Member of Parliament for Tregony, Truro and Penryn, and was made the 1st Viscount Falmouth. Edward, however, as a third son, knew he was unlikely to inherit Tregothnan, and having spent his boyhood in the bustling harbour of nearby Falmouth, where the anchorage at Carrick Roads was full of the ships of the Royal Navy and the Royal Mail packet service, in 1723, aged 12, he joined the Royal Navy.

Edward Boscawen's first ship, the HMS *Superbe*, was sent out to the Caribbean under the command of Admiral Francis Hosier, and while Boscawen was serving in the Caribbean he was promoted to midshipman, then to lieutenant. By 1738 he was in command of HMS *Shoreham* and was involved in the preparations for the conflict with Spain that became the War of Jenkins' Ear. The British plan called for combined operations against the Spanish colonies in the Caribbean and on the west coast of South America. Under the command of Admiral Edward Vernon, Boscawen performed with distinction in the siege of Porto Bello, an important Spanish port in what is present-day Panama. He also fought

---

7   Ibid.
8   Ibid.
9   Ibid.
10 Stewart, William. *Admirals of the world: a biographical dictionary, 1500 to the present.* Jefferson: McFarland, 2009, p.36.
11 The Whig political party stood in opposition to the Tory party and was in favour of a constitutional monarchy as opposed to absolute rule.

on shore at Cartagena de Indias, leading a large force of seamen and Royal Marines. As a reward for his services he was promoted to the command of HMS *Prince Frederick* on which he returned to England, and to Cornwall. He did not visit the Caribbean again, going on to serve in the Mediterranean, India and North America.

Although the demands of his naval service left him little time to take an active part in parliamentary proceedings, soon after his return to Cornwall he became Member of Parliament for Truro, a position he held until his death. He spent his entire life in the Royal Navy and went on to become Admiral Boscawen, Lord Commissioner of the Admiralty, General of the Marines, and a member of the Privy Council. He was sometimes known as 'Old Dreadnought' after the ship HMS *Dreadnought* that he once commanded and because of his fearless approach to leading his men. The admiral was also known as 'Wry-Necked Dick' from his habit of inclining his neck to one side, a pose noticeable in an undated portrait of him painted by Sir Joshua Reynolds.

Admiral Edward Boscawen.
Painter: Sir Joshua Reynolds. Date: unknown.

Boscawen died from typhoid fever in January 1761 while sailing off the coast of France, and was buried in the parish church of St Michael Penkivel, the village that stands outside the main gate of the Tregothnan estate.

One of his sons, William, also joined the Royal Navy and served on the Jamaica Station. Unfortunately, he drowned while visiting Decoy Estate, the favourite Jamaica residence of Sir Charles Price, a member of the wealthy Price family who came from Penzance in Cornwall.[12]

Richard Spry (1715–1775)[13] was a near contemporary of Edward Boscawen. Born at Place House in St Anthony in Roseland in south Cornwall, he was the second son of George Spry, whose business interests centred around tin mines and shipping. Place House was only a few minutes by boat across a nearby creek from the village of St Mawes, and from St Mawes, Spry would have had a good view of the entrance to Falmouth Harbour where, like Edward Boscawen, he would have become familiar with the ships of the Royal Navy and the Royal Mail packet service as they began and ended their voyages. The family owned a cutter, which his father used when business took him to Falmouth or Truro, and Richard went along at every opportunity, missing nothing as the cutter:

> *beat away to the westward, sailing among the big vessels that anchored in Carrick Roads ... Wherever you went there would be the sight and sound of ships ... Most important of all were the packet ships. Some forty years before, Falmouth had been appointed the chief station for His Majesty's mails. By now there was a fleet of smart well-manned vessels ... [and] stories of their fast passages and heroic actions against pirates and privateers were already becoming local legends.*[14]

As Richard had an elder brother, he did not expect to inherit his father's house and estate, and in 1733, aged 18, he joined the Royal Navy. By 1740

---

12 For more about the Price family, see: Chapter 2: Jamaica and the Cayman Islands; Chapter 1: The British Leeward Islands; and Chapter 9: Copper and Guano: the Mines of Virgin Gorda and Sombrero.
13 O'Toole, Laurence. *The Cornish captain's tale*. Redruth: Dyllansow Truran, 1986.
14 Ibid. p.15.

he had reached the rank of lieutenant, and early in 1743 was appointed to HMS *Superbe*, the ship on which Boscawen senior had first sailed to the Caribbean, now under the command of Sir Charles Knowles. Knowles gave Richard command of the bomb ship[15] HMS *Comet*, and sent him north to Boston to refit.

Returning to the Caribbean aboard the refitted *Comet* in February 1745, Richard was pursued by a Spanish privateer, the *Galga*, a ship much larger than his own. After a stubborn fight the *Comet* was so damaged that the commander of the *Galga* gave orders for the *Comet*'s crew to be taken off, and the ship to be sunk. Spry and his crew were taken on board the *Galga*, but before the *Comet* could be sunk the arrival of Royal Navy ships out of Antigua's English Harbour caused the *Galga* to sail away with Spry and his men on board as prisoners. Two months later they were put ashore in Havana, Cuba. Here Spry was treated well by Spanish naval officers who, expecting that he would be a prisoner for some time, freely shared with him details of the movements of the Spanish and French convoys bound for Havana. They told him that the next convoys would be sailing along the south coast of Cuba to avoid the Royal Navy cruisers that expected them to sail along the north coast, and gave him details about the transport of the vast sums of gold from Spain's New World possessions which were shipped to Havana before sailing in convoy to Spain. But after spending only two months in Havana, Spry was unexpectedly returned to England as part of an exchange of prisoners, and was able to give details of Spanish naval plans for the Caribbean to his delighted superiors. 'While I was in Havana', he writes:

> *five sail of their Men of Warr arrived having been at Porto Rico to bring from thence the 'Principe', a Ship of 66 guns who was disabled on her passage to Old Spain with Admiral de Torres Squadron. Who sailed from the Havana last November with 4 men of Warr having on board Nine Million Pieces of Eight registered. Admiral Reggio will certainly sail next November with 4 sail more, from 64 to 76 Guns,*

---

15 Bomb ships were designed for bombarding (hence the name) fixed positions on land. They were armed with mortars mounted forward near the bow and elevated to a high angle, so that their fire projected in a ballistic arc.

all new ships, but sail very heavy. Of the 4 Ships that sail'd with De Torres, only two carry'd any money, the other two were design'd to Stand the Attack should they meet any of our Cruizers, while those with the Money made off; and Notwithstanding, De Torres went in one of the Money'd Ships, yet was his Flag hoisted on board one of the others to deceive our Ships. Reggio will do the same when he goes home.[16]

On the death of his elder brother in 1756, he unexpectedly inherited Place House and its estate, and here, after King George III promoted him to rear-admiral and gave him a knighthood, he retired. When he died in November 1775, he was buried at the parish church of St Anthony in Roseland. Remembered as a good officer with a distinguished service record, he was also apparently known 'as an inveterate perpetrator of disagreeable hoaxes'![17]

Unlike Boscawen and Spry, who both came from the Falmouth area, John Eliot (1742–1769)[18] was born at Port Eliot,[19] a grand house in southeast Cornwall, about 10 miles from Plymouth Dock (now Devonport), the Royal Naval dockyard designed by Edmund Dummer (1651–1713) when he was Surveyor of the Navy. Dummer would later become one of the pioneers of the Falmouth Royal Mail packet service.[20]

Eliot was the third son of Richard Eliot, an important politician in the nearby boroughs of St Germans and Liskeard, while his grandfather, William Eliot, had been a naval officer in his day. Aged nine, John joined the Royal Navy in 1752 aboard HMS *Penzance*, which sailed for St John's, Newfoundland. He then transferred to HMS *Vanguard*, which remained at Plymouth Dock throughout the winter of 1754, and sailed with her

---

16 Ibid., p.46.
17 'Spry, Sir Richard (1715–1775).' *Dictionary of national biography*, pp.432–433 (Vol.53 1898). Accessed 6 February 2015, https://ia601607.us.archive.org/34/items/ DictionaryOfNationalBiographyVolume53/DictionaryOfNationalBiographyVolume53.pdf
18 Research into the life of John Eliot was based on the following article: Rea, Robert R. 'The naval career of John Eliot, Governor of West Florida.' *The Florida Historical Quarterly*, pp.451–467 (Vol.57, No.4, April 1979).
19 One of the few grand houses of Cornwall that is still in private hands: http://www.porteliot.co.uk/
20 For more on Edmund Dummer, see Chapter 4: The Falmouth Packet Service.

during most of 1755 and 1756, as Britain entered the Seven Years' War against France. Early in 1757, he transferred to HMS *Marlborough*, the flagship of Rear-Admiral Thomas Cotes, and sailed from Portsmouth for Port Royal, Jamaica, where Cotes took over command of the Jamaica Station. The ship's company had been looking forward to taking part in action against the French, but:

> *unfortunately Marlborough's first cruise [in search of the enemy] proved her to be such a poor sailor in the light Caribbean breezes that she was unable to make headway against the Jamaican currents. While others gained glory and took prizes, Cotes's flagship remained idle and in October was finally tied up at the wharf, her guns removed.*[21]

Eager to fight, Eliot asked the rear-admiral for permission to transfer to another ship. Permission was granted and he joined HMS *Augusta* as third lieutenant. The *Augusta*, under the command of Captain Arthur Forrest, had just returned to Port Royal in need of repairs after a successful encounter with a French naval squadron off the French possession of Saint-Domingue (which, in 1804, declared its independence and became the Empire of Haiti). Once ready to sail, the *Augusta* returned to sea and Eliot soon saw plenty of action! On Christmas Eve, they fought the French off Mayaguana, the most easterly island of the British colony of the Bahamas. In January 1758, they did some damage to French merchantmen anchored off Cape Tiburon, the peninsula on the south coast of Saint-Domingue, and by June the *Augusta* had taken several prizes and needed extensive repair. Eliot transferred to HMS *Viper*, under the command of Captain Housman Bradley, and when in January 1759 Captain Bradley died suddenly Eliot was given temporary command. In April 1759, Rear-Admiral Cotes appointed Eliot lieutenant of HMS *Hornet*, and two months later, in convoy with other ships, Eliot left Jamaica for England.

After his successful tour of duty on the Jamaica Station, Lieutenant Eliot was promoted to commander of HMS *Hawke*, a small, 12-gun,

---

21 Rea, Robert R. 'The naval career of John Eliot, Governor of West Florida.' *The Florida Historical Quarterly*, p.454 (Vol.57, No.4, April 1979).

sloop. She was captured by the French privateer *Duc de Choiseul*, and Eliot and his crew were made prisoner. When they were exchanged for French prisoners, and Eliot returned to England, he had to appear at an enquiry into the fate of the *Hawke*. Cleared of all blame, Eliot went on to command other vessels in the Baltic and the Mediterranean.

In 1767, still a young man of 24, he was made Governor of West Florida. Florida had only recently become a British possession, ceded by Spain in 1763 following Britain's successful attack on Havana in the Seven Years' War. Given his youth and lack of experience in the field of colonial administration, his posting was unexpected; it was largely due to the influence of his brother, Edward, and his uncle, Robert Nugent, who both sat on the Board of Trade and Plantations, the body responsible for administering Britain's colonial affairs.[22] On his way to take up his post in Pensacola, now designated the capital of West Florida, Eliot stopped at the island of St Christopher, where he: 'seems to have purchased two negro slaves, as Susan and Kattie were added to his party roster on March 8'.[23]

During the voyage, Eliot began to suffer from violent pains in his head. These continued as he took up his governorship, and on 1 May he had an attack 'with greater violence than before ... [which] totally deprived him of his senses.'[24] The next morning, Eliot's body was found in his study at Government House. He had hanged himself. It is thought that during the last year of his life he may have developed a brain tumour which caused his severe head pains and in turn resulted in an emotional breakdown which led him to take his life. He was 26 years old.[25] It was a sad end to a promising early career.

While John Eliot is not generally well known, his near-contemporary, William Bligh (1754–1817), is widely remembered for the mutiny of members of his crew while he was in command of HMS *Bounty*. Bligh had been born at Tinten Manor in the parish of St Tudy, which lies in the River Camel valley in north Cornwall, but his father, an excise officer,

---

22 Rea, Robert R. 'The naval career of John Eliot, Governor of West Florida.' *The Florida Historical Quarterly*, p.465. (Vol.57, No.4, April 1979).
23 Ibid, p.466.
24 Ibid, p.466.
25 Ibid, p.467.

was based in Plymouth, Devon, where the family spent much of their time.[26] Bligh first went to sea at the age of seven, serving as the captain's personal servant on board HMS *Monmouth*. In 1770, he became an able seaman and then midshipman on HMS *Hunter*, later transferring to HMS *Crescent*. In 1776, he joined Captain James Cook aboard HMS *Resolution* and, promoted to sailing master, he accompanied Cook on his last voyage to the Pacific. For the next few years Bligh served on several ships, reaching the rank of lieutenant. He then served for five years in the Merchant Service before returning to the Royal Navy in 1787.

On his return he was put in command of HMS *Bounty*, bound for the South Seas. The purpose of the voyage – the result of lobbying by West Indian plantation owners – was to transport breadfruit and other potentially useful plants from the South Seas to British colonies in the Caribbean, where the breadfruit would be used as a cheap source of food for those enslaved on the plantation. The voyage had the backing of the botanist Sir Joseph Banks, a patron of the Royal Botanic Gardens at Kew and President of the Royal Society. Breadfruit and other plant specimens were collected in Tahiti, and the famous mutiny took place soon after the *Bounty* had left the island. Cast adrift by the mutineers in an open longboat with little food, Bligh and eighteen members of his crew managed to sail 3,618 miles to safety in Timor: an amazing feat of navigation. Returning to London, Bligh was cleared of any wrongdoing and was promoted to captain.[27]

The *Bounty's* mutineers threw the breadfruit and other plants collected by the expedition overboard, so none reached the Caribbean; but the British government's interest in transporting useful plants to their Caribbean possessions continued, and a second expedition, again under the command of Bligh, left for Tahiti in 1791 aboard HMS *Providence* and HMS *Assistant*.[28] This time the expedition was successful: 2,126

---

26 Cornwall Calling. *Captain William Bligh, mutiny on the Bounty fame.* Accessed 15 February 2015, http://www.cornwall-calling.co.uk/famous-cornish-people/bligh.htm
27 Australia. State Library of New South Wales. *Papers of Sir Joseph Banks, series 45.* Accessed 15 February 2015, http://www2.sl.nsw.gov.au/banks/series_45/45_view.cfm
28 Australia. State Library of New South Wales. *Papers of Sir Joseph Banks, series 50.* Accessed 15 February 2015, http://www2.sl.nsw.gov.au/banks/series_50/50_view.cfm

breadfruit plants were collected in Tahiti, planted in pots and tubs, and stored aboard the *Providence*.

While many of the breadfruit plants died on their long journey aboard the *Providence*, the expedition's gardener managed to deliver 678 healthy plants to the Caribbean, where the British government had set up two botanical gardens. One was the St Vincent Botanic Gardens, established in 1765;[29] the other was the Bath Botanical Gardens

William Bligh.
Painter: J. Ruffell.
Engraver: J. Condé. Date: 1792.

Transplanting of the bread-fruit trees from Otaheite.
Painter and Engraver: Thomas Gosse. Date: 1796.

---

29 BGCI. *About the St Vincent and the Grenadines Botanic Gardens.* Accessed 13 February 2015, http://www.bgci.org/garden.php?id=314

in Jamaica, established in 1779.[30] Under the guidance of the Royal Botanical Gardens at Kew, the curators of those two gardens were given the responsibility of developing plant collections for study and for useful propagation. They were also responsible for distributing plants that had potential use, either as cash crops or as sources of food.

St Vincent was Bligh's first stop, and in early 1793 he handed over a number of plants to the curator of its gardens, Dr Young, who successfully transplanted them. They subsequently grew into fruit-bearing trees, and their descendants still grow in the gardens and elsewhere on the island. The *Providence* then sailed for the Jamaica Station at Port Royal, where the arrival of the breadfruit caused considerable excitement among members of the local community, so much so that the officers aboard the *Providence* began to complain about the popularity of their cargo, as:

> [the] ... *floating forest [of breadfruit plants is so] eagerly visited by numbers of every rank and degree [that] the Common civility of going around the Ship with them and explaining the Plants became by its frequency rather troublesome.*[31]

Leaving Port Royal, Bligh sailed eastwards along the coast for Port Morant, near the south-east tip of the island and the nearest harbour to Bath. Here he delivered 346 breadfruit plants, which were carried overland for the last six miles of their long journey to the Bath Botanical Gardens.[32]

The introduction of breadfruit to the Caribbean as a source of cheap food for the enslaved initially failed. Maize, yams, plantains and cassava remained the preferred form of starch, and it was not until after Emancipation and the subsequent growth of small, largely subsistence,

---

30 Jamaica National Heritage Trust. *Bath Botanic Gardens*. Accessed 13 February 2015, http://www.jnht.com/site_Bath_Botanic_Garden.php
31 Alexander, Caroline. 'Captain Bligh's cursed breadfruit.' *Smithsonian Magazine* (September 2009). Accessed 1 February 2015, http://www.smithsonianmag.com/travel/captain-blighs-cursed-breadfruit-41433018/?no-ist
32 Ibid.

farms in the British islands that breadfruit began to play a significant part in the local diet.[33]

Returning to England, Bligh captained several naval vessels that saw service in Europe, but he never returned to the Caribbean. In 1805 he became Governor of New South Wales, Australia, and by the time of his retirement in 1814 he had reached the rank of vice-admiral. He did not return to Cornwall, but spent his retirement at the Manor House, Farningham, in Kent. He died in London on 7 December 1817, aged 64.

Although today Captain Bligh is one of the best remembered of the 18th-century Royal Naval officers, to his contemporaries it was Admiral Edward Pellew, 1st Viscount Exmouth (1757–1823) who was a far more well-known and popular figure.[34] Edward's grandfather, Humphrey Pellew, the son of a naval officer, was a merchant seaman and ship owner of considerable wealth. He was in part responsible for developing the village of Flushing that lies across the Penryn river from Falmouth and was home to many of the Royal Mail packet service captains. Humphrey's son, Samuel, joined the Royal Mail packet service in Falmouth, and married Cornishwoman Constance Langford. When Samuel was promoted to captain of one of the Dover packets, the family moved to Dover, in the county of Kent, and here their children, including Edward and his brother Israel, were born. Following Samuel's death, Constance remarried, and the family moved back to Cornwall, settling in Penzance.

Israel Pellew (1758–1832), like his brother Edward, joined the Royal Navy, and in 1771, when he was 13, sailed for the Jamaica Station aboard the sloop HMS *Falcon*. Having spent five years in Jamaica, in 1776 he moved to the North American station, and by 1797 had been promoted to captain. Aboard HMS *Cleopatra*, he returned to the Jamaica Station, where he took part in a mostly unsuccessful attack on Spanish vessels anchored off Levisa Bay, in the north-east of Cuba, during which he

---

33 Watts, David. *The West Indies: patterns of development, culture and environmental change since 1492.* Cambridge: Cambridge University Press, 1987, p.505.
34 Much of the information on the Pellew family is sourced from Parkinson, C. Northcote. *Edward Pellew, Viscount Exmouth, Admiral of the Red.* London: Methuen, 1934. Accessed 28 February 2015, http://www.pellew.com/Exmouth/Exmouth per cent20003/Cover per cent20Page.htm

managed to capture only one small Spanish galley; many of his crew were killed or injured before his ship was driven off. His run of bad luck continued when the *Cleopatra* ran aground off Abaco Island in the Bahamas. He was unable to free his ship for three days, until he threw all his guns and some of the ballast overboard and managed to refloat her. His later voyage to the Caribbean had a more positive outcome. In 1804, he was given command of HMS *Conqueror*, and took part in the Trafalgar Campaign. *Conqueror* participated both in the chase across the Atlantic in search of the French fleet, which had sailed to the island of Martinique, and in the return chase to Cadiz, fighting well at the Battle of Trafalgar under Admiral Horatio Nelson's command.

It was to the *Conqueror's* Captain Atcherley that the commander of the combined French and Spanish fleets, Admiral Pierre-Charles Villeneuve, surrendered. Villeneuve asked – in English:

'To whom have I the honour of surrendering?'

Atcherley answered: 'To Captain Pellew of the *Conqueror*.'

To which Villeneuve replied: 'I am glad to have struck to the fortunate Sir Edward Pellew.'

'It is his brother, Sir,' said Atcherley.

'His brother! What! Are there two of them? Hélas!' Villeneuve replied.[35]

Israel was wounded in the Battle of Trafalgar but recovered and continued to serve in the Royal Navy until 1830, when he retired as a full admiral, living in Plymouth until his death two years later.

When Israel and Edward Pellew

Admiral Sir Israel Pellew.
Painter and date unknown.

---

35 Warwick, Peter. *Trafalgar: tales from the front line.* Newton Abbot: David & Charles, 2011, p.236.

were at the height of their respective naval careers, two of Edward's sons joined the Royal Navy: his eldest son Pownoll (1786–1833) and his younger son Fleetwood (1789–1861). Pownoll spent part of his career in the Caribbean. Having joined the Navy at the age of twelve, he served as a midshipman under his father, and thanks in part to his father's influence attained the rank of commander at the early age of seventeen. He was then sent to the Caribbean and given the command of HMS *Fly* under Admiral Dacres. His father was apparently most concerned about Pownoll's well-being, as he found time to pen a notebook full of advice, which he sent out to his son in Jamaica. In it he writes:

> *From your affectionate Father to his Dutiful Son*
>
> Avoid as certain destruction both of Soul and Body all excesses of whatever Nature they may be, in the Climate you are going to you must use great Caution to avoid all the Night dews – and when you are exposed by Night never permit your breast to be uncovered or your neck exposed without something tied round it – Never stop upon Deck unless covered by something to keep off the Dew. It is equally necessary to avoid the Sun in the Middle of the Day from wh, much danger is to be expected; it may at a moment produce Giddyness of head, sicknefs and fever – take great care never to over-heat your blood by drinking or exercise – never go out shooting on any account or riding in the Sun and be very particular never to check perspiration or sit in a draft of Wind so as to produce it – altho it is so pleasant to the feeling it is almost certain Death. At night always sleep in Calico – be you ever so hot – it is a great security against the diseases of that Country. On your first arrival be extremely careful not to indulge in eating too much fruit – and do not go into the Water when the Sun is high. Take great care to keep your body regular and never pass a day without Evacuation – the moment you feel your Body-bound take directly a pill or two of those you carry (323) of the size of a large pea. And should you ever feel unwell instantly take a strong Emetic or a good dose of Physic. If you are seized with a flux take directly a large dose of Rhubarb and apply directly to your Surgeon. Always wear a

piece of White paper inside your hat. If you should take prizes I need scarcely recommend you to treat your Prisoners with kindness, but be very careful to keep safe and proper Guards over them – An Officer who suffers his Prisoners to retake his Ship can never recover the Stain on his Character ...

Be extremely Cautious and Correct in your Conduct. The first impression of your Character will be formed from it and the companions of your choice; always endeavour to keep in with the Captains and Admiral as much as possible, behaving with quiet Modesty – you will always learn something in their Company and they will soon respect and esteem you.

Never become one of the Tavern parties on shore, they always end in drunkenness and Dissipation.

In your Command be as kind as you can without suffering imposition on your good Nature, be steady and vigilant. Never neglect any opportunity of writing to your Mother Who deserves your utmost love and attention for her unceasing goodness to you and all your family. I hope you will believe I shall be equally glad to hear of you. I am sure you will never dishonour yourself or your family or the Service of your King.

In your Expenses be as frugal as you can. You know the situation of your Father and how many calls he has for Money . . . Be attentive to your person and dress. Nothing recommends a young Man more to notice. If you meet Capt. O'Brien tell him I ordered you to ask his protection. Admiral Dacres will be as a Father to you, never fail to consult him and ask his advice on any occasion of difficulty. Take great care to examine all papers you put your name to and be satisfied of the truth of them and avoid any accident on this point, never sign a paper when bro't to you in a hurry – if it is one of account – but desire it to be left for our perusal. Get into a habit of signing your name well and [in] one uniform manner and at least once a Month look over your Ship's Books and the diff't Officers expenses – and do not pass by any extraordinary Expense without strictly investigating the circumstance, as it is your Duty to be as honest and careful for the

King as for yourself. Mr Hemming has wrote a recipe for some pills for you to use occasionally when you are at all Costive. I have used them many years and found them safe and easy-do not fail to get a good quantity of them made up at Cookwortheys at Plymouth, to take with you and always remember to have the recipe back again and keep it in this Book.

Never fail to keep the Ships reckoning yourself and observe both by Day and Night, it is a great Duty for you have in charge the Lives of hundreds. I hope you will never from idleness excuse yourself from this sacred Duty and never lay down to rest without sending for your Master and together with him mark the Ships place in the Chart – do not let any false Modesty or Shame prevent you from this or asking his aid in working your Lunars – it is madness to do so in the extreme and must ultimately end in the ruin of any Young Officer who practises it.[36]

In spite of all this good advice from his father, Pownoll was not destined for a successful career in the Royal Navy. In 1805, a few months after receiving his father's notebook, he lost the *Fly* on the Carysford Reef, a 4-mile-long (6.5 km) reef off Key Largo in the Florida Keys. Pownoll was court martialled, and had to answer for the loss of his ship; but he was honourably acquitted and later joined his father, now Commander-in-Chief of the Navy in the East Indies, in Madras, India. Pownoll did not stay in the service, but decided to return to England where he turned his attention to a political career and became Member of Parliament for Launceston, in Cornwall. On the death of his father in 1833, he succeeded to the title of Viscount Exmouth, but was not able to enjoy the privileges of his title for long: he died eleven months later at the age of forty-seven.

Pellew is the name of a small island, also known as Monkey Island, or Princess Island,[37] which lies off the north-east coast of Jamaica, near the town

---

36 Parkinson, C. Northcote. *Edward Pellew, Viscount Exmouth, Admiral of the Red.* London: Methuen, 1934. Chapter 10. Accessed 28 February 2015, http://www.pellew.com/Exmouth/Exmouth per cent20003/Cover per cent20Page.htm

37 Jamaica Environment Trust. *Pellew Island.* Accessed 3 March 2015, http://www.jamentrust.org/advocacy-a-law/campaigns/pellew-island.html

of Port Antonio. It was supposedly named after Edward Pellew,[38] although it is more likely that it was named after Israel or Pownoll Pellew, as both spent time on the Jamaica Station. Alternatively, the island may have been named after a French recluse named Jacques Peleau, who lived on the island in the early 20th century, surviving on a diet of seafood and coconuts.[39]

The Pellews' were not the only family to produce several distinguished Cornish naval officers. Three members of the Reynolds family are also remembered for their naval careers.[40] Robert Carthew Reynolds the Elder (1745–1811), was born in the village of Lamorran near to the River Fal, and while the Seven Years' War was still in progress he joined the Royal Navy, aged fourteen. In 1877, following the outbreak of the American Revolutionary War, he was promoted to lieutenant, and served in the English Channel Fleet until 1783, when he was sent out to the Caribbean as commander of HMS *Dolphin*. After three years of service in the Caribbean he left for the Newfoundland Station in command of the sloop HMS *Echo*, and did not return to the Caribbean. Like many of his fellow Cornish officers he at one time served under Sir Edward Pellew. While onshore he built Penair Place – not too far from Lamorran, where he had been born – and which became the family home.

His elder son, Robert Carthew the Younger, (1782–1804) also joined the Navy. Having attained the rank of captain, he was sent out to the Caribbean during the Napoleonic Wars, where he took part in the 1804 action off Martinique but was fatally wounded. His younger brother Barrington (1786–1861) went to sea with his father during the French Revolutionary Wars when he was nine years old, but he never served in the Caribbean. He went on to become an admiral.

Several members of the Cole family of Marazion also joined the armed services and were posted to the Caribbean.[41] Humphrey Cole

---

38 Jane Austen Society. *Admiral Edward Pellew: The true history of this most novel Captain*. Accessed 3 March 2015, http://www.janeausten.co.uk/admiral-edward-pellew-the-true-history-of-this-most-novel-captain/
39 Ibid.
40 Email from Tony Pawlyn, Senior Researcher, Bartlett Library, National Maritime Museum, Cornwall, dated 6 April 2015.
41 *Cornwall story [the Cole family]*. Accessed 6 March 2015, http://homepages.paradise.net.nz/howardco/international/cornwall/cornwall_story.htm

(1756–1796), joined the army and achieved the rank of major, but died at an early age while serving in Jamaica. His brother Francis Cole (1760–1798) commanded HMS *Trepassey* on the Jamaica Station, taking part in the American Revolutionary War. A third brother, Christopher Cole (1770–1836),[42] first went to sea, aged nine, on HMS *Royal Oak* under Captain Sir Digby Dent. On board was yet another brother, John, an Anglican priest who was chaplain of the *Royal Oak* and would later pursue an academic career, becoming Vice-Chancellor of Oxford University. Christopher Cole later moved to HMS *Russell*, the flagship of Commodore Sir Samuel Drake, and sailed to the Caribbean. In April 1781, while serving on the *Russell*, he fought against the French at the Battle of Fort Royal, off the island of Martinique. He then sailed aboard HMS *Princessa*, and in January 1782 saw action at the Battle of St Kitts,[43] when the British fleet, under the command of Sir Samuel Hood, met the larger French fleet, commanded by the Comte de Grasse. The Comte had attacked the British islands of St Christopher and Nevis, and had landed 6,000 men on St Christopher, laying siege to the fortress on Brimstone Hill. Hood managed to outmanoeuvre de Grasse but was unable to prevent the island from being surrendered to the French. Hood then left St Christopher to join the fleet of Admiral George Rodney. Jamaica was de Grasse's main target, but as he left Martinique, heading for Jamaica, he met Rodney's fleet off the Saintes, the small islands between Guadeloupe and Dominica. The Battle of the Saintes, in which Christopher Cole took part, resulted in a major victory for Britain, ending any further French threats to British possessions in the Caribbean.

Christopher Cole then joined his brother Francis aboard the *Trepassey*, and sailed with him to Halifax, later returning to the Caribbean with HMS *Sans Pareil*, the flagship of Vice-Admiral Lord Hugh Seymour, to take part in the French Revolutionary Wars. In August 1799, a British force under the command of Lieutenant-General Thomas Trigge and Vice-Admiral Seymour captured the Dutch colony of Surinam (now the independent nation of the Republic of Suriname) on the north-east coast

---

42   *Dictionary of national biography*. Supplement, vol.2. London: Smith, Elder and Co., 1901, pp.40–41.
43   Official name St Christopher.

Captain Sir Christopher Cole.
Painter: Margaret Sarah Carpenter.
Date: between 1820 and 1824.

of South America. Among the prizes won by the British was the French corvette *Hussar*. The *Hussar* was renamed *Surinam*, and Christopher Cole, in recognition of his service, was appointed her commander. *Surinam* then served on the Leeward Islands Station. Here, Cole distinguished himself by pursuing and capturing two French privateers and recapturing a merchant schooner.

He also introduced new regulations aboard his ship, which kept his men in good health, an improvement that Seymour made the subject of an official recommendation to the Admiralty. In 1801, Seymour died from a fever, but Cole gained the good opinion of Seymour's successor Sir John Thomas Duckworth, who promoted him to his flagship HMS *Leviathan* and later to the frigate HMS *Southampton*. In 1802, with the signing of the Treaty of Amiens, France, Britain, Spain and the Netherlands[44] were temporarily at peace, and the *Southampton* was ordered home to Britain, where her officers and crew were paid off.

---

44   Known as the Batavian Republic since its invasion by France in 1795.

Christopher Cole later joined Edward Pellew in the East Indies, before returning to Britain and retiring in 1814. In recognition of his services he was made a Knight Commander of the Order of Bath. He was also given the Order of Maria Theresa by the Austrian Empire, and the Order of St George by the Russian Empire. He went to live in Killoy, near Cardiff, in Glamorganshire, Wales, the home of his wife Mary Lucy, née Talbot. Here he became Member of Parliament for Glamorganshire. He died in 1836.

Another distinguished Cornish naval officer was Charles Vinicombe Penrose (1759–1830).[45] He was born in the Falmouth area, near Penryn, and was admitted to the Royal Naval Academy in Portsmouth in 1772. He then served in the Mediterranean, and following the end of the American Revolutionary War spent some years onshore. He declined to make use of the political influence of the local Penryn politicians to advance his naval career, and so when he returned to sea in 1790 he was still a lieutenant.[46] He took part in the French Revolutionary Wars, fighting during the capture of the island of Martinique from the French in 1794. Five years later he returned to the Caribbean, joining fellow Cornishman Christopher Cole aboard HMS *Sans Pareil*. He remained with the *Sans Pareil* until the death of her commander, Vice-Admiral Lord Hugh Seymour, when he transferred to HMS *Carnatic*. Here he remained until the Treaty of Amiens brought an end to the French Revolutionary Wars in 1802, when he returned to Plymouth.[47] He went on to be become Commander-in-Chief of the Mediterranean Fleet, retiring in 1819, when he went to live in Lostwithiel, which lies at the head of the River Fowey estuary. He died at his home in January 1830.

His nephew, also named Charles Vinicombe Penrose, joined his uncle in the Caribbean in 1800 as second lieutenant of HMS *Amphitrite*. He contracted a fever while on shore at St Pierre, Martinique, in 1809 and, in spite of careful nursing by the ship's doctor and his uncle, died a few days later.[48]

---

45 Penrose, John. *Lives of Sir Charles Vinicombe Penrose and Captain James Trevenen*. London: John Murray, 1850, pp.3–4.
46 Ibid., pp.10–12.
47 Ibid., pp.17–18.
48 Ibid., p.162.

Sir Charles Vinicombe Penrose.
Lithographer: Richard James Lane.
Date: about 1825–1850.

Fighting with the elder Charles Penrose during the 1794 capture of Martinique was James Carthew (1769–1855).[49] Born at Tredudwell Manor, near Fowey, he entered the Navy in 1780 aged 11, and from 1782 to 1786 served in the Caribbean as a midshipman aboard HMS *Syren* and HMS *Adamant*. He then returned to Britain, and was posted to Newfoundland before returning to the Caribbean in 1793. Now a lieutenant aboard HMS *Solebay*, he fought ashore during the first capture of Martinique. He was then posted back to Newfoundland, and went on to Europe before returning to the Jamaica Station in 1801. While in Jamaica he served on HMS *Shark*, and then commanded HMS *Garland* followed by HMS *Crescent* until the Treaty of Amiens in 1802 brought a temporary peace. By 1808, Carthew was back in the Caribbean as the commander of

---

49   O'Byrne, William R. *A naval biographical dictionary: comprising the life and services of every living officer in Her Majesty's Navy, from the rank of Admiral of the Fleet to that of Lieutenant, inclusive.* Vol.1. London: John Murray, 1849, p.176.

HMS *Gloire* and took part in the second capture of Martinique. Unlike his countryman, Commander Robert Reynolds, Carthew survived the fierce fighting and went on to command the British squadron in the Caribbean. Having reached the rank of admiral in 1853, he retired to his home at Tredudwell, where he died at the advanced age of 86.

Richard Darton Thomas (1777–1857) was a young man of seventeen when, with fellow Cornishmen Charles Penrose the Elder and James Carthew, he took part in the first capture of Martinique. Born in Saltash near the Tamar river, which divides Cornwall from Devon, he joined the Royal Navy in 1790 at the age of thirteen, becoming a midshipman in 1792 and a master's mate in 1793.[50] In that year, he was sent out to the Caribbean, where he took part in action against the French-owned islands of Tobago and Saint Lucia. He then joined HMS *Boyne*, under Sir John Jervis, then Commander of the Leeward Islands Station. Off Martinique, Thomas commanded a boat in the attack on Fort Royal, the last action he would see in the Caribbean. His later career was spent in the Pacific, and

Admiral Richard Darton Thomas.
Painter: unknown. Date: about 1837.

---

50 Baring-Gould, S. *Cornish characters and strange events*. London: Bodley Head, 1909, p.259.

he rose to the rank of admiral in 1854, dying at his home in Stonehouse, Devon, three years later.

Not all the Cornish Royal Navy officers who served in the Caribbean were employed in a fighting capacity. Some, including Lieutenant George Bennett Lawrence (1818–1853), undertook other roles. Lawrence had been born in Lostwithiel, the same small town to which Sir Charles Vinicombe Penrose would retire in 1819. Lawrence was a survey officer, whose task was to survey all the reefs and passages around the various Caribbean islands and to prepare accurate navigation charts which would enable British ships to complete their voyages more quickly, and in greater safety. At the age of thirty-five, while surveying the Virgin Islands, he unexpectedly died. As *The West Briton* newspaper reported, he was good at his job, and his talents would be sorely missed:

This gallant and talented surveying officer died at St. Thomas's on Sunday morning, the 15th of January. We learn from the St. Croix Avis that the funeral took place the same evening ... The same paper adds the following: – 'The death of Lieutenant Lawrence is a public loss, not alone to his nation, but to the service of navigation in general. For some years past he has been employed in surveying the Virgin Islands, including Crab Island [51] *and Culebra with all their reefs and passages, and which having lately completed, he came to this island to survey its coasts and reefs also. In this occupation, which necessarily exposed him to great fatigue, his valuable life was closed ... His skill and talents as a surveyor are conspicuous in those charts of the British Virgin Islands which are already published, and equally so in his surveys of the Danish islands, St. John's, St. Thomas's, and the numerous small islands and channels connected with them, which were shown to the writer by Lieut. Lawrence himself, and which when published, accompanied with the numerous beautiful views he has taken, will leave nothing further for the navigator to desire; but his surveys were not confined to these islands, for his field of action has extended over the West Indies generally, the Bahamas, the Gulf of Mexico, and other places, so that*

---

51 Now called Vieques.

grief and regret become the more acute, that a life so honourably and usefully employed should have so suddenly terminated.'[52]

Cornishmen were not only well represented among the officers who served in the Caribbean; they were also frequently found among the petty officers and the hands. We rarely know much about the details of their lives, but Robert Jeffery,[53] who was born in Fowey in 1789, is an exception. When he was seven years old, his family moved to Polperro, and he went to school in nearby Looe, probably attending the charity school there. He would have been taught reading, writing and mathematics, but with an emphasis 'in the mathematics on those branches which relate to navigation.'[54] In Cornwall a knowledge of navigation was an important skill for those who would earn their living on the sea, whether in the Royal Navy, in the Royal Mail packet service, as a privateer, as a smuggler or as a pilchard fisherman. When Robert was twelve, his father John died, and his mother Honor married Polperro's blacksmith, Benjamin Coad, who took on the responsibility of teaching his stepson the smithy's trade. After six years of working for Coad, Jeffery decided he wanted to go to sea.

He was attracted to the ships owned by the privateers who, during the Napoleonic Wars, often used the sheltered harbour of Polperro as their base: it was a convenient place to start their search for French enemy ships. Polperro was also popular with the privateer captains because it was one of the Cornish ports where crew could readily be found that knew something of the sea. With his blacksmithing skills, Jeffery had no difficulty in finding a ship, because their weapons and the metal fixtures and fittings on board needed continual attention to counteract the corrosive effects of seawater. The privateer *Lord Nelson* was anchored in the harbour, and with Jeffery on

---

52 'The late Lieutenant George Bennett Lawrence, Commander of the surveying brig 'Scorpion', and formerly of Lostwithiel.' *West Briton* (11 March 1853). Accessed 8 March 2015, http://freepages.genealogy.rootsweb.ancestry.com/~wbritonad/cornwall/1853/misc/mar.html

53 Much of the information about Robert Jeffery comes from James Derriman's book *Marooned: the true story of Cornishman Robert Jeffery*, and Robert Jeffery's own account of his experience: *A narrative of the life sufferings and deliverance of R. Jeffery, who was put on the desolate rock of Sombrero, Dec 13, 1807, with portrait.*

54 Derriman, James. *Marooned: the true story of Cornishman Robert Jeffery*. 2nd ed. Clifton-Upon-Teme: Polperro Heritage Press. 2006, p.10.

board she weighed anchor and sailed along the Cornish coast to Falmouth, where she passed near to HMS *Recruit*. The *Recruit* needed a crew of 121, but while she was lying off Falmouth she had only 100 crewmen aboard. Unfortunately for The *Lord Nelson*, the Royal Navy was at that time so short of manpower that press gangs were sent on board merchant ships and privateers to find crew: the *Lord Nelson* was boarded by men from the *Recruit*, and despite objections from the *Lord Nelson's* commander ten men were impressed. One of these was Jeffery.

Jeffery joined an unhappy ship. Her commander, the Hon. Warwick Lake, had a reputation for inflicting severe punishment on his men for the least infringement of the rules. Desertion was frequent in the Royal Navy of the time, but on the *Recruit* it was especially high.[55] Two days after Jeffery was brought on board, and before the *Recruit* left Falmouth to join the Leeward Islands Station, two Royal Marine sentries, a quartermaster and three seamen took the cutter from the stern of the ship and escaped. Still short of eleven crew members, the *Recruit* set sail. After calling at the island of Madeira for wine and provisions, she sailed south for the coast of the Guianas,[56] then set her course back north to Barbados. En route Jeffery helped himself to a bottle of rum from the gunner's cabin, and was reported to the captain, who put him under arrest, kept him in irons for two days, and then had him flogged with a cat-o-nine-tails. He was one of eight men flogged that day:

> *Three men each received 12 lashes. Four, including Jeffery, took 24 lashes and the eighth man, a marine, was given no less than 48. The bosun's mates, whose duty it was to wield the cat, must have exhausted themselves by the time they had inflicted the total of 180 lashes, even though the practice was for them to change over after each two dozen.*[57]

---

55 Ibid., p.13.
56 Present-day Guyana, Suriname and French Guiana, on the north-east coast of South America.
57 Derriman, James. *Marooned: the true story of Cornishman Robert Jeffery*. 2nd ed. Clifton-Upon-Teme: Polperro Heritage Press. 2006, p.14.

The following day the *Recruit* anchored in Carlisle Bay, the main harbour adjoining Bridgetown, the capital of Barbados. The ship began a cruise of the Leeward Islands, patrolling north past St Lucia and Guadeloupe and then sailing east past Puerto Rico to the Virgin Islands. Jeffery again got himself into trouble, taking two quarts of spruce beer[58] intended for the midshipmen's mess. He was reported by the sailor with whom he had shared the beer, and was ordered to appear before Captain Lake. The *Recruit* was then in the Anegada Passage, the main sea route between Europe and the Caribbean, which lies to the east of the Virgin Islands. Mid-passage lies the islet of Sombrero, named by the Spanish because of its shape, resembling a hat. Captain Lake ordered that Jeffery should be marooned on Sombrero. It was a dry, barren, uninhabited and isolated spot, the nearest islands being Anguilla, 38 miles (61 km) to the south, and Anegada, 55 miles (88.5 km) to the west. He was left there with no food, no water and no clothes, although once he was ashore his shipmates gave him a pair of shoes, a knife and some handkerchiefs with which to attract the attention of any passing ship.

Word of Jeffery's punishment reached Admiral Sir Alexander Cochrane, then Commander-in-Chief of the Leeward Islands Station. Two months after Jeffery had been marooned, Cochrane ordered Captain Lake to return to Sombrero and collect whatever might be left of Jeffery. Lake found no sign of Jeffery or his remains, and was ordered to appear before a Board of Inquiry, which found that Lake was unfit to command for reasons of health and ordered that he be returned to Britain. News of Jeffery's marooning then reached the Admiralty. They ordered an investigation and in 1809 sent a ship to survey Sombrero and report on the possibility of survival for anyone stranded there. Again, no sign of Jeffery was found. On receiving the report, the Admiralty decided that Captain Lake should face a court martial, following which he was found guilty of attempted murder, and dismissed from the Navy.

---

58   Spruce beer is a beverage flavoured with the buds, needles or essence of spruce trees, a natural source of vitamin C. The drink originated with the native peoples of North America, who used it as a cure for scurvy during the winter months when fresh fruits were not available. This method of treating scurvy was later picked up by the Royal Navy, and spruce was regularly added to ship-brewed beer during the eighteenth century.

In fact, unknown to the Royal Navy or the Admiralty, after surviving on Sombrero for nine days Jeffery had been seen by the United States schooner *Adams* and rescued. The schooner took him back to her home port of Marblehead, Massachusetts, a coastal town full of sailors and fishermen, where he decided to stay, and returned to his trade of blacksmithing.

News of Jeffery's marooning and subsequent events at the Admiralty now reached the British Parliament, where it ignited concerns about the punishment handed out by Royal Navy commanders. One of these politicians was Samuel Whitbread, a member of the Whitbread Brewery family and Member of Parliament for Bedford, the county town for Bedfordshire. Samuel was Leader of the Whig Party, and a reformer: a champion of religious and civil rights, a proponent of the abolition of slavery, and in favour of a national education system. The case of Robert Jeffery appealed to Whitbread, and he managed to track Jeffery down to his home in Marblehead and have him repatriated to Britain. When Jeffery arrived at Portsmouth, he was met by Whitbread and brought to London, where the Admiralty issued him his discharge papers. Jeffery could have brought a civil or criminal case against Lake, a course of action Whitbread may have encouraged him to take. Members of the Lake family were, on the other hand, understandably eager to settle matters out of court. Jeffery was accordingly:

> met by an agent of the noble family concerned [the Lake family], and overtures were made, accompanied by expressions of regret and sympathy evidently unfeigned. He [Jeffery] wisely consented to forego any further prosecution of the matter on the payment of six hundred pounds.[59]

Jeffery's exploits received wide publicity. He returned to his family in Polperro, but soon realised he could make a living out of his experience after:

> he was induced by some traders in notoriety, and a few foolish though well-meaning neighbours, to turn to profit the interest with which his

---

59 Couch, Jonathan. *The history of Polperro: a fishing town on the south coast of Cornwall, being a description of the place, its people, their manners, customs, modes of industry, &c.* Polperro: Simpkin, Marshall and Co., 1871, p.98.

adventures had invested him, and he proceeded to London, where, showing himself on the boards of some of the minor theatres, 'Jeffrey [sic] the Sailor' was for a time one of the sights of the town.[60]

In 1811, he published an account of his adventures entitled *A narrative of the life sufferings and deliverance of R. Jeffery, who was put on the desolate rock of Sombrero, Dec 13, 1807, with portrait.* He also sat for his portrait, in which he appears in the style of the then popular image of the Romantic Poet, with carefully coiffed hair, serious gaze, ruffled shirt and casually tied cravat.

After a few months in London, he returned to Polperro with enough money to buy a small schooner, which he planned to use as a coastal trader, but during his time in the city he had contracted tuberculosis and his health was already declining. He died in 1815, leaving a young wife and daughter.[61]

Robert Jeffery.
Engraver: James Godby after a painting by
E.M. Jones. Date: 1811. Reproduced with permission
of the National Portrait Gallery, London.

---
60   Ibid., p.98.
61   Ibid., p.98.

Although the Royal Navy was a powerful force in the defence of Britain's empire, the conflicts of the early 18th century brought the need to expand Britain's standing army:

> [Up] to that period ... there was only a very small regular Army, our standing force being the Navy, and all, or nearly all, the troops were raised as adjuncts of that service, and trained on board ship, to be landed as occasion demanded ... The naval and military forces of the country were not sufficiently strong to stand the strain of a long campaign, or indeed any campaign at all; it therefore became necessary to raise men to meet any danger that might threaten the country.[62]

The Caribbean was not a popular destination for the army, and men did their best to avoid being sent there because, all too often the regiments:

> were, by epidemics, climatic causes, want of proper accommodation, proper diet, proper medicines, and mere ordinary care on the part of those in power, reduced in a few years to mere handfuls of effective men.[63]

One regiment that survived the rigours of a Caribbean posting was the Duke of Cornwall's Light Infantry. Officially formed in 1881, it can trace its history back to the founding of the two regiments that were amalgamated to form the Duke of Cornwall's in that year: the 32nd and 46th Regiments of Foot.

In 1702, Colonel Edward Fox, then Lieutenant-General of the Leeward Islands, had raised a regiment known as Colonel Fox's Regiment.[64] In 1751, Colonel Fox's Regiment was renamed the 32nd Regiment of Foot.

---

62 Swiney, G.C. *Historical records of the (32nd) Cornwall Light Infantry now the 1st Battalion Duke of Cornwall's L.I. from the formation of the regiment in 1702 to 1892*, p.1. London: Simpkin, Marshall, Hamilton, Kent and Company, 1893. Accessed 14 March 2015, https://play.google.com/books/reader?printsec=frontcover&output=reader&id=Hob4Cs7dqNoC&pg=GBS.PR3
63 Dalton, Charles. 'Soldiering in the West Indies in the days of Queen Anne.' *Journal of the Royal United Service Institution*, p.70. (Vol.42, Issue 1, 1898).
64 Ibid., p.67.

In 1782, all British regiments without royal titles were awarded county titles to encourage recruitment from the region after which they were named. The 32nd Regiment of Foot became the Cornwall Regiment of Foot, while the 46th Regiment of Foot became the South Devonshire Regiment of Foot, although both regiments were still known by their numbers. In practice, rather than the Cornwall Regiment recruiting its men from Cornwall, and the South Devon Regiment from South Devon, recruiting was still very much based on obtaining men wherever they could be found.[65]

In 1796, the Cornwall Regiment of Foot sailed to the Caribbean with Sir Ralph Abercrombie, where they fought in Saint-Domingue (now Haiti) during the French Revolutionary Wars and saw action in the Bahamas. One of the Cornwall Regiment's soldiers was one Anthony James. He had been born in about 1767 in the hamlet of Cury, on the Lizard peninsula, and had learnt to play the fiddle when young, earning his living playing music at dances and singing to entertain. Later he married a local girl, with whom he had a son. Like Robert Jeffery, he did not join the armed forces from choice. Impressment was used as much in the army as it was in the Royal Navy and the 32nd, short of men, was 'recruiting' in the area. As James later reported, he met the recruiting sergeant and some of his fellow soldiers:

> *The soldiers were up Cross Lane, [at] the Wheel Inn, and they seemed to have money to burn, enough to buy me ale. When I woke up there were shackles on my ankles and I was on my way to Devonport [Plymouth, Devon]. Since then I've been halfway round the world with the 32nd Regiment of Foot. They kept us overseas so we wouldn't run away: Cork, Haiti [sic] and the Bahamas. I only got home 'cause Johnny Frenchman put chain shot in the rigging of our transport and a spar fell on my head.*[66]

---

65 Snell, Lawrence S. *A short history of the Duke of Cornwall's Light Infantry 1702–1945.* Aldershot: Gale and Polden, 1945, p.28.
66 O'Connor, Mike. *Cornish folk tales.* Stroud: The History Press, 2010, p.47.

Blinded by the spar, James was repatriated to England and provided with a military pension. In winter he lived at Stoke Military Hospital in Devonport, but in summer he returned to Cornwall with his fiddle. Guided by his son, he became a travelling 'droll teller' or storyteller, living on his songs and tales.[67]

The 32nd had its own regimental march, called 'One and All', which is the motto of Cornwall. This march, it is said, was: 'written by a lady residing near Bodmin (in Cornwall), and to have been adopted by the regiment early in the year 1811.'[68] After 1881, when the Duke of Cornwall's Light Infantry Regiment was formed by amalgamating the 32nd Cornwall Light Infantry Regiment of Foot, with the 46th South Devonshire Regiment of Foot, Victoria Barracks in Bodmin became the home of the regiment, continuing to serve in that role until the end of the 19th century.

One Cornishman who joined the army by choice, although not in a fighting capacity, was John Davy (1790–1868). Born in the town of Penzance on the south coast of Cornwall, as a young man he assisted his elder brother Humphry at the Royal Institution of Great Britain, before moving north to Scotland to study medicine at the University of Edinburgh. Brother Humphry later developed a safety lamp for miners; it enabled the lamp to operate without allowing the heat from its flame to explode the methane gas often found in mines: a danger that had caused many accidents and deaths.

On graduating from Edinburgh University, John Davy joined the British Army Medical Department, and became Inspector General of Hospitals. He travelled widely throughout Britain's colonial possessions, and was stationed in India and Ceylon before moving on to Barbados, where he was stationed between 1845 and 1848.[69] During his tour of duty, he had an opportunity to visit several of the surrounding islands and

---

67 Ibid., p.1.
68 Dalton, Charles. 'Soldiering in the West Indies in the days of Queen Anne.' *Journal of the Royal United Service Institution*, p.314. (Vol.42, Issue 1, 1898).
69 Davy, John. *The West Indies, before and since slave emancipation: comprising the Windward and Leeward Islands Military Command; founded on notes and observations collected during three years residence*, p.ii. London: W. & F.G. Cash, 1854.

published several papers on his observations. While in Nevis, he analysed the water in the mineral baths there and commented:

> *the baths have proved very beneficial in obstinate cases of chronic rheumatism. Our great naval hero, Lord Nelson, it is likely used them; for, when in infirm health, we are informed, he recruited it in this island, residing at a spot about two miles distant from the baths, in a house the property of the uncle of Mrs. Nesbit, a native of Nevis, whom he married at this time.*[70]

Davy also took an interest in local agriculture, and was made an Honorary Member of the General Agricultural Society of Barbados. He once presented a paper to the society on the importance of manure, beginning:

> *Gentlemen, – In the discourse I am about to have the honour to address to you, it is my intention to bring under your notice the subject of manures. To you, as practical agriculturists, I need not insist on, or endeavor to point out its importance; one word may suffice to convey an idea of it, and even an adequate idea, viz., that manures are the food of plants.*[71]

He also had views on the business of agriculture in relation to sugar estates and their use of slave labour, and in 1854 he published a book entitled: *The West Indies, before and since slave emancipation: comprising the Windward and Leeward Islands Military Command; founded on notes and observations collected during a three years residence.*[72] He had strong views on racial equality and wrote that he had undertaken:

---

70 Davy, John. 'On the mineral water of the Baths of Nevis, in the West Indies; in a letter addressed to Prof. Jameson.' *Edinburgh New Philosophical Journal*, p.5. (Vol.XLIII, April/October 1847).
71 Davy, John. 'A discourse [on agriculture]' [Minutes of the Meetings of the] Agricultural Society of Barbados, p.289 (1847).
72 Davy, John. *The West Indies, before and since slave emancipation: comprising the Windward and Leeward Islands Military Command; founded on notes and observations collected during a three years residence.* London: W. & F.G. Cash, 1854.

John Davy.
Painter unknown. Date unknown.

to vindicate the character ... in regard to the negroes of African descent and the people of colour of mixed races – having the firm conviction that the low and the degraded state in which they were sunk and from which they are but slowly emerging, has been owing not to any inherent inferiority of nature or of mental capacity, but to the dire circumstances of their former condition in the state of slavery.[73]

Davy left the Caribbean to retire to Ambleside in the Lake District of northern England, where he died aged 78.

As the 19th century ended, Britain, France and Holland continued to administer their Caribbean possessions, but the influence of Spain as a colonial power in the Caribbean continued to wane. Spain had lost her South American possessions during the earlier part of the century, and now the Spanish–American War (1898) ended Spanish control of the islands of Cuba and Puerto Rico. Representatives of Spain and the United States signed a peace treaty in Paris on 10 December 1898, which established the independence of Cuba and ceded Puerto Rico to the United States. Thus for the first time, the United States joined Britain and France, and to a lesser extent Holland, as an influential power in the Caribbean.

---

73   Ibid., p.iii.

4

The Falmouth Packet Service

By the end of the 17th century the Mathews of St Christopher, the Webbes of Nevis, the Prices of Jamaica and the Kendalls of Barbados, along with their agents and merchants in London, were eager to exploit the potential of increased trade with the 'Mother Country'. A necessary component of any such development was a regular and reliable communication system between England and her colonial possessions in the Caribbean. The Post Office had introduced an international service delivering mail between England and Europe in the mid-17th century, but given the cost of establishing and maintaining a regular mail delivery to and from the Caribbean was reluctant to expand operations to the islands.

The year 1701 saw the beginning of the War of Spanish Succession[1] and the conflict soon spread to the Caribbean where the treasure fleets of Spain and Portugal were targeted by enemy vessels, and privateers[2] raided colonial settlements for goods and slaves. Military forces were sent out to defend England's possessions, and the English government began to appreciate the need for safe and reliable communication of intelligence between its commanders in the field. As there was still concern about the

---

1   See Appendix 4 for an overview of major 18th- and 19th-century conflicts that impacted the Caribbean.
2   A privateer was a private person or ship authorised with letters of marque issued by a national government to attack enemy vessels during wartime. Privateering was a way of mobilising armed ships and sailors without having to spend treasury resources. The cost was borne by private investors. The profit was from the prize money earned from captured cargo and ships, which was shared among the investors, and the officers and crew of the privateer.

investment cost of setting up and managing a Caribbean network, it was decided to consider any reasonable project proposal made by a private investor.

Edmund Dummer, an experienced English naval engineer and shipbuilder, soon produced such a proposal. He had spent most of his working life in the navy, rising to become an assistant surveyor and then Surveyor of the Navy. He designed and supervised the construction of the Royal Naval dockyard at Plymouth, designed the extension of the dockyard at Portsmouth, and conducted a survey of the defensive capabilities of England's south ports. He also supervised the construction of several boats for the Post Office Mail Service which ran between Harwich and the Netherlands. This project was successful, so the English government asked him to submit proposals for the design of boats to carry the mail between Falmouth and Corunna (A Coruña in Galicia, northwest Spain), and to manage the implementation of a similar service between Falmouth, Corunna and Lisbon. Aware that the objective of the Caribbean communication service was primarily to provide intelligence to support English military action in the region, Dummer wisely named his proposal 'A Scheam for Forreign Advice' and laid out the requirements for providing a monthly service between England and the islands of Barbados, Antigua, Montserrat, Nevis and Jamaica.

Dummer now set about gaining the support of those who could influence the government to approve his proposal. As Member of Parliament for Arundel, West Sussex, for some years, Dummer had developed good working relations with several senior members of the government, including: Robert Harley, Speaker of the House of Commons; Cornishman Sidney Godolphin, First Lord of the Treasury; Lord Nottingham, Secretary of State for the Southern Department – whose responsibilities included England's North American and Caribbean possessions; and the powerful Duke of Marlborough. Once Dummer had persuaded these gentlemen to support him, the proposal was soon put before the Council for Trade and Plantations for its consideration. Negotiations were concluded by June 1702, when the proposal was approved, and the service was inaugurated on 21 October in the same year.

The town of Falmouth, on the south coast of Cornwall, was chosen as the base for the new route. Most of the mail bound for the Caribbean originated in London, the hub of government and commerce, but as the King's Great Post Road connecting London and Falmouth was little more than a track there was concern about the speed and reliability of transporting the mail to Falmouth. But Falmouth had advantages that outweighed the issue of transportation. In its assessment of Falmouth, the Post Office noted:

> *The extreme westerly position of Falmouth Harbour gives it an advantage which is rendered obvious by a single glance at the map. From no other harbour in this country can an outward-bound vessel clear the land so quickly. No other is so soon reached by one homeward-bound and running for shelter. On the darkest nights, and in dense fog, ships unacquainted with the harbour may enter it in safety, so easy is it of access; and sailing vessels can leave it in any wind, save one blowing strongly from the east or south-east.*
>
> *It is, in fact, the safest anchorage in the country, protected from the full strength of the Atlantic rollers and bounding in sheltered creeks where vessels might be in practical immunity from the worst of storms.*[3]

The entrance to the harbour was guarded by the two fortresses of St Mawes Castle to the east and Pendennis Castle to the west, making it difficult for marauding privateers to gain access – and in addition Falmouth had, since 1688, been used as the home port for the Post Office's mail service to Spain and Portugal, so much of the infrastructure was already in place. The influence of First Lord of the Treasury, Sidney Godolphin, a member of a respected Cornish family, who was keen to encourage the development of his home county, may also have played a part in the choice of Falmouth as the base for the packet service. (Correspondence and dispatches of the day were folded and sealed in packets, and the word 'packet' was soon used to describe both the mail service and the ships that transported the mail.)

---

3   Mudd, David. *The Falmouth packets*. Bodmin: Bossiney Books, 1984, pp.5–6.

While Dummer was skilled at lobbying for support of his proposal, it soon became clear that he was unable to manage the project efficiently. Correspondence concerning passage from Falmouth to Barbados for one Thomas Tudor, an employee in the public service of Barbados, gives an illustration of financial procedures and the complications involved in meeting a simple request. In late 1706, the Secretary of State, Sir Charles Hedges, requested free passage on the next packet ship bound for Barbados for a Mr Tudor who, along with the packet on which he was a passenger, had been captured by a French privateer. He was temporarily imprisoned in France and then returned to England as part of an exchange of prisoners when the Secretary of State asked that Tudor be allowed a free passage back to Barbados. Postmaster General, Sir Thomas Frankland and Secretary of the Post Office, Sir Robert Cotton, informed Sir Charles:

> *that the cost of the West Indies boats are on a different footing to the others belonging to the post office. By the contract with Dummer for the maintenance of five boats in that service, her majesty [Queen Anne] pays him £12,500 per annum, of which Dummer undertakes £8,000 shall be raised by the carriage of letters and freight ... There has hitherto been a considerable deficiency in the £8,000, which has to be made good by Dummer from letters and passengers; and therefore, if free passage is given to anyone, her majesty has to make good to Dummer the fare of £12.*[4]

Hopefully Thomas Tudor received his free passage and returned safely to Barbados.

The loss of seven packet ships, taken as prizes by enemy privateers, added to Dummer's financial problems and this, combined with his poor management, caused the business to fail towards the end of 1711. The end of the War of Spanish Succession in 1713 removed the need

---

4   Rumble, A., C. Dimmer and C.S. Knighton, ed. *Calendar of state papers, domestic series, of the reign of Anne, preserved in the Public Record Office: IV October 1705–December 1706.* Martlesham: Boydell Press, 2006, SP348/71.

for the British government[5] to give serious consideration to providing a Caribbean mail service, so the service ceased and communication with the Caribbean once again relied on individual naval or merchant vessels.

Continued rivalry for dominance among the European powers led to the outbreak of the Seven Years' War in 1754 and as this conflict also spread to the Caribbean the need for a regular communication service to provide military intelligence once more came to the fore. By 1755 the packet service was reintroduced – but this time, rather than relying on one contractor the Post Office contracted private ships on an individual basis; by 1776 six packets were sailing to and from the Caribbean. In the early 1780s, under pressure from the Treasury to save money on contracting fees, the Post Office became a packet ship owner, but as its decision makers were not accustomed to ship management this scheme was not a financial success and there was a return to contracting private ships individually.

Many of the packet captains were Cornish and lived at Flushing, just across the Penryn river from Falmouth, where they were important members of the community:

> *they were men of some style, cutting a dash in fine uniforms. With a number of regular naval officers living in the locality, the place literally sparkled with gold epaulets, gold lace hats, and brilliant uniforms. As there was no official packet service uniform the commanders assumed a style of uniform dress that was barely distinguishable from those won by the Royal Naval officers. This practice caused annoyance in naval circles.*[6]

As the packet service grew, so the people of Falmouth and the surrounding area found employment, and the town became a bustling port, able to provide a whole range of local support services:

---

5   After the Acts of Union between England and Scotland had been passed in 1706 and 1707, the Kingdom of England (including Wales) became the Kingdom of Great Britain.
6   Pawlyn, Tony. 'Packet Commanders.' In Pawlyn, *The Falmouth Packets 1689–1851*, p.42. Truro, Truran Books, 2003.

In direct support of the packets there were the: insurance brokers, sail-makers, block-makers, pennant and flag makers, rope-walkers, cord-winders and riggers, chandlers, chart and stationery printers; anchor-smiths, ship surveyors, dock proprietors, shipwrights, boat-builders, ship-carpenters and sawyers, along with innumerable boatmen, whose frail craft scuttled to and from all parts of the Fal estuary on untold errands, servicing every need of the packets. On the provisions side there were the wholesale butchers, dairy men, poultry men, salt-provision merchants, ships bread and biscuit makers, fresh produce merchants and wine and spirit merchants. On the periphery, but inextricably linked, were the innkeepers, hoteliers, barmaids and porters, chambermaids and pot-boys, coachmen, wagoners, farriers, harness makers, cartwrights, wheelwrights, blacksmiths, stable proprietors and forage merchants, farmers, swineherds and milkmaids. And just one step removed from them ... were all the other local services: builders, labourers, street-cleaners ... shop keepers and their assistants, tailors, hawkers and the like.[7]

In the early days, overall responsibility for the Falmouth packet service was London-based and lay with the Postmaster General. The Secretary of the Post Office was responsible for its day-to-day management with the assistance of a Falmouth-based packet agent, while overseas agents were employed to receive the mail at the various ports of destination. During the early 1790s, as the service grew more complex, additional staff were employed, including a London-based Inspector of Packets: by the early 19th century over thirty packet ships and about 1,200 packet men were employed in Falmouth.

Packets leaving Falmouth with mail were required to be fully manned and ready to leave on the day before they sailed. This prevented crews from remaining ashore until the last minute and delaying the ship's departure. The mail for the overseas agents was sorted into bundles, wrapped first in brown paper then in oiled cloth, and packed into leather portmanteaux. As the mail often contained secret military information, before each

---

[7] Pawlyn, Tony. *The Falmouth packets 1689–1851*. Truro, Truran Books, 2003, p.23.

A 19th-century print of Falmouth Harbour.
From the author's collection.

voyage each portmanteau was weighted down with heavy pieces of iron. If a packet ship went into action against a privateer, the weighted mail was hung over the stern so that it could be quickly cut away and, as it was weighted, would rapidly sink.

On the day the packet was waiting to sail:

> *as soon as the Mail was ready, a signal was made at the [Post] Office and answered by the Packet and the topsails were sheeted home. The Captain and a Boat's crew were allowed to remain ashore to take the mail aboard. A Boat with a Clerk from the Office had been previously sent to muster the Crew who were awaiting the Captain and the mail. The Packet slipped from her moorings and proceeded to sea as soon as all were aboard.*[8]

Smaller boats, based in Barbados, were introduced to provide an intra-regional mailboat service within the Caribbean, collecting and delivering mail to and from the packets' major ports of call. The cost of introducing

---

8   Philbrick, M.E. 'The Falmouth packet service [Part 1].' *Postal History: the Bulletin of the Postal History Society*, (No.207, 1978), p.18.

A typical packet ship of the early 19th century – the *Francis Freeling* (named after Francis Freeling, Secretary of the Post Office from 1798 to 1836). Courtesy of the Bartlett Library, National Maritime Museum, Cornwall.

this local mailboat service was much less than the cost of adding to the number of larger packet ships sent out from Falmouth, and the Post Office anticipated that much of the cost of introducing the small mail boats would be offset by an improvement in service: the mail leaving Falmouth arrived at its destination more quickly, the correspondents had more time to write and send their response, and the packet ships' voyages from Falmouth would be shorter.

The Jamaica Packet sailed on the Sunday after the first Tuesday of the month, and the Leeward Islands Packet went on the Sunday after the third Tuesday of the month. Now, instead of delivering and collecting mail at each island, the first packet of the month – the Jamaica Packet – called at Barbados, went straight on to Jamaica, then returned to Falmouth via the Bahamas. But the second packet of the month – the Leeward Islands Packet – having called first at Barbados, went on to visit the various Leeward Islands before returning to Falmouth. As it was important that the packets operate as economically as possible, the Postmaster General issued detailed regulations on estimated voyage times expected, preferred routes to be taken, and length of time the boats were expected to spend in each port. The regulations for the Jamaica Packet, which carried mail not only for Barbados and Jamaica but for the Windward Islands, for Demerara, Berbice and La Guayra on the north coast of South America, and for St. Thomas, include the following:

> *After landing her mails for Barbadoes, &c. proceeds (in the event of her arriving before 12 o'clock,) the same day, with the English and Barbadoes mails to St. Vincent and Grenada, and from thence direct to Jamaica; but should she arrive after twelve o'clock, she remains at Barbadoes until the following evening.*
>
> *The day after arrival of this packet, the mail-boats invariably sail, in the following order, viz:-*
>
> *No.1 Demerara direct: after landing her mails there, she proceeds, the next tide, to Berbice, where she remains for three days. She returns to Demerara, and from thence to Barbadoes. This boat may be expected to return in about fifteen days from the day she left Barbadoes.*
>
> *No.2 St. Lucia, touching at the whole of the islands northwards to St. Thomas's. She remains at each of the same islands six hours (and from thence) to Barbadoes. In 21 days she may be looked for at Barbadoes.*
>
> *No.3 Tobago, Trinidad, Grenada, and St. Vincent, remaining 24 hours at each island, and returns direct to Barbadoes. Fifteen days is the usual time in which this route is performed.*
>
> *No.4 La Guayra [in the Spanish Vice-Royalty of New Granada – present day Venezuela]; remains there one week, and from thence proceeds to St. Thomas's, where she remains six hours. This boat returns direct to Barbadoes, and is considered due in 28 days from the time of her leaving Barbadoes.*[9]

---

9   Martin, R. Montgomery. *Possessions in the West Indies.* Vol. 2 of *History of the British Colonies.* London: Cochrane and M'Crone, 1834, pp.515–516.

The communication of military intelligence remained a key reason for the development of the packet service. Packet captains were under orders from the Post Office to keep themselves informed of the local situation in every country they visited, and to report in detail to the British government about any ongoing military or naval operation. Returning packet ships went straight to Falmouth, and news of all the latest developments in conflict and commerce were known about and discussed in the town and its vicinity long before the news reached London.

As the packets voyaged to and from the Caribbean, they often drew the attention of enemy vessels and privateers, be they French, Spanish or Dutch. The duties of the captain of a mail packet in the event of enemy action were clear:

You must run where you can, you must fight when you can no longer run, and when you can fight no more, you must sink the mails before you strike.[10]

In October 1782, during the American Revolutionary War (1775–1783), the packet *Antelope* was sailing off the island of Cuba when she sighted two French privateers who gave chase.[11] Obeying the Post Office regulation to 'run while you can' *Antelope* began to head back to port to avoid trouble, but before she could reach safety the wind failed and the French privateer *Atlante* was able to come alongside and attack. During the battle, the *Antelope's* officers were killed or wounded, and the boatswain, John Pascoe – a good Cornish surname – took over command. After a fierce battle, *Antelope* forced the *Atlante* to surrender and, with her prize in tow, put into Annotto Bay on the north-east coast of Jamaica. To honour the bravery of the *Antelope's* crew, Jamaica's House of Assembly agreed to vote 500 guineas (£525) to them.[12]

---

10 Laakso, Seija-Riita. *Across the oceans: development of overseas business information transmission, 1815–1875.* Helsinki: Finnish Literature Society, 2006, p.30.
11 In 1778, France had signed an alliance with the newly declared nation of the United States of America and then fought on the side of the United States against Britain.
12 Falmouth Packet Archives 1688–1850. Accessed 4 August 2014, http://www.falmouth.packet.archives.dial.pipex.com/

In October 1807, during the Napoleonic Wars (1803–1815), the packet ship *Windsor Castle* was approaching Barbados when she was chased by the French privateer *Le Jeune Richard*. In command of the *Windsor Castle* was twenty-six-year-old Cornishman William Rogers, as acting captain. Rogers had been born in Falmouth in 1783, and had gone to sea on the packets at an early age. By the time he joined the *Windsor Castle*, he had led an adventurous life: aged fourteen, on his first packet voyage aboard the *Countess of Leicester*, he was made a prisoner of war when the ship was captured by a French frigate, and a few months later was one of a group of British prisoners exchanged for French prisoners and returned to Falmouth. He next joined the *Carteret*, bound for the Caribbean, which was taken by the French privateer *Bellona* on her second return journey from Jamaica. Exchanged again, he was back in Falmouth in time to join the *Duke of Clarence*, bound for the Caribbean. Captured yet again, this time by a Spanish privateer, he was taken to Tenerife in the Canary Islands. Rogers managed to escape and boarded an American ship which brought him to London in May 1801. He then sailed briefly on the *Penelope*, bound for Jamaica, before joining the *Duke of Kent* in March 1802 as a mate. *The Duke of Kent* was captured by a French privateer in May 1804 and taken to Guadeloupe, where Rogers stayed for three weeks before once again being freed as part of an exchange of prisoners.[13]

Back in Falmouth Rogers, having been given command of the *Windsor Castle*, sailed her to the Caribbean. Given his all too frequent experiences of capture by an enemy privateer, when *Le Jeune Richard* attacked and it was clear that the *Windsor Castle* could not escape, Rogers chose to fight. *Le Jeune Richard* was better armed and manned than the *Windsor Castle*, yet Rogers and his crew not only succeeded in repelling the privateer but managed to capture their attacker. Rogers and his crew returned to England as heroes, and the capture of *Le Jeune Richard* was painted by the artist Samuel Drummond.

---

13 *European Magazine, and London Review.* (Volume 53, 1808), pp.163–164. Accessed 21 January 2015, https://books.google.com.ag/books?id=6McPAAAAQAAJ&q= per cent22the+european+magazine+and+london+review per cent22+volume+53&dq= per cent22the+european+magazine+and+london+review per cent22+volume+53&hl=en&sa=X&ei=1-SVP2VH4jlgwSUnIPACA&ved=0CCAQ6AEw AQ

William Rogers capturing the *Jeune Richard*,
1 October 1807, by Samuel Drummond, 1808.
Courtesy of the National Maritime Museum, Cornwall.

Rogers was promoted to captain, awarded two swords of honour and:

When the account of this truly gallant action was received in the metropolis [London], a subscription to relieve the widows and orphans of those brave men who had so nobly lost their lives in the discharge of their duty, was instituted ... Mr. Dougars [?] of Tortola, and the officers of the Belleisle (Admiral Cochrane's flag-ship)... presented to Captain Rogers a purse of fifty pounds, as a token of their approbation of his conduct. Indeed, so highly was the public sensibility excited by the glorious action ... that a subscription in favour of the heroes who had fought and bled for their country, and for the wives and families of those that had fallen, was opened in all the West India Islands; one hundred pounds was voted by the Patriotic Fund; and we learn that a subscription for the above-mentioned purpose [was opened] in Liverpool.[14]

A packet crew could not, however, rely on the occasional monetary reward for bravery to augment their wages, and the trading of purchased goods – or 'adventuring' – was a regular part of their life as packet men. There were regulations which specifically prohibited such private trading, but when the quantity of trading goods carried by the crew was not large the regulations were not enforced:

> *Indeed, so recently as 1798, in a code of new regulations applicable to the Packet station at Falmouth, the trade had been explicitly recognized, and the only instruction given to the agent in regard to it was that he must satisfy himself that no Packet carried so large a quantity of goods, or stowed them in such a manner, as to put her out of trim. The Post-Office always looked unfavourably on this trade; and from time to time sought the assistance of the Treasury in abolishing it, and restricting the Packets to their proper use. But in those days of constant war, when the seas were unsafe for merchant vessels, and the ports now of one nation, now of another, were closed to English ships, the Government held that it would be inopportune to stop a commercial outlet on which so many merchants in Bristol and other towns in the west depended for a chief part of their trade; and so the irregular system went unchecked.*[15]

Goods carried out to be sold in the Caribbean included cheese, potatoes, boots, shoes and fighting cocks. There was a great demand for fighting cocks, most probably from the Spanish colonies where cock fighting was a popular sport. The packet men sometimes sold goods on their own behalf, and

---

14 *European Magazine and London Review.* (Volume 53, 1808), p.165. Accessed 21 January 2015, https://books.google.com.ag/books?id=6McPAAAAQAAJ&q= per cent22the+european+magazine+and+london+review per cent22+volume+53&dq= per cent22the+european+magazine+and+london+review per cent22+volume+53&hl=en&sa=X&ei=1-SVP2VH4jlgwSUnIPACA&ved=0CCAQ6AEwAQ

15 Norway, Arthur H. *History of the Post Office packet service between the years 1793–1815 compiled from records, chiefly official.* London: Macmillan, 1895, p.94.

sometimes on behalf of a Falmouth merchant with whom they maintained a regular working relationship.[16] The goods were sold in the various ports where the packet ships docked, either to merchants who auctioned them off, or to numerous local market women. In Antigua, as Mrs Lanaghan, that observant recorder of 19th-century Caribbean life, writes:

> *among those black women resident in the capital [St John's], are to be found an immense number of hucksters; indeed, in every street at every corner, they are to be met with. These persons deal in different articles; some in cloth of various fabrics, threads, tapes, laces, &c., and others in fruits, vegetables, soap and candles. Some of these hucksters occupy small shops of about fourteen feet square, (which, by the bye, in most cases they are obliged to use as their sleeping, dining, and dressing room as well,) where they vend their different wares; while others frequent the markets, or walk about the town or country with their goods.*[17]

It is said that it was Cornish seamen who brought the Cornish pasty to the Caribbean, sharing recipes as they traded with the hucksters. The hucksters adapted it to their taste, and added the meat patty – still a Caribbean favourite – to the range of foods they sold. Once the packet men had sold their goods, they made purchases for the return to Falmouth. A wide variety of textiles, tobaccos and wines were smuggled into that port duty free, and there were, in and around Falmouth, many women who, like the hucksters in the Caribbean, were eager to buy and sell these imported bargains:

> *a whole corps of female pedlars was in existence, locally named 'troachers,' who trudged the country and hawked about the goods of Jamaica or New York from farm house to country mansion.*[18]

---

16   Ibid, p.95.
17   Lanaghan, Mrs. *Antigua and the Antiguans: a full account of the colony and its inhabitants from the time of the Caribs to the present day, interspersed with anecdotes and legends ... in two volumes.* London: Saunders and Otley, 1844, p.145.
18   Norway, Arthur H. *History of the Post Office packet service between the years 1793–1815 compiled from records, chiefly official.* London: Macmillan, 1895, p.95.

When it came to trading, the general view of the Falmouth community – as throughout Cornwall – was that free trade was fair trade. This convenient arrangement was upset in late 1810 when, following a particularly thorough inspection and impounding of trading goods by customs officers, the crews of two packets refused to put to sea. There was a noisy demonstration on shore in support of the packet men; other crews threatened to refuse to put to sea, and when the demonstration turned violent the Riot Act was read. In punishment for the refusal of the Falmouth packet men to man its ships the Post Office moved the packet station to Plymouth. The good citizens of Falmouth were appalled at the loss of the packets, on which their prosperity depended and, with the support of 'the High Sheriff, Noblemen, Gentlemen and Clergy, of the County of Cornwall,' [19] in January 1811, they successfully petitioned the Postmaster General to return the service to Falmouth. Once again the packets sailed from Falmouth, and once again private trading was the unofficially accepted means of adding to the packet men's income.

Packet captains, too, profited from private trading, and the Post Office occasionally saw the need to make the legal situation clear. A circular from the Falmouth agent dated 15 January 1818 reads:

Captain Graham Commander of the Marchioness of Salisbury Packet, having taken on Board his Ship at Jamaica, a large quantity of Cochineal on Freight, under the erroneous idea that he was authorized so to do, it was seized by the Officers of the Customs at Falmouth, and given up by the Commissioners upon payment of the Tonnage Duty and satisfying the seizing Officer.

Although it ought to be well known to all Commanders, that it is illegal for the Packets to carry Merchandise of any description, (Bullion excepted) unless there may in special cases, be a Licence from the Board of Customs, I am directed by the Postmaster-General to promulgate the Law on this Head, to all Commanders, that no plea of want of Information may be urged on and future occasion.[20]

---

19   National Maritime Museum Cornwall. *Falmouth packet letters* [file].
20   Ibid.

No doubt the circular was widely ignored.

Packet captains also added to their income by carrying passengers, the Post Office receiving a percentage of the profit made on each passenger. Two levels of service were offered, cabin and steerage, and in 1810 the cost in the then British currency of pounds, shillings and pence[21] was as follows.[22]

Stations	Voyages	Cabin £ s d	Steerage £ s d
Jamaica	Falmouth to Barbados or Martinique	53 11 0	29 8 0
	Falmouth to Curaçao	58 16 0	32 0 0
	Falmouth to Jamaica	58 16 0	32 0 0
	Jamaica to Falmouth	53 11 0	29 8 0
Leeward Islands	Falmouth to Dominica	54 12 0	19 18 0
	Falmouth to Guadeloupe	55 13 0	30 9 0
	Falmouth to Antigua	57 15 0	31 10 0
	Falmouth to Montserrat	58 16 0	32 0 6
	Falmouth to Nevis or St Kitts	60 18 0	33 1 6
	Falmouth to Tortola or St Thomas	63 0 0	34 2 6
	From any of the Leeward Islands to Falmouth	53 11 0	29 8 0
Surinam	Falmouth to Surinam	56 14 0	30 19 6

---

21 Twelve pence to the shilling, twenty shillings to the pound.
22 Pawlyn, Tony. *The Falmouth packets 1689–1851*. Truro, Truran Books, 2003, p.128.

	Surinam to Falmouth	53 11 0	29 8 0
Berbice	Falmouth to Berbice	57 15 0	31 10 0
	Berbice to Falmouth	53 11 0	29 8 0
Demerara	Falmouth to Demerara	58 16 0	32 0 6
	Demerara to Falmouth	53 11 0	29 8 0

Travel via the packet service was expensive for the period: at today's prices, to travel cabin class from Falmouth to Jamaica cost the rough equivalent of £3,640, while to travel steerage cost about £1,980.[23] Passengers to the Caribbean were usually wealthy planters and their families and friends, plus government officials and foreign dignitaries. Later in the 19th century, as Cornish miners were contracted to work in Caribbean mines, they too travelled on the packet ships.

Regulations for travel were clearly defined by the packet agent:

Female servants pay as Cabin Passengers: Children under 12 months of Age go free of Charge; under 4 Years of Age pay as Steerage; above 4 Years as Cabin Passengers. The Passengers by all except the Lisbon Packets, provide Bedding; and from the West Indies lay in their own Stock. 400 Lbs [sic]. Any Commander of a Packet demanding more than the above authorized Rates, will incur the high displeasure of my Lords the Postmaster General.[24]

In addition to passengers, the other legitimate commodity carried by the packet ships and from which both the Post Office and the packet captains made a profit, was bullion. During the 18th century, bullion was mostly carried on the Lisbon route, but in the early 19th century the Caribbean packet service extended its Jamaica route to the wealthy city of Cartagena

---

23   Lawrence H. Officer and Samuel H. Williamson, 'Five Ways to Compute the Relative Value of a UK Pound Amount, 1270 to Present,' MeasuringWorth, 2014. Accessed 18 August 2014, http://www.measuringworth.com/ukcompare/
24   Pawlyn, Tony. *The Falmouth packets 1689–1851*. Truro, Truran Books, 2003, p.128.

de Indias, on the northern Caribbean coast of what was then the Spanish Viceroyalty of New Granada and is now Colombia. Bullion was a valuable cargo, and by 1810 the value of bullion freight shipped out of Cartagena had grown to exceed £1.1 million.[25] After 1811, when Cartagena declared independence from Spain, the city and its surrounding area began to experience a period of economic instability, and this had a negative impact on the bullion trade.

The packet ships also carried large and valuable amounts of bullion from Havana, in Cuba. They made regular shipments and, on one occasion when he was in port, the captain of the Royal Navy Sloop *Columbine* noted that 'the two Post-office packets, *Pigeon* and *Lady Mary Pelham*, were loaded with upwards of a million dollars [in bullion].[26]

Bullion landed at Falmouth was taken to London by road on wagons drawn by six or eight horses travelling at a walking pace and escorted by armed militia. The journey took about six days, and – surprisingly, given the regularity of the transfer of bullion and the slow pace of the journey – there were few successful robberies. The main carrier was the Exeter-based company of Russell and Company, whose evocative moniker, 'Russell's Flying Waggons', may have contributed to its success in winning the contract.

In 1814, Lord Melville, First Lord of the Admiralty, became alarmed at the frequent loss of packets to enemy privateers. The Royal Navy had recently been asked to provide a few small vessels to supplement the packet ships and as the Navy now had some experience in operating the packet service and its ships were better able to defend themselves than the lightly armed civil packet ships, Melville proposed that the navy should take over the service from the Post Office. Initially nothing came of his proposal, but when at the end of the Napoleonic Wars the navy found itself with idle ships and unemployed seamen and officers, Melville resubmitted his proposal. He saw that the packet service could provide work for both idle ships and idle men, and believed the navy could run the service more efficiently and with a smaller number of ships than were contracted by the Post Office.

---

25 Ibid, p.95.
26 Ibid, p.94.

The British government was convinced by his arguments, and in April 1823 control of the Falmouth packet service was transferred to the Royal Navy. The contract packets and their crews were not laid off, but as their contracts expired they were replaced by Admiralty-owned brigs commanded by a Royal Navy officer and manned by naval crews. Unfortunately, however, the Admiralty brigs were not suited to packet duties: they had been built to be manned by a crew of eighty or more but after they had been adapted to meet the needs of the packet service their crews were reduced to about thirty. In an emergency there were not enough men to reduce sail quickly, so in sudden squalls the brigs tended to capsize and founder. During the first years of the Royal Navy Packet Service at least eight brigs were lost at sea, most disappearing without trace. As the number of ships lost continued to increase they came to be known as 'coffin brigs'.

In the early 1830s, the Admiralty introduced steam vessels to the Falmouth packet service. The first steam packets were far from efficient: they frequently suffered from mechanical breakdowns, used huge quantities of coal to produce steam, and had to rely on bunkering stations that were too few and far between. On some of the Caribbean intra-regional routes, however, small steamers replaced the sailing vessels, mainly sailing between Jamaica and St Thomas (then part of the Danish West Indies, now part of the United States Virgin Islands).

While the Admiralty was striving to improve the Caribbean packet service, James MacQueen, a sugar plantation manager at Westerhall Estate on the island of Grenada, was becoming increasingly frustrated with its efforts. An outspoken anti-Abolitionist, he lived and worked in Grenada from 1797 until 1830, and during both his business and leisure activities corresponded with and visited the surrounding islands. He found the delivery of mail and the availability of passenger berths unreliable, and when he returned to his native Scotland he began to develop proposals which he believed would make the packet ships more efficient. In late 1837, he submitted his proposals to the British government, where they were enthusiastically received. Encouraged by this response, he focused on gaining the support of potential investors with an interest in the

Caribbean, including Thomas Baring, who would later be approached to invest in the development of the copper mine on Virgin Gorda.[27] In January 1838, he submitted an outline plan to the Treasury. This was accepted and it was agreed that the British government, through the West India Committee, would subsidise the founding of a private company, to be called the Royal Mail Steam Packet Company (RMSPC). James MacQueen was appointed as the Company's General Superintendent of Affairs with the remit of providing a line of specialised steamships to carry mail and passengers: 'to and from Great Britain and the West India Islands and North and South America and other foreign parts.'[28]

The RMSPC was granted a charter by Queen Victoria on 26 September 1839, and on 20 March 1840 the RMSPC and the Admiralty signed a contract agreeing to provide a twice-monthly service to the Caribbean. At the time of signing, however, the RMSPC possessed not a single vessel! It was given twenty months to provide both the ships and the support facilities needed to provide the service: coal bunkers, coal, water, provisions and repairs. The newspapers of the day thought the task impossible, but the company enthusiastically set to work. The authorised share capital was £1,500,000, and stock was issued at £60 per 100 shares, raising no less than £9,000,000. To meet the deadline, shipbuilding orders were spread among various British shipyards, while to help put support facilities in place as quickly as possible the foreign secretary, Lord Palmerston, provided MacQueen with a letter of introduction to various island councils so that he could: 'make the necessary arrangements for carrying on the important public service which the Company has undertaken to perform under contract with Her Majesty's Government.'[29]

The RMSPC managed to meet the terms of its contract: by late 1841 it had a fleet of fourteen paddle steamers for the transatlantic Caribbean

---

27 For more about Thomas Baring, see Chapter 9: Copper and Guano: the Mines of Virgin Gorda and Sombrero.
28 Merchant Navy Officers. *Royal Mail Steam Packet Company 1839–1913*. Accessed 6 August 2014, http://www.merchant navyofficers.com/rm.1.html
29 Anim-Addo, Anyaa. 'Steaming between the islands: nineteenth-century maritime networks and the Caribbean archipelago.' *Island Studies Journal*, (Vol.8, No.1, 2013), p.25.

service and three schooners for the intra-regional service. The company established Southampton as its home base, and set up the Caribbean-based port facilities required to run the service. The inaugural voyage from Falmouth to the Caribbean, bound for Berbice, Havana, New York and Halifax, took place on 3 January 1842. A second steamer left harbour to:

> *the Island of Barbados and after such interval from her arrival there (not exceeding six hours) as the Governor [of the island] or Senior Naval Officers present may require, such steam vessel as aforesaid shall forthwith proceed, with the said mails on board, to the Island of Grenada, and there remain so long only (not exceeding twelve hours) as the Governor of Senior Naval Officer present may require and thence proceed, with the said mails on board, to the Island of Santa Cruz [now St Croix], from Santa Cruz to St. Thomas, from St. Thomas to Nicole Mole [Cape Nicolas Mole], in the Island of Hayti, from Nicole Mole to Santiago de Cuba, and from Santiago de Cuba to Port Royal in the Island of Jamaica.*[30]

Powered by steam, these new packet ships had no need of a favourable wind to send them on their way from Falmouth to the Caribbean. But if the service was to run efficiently, the strategic coaling stations on the steam ship routes would have to be well maintained, so that the steamers could quickly take on coal before steaming on to their next port. From the early 1840s through to the 1850s the coaling stations in the Caribbean were based on the islands of St Thomas, Grenada, Jamaica and Cuba.

When the RMSPC began using St Thomas as a coaling station, the island was a Danish possession. Denmark did not abolish slavery until 1848 and the bearers who carried coal onto the steam ships in the harbour at Charlotte Amalie, the capital of St Thomas, were enslaved men and women hired out to the RMSPC by their owners. A junior officer on board one of the steam packet ships wrote:

---

30   Merchant Navy Officers. *Royal Mail Steam Packet Company 1839–1913*. Accessed 6 August 2014, http://www.merchant navyofficers.com/rm.1.html

A Royal Mail Steam Packet Company ship taking on coal in
St George's Harbour, Grenada, in about 1846.
Courtesy of the Bartlett Library, National Maritime Museum, Cornwall.

> *I saw the ladies and gentlemen employed at the work were kept moving by a white man with a whip in his hands; the ladies also carried baskets on their heads which held 112 lbs. coal ... and had to move smartly with their load, or the whip came into requisition.*[31]

In the British Caribbean colonies the enslaved were emancipated in 1834, but the British government was amenable to ignoring the illegal use of enslaved men, women and children by British business interests on St Thomas, just as it was when British-registered companies investing in the Spanish colony of Cuba's El Cobre copper mine – where enslavement was still legal – used enslave labour contracted from their local owners.[32]

---

31 Anim-Addo, Anyaa. '"A wretched and slave-like mode of labor": slavery, emancipation, and the Royal Mail Steam Packet Company's coaling stations.' *Historical Geography*, p.65 (Vol.39, 2011).
32 See Chapter 8: Gold and Copper: the Mines of Cuba and the Dominican Republic.

Loading a steam ship with coal by hand was hard, dirty work, and conditions did not much improve after the enslaved on the Danish islands were emancipated. It was work:

> done by negresses, for a negro must be very badly off indeed before he would condescend to do such work. The coals are carried in baskets on the head ... and the payment is 3d. per dozen baskets if coaling by day, but double that, or 6d., if at night ... By this method the steamers are supplied with about 200 tons of coal in from eight to ten hours. A tallyman sits near the gangway, whose business it is to keep an account of the number of baskets brought by each person. To aid him, each woman carries a piece of tin at her waist, with her number painted upon it, and she turns towards the tallyman as she passes so as fully to display it. He then drops a pea into a perforated tin lock-up box over that number; and, when the work is done, the peas are counted, and the ladies are paid immediately.[33]

Coaling a Royal Mail steam packet at Kingston Harbour, Jamaica.
Illustrated London News, 25 November 1865.
From the author's collection.

---

33 'Kingston, Jamaica.' *Illustrated London News* (25 November 1865).

The home port for the RMSPC was Southampton, but its vessels were obliged to call at Falmouth to receive and deliver the mail, as they were still being sent there by carrier from London. But a railway service was established between London and Southampton in 1840, and in September 1843 the Post Office gave approval for the mail to be sent to and from Southampton direct. The Cornwall Railway had made plans to connect London and Falmouth to provide a connecting mail delivery service for the steam packet ships, but the section from Plymouth to Truro was not opened until May 1859 and the extension from Truro to Falmouth only opened in August 1863. It was far too late. Falmouth was abandoned by the RMSPC in 1843, and as there was no longer any need for the services that Falmouth supplied to the packet ships the town began to decline.

5

Barbados, the British Windward Islands and Trinidad[1]

The Rev. Nicholas Leverton was said to have lived a 'troublesome and unsettled life,'[2] an observation which is an understatement. Leverton was born in about 1610 in the village of St Eval, about 4 miles (7 km) west of Padstow, on the north coast of Cornwall.[3] A bright boy, he went up to Exeter College, Oxford, from where, despite being 'addicted rather to youthful diversions,'[4] he graduated with a Bachelor of Arts degree.[5] In December 1632, he was ordained deacon at Exeter Cathedral by Bishop Joseph Hall, a Puritan sympathiser who encouraged Leverton towards his own religious beliefs.[6] Leverton then returned to Cornwall, to run the school in the village of St Endellion, which lies about 2 miles (3 km) east of Padstow, but by 1634 he was ready to expand his horizons. He made his way to Plymouth and booked a passage on a ship bound for Barbados.[7]

---

1 See Appendix 5 for a background history of Barbados, the British Windward Islands and Trinidad.
2 *The life of Nicholas Leverton*. Accessed 1 June 2016, http://wesley.nnu.edu/john-wesley/christian-library/a-christian-library-volume-15/the-lives-of-jospeh-woodward-nicholos-leverton-sir-nathanael-barnardiston-and-samuel-fairclough/ [sic]
3 *Rev. Nicholas Leverton 1610–1662: life and death of a Non Conformist*. Accessed 1 June 2016, http://www.nickleverton.com/life-and-death-story.html
4 Ibid.
5 *The life of Nicholas Leverton*. Accessed 1 June 2016, http://wesley.nnu.edu/john-wesley/christian-library/a-christian-library-volume-15/the-lives-of-jospeh-woodward-nicholos-leverton-sir-nathanael-barnardiston-and-samuel-fairclough/
6 *Rev. Nicholas Leverton 1610–1662: life and death of a Non Conformist*. Accessed 1 June 2016, http://www.nickleverton.com/life-and-death-story.html
7 Ibid.

On Barbados he was made welcome and was 'soon placed in one of their Churches ... officiating about half a year in which time he got acquaintance if with none of the best yet likely as good as any were then there to be had, for ... the people there were very debauched, [and] their manners somewhat ingrate and fulsome to him.'[8] As the people of Barbados did not please him, he was relieved when in 1637 he was offered the post of chaplain to a group of Puritan colonists southbound for the island of Tobago. The attempt at settlement was funded by fellow Puritan Robert Rich (1587–1658), Earl of Warwick, who sponsored not only several early attempts at colonisation but many of the English privateers who operated throughout the Caribbean.

But the attempt at settlement was a disaster. When the group landed on Tobago they were attacked by the island's indigenous population and managed to lose the longboat that had carried them from their ship to the shore. By the time they managed to return to their ship about half of them, including the ship's captain, had been killed, and Leverton had been badly wounded in the head by an arrow. It was at first thought unlikely that he would live, but while they waited offshore to see if any other members of their group remained alive and would require assistance to reach the ship he recovered. The remaining would-be colonists now had to plan their next move. They could not return to Barbados because:

> it lay to windward as also the other English plantations, and their ship being old and rotten could not sail upon a tack. But if it had been fit to cruise, that kind of sailing would have required much time, and their victuals being far spent they could not hold out. Only one visible hope they had to be preserved, and that was to make for the Isle of Providence which, though it lay at great distance ... that is 500 leagues or so ... because it lay to the leeward they hoped to get there before all their victuals were spent. Nor yet was this course void of very great danger, for though they had good charts on board to direct them, yet only one man of the company had been ever there and he only was able to tell them it was the same island if they should happen

---

8   Ibid.

to strike right upon it; and if they should miss it and fall among the Spaniards they could expect nothing but destruction ... However there being but this one way open there was no room for deliberation what to choose. They therefore took course committing themselves to merciful providence which failed them not in this great exigency, but safely brought them to their desired port.[9]

Providence lies about 120 miles (200 km) east of the coast of present-day Nicaragua, and a colony had been established there in 1631 by the Earl of Warwick. It was managed by the Providence Island Company, a joint-stock company that included many prominent English Puritans whose goal was to make Providence the leading Puritan colony in the New World. Since its climate was far superior to that of the Massachusetts Bay Colony which had been founded the same year, they thought this would be achieved without too many challenges. The colony also operated as a base from which Warwick's privateers sailed against Spanish ships and settlements in the region.

Leverton and his companions were welcomed to Providence and settled down to contribute to the peaceful development of the colony, but dissension soon arose when the Governor of Providence, Nathaniel Butler, returned to England, leaving the island in the care of his deputy, Captain Carter. Carter was unpopular, and the council refused to accept him, nominating one Captain Lane in Carter's place. Carter then armed:

many of the under sort of people... [who] broke in violently upon the council and apprehended Captain Lane and Mr. Holliard who had formerly been a magistrate and Mayor of Banbury, and the two Ministers, for the Ministers were wont to sit in their council. These, it seems, he thought the greatest obstruction of his preferment ... After a strict imprisonment for some days ... he shipped them away for England by one Captain Jackson who was a privateer on those coasts and then in their harbour. By this Captain he sent a charge against

---

9   Rev. Nicholas Leverton 1610–1662: life and death of a Non Conformist. Accessed 1 June 2016, http://www.nickleverton.com/life-and-death-story.html

them to the Lords that had the patent, and especially an information to the then Archbishop Laud about their opposition to the liturgies and ceremonies of the Church of England.[10]

By the time Leverton and his fellow prisoners reached England in early 1641, the political situation had changed: Archbishop Laud, a supporter of the Church of England, was in prison, and the Puritan faction, the Earl of Warwick among them, was on the rise. So the prisoners were released, welcomed by Warwick and the other proprietors of Providence, and encouraged to return to the island. Lane and Leverton agreed to the proposal and left with a well provisioned ship. Leverton was employed to take care of the spiritual needs of the colonists and it looked as if his career was now decided, but peace and stability once again evaded him. As the ship approached Providence, it became clear that the island had been seized by Spain in their absence and that the Puritan colony was no more. They wisely put back out to sea as quickly as possible and for the next two years they sailed the Caribbean, facing a series of perilous adventures that nearly ended their lives:

> They had many preservations, almost miraculous, from famine, from the Spaniards, and in violent storms. Twice they lost their ship, and were providentially taken up, once by a Frenchman, and another time by a Dutchman ... At length they resolved to return home, and by the assistance of a French vessel arrived safe at St. Christopher's; and thence Captain Lane, and some of the men, proceeded directly to England. Mr. Leverton and some others inclined to settle there; but finding the dissoluteness of the place, and seeing little hope of doing good among them, after four or five months' trial, he took the opportunity of a French frigate to return to Europe.[11]

---

10 Ibid.
11 *The life of Nicholas Leverton*. Accessed 1 June 2016, http://wesley.nnu.edu/john-wesley/christian-library/a-christian-library-volume-15/the-lives-of-jospeh-woodward-nicholos-leverton-sir-nathanael-barnardiston-and-samuel-fairclough/

If Leverton was expecting an uneventful voyage back to England, he was to be disappointed:

A dead calm continuing long at sea, all their victuals were spent. For many days they had but eight spoonfuls of peas, and a pint of water, per man ... At length, upon keeping a day of solemn prayer, no sooner was it ended, but they discovered a ship and upon making towards it, found it an English merchant-man; bound for Bermuda, who took all the English on board, and plentifully supplied the French for their voyage home. On board this ship was the Governor of Bermuda, who acquainted Mr. Leverton, upon converse with him, that the ship's coming there at that time was by a very uncommon providence.[12]

Soon after Leverton reached Bermuda, he made the acquaintance of a young woman called Anbitt Reyner, daughter of a local planter. In 1642, after a short courtship, they married, and Leverton settled down to enjoy married life and preach to the people of Bermuda. This short period of enjoyment and stability was cut short when he developed a serious illness and was advised to return to England if he hoped to recover. He once more boarded ship, reaching his home port in early 1644. Having regained his health, he found employment as the Minister of Heveningham in Suffolk, and was able to send for his wife, who had remained in Bermuda. By 1649, he was on the move again, this time back to Cornwall, where he became Minister of St Tudy,[13] a parish in the River Camel valley, about 17 miles (27 km) east of his place of birth, St Eval.

Over the next ten years Leverton ministered to the spiritual needs of the people of St Tudy, but when the monarchy was restored under Charles II, Leverton's peaceful life was once more interrupted. As a Puritan and a supporter of the Parliamentarians, he was ejected from his living in St Tudy and forced to leave the village. Fortuitously, he soon received a letter from one Mr Oxenbridge, who he had known in Bermuda. Oxenbridge had heard of Leverton's troubles in Cornwall, and wrote that Lord

---

12 Ibid.
13 St Tudy was the birthplace of another Cornishman who travelled the world: Captain William Bligh.

Willoughby of Parham, who in 1650 had sent an expedition to found a colony in Surinam on the north-east coast of South America, had been made the new colony's governor, and that: 'he [Willoughby] was desirous to send over some fit person to be Minister there, for that at that time the colony was wholly destitute of any.'[14] Would Leverton be interested in the post? Never one to turn down a new adventure, Leverton accepted the offer, and in early 1662 set forth for the Caribbean with his wife and family.

When he arrived in Surinam, he seemed in good spirits, but soon: 'his old distempers returned upon him ... [and] his cheerfulness upon his new settlement after so many troubles, did rather make him seem to be well than at all render him so.'[15] After spending only a few weeks in Surinam in 1662, perhaps worn out by a tumultuous life which had taken him back and forth between the Caribbean and England and from one end of the Caribbean to the other, he died. He was 52 years old.

Thomas Kendall (1609–1666), like Leverton, was an early settler on Barbados. He was born at Treworgey, in Duloe near Looe on the south coast of Cornwall, where the family had lived since the early 14th century. Unlike Leverton, Kendall stayed on Barbados and in 1648, in partnership with his brother-in-law Thomas Modyford (later Governor of Jamaica), bought 400 acres of land in the parish of St John on the east coast of Barbados, then known as Buckland Plantation. He also bought land in Jamaica.[16]

Like other early settlers Kendall first worked his land with the assistance of imported indentured labourers. Among those sent to Barbados were some Cornishmen, including: Thomas Stephens, who was indentured to Richard Lukins for three years in 1657; Arthur Tirriby from St Teath, a yeoman farmer indentured to Thomas Gwin for seven years in 1658; John Babb, a mariner from Cummerford, indentured to Richard Roberts for four years in 1659; and John Perflit, a yeoman farmer from Padstow who was indentured to William Hammonds for four years

---

14 Ibid.
15 Ibid.
16 The Kendall properties in Jamaica and Barbados both became known as Kendal, not Kendall Plantation.

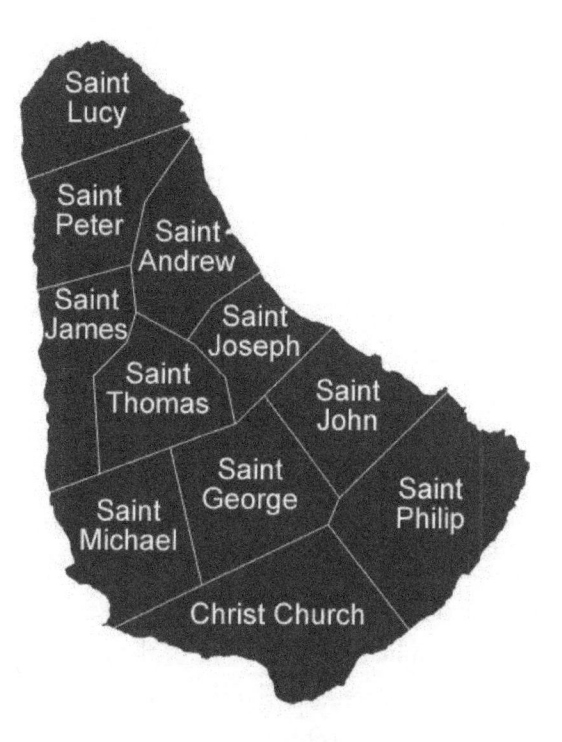

The parishes of the island of Barbados.

in 1659.[17] The colony's servants and indentured labourers were often speakers of various regional dialects, and as Bristol was the major port for shipment to Barbados, many colonists came from the surrounding counties, in particular from Somerset, Devon, Cornwall and Dorset. The early introduction of these regional dialects is thought to have had a lasting impact on the spoken language of Barbadians.[18]

Thomas Kendall did not live long enough to see the development of his lands into thriving plantations. He died towards the end of 1666, leaving his estate to his surviving sons. On the death of his elder son, John, in 1684, his Caribbean properties were inherited by his younger son, James.

---

17   Cooper, Cliff. 'Barbados connection.' *Cornwall Family History Society Journal*, p.7. (No.79, March 1996).
18   Neumann-Holzschuh, Ingrid, and Schneider, Edgar Werner. *Degrees of restructuring in Creole languages*. Amsterdam: John Benjamins Publishing, 2000, pp.224–226.

James Kendall (1647–1708) had first pursued a career in the army, serving in the Coldstream Guards until 1685, the year of the Monmouth Rebellion. After the rebellion failed, Kendall, possibly because of his Barbados connections, was made responsible for organising the transport of 100 of the rebels 'attainted of high treason'[19] from England to Barbados, where they were sold as slaves for ten years or longer. Among the purchasers was Nicholas Prideaux.[20] He was a member of an old and prominent family whose Cornish roots stretched back to the Norman Conquest of 1066, when they were granted the Iron Age fort of Prideaux Castle near Fowey in Cornwall, together with a manorial holding in the Luxulyan Valley nearby. One branch of the family later lived at Prideaux Place just outside of Padstow. When Nicholas Prideaux settled on Barbados, he became a merchant in Bridgetown and the Royal African Company's agent for the sale of slaves. He later leased a plantation in the parish of St Thomas and became President of the Barbados Council.[21]

In 1685, Kendall was elected to Parliament as the Member for West Looe, retaining his seat until 1690, when he left England to take up the post of Governor of Barbados. Soon after settling into the governor's mansion, he met Walker Colleton, the daughter of Colonel Thomas Colleton and niece of Sir Peter Colleton, one of the most influential planters on the island. Walker was about twenty at the time and had recently been orphaned. She became bachelor Kendall's housekeeper, moved into the mansion and soon became pregnant by him. Their son was named James Kendall, after his father.[22]

In 1692, Governor Kendall was given the responsibility of planning an attack on the French, who were becoming an increasing threat to England's Caribbean possessions. He was able to work productively with

---

19 Hotten, John Camden. *The original list of persons of quality: emigrants, religious exiles, political rebels. Serving men sold for a term of years, apprentices, children stolen, maidens pressed, and others. Who went from Great Britain to the American plantations, 1600–1700*. New York: Empire State Book Company, 1874. Kindle edition. Accessed 21 May 2016.
20 Ibid.
21 Galenson, David W. *Traders, Planters and Slaves: Market Behavior in Early English America*. Cambridge: Cambridge University Press, 2002, p.191.
22 Buchanan, J.E. 'The Colleton family and the early history of South Carolina and Barbados: 1646–1775.' PhD diss., University of Edinburgh, 1989, p.209.

the Barbados Council and Assembly to plan and implement his ideas successfully, and the French were defeated. But by the summer of 1693, Kendall and the Assembly were no longer on good terms. This was partly because the Assembly refused to meet the cost incurred by the French defeat, but the main cause was the hostility of several of the colony's leading figures to a 1692 Act which required Assembly members to take the Church of England sacrament. Those opposing Kendall, who included the powerful Sir Peter Colleton, were able to have Kendall removed from office by the end of 1693. He was subsequently made a member of the Barbados Council, which would have allowed him to remain at Kendal Plantation, but with property in Jamaica he had hopes that he would be appointed Governor of Jamaica. This post was, however, denied him, so taking Walker Colleton with him he returned to Cornwall, arriving in Falmouth in May 1695. He settled back into life as an absentee planter and a Cornish gentleman of some means, while Walker took the name of Kendall and continued in her role as housekeeper and mistress.

Soon after Kendall returned to Cornwall, he was appointed a commissioner in the office of the Lord High Admiral, and in the 1695 election he was returned as Member of Parliament for West Looe. His success in the election was in part due to the influence of his niece Mary, the heiress of Killigarth Manor and its estate – but after a subsequent disagreement she made sure that Kendall lost his seat in the 1702 election. In return he disinherited her in his will, and when he died – from apoplexy – in July 1708 Mary received nothing. His estate, which was worth £40,000 and included his plantation in Barbados, went to Walker Colleton, and she in turn left it to their son, James.[23] It would not stay in the family long, as in about 1710 the Barbados Kendal Plantation was sold to Samuel Osborne.[24]

Another of the early Cornish governors of Barbados was Sir Bevil Granville (1631–1706). His family came from Stowe House, Kilkhampton, in north-east Cornwall, and were descended from the explorer and naval captain Sir Richard Grenville (1542–1591). With

---

23   Ibid., p.209.
24   *Kendal Plantation.* Shilstone Memorial Library, Barbados Museum & Historical Society vertical file.

an eye to adding prestige to their name, the family changed the spelling from Grenville to Granville, because of possible connection to members of the Norman aristocracy who had come from Granville in Normandy. Sir Bevil was a Tory Member of Parliament for Fowey in 1685, 1695 and 1698, and for Lostwithiel in 1690.[25] A military man, he spent most of his career in Europe, particularly in Flanders, before being made Governor of Pendennis Castle, Falmouth, in 1695. When he returned to Flanders he was unpopular with his fellow officers, who accused him of illegal practices. In May 1702, Queen Anne made him Governor of Barbados and he arrived in the colony in March 1703. The beginning of his governorship proved difficult as he almost immediately fell ill, probably from yellow fever, and was unable to manage the island's affairs until his unexpected recovery some weeks later. When he did begin to govern he proved to be as unpopular with the settlers as he had been with his fellow officers in Europe. Local planters complained of his tyrannical behaviour, and although after a hearing by the Barbados Council he was acquitted of any wrongdoing, he was recalled to England in 1706. Still unwell, he died at sea during his homeward passage.[26]

Nathaniell (or Nathanell) Trevanion (or Trevanyon) came to Barbados in about 1679 or 1680 and set up business as a merchant.[27] [28] While there is no reference to a Cornish birth, his surname is typically Cornish, and the Trevanion family has a long Cornish history: its estate – in St Michael Caerhays, on the south coast of Cornwall – was included in the Domesday Book of 1086.[29] Once established as a successful merchant,

---

25 *Granville (Grenville), Bevil (1665–1706)*. Accessed 15 May 2016, http://www.historyofparliamentonline.org/volume/1660–1690/member/granville-(grenville)-bevil-1665–1706
26 Luttrell, Narcissus. *A brief historical relation of state affairs from September 1678 to April 1714*. 6 vols. Oxford: Oxford University Press, 1857. Accessed 15 May 2016, https://catalog.hathitrust.org/Record/011539870
27 Sanders, Joanne McRee. *Barbados records: wills and administrations volume II, 1681–1700*. Baltimore: Clearfield, 2011, p.533.
28 Brandow, James C. *Omitted chapters from Hotten's original lists of persons of quality ... and others who went from Great Britain to the American plantations 1600–1700: census returns, parish registers, and militia rolls from the Barbados Census of 1679/80*. Baltimore: Genealogical Publishing Co., 1982, p.120.
29 *St Michael Caerhays*. Accessed 20 May 2016, http://www.genuki.org.uk/big/eng/Cornwall/StMichaelCaerhays/

Trevanion expanded his business interests. He joined the plantocracy of Barbados, acquiring 173 acres in the parish of St Philip and 25 acres in the parish of St John. In his later years he bought a third plantation,[30] also in the parish of St John, which he left to his eldest daughter and heiress, Mary. She married William Fortesque, and after their marriage the plantation became known as Fortesque Plantation. By the time Trevanion died in 1692, however, he was living in financially straitened circumstances, apparently because of the marriage of his daughter Elizabeth to one Samuel Cox, and he requested to be buried:

in St. Philips Vestry house in the grave where kinsman David Moyle was buried or ye grave where Col. William Fortesque [his son-in-law] was buried ... [as there have been] late bad times since the intermarriage of [my] dau Elizabeth Cox with Samuel Cox.[31]

In 1763, Barbados was given administrative responsibility for the islands ceded to Britain at the end of the Seven Years' War: Dominica, Grenada and the Grenadines, St Vincent, and Tobago. The Governor of Barbados became Governor-General of Barbados, Grenada and the Grenadines, St Vincent, and Tobago, while each island had its own lieutenant-governor and its own Assembly: an arrangement that gave some autonomy to the individual members. In 1833, these islands became the Windward Islands Colony. In 1838, both the island of Trinidad, acquired in 1802 from Spain, and that of St Lucia, acquired in 1814 from France, became members. But Trinidad's membership was brief, as in 1840 the island left the group and became a separate colony.

The Windward Islands Colony was unpopular both in Barbados, which wished to retain its long-established separate identity, and with the other members of the group, who resented being administered by Barbados. Nevertheless, the union survived until 1885, when Barbados returned to its former status as a separate colony. Grenada then became

---

30 Campbell, P.F. 'Richard Ligon.' *Journal of the Barbados Museum and Historical Society*, pp.235–236 (Vol.37, 1985),.
31 Sanders, Joanne McRee. *Barbados records: wills and administrations volume II, 1681–1700*. Baltimore: Clearfield, 2011, p.533.

the island with administrative responsibility for the Windward Islands Colony, with a governor-general based in Grenada. Tobago left the grouping in 1889, when it became part of the colony of Trinidad.

When Grenada became a British colony in 1783, the first person to hold the position of Governor of Grenada and the Southern Grenadines, the small islands which lie to the north of Grenada, was Edward Mathew (1728–1805). He was the brother of Daniel Mathew, who owned plantations in St Christopher, Antigua and Tobago, the son of William Mathew, Governor of the Leeward Islands, and great-grandson of Abednego Mathew who, in the middle of the 17th century, had left St Kew in Cornwall to settle on St Christopher.[32] Edward Mathew had been born in Antigua, and he made his career in the army. He joined the Coldstream Guards, and served in Europe before becoming equerry to King George III in 1762, a position he held until 1776. He fought with distinction in the American Revolutionary War, attaining the rank of major-general, before being appointed commander-in-chief of the armed forces in the West Indies in 1782.[33]

As Grenada's first governor after the end of French occupation, one of his first tasks was to survey the existing fortifications that stood above the island's capital, St George's on Richmond Hill. He found that most of the defences could not be salvaged and needed to be replaced, reporting that even the principal redoubt:

is in a most ruinous condition, it was originally so ill-constructed, that the French were apprehensive that the firing of its own guns would bring it down ... The soil is very loose ... so that it will not long resist the violent rains of the Country unless established in Masonry.[34]

The new fortifications, including a fort named Fort Mathew after the governor, were constructed by the Carolina Corps, a battalion raised in 1779 in South Carolina from a cadre of free black men who had fought

---

32 For more information about the Mathews family, see Chapter 1: The British Leeward islands.
33 Chilvers, Allan. *The Berties of Grimsthorpe Castle*. Bloomington: AuthorHouse, 2010, p.182.
34 Fort Mathew. Accessed 19 May 2016, http://www.forts.org/fort_mathew/index.html

on the side of the British in the American Revolutionary War. At the end of the conflict they were transferred to Grenada and remained there until 1793. They later became the First West India Regiment, returning to Grenada in 1796 as part of the garrison based in St George's.[35]

Along with the improvement of Grenada's defences, Governor Mathew had to manage the much more complex issue of the latent hostility that existed between the French Roman Catholic and the British Protestant inhabitants. The more strident of the British Protestants, led by the Scottish planter Ninian Home, began a sustained social and political attack on the French. Legal steps taken against the Roman Catholics included the seizure of Roman Catholic church buildings, and the voiding of the registration of births, marriages and burials that had taken place outside of the Anglican Church. The political situation was particularly difficult for any members of the French free coloured population who wished to stand for political office, as a ruling had also been made that all candidates had to be white males over 21, natural-born British subjects and Protestants.[36]

Edward's father William had governed as an autocrat during his years as Governor-General of the Leeward Islands; his management style left him out of favour with both the local planters and the colonial government. Edward had inherited the same lack of diplomatic skill, and was described as: 'hot tempered and autocratic … a stern presence [and] dictatorial.'[37] He was, for instance, against the practice of allowing the enslaved to grow crops for their own use and for sale at the local market. Mathew believed they stole crops from their masters and then sold them as their own produce. Hence, the enslaved were prohibited from growing any indigo, cotton, ginger, coffee or cocoa, from holding Sunday markets, and from participating in any other 'licentious meetings'.[38]

Despite his unpopularity, Mathew was appointed as governor a second time by George III. But the king, now suffering from loss of

---

35 Ibid.
36 Ashie-Nikoi, Edwina. 'Beating the pen on the drum: a socio-cultural history of Carriacou, Grenada, 1750–1920'. PhD diss., New York University, 2007, pp.31–32.
37 Chilvers, Allan. *The Berties of Grimsthorpe Castle*. Bloomington: AuthorHouse, 2010, p.168.
38 Ibid.

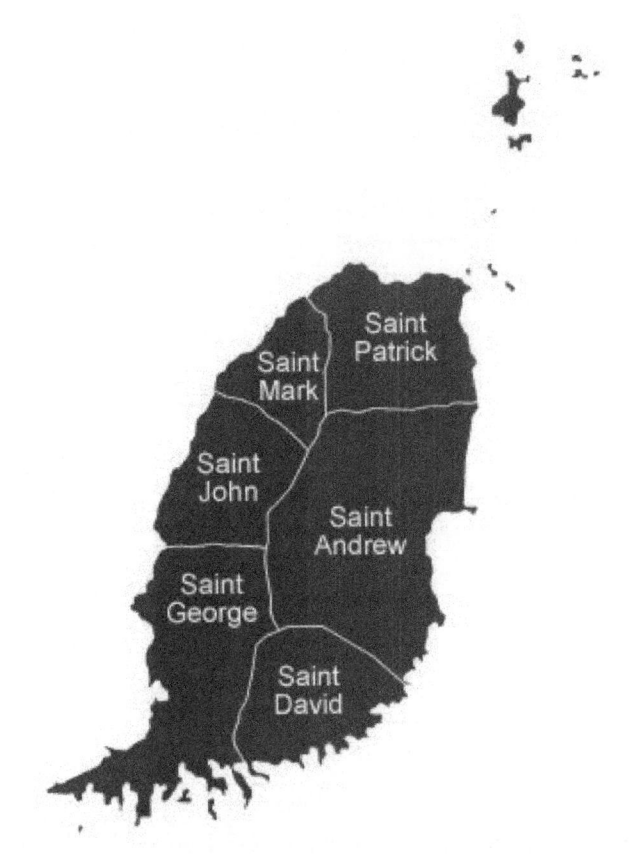

The parishes of the island of Grenada.

memory and fits of madness, forgot to clear Mathew's salary with the Treasury, a matter which Mathew never resolved. Shortly after his death, the Treasury billed the Mathew family £24,000 for repayment of his salary and all the expenses from his second term. This his heirs duly paid.

Mathew's dictatorial style of leadership helped lay the seeds of discontent which, shortly after his departure to England, exploded in what is known as the Fédon Rebellion. Born in Grenada, or possibly Martinique, Julien Fédon was the son of a white French jeweller and a free black woman.[39] A successful planter, he lived with his wife on Belvedere Estate in the Parish of Saint John. Fédon was influenced by the success of the French Revolution, and became

---

39   Jacobs, Curtis. *The Fedons of Grenada, 1763–1814*. Accessed, 14 June 2016, http://www.open.uwi.edu/sites/default/files/bnccde/grenada/conference/papers/Jacobsc.html

leader both of the French-speaking free coloured members of the population and of some of the island's enslaved people. In March 1795 his followers rose up in support of Republican France. Their objectives were to get rid of British colonial rule, return Grenada to France, and free the enslaved and make them French citizens. Fédon and his supporters fought the British in a conflict that raged across the island for more than a year, capturing and killing several prominent British planters and administrators, including Mathew's successor, Governor Ninian Home, the erstwhile leader of the anti-French movement.[40] Fédon's movement was eventually defeated, and several of his followers were arrested and hanged, but Fédon was never found.

When Edward Mathew returned to England it was not to Cornwall but to Laverstoke in Hampshire. Here he lived with his wife Lady Jane Bertie and their six children in the Old Manor House. Their eldest daughter, Anne, married a neighbour's son, James Austen, brother of the novelist Jane Austen; it is said that she based the autocratic character of General Tilney, who appears in her 1798 novel *Northanger Abbey*, on Edward Mathew.[41]

Edward's brother, Daniel Mathew, the owner of plantations on St Christopher and Antigua,[42] had meanwhile extended his holdings to include properties in Tobago. He had bought them during the early part of the 1770s when there was considerable unrest on the island and little competition from other buyers: at that time the enslaved had successfully attacked the barracks on Courland Point, capturing ammunition and killing two soldiers and several members of the Council.[43] The rebellion lasted a week, and was only put down with the help of military assistance from neighbouring islands. In 1771, several more insurrections occurred, mostly in the north-east of the island, and British soldiers were hard put to gain control of the situation. Their commanders realised that the traditional red jackets they wore made them too conspicuous, reporting

---

40 *Julian Fedon.* Accessed 19 May 2016, http://culture.gd/index.php/aunty-tek-spiceword-festival-gallery/16-hry/228-julien-fedon.
41 Chilvers, Allan. *The Berties of Grimsthorpe Castle.* Bloomington: AuthorHouse, 2010, p.182.
42 See Chapter 1: The British Leeward Islands.
43 Paquette, Robert L., and Stanley L. Engerman. *The Lesser Antilles in the Age of European Expansion.* Gainesville: University Press of Florida, 1996, p.116.

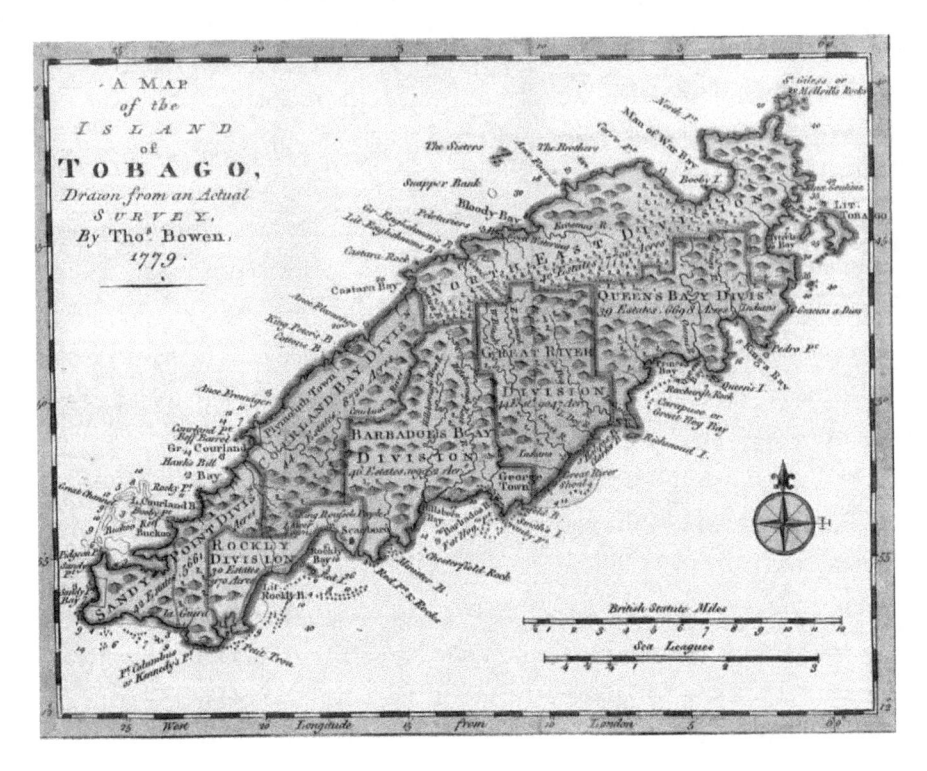

Thomas Bowen's 1779 map of Tobago, showing the island's subdivisions.

that the 'Glaring colour of the cloathing greatly hurts the service'.[44] Their men were henceforth dressed in green jackets and trousers, but it was to be another 100 years before the rest of the British army realised that their men would be less likely to be shot at if they were less visible. In 1774, the enslaved rose up again, this time on two plantations at Queen's Bay on the south-east coast, where about fifty enslaved men killed two whites and captured some arms.[45]

In February 1771, Daniel Mathew bought Steele Town Plantation from Sir William Young.[46] Steele Town lay on the north-west coast of Tobago, in the Sandy Point Division, and Sir William had bought it only shortly

---

44 Ibid., p.116.
45 O'Shaughnessy, Andrew Jackson. *An Empire Divided: The American Revolution and the British Caribbean*. Philadelphia: University of Pennsylvania Press, 2000, pp.39–40.
46 Glamorgan Record Office. *Family and estate papers of the Mathew family of St Kew, Cornwall and of the Caribbean islands*, DMW/49.

beforehand from Joshua Steele, who with his brother Richard had been the original grantee of the property and named it Steele Town.[47] Mathew renamed the property Felix Hall after his country residence in England.[48]

The development of Felix Hall Plantation, like most of the new sugar estates on Tobago, demanded plenty of labour, and Daniel Mathew, like many plantation owners with estates on other islands, transferred his enslaved workers to where they were most needed. At Felix Hall:

> *as there was only Ten Negros got with the Estate, 3 of which was children at their Mother's breasts ... there was 35 brought from Antigua, 16 of which were New Negroes [slaves newly arrived from Africa].*[49]

Mathew twice shipped enslaved labour from his estates in Antigua to Tobago, once in January 1771 and again in December of that year.[50] As development of the property got under way his attorney (manager) reported:

> *The condition of this Lott when taken over, was 60 acres 12 of which was in Plantains, 3 in Yams, Potatoes and Eddoes, 2 in Guinea Grass & one acre in cane, but these all destroyed by the Rebellious Negroes during the late Insurrections and the rest of the Land grown up in long grass; and small bushes; – In order to make some sugar in the year 1773 I holed land to plant canes immediately for a nursery that they might be old enough to cut for the Plants to put in for the crop ... When the Estate was taken possession of for Mr. Mathew; all the stores and Negro Houses but one, having been burnt by the Rebells in the Insurrection, the first thing to be done was to get timber and wattles and carry thatch, to create Negro Houses, for they were obliged to be lodged in a small Dwelling House (not more than 30 feet long) along with the white People which was much crowded.*[51]

---

47 Ibid., DMW/49.
48 Ibid., DMW/47–49.
49 Ibid., DMW/56.
50 Ibid., DMW/50.
51 Ibid., DMW/56.

By 1774, Daniel Mathew was the co-owner of Mount Mathew, also in Sandy Point Division. This plantation, like Steele Town, had first been granted to Richard and Joshua Steele, and had previously been known as Mount Irvine, named after Charles Irvine, one of the previous co-owners.[52] Mount Mathew would later be bought by the son of Charles Irvine and once again become Mount Irvine, the name by which the area is known today.[53]

At the time of Daniel Mathew's death in 1777, Tobago was exporting great quantities of sugar, rum, cotton and indigo, with sugar production peaking during the late 18th and early 19th centuries. France briefly took possession of the island between 1781 and 1793, and again between 1802 and 1803, but although this caused some temporary instability the sugar industry continued to do well. Decline set in after 1807, when it became illegal to trade in enslaved people in the British colonies, and continued after Emancipation in 1834: Tobago planters, as on other islands, struggled to survive both these developments and the falling price of sugar.

The newly freed men and women on Tobago, as throughout the Caribbean, became disenchanted when Emancipation not only failed to give them the rights they had envisaged but withdrew their customary privileges, such as the right to grow crops on the provision grounds of the estates, with access to land now depending on the payment of rent. Many felt that they should be allowed to use land rent free, but even if they were willing to pay rent they had difficulty in acquiring land from the plantation owners, who were unwilling to split their plantations up into small plots.[54] The reduction of wages that were already low, plus the irregularity of wage payments, became important issues, as planters became short of both capital and funds to meet the running costs of their estates. Another grievance was the linking of the payment of wages to debts outstanding at the estate shops where the labourers bought their goods.[55] The devastating hurricane of 1847 added to the planters' financial problems and the labourers grievances:

---

52 Nardin, Jean-Claude. *La mise en valeur de l'ile de Tobago (1763–1783)*. Paris: Mouton, 1969, p.332.
53 Phillips, David. *La Magdalena: the story of Tobago, 1498–1898*. New York: iUniverse, 2004, p.152.
54 Brereton, Bridget. 'Post-emancipation protest in the Caribbean: the 'Belmanna Riots' in Tobago, 1876.' *Caribbean Quarterly*, p.115 (Vol.30, No. 3/4, September–December 1984).
55 Ibid., pp.111–112.

sugar lands and plantation infrastructure across the island were destroyed to such an extent that they never fully recovered.[56]

In 1876, the estate labourers on Roxborough Plantation, on the south coast of the island overlooking Queen's Bay, began to express their grievances by setting fires on the estate. Police were sent to arrest the suspected arsonists, but a crowd of labourers gathered and resisted the arrests. One of the policemen, Corporal Belmanna, fired into the crowd, killing a woman and injuring a man. This triggered a major riot, and the police retreated to the estate's court house, which the crowd attacked. The labourers demanded that Belmanna be handed over to them. He agreed to leave the building, but under escort as a prisoner to be tried for murder. As he left the court house, however, the crowd managed to seize him from his escort, beating him so severely that he later died from his injuries.[57]

The general unrest that spread across the island after what became known as the Belmanna Riots was the final blow to the island's sugar industry. The economy, already in decline, did not recover, and in 1889, no longer viable as a separate colony, Tobago was amalgamated with the island of Trinidad. Daniel Mathew had initially willed his Tobago estates, along with those in Antigua, to his younger son, George Mathew, but he later changed the legacy, directing that they be sold. In exchange, George received £10,000 and the money to purchase a lieutenancy in the army. The descendants of George Mathew, including George's son George Benvenuto Buckley Mathew,[58] who inherited the Mathew estates in St Christopher, may well have been relieved that Daniel Mathew had altered his will.[59]

---

56 Trinidad and Tobago. Office of the Prime Minister. Tobago hurricane of 1847. Port-of-Spain: Office of the Prime Minister, 1966.
57 Brereton, Bridget. 'Post-emancipation protest in the Caribbean: the 'Belmanna Riots' in Tobago, 1876'. *Caribbean Quarterly*, p.112–113 (Vol. 30, No. 3/4 September-December 1984).
58 See Chapter 1: The British Leeward Islands.
59 One source identifies the Robley family, influential members of the Tobago planter class, as being of Cornish heritage (Phillips, David. *La Magdalena: the story of Tobago, 1498–1898*. New York: iUniverse, 2004, p.115), but other references place them as having originated in Cumberland (Robley genealogy. Accessed 23 May 2016, http://www.robley.org.uk/ and Legacies of British slave ownership. Accessed throughout 2015, https://www.ucl.ac.uk/lbs/). The latter references appear to be correct, so unfortunately the Robleys cannot be included in these pages.

Like Tobago, Trinidad was one of the later islands in the Caribbean to develop a thriving sugar industry. By 1797, when Trinidad was taken by Britain, the island was established as a sugar economy, and development increased after it became a British Crown Colony in 1802. Much of Trinidad's sugar and rum was transported to the Mother Country on the West Indiamen – strong, ocean-going merchant ships, designed to weather the Atlantic storms, which sailed between Britain and the Caribbean. One Cornishman who sailed on the West Indiamen was James Silk Buckingham (1786–1855). He was born at Flushing, near Falmouth, where he grew up surrounded by the comings and goings of the packet ships, and the ships of the Royal Navy that anchored at Carrick Roads, off Flushing.

Buckingham initially went to the Caribbean as first officer aboard the *Titus*, bound for Trinidad.[60] He sailed from the West India Docks in London, which had been built on the Isle of Dogs in response to the demands of West Indian planters, agents and ship owners who were alarmed at the level of theft and delay that occurred when ships used London's riverside wharves. To improve security, the West India Docks were enclosed by a high wall, night watchmen guarded each of the six warehouses against vandalism and theft, and a military guard was appointed to secure the site. By a clause in the Act of Parliament that enabled their construction, West Indiamen sailing to and from the Port of London were bound to use these docks.[61]

When the *Titus*, with Buckingham aboard, was about a week out of London she was chased by a fast French privateer, an encounter that Buckingham describes, giving an insight both into the experience of being captured by a privateer and into the type of cargo the West Indiamen carried on their outward voyage to the Caribbean. 'She was soon alongside of us' he writes:

---

60 Buckingham, James Silk. *Autobiography of James Silk Buckingham; including his voyages, travels, adventures, speculations, successes and failures …* Vol.1. London: Longman, Brown, Green and Longmans, 1855, p.215.
61 *West India Docks (1803–1980)*. Accessed 30 May 2016, http://www.portcities.org.uk/london/server/show/ConFactFile.83/West-India-Docks.html

The West India Docks in 1837.
Engraved by FW Topham after a picture by R Garland.

and, with the French flag at her peak, declared herself to be La Josephine, of Nantes, showing, at the same time, a formidable battery of long brass twelve-pounders run out for action, with matches lighted, and all prepared for a heavy broadside. A boat soon came on board, and, as we had but two guns, chiefly of use for signals rather than defence, and a crew of twenty men to oppose to her 200, resistance would have been folly; so we surrendered to her as a prize. An examination of our papers showed the nature of our cargo, – chiefly English manufactures of the coarser kind, with tools and implements for estates worked by the negroes, – things of so little value for sale in France as to make it hardly worth while for the captors to take us into port ... They contented themselves, therefore, with taking chiefly articles from the cabin, including the captain's and my own private adventure, consisting of article adapted for the higher classes of West Indian society ... They also took our sextants, quadrants and compasses, with most of our charts, threw the only two guns we had over-board, and then left us to our fate. We were sadly mortified at

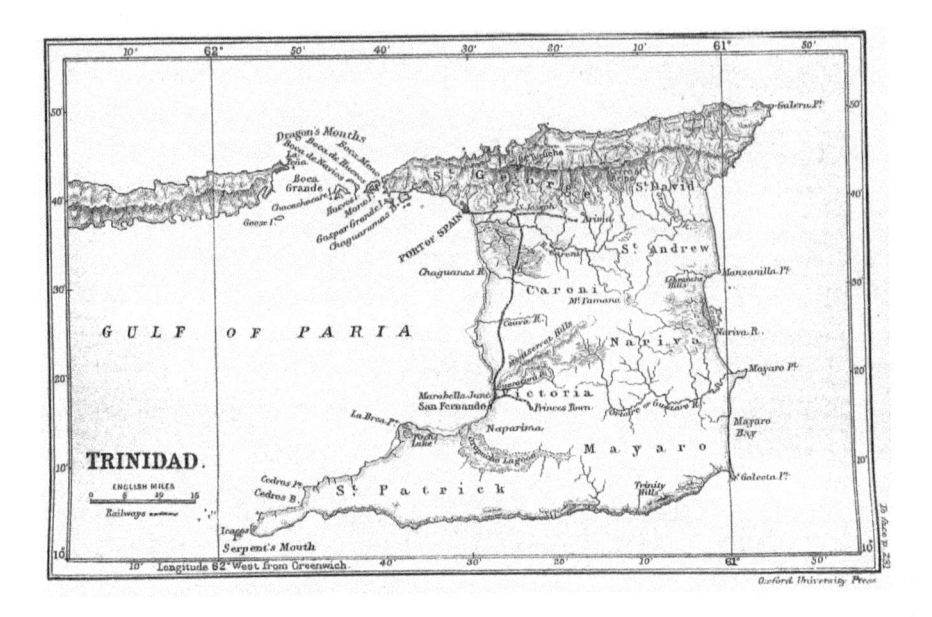

An 1888 map of Trinidad.
Image extracted from page 260 of volume 2 of *A Historical Geography of the British Colonies*, by Charles P. Lucas. Original held and digitised by the British Library.

being thus stripped of so much that was essential for our safety, though glad to escape imprisonment in France at any price.[62]

Without so much as a compass, the *Titus* reached Trinidad four weeks later: 'steering in through the intricate passage of the Dragon's Mouth'[63] and anchoring off Port-of-Spain.

While Buckingham was charmed with the scenery of Trinidad and the hospitality of its inhabitants, he was shocked by:

the constant sight of naked negroes working in gangs, many with chains on their legs, leaving sores by their friction, and others with iron collars with great hooks projecting outwards from them on all sides, to prevent the wearers from escaping through the forests or jungles. In

---

62 Buckingham, James Silk. *Autobiography of James Silk Buckingham; including his voyages, travels, adventures, speculations, successes and failures ...* Vol.1. London: Longman, Brown, Green, and Longmans, 1855, pp.216–218.
63 Ibid., p.218.

my youthful enthusiasm for liberty, and with more zeal than prudence perhaps, I took frequent occasion to express my abhorrence ... fully convinced that if the same motives of good wages and kind treatment were applied to the negroes as to other men, they would work far better when they were to be benefitted in proportion to their labour, than if they saw all the profits of their labour taken from them by their masters. [Mr Vance, Buckingham's host in Trinidad] doubted this, as apparently did everyone else at that period in his position. But my convictions were as strong on this subject as at any subsequent period of my life; and I could not refrain from pressing this conviction on others.[64]

Leaving Trinidad on board the *Titus*, Buckingham sailed north to St Thomas, via Tobago, to meet the convoy for the homeward-bound Windward Islands Fleet. He observed that keeping ships with different capabilities together in a fleet during the long journey back to England was: 'tedious and intricate, with squally weather, which required a constant look-out, and frequent tacking, reefing, and shortening and making sail'.

Buckingham's first voyage to the Caribbean as a captain was in 1807[65] aboard the *Surrey*. He was twenty-one years old. He again sailed as part of a convoy, but after some initial bad weather, when he felt the weight of his responsibility as he manoeuvred his ship to safety, this journey proved to be more agreeable than his return from Trinidad:

We sailed with the convoy ... and rolled away down the channel with at least 300 sail of vessels ... and it was an animating and agreeable spectacle to witness so much order, so many fine vessels, such frequent interchange of signals, such vigilance in the sloops of war, scouring the horizon on all sides on the look-out for French privateers ... The Mediterranean fleet left us soon after clearing the channel, steering southward, and the South American fleet a few days afterwards,

---

64   Ibid., pp.221–222.
65   *James Silk Buckingham*. Accessed 30 May 2016, http://spenserians.cath.vt.edu/BiographyRecord.php?action=GET&bioid=4462

James Silk Buckingham.
Attributed to Clara S. Lane, about 1850.

steering south west, while, as the remnant bound for the West Indies, we continued on our way.[66]

Buckingham soon left the sea for a life of travel, writing of his adventures in the Middle East, and later settling in India. Here, true to his word, he continued to press his convictions on others. In 1818, he began to publish the *Calcutta Journal*, in which he was openly critical of the business dealings of the East India Company. By 1823, the company had managed to quieten his voice: the *Calcutta Journal* was closed down and the governor-general expelled him from India. He continued to fight for a more liberal press, and in 1834 his case was brought before a Special Committee of the British House of Commons. He won his case and was awarded a pension of £500 in compensation: that the pension was to be paid by the East India Company must have given Buckingham no little satisfaction.

---

66   Buckingham, James Silk. *Autobiography of James Silk Buckingham; including his voyages, travels, adventures, speculations, successes and failures …* Vol.1. London: Longman, Brown, Green and Longmans, 1855, pp.273-274.

Among a later generation of merchant ship captains who traded with Trinidad was Cornishman Henry Blewett (1836–1891). He captained the *Naparima*, owned by Scruttons, a firm of ship owners and insurance brokers founded by the Scrutton family in 1802. In 1864, he sailed the *Naparima* for Port-of-Spain carrying both cargo and passengers. When the passengers had disembarked and the cargo had been unloaded, sugar and cocoa were taken aboard and the ship sailed south across the Gulf of Paria to anchor off the village of La Brea. She had come to collect a sample of asphalt from the nearby pitch lake.[67]

The idea of shipping asphalt from Trinidad to Britain had come about because of the business relationship between Scruttons and Joseph Previte, a ship insurance broker who had set up his business next door to the Scruttons office in Cornhill, in the centre of the City, London's financial district. Admiral Lord Cochrane, who served as Commander-in-Chief of the North America and West Indies Station from 1848 to 1851,[68] had brought back a small sample from the pitch lake to England. He thought it had possibilities for commercial use in road construction, and convinced Previte of the feasibility of the project. Previte then contracted Scruttons to bring some of the asphalt to London for testing, and as the *Naparima* was already sailing regularly between London and Trinidad she was chosen for the job. Concerned about the possibility of the pitch contaminating his cargo of sugar and cocoa, Blewett had the asphalt sample packed in six of the large wooden casks known as puncheons, and loaded into his hold, delivering them safely to Previte. Tests proved how useful the asphalt could be, and Previte subsequently leased part of the lake with the right to extract. The trade developed quickly, and by 1867 Scruttons had purchased an additional vessel for shipping the asphalt.[69]

---

67 The name *Naparima* comes from an Amerindian word *anaparima*, meaning 'single hill', the historical name for the hill in the nearby town of San Fernando, founded as *San Fernando de Naparima* by Spanish Governor Don José Maria Chacón in 1784. *Brea* is Spanish for 'pitch' or 'asphalt'.
68 The Royal Navy's North American Station was separate from the Jamaica Station until 1830, when the two combined to form the North America and West Indies Station.
69 Parsons, Jack and Nora Parsons. *Cornish fisherboy to Master Mariner: the life of Henry Blewett 1836–1891. Part two 1861–1866: Mate and Master Mariner*. Bournemouth: Bournemouth Local Studies Publications, 1993, pp.29–31.

Blewett had been born in Mousehole, a fishing village near to Penzance, which lies on the shore of Mount's Bay on the south-west coast of Cornwall. He and his parents and siblings were committed Wesleyan Methodists and regularly attended their local chapel, a practice that Henry Blewett would continue wherever his trading voyages took him. His early working days were spent with the local fishing fleet, but after a few years he decided he wanted to see more of the world and joined the Merchant Navy. His first voyage to the Caribbean was as an ordinary seaman aboard the *Melbourne* where, as was often the case during the mid-19th century when the local mining industry was beginning to fail, he was one Cornishman among many: although the crew had signed on in London, most of the men on board, including the captain, were Cornish.[70]

The *Melbourne* left for British Honduras (now Belize) in October 1854, probably carrying implements and equipment needed by the Honduran settlers. She returned with a cargo that mostly comprised equatorial hardwoods, including mahogany, logwood and rosewood: the colony's most important exports. Blewett then went to India, the Mediterranean and Canada, before returning to Cornwall to sail on one of the coastal schooners which took Cornish copper ore to the smelters of Swansea, and returned to Cornwall with Welsh coal to power the copper mines, brickworks and limestone quarries that lined the banks of the Tamar river.

After a brief return to the local fishing fleet, he joined the Scrutton-owned *Amber Nymph* as bosun and second mate. Scruttons had entered into partnerships with prominent Caribbean sugar producers and merchants, creating a niche for itself in British Guiana, on the north-east coast of South America, and on several of the islands; this was a business move that helped to ensure a market for its goods in the Caribbean and a ready cargo of sugar products available for the return voyage.[71] The ships on which Blewett sailed were often captained by a Cornishman, and the *Amber Nymph* was no exception: her captain was John Madron from Mousehole.[72] In October 1860, the ship set sail for New Amsterdam

---

70 Ibid., p.21.
71 Ibid., pp.53–56.
72 Ibid., pp.52–53.

in British Guiana.[73] By 1860, the sugar exported annually from British Guiana had reached about 54,000 tons, at least twice as much as the amount exported from either Barbados or Jamaica. After slavery came to an end, indentured labourers from the British colonies of India and Hong Kong were introduced to work the sugar plantations on several of the British possessions, including British Guiana and Trinidad and, on his arrival in New Amsterdam, Blewett would have noticed the number of people of Asian descent working there, some of whom had left the plantations to establish themselves as shopkeepers and tradespeople.[74]

Blewett's next voyage aboard the *Amber Nymph* was to the island of Dominica, where port facilities at Roseau, the capital, were rudimentary and ships had to anchor offshore. Each item of cargo then had to be hoisted into small canoes and taken ashore, and return cargo had to be hoisted individually from the canoes and loaded into the hold: unsurprisingly, a typical turnaround time was one month. Blewett's return journey to London went smoothly, and once unloading was complete he went home to his family. The Cornishmen working for Scruttons formed a small community on Bromehead Street in Stepney, from where they had easy access to the West India and London Docks.

By age twenty-four Blewett was a certified mate, and in December 1861 he sailed for the island of St Vincent aboard the *Spheroid*. Like Roseau in Dominica, Kingstown, the capital of St Vincent, had no wharf and all vessels had to anchor offshore. While the long business of unloading her cargo via small boats and canoes was under way, the goods she brought were eagerly awaited by the estate owners and shopkeepers ashore. One of the local newspapers advertised that: 'A. Dalrymple and Co. Daily expect on the SPHEROID: one case of diaries; Two trunks of Wellington Boots; 4,000 yards Cambric Prints; Gents' Belts; Venetian Ladders.'[75] Another newspaper advertised that Mr Plumridge would have available from the same vessel:

---

73 Ibid., pp.58–59.
74 Ibid., p.60.
75 Parsons, Jack and Nora Parsons. *Cornish fisherboy to Master Mariner: the life of Henry Blewett 1836–1891. Part two 1861–1866: Mate and Master Mariner*. Bournemouth: Bournemouth Local Studies Publications, 1993, p.11.

Hunting and dogs whips, Riding Whips, Reins, Collars, Spades, Shovels, Farm Implements, Iron Hoops, Nails etc. Ladies and Girls' miscellaneous hats, trimmed and untrimmed [and, a week later] Ham, Cheese, Raisins, Sago, Groceries, Hardware, Stationery, Perfumery.[76]

In 1864, Blewett passed his examination that certified him as a master mariner, and in 1866, after several temporary commands that took him to Barbados and Trinidad, he was given command of the *Roseau*. St Vincent became his regular port of call, and between 1866 and 1881 he made thirty-five voyages to and from St Vincent: it would become his second home.

On 29 October 1866, during one of his early layovers in St Vincent, Blewett witnessed a fire that destroyed a good part of Kingstown. He and his crew helped to put out the blaze, but the damage was significant, and as the ship's papers were destroyed in the fire his departure was delayed until replacements were prepared by the shipping master. Eventually, after bad weather had further delayed her departure, the *Roseau* was able to leave with a cargo of sugar, rum, molasses, arrowroot, cocoa and cotton.[77] Arrowroot would later become an important export for the island.

By the 1870s, Cornish captains began to hire Caribbean crew, and Vincentians began to make an appearance on Blewett's crew lists. They often signed on for a single voyage to Britain on the understanding that they would be hired for the return voyage to St Vincent, but occasionally they stayed on for more than one voyage. Some had no previous experience of working at sea, so were signed on as ordinary seamen, but others were taken on as able seamen or cooks, and one sailed as the *Roseau's* bosun.

On several occasions Blewett's wife and family sailed with him to St Vincent, where they regularly attended the Methodist chapel in Kingstown. Indeed, the family was so much a part of local society that Blewett paid an annual rent for a pew in the chapel.[78]

During the 1870s, Scruttons' sailing ships began to struggle to operate at a profit. As competition increased from other sugar islands and from

---

76 Ibid., p.12.
77 Ibid., p.12.
78 Ibid., p.70.

the subsidised sugar beet being grown in Europe, the sugar trade on St Vincent began to decline, and as the prosperity of the island began to decline, shopkeepers and estates could less easily afford to import goods. The firm made efforts to diversify its cargo, looking for new opportunities from which it might make a profit: in 1871 for example, the *Roseau's* return cargo included tamarind, preserves, nuts and yams. The London market for sugar was poor, so Scruttons looked for alternative buyers in new markets[79] and on their return journey, its ships would sometimes dock in Greenock in Scotland, or Queenstown in Ireland. By the end of the decade the company even experimented with a different route for the *Roseau*: Blewett tried sailing from Cardiff, in south Wales, with a cargo of coal bound for the steamship coal bunkers of Cape Town, South Africa, before sailing back across the Atlantic to St Vincent. But as little cargo was available for loading at Cape Town, the voyage operated at a loss and the experiment was not repeated.

Scruttons were by this time convinced that steamships would replace sailing ships, so the company set up a syndicate to share the cost of the investment needed to introduce a steamship service, and when its new steamships were ready it introduced routes from both London and Glasgow to British Guiana and Trinidad. Over the next few years, the sailing ships were sold off and there was a reduction in the number of captains' positions available. So the captains were faced with the possibility of unemployment, and some made the change to steamships, Blewett among them. After he left the *Roseau* in 1881, he joined the steamship *Nith*, but after she sank he returned to his local fishing fleet in Cornwall, where he owned and ran his own fishing lugger. But then, missing his old life, he returned to the Merchant Navy aboard the *Dunphaile Castle*, when he was again shipwrecked. Finally, serving on the steamship *Umtata* in 1891, he was wrecked yet again, this time off Madras, in India. He died in a hospital in Madras, far from his beloved St Vincent.

---

79   Ibid., pp.51–52.

6

Gold and Diamonds: The Mines of British Guiana and Aruba[1]

James Jewell and Edwin Nicholls were convinced they would make their fortune in the goldfields of British Guiana. Both born in Penzance, where in his youth Jewell had been apprenticed to a local cabinet-maker and Nicholls had worked as a carpenter, they had been away from Cornwall for some years and had recently been 'engaged in the salt trade in Trinidad'.[2] Neither Jewell nor Nicholls appear to have had any previous mining experience, but in 1887 they signed a six-month contract to work for a mining company prospecting in Essequibo.[3]

Gold mining was a fairly recent development, as substantial gold deposits had only been discovered during the 1860s. British investors soon began to show an interest, establishing the British Guiana Gold Company which in 1863 discovered gold-bearing quartz on the Cuyuni river. The Cuyuni rises in neighbouring Venezuela, forming part of that country's international boundary as it flows into the north-east of British Guiana – now Guyana. The company's operations began to produce profitable results, but were halted because of an ongoing boundary dispute with Venezuela.[4]

1　See Appendix 6 for a background history of British Guiana and Aruba.
2　'Two Penzance men drowned' *The Cornishman*, p.4 (14 July 1887). Although the newspaper article notes that the men were working for a company prospecting in Demerara, the Cuyuni river is actually in Essequibo. (The colony as a whole was sometimes referred to as Demerara, which probably accounts for the wording of the piece.)
3　Ibid.
4　Thomas, Clive. *Too big to fail: a scoping study of the small and medium scale gold and diamond mining industry in Guyana*. df. Ed. Turkeyen: University of Guyana, 2009, p.2. Accessed 31 July 2016, http://guyanaminers.com/document/too-big-fail-scoping-study-small-and-medium-scale-gold-and-diamond-mining-industry-guyana

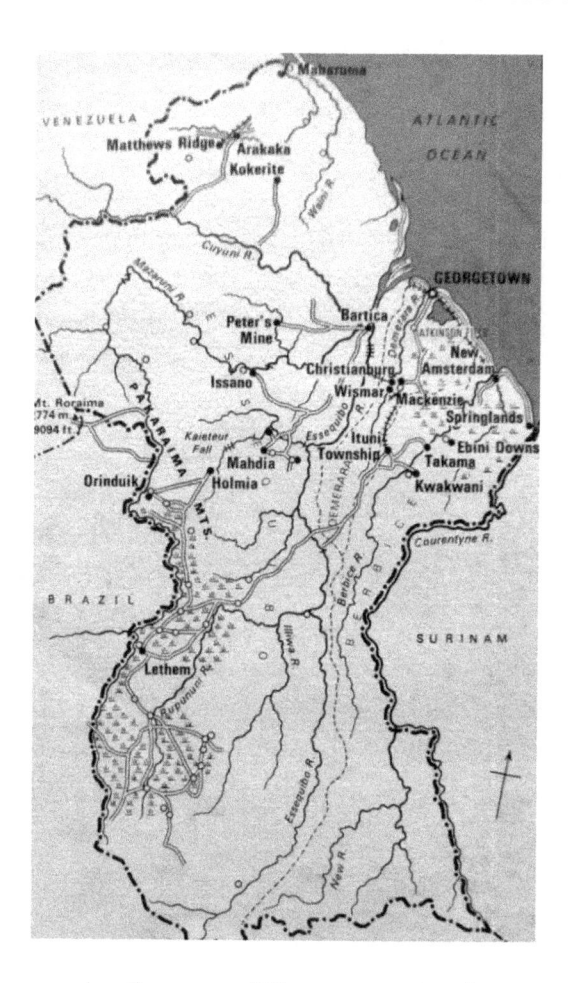

A 1960s map of Guyana, previously
British Guiana, showing the main rivers.
From the author's collection.

Many of the first miners who flocked to the interior of British Guiana were were recently freed from enslavement and saw gold mining as a quick means of improving their standard of living, a better option than either working the land as small farmers and employees of the sugar plantations, or moving to town to become hucksters and shopkeepers.[5] They went into the interior of the colony to try their luck, setting up camps wherever they found gold, and establishing more permanent bases where they found

---

5   Josiah, Barbara P. *Migration, mining, and the African diaspora: Guyana in the nineteenth and twentieth centuries.* New York: Palgrave Macmillan, 2011, p.1.

particularly rich gold deposits. Mahdia was such a settlement, established in 1884 by men from Berbice and East Coast Demerara who were mining gold from nearby Omai and Eagle Mountain.[6]

The local miners became known as 'pork-knockers': the 'pork' was generally considered to have originated from their reliance on salt or pickled pork as a main item of their diet, and the 'knockers' was a local word meaning 'hungry eaters'.[7] Pork-knockers became important contributors both to the local mining economy and to the folklore of the country, their exploits told in song and story over the years.

As news spread of the gold to be found, local miners were joined by men from islands in the Caribbean and from further afield, beginning the international gold rush of which James Jewell and Edwin Nicholls belatedly became a part. As *The Cornishman* newspaper reported in June 1879:

> *Large numbers of Cornish miners, of miners from California and British Columbia, and labourers from the different West India Islands have been attracted to these fields ... One man, it is stated, in four weeks gathered upwards of 40 lbs weight of pure gold with very little labour, and similar instances of the abundance of the metal are numerous.*[8]

When Jewell and Nicholls arrived in Georgetown, the capital of the colony, they began their trek to reach the gold fields, first taking a small steamer heading westwards along the coast from Georgetown, then taking a boat up the Essequibo river to the mining town of Bartica.[9] In the early days of the British colony, Bartica had been the site of an Anglican mission, but as the gold rush took hold the government needed a centre from which it could regulate the growing industry. The town was established in 1887, the year Jewell and Nicholls arrived. Here the miners registered their claims, government officers inspected and licensed the boats that carried

---

6 Sutherland, Gaulbert. 'Mahdia.' *Stabroek News*. (1 September 2013). Accessed 11 August 2016, http://www.stabroeknews.com/2013/features/sunday/beyond-gt/09/01/mahdia/
7 Allsopp, Richard. *Dictionary of Caribbean English usage*. Kingston: University of the West Indies Press, 2003, p.450.
8 'Gold in South America.' *The Cornishman*, p.6 (3 July 1879).
9 White, Walter Grainge. *Notes and comments on my trip to the diamond fields of British Guiana*. Georgetown: White, 1902, p.36.

the miners to the gold fields, and magistrates adjudicated on mining disputes. In the days of the Anglican mission, a church had been built in Bartica, and there the miners could attend to their spiritual needs – and should they not survive their mining adventure they could find a place of burial. The town had a hotel, where a miner with financial resources would be well looked after, and there were stores where he could find all the clothing, mining equipment and food supplies he might need. There was also a hospital to take care of the sick, whether they were suffering from malaria, yellow fever or a mining accident, and there was a jail where the disorderly could be locked up. There were also plenty of bars and brothels to provide entertainment.[10]

For Jewell, Nicholls and the other prospectors, the dangerous part of the journey to the gold fields began after leaving Bartica. Only small boats powered by oarsmen and directed by an experienced captain could make the journey up-river. The explorer Walter Grainge White, writing in 1902, wrote of the challenges:

[Soon after leaving Bartica] in the process of hauling [the boat up over a cataract], one of the men got washed off the warp[11] and was carried down by the stream. Fortunately, he managed to grab a bush-rope, as he was being swirled along, and he was thus enabled to swing himself on to the island, close to which we were hauling. After getting over this fall, the work became much harder, and the men had to bend with a will to their blades. The river now becomes bescattered with islands, islets, boulders and rocks, of many shapes and sizes. Fall after fall and rapid after rapid is encountered, and the scene presented is one of indescribably, wild confusion. With a roar and a bound the torrents burst between and over the obstructions, bubbling and spitting, like water in a cauldron under which a huge fire is blazing.[12]

---

10 Allicock, Dmitri. 'Bartica: the gateway to Guyana's interior.' *Explore Guyana*, pp.56, 59 (2015).
11 The rope attached to the boat at one end and held at the other end by the boat crew on shore. The crew haul on the warp to pull the boat along, or up over a rapids or cataract.
12 White, Walter Grainge. *Notes and comments on my trip to the diamond fields of British Guiana*. Georgetown: White, 1902, p.14.

Hauling up a cataract.
Drawing by Charles Barrington Brown from: Brown, Charles Barrington, *Canoe and camp life in British Guiana*. London: Edward Stanford, 1876, p.33.

Depending on conditions, the journey up-river could take as long as fourteen days. White went on to complete his journey, but Jewell and Nicolls were not so lucky. Having reached the Cuyuni river, where rich finds were made between 1886 and 1888,[13] they were shooting some falls when:

> the boat was upset, and Jewell, Nicholls, and their clerk, a creole named Thierens, were drowned. Four of the Indian boat hands managed to get ashore, and brought back news of the disaster.[14]

Jewell was thirty-five years of age, Nicholls forty-four.

The dangers of the journey up-river to the gold fields found expression in the local folk song 'Itaname', which speaks to the fear of the miners as they had to navigate up yet another cataract:

---

13 Harrison, J.B. *The geology of the goldfields of British Guiana*. London: Dulau and Co., 1908, p.5.
14 'Penzance men drowned in America.' *The Cornish Telegraph*, p.5 (14 July 1887).

> Oh captain, captain, put me ashore!
> I don't want to go any more.
> Itaname too high fuh me!
> Itaname gun friken me![15]

As overseas investors showed an increased interest in the gold fields of British Guiana, they began to send mining experts on exploratory visits to the interior of the colony. In 1888, a group of investors calling themselves The London Syndicate wanted to survey their mining concessions at Karacoon (sometimes spelt Caracoon), upstream from Bartica. An important member of the syndicate was Charles Barrington Brown, who in 1870 was one of two geologists appointed by the British government to survey the colony. He is probably best remembered as the first European to see Kaieteur Falls, the spectacular fall on the Potaro river. Impressed by the results of his survey, he decided to invest in the potential of the colony's gold resources.[16] The man selected to complete the Karacoon survey was Mine Captain Thomas Kitchen, who was born in about 1854 in Tresowes (or Tresowas), Germoe, near the town of Helston in West Cornwall.[17] Like many of his fellow Cornishmen, Captain Kitchen started his working life as a miner in his home county, and:

> *by his enterprise and ability, he had early in life raised himself from a miner's life to that of a [mine] agent and [mine] inspector … While quite a young man he went to the United States and succeeded so well that he soon sent home for a brother … Captain Kitchen had also been entrusted with very responsible work in Venezuela and India.*[18]

---

15 *Some folk songs of Guyana: Itaname*. Accessed 7 August 2016, http://silvertorch.com/folksongs-of-guyana.html#Itaname
16 *Charles Barrington Brown, Assoc., R.S.M., F.G.S.* Accessed 15 August 2016, http://journals.cambridge.orgactiondisplayFulltext?type=1&fid=5114932&jid=GEO&volumeId=4&issueId=05&aid=5114928
17 'Death of Captain Kitchen, of Germoe.' *The Cornishman*, pp.4–5. (2 August 1888).
18 Ibid.

Thomas Kitchen's diary gives us an insight into the daily life of a gold miner in the interior of British Guiana.[19] On 6 February 1888, he took the overnight train to London and went to meet the members of the syndicate, who were optimistic that the enterprise would be a great success. He then travelled to Southampton, where he boarded the steamship *Para*, bound for Barbados. Disembarking at Bridgetown, he stayed at the Marine Hotel, a new and well-appointed 200-room hotel in Hastings, a village on the south-west coast of the island. He then boarded another steamer, bound for Georgetown, where he was met by the syndicate's local agent, Mr Conrad. After their business meeting, Conrad took him to a comfortable hotel and introduced him to the Georgetown Club, where the elite of colonial society met to relax and discuss the events of the day. After a few days' rest Kitchen travelled from Georgetown to Bartica, and then went a short distance up the Essequibo to the syndicate's Karacoon concession. Here he examined the outcrops of ore to assess their potential for gold production, recording in his diary that they were 'worth a trial.'[20]

Returning to Georgetown, he supervised the unloading of the mining machinery he had bought on behalf of the syndicate before leaving home. He bought supplies from a chandlery and contracted a carpenter to build a manager's house for himself and a bunkhouse for the miners at Karacoon. Knowing that Kitchen was offering employment, a crowd of men and boys gathered hopefully in front of him, and from these he chose twelve to work the concession. At the Georgetown dock the new employees packed the equipment, the supplies and their personal possessions ready for shipment, and settled down to wait overnight for the arrival of the morning steamer which would take them as far as Bartica. As many other men were eager to try their luck in the gold fields and were only too ready to relieve Kitchen's men of their equipment and supplies, the twelve took it in turns to act as watchman to ensure that they were not robbed. When the steamer arrived, they loaded everything on board and made their way along the coast and up the Essequibo to Bartica. Here everything was

---

19 *Thomas Kitchen: a Cornish mining adventure in British Guiana.* Accessed 31 July 2016, http://www.cornishreunited.com/thomas-kitchen-a-cornish-mining-venture-in-british-guiana/
20 Ibid.

unloaded, and while Kitchen spent the night in a hotel the men slung their hammocks and slept under the trees.

Next morning, they went up-river to Karacoon, where the men began to cut a track to the outcrop of ore which they hoped would contain gold. They prepared the ground for their accommodation, which was quickly constructed by the carpenter and workmen he had contracted in Georgetown, who arrived with a pontoon stacked with lumber. Meanwhile, the concession was mapped and a quartz-crushing mill set up to pulverise the ore. Some coloured quartz, promising the presence of gold, was found in the outcrop, so four men were sent back to Bartica to buy blasting powder to blast the ore out of the outcrop. But unfortunately, little gold was found in the ore.

Kitchen decided to halt the search for gold-bearing ore, instead sending the men to a nearby creek to see if they could find any alluvial gold. But they found only small quantities, and Kitchen wrote in his diary: 'I am first rate, but should feel more comfortable if we could find a little more gold.'[21] The men, however, were disappointed at their lack of success and started to become disillusioned when the delivery of provisions, which were supposed to arrive from Bartica every week, became irregular and the camp diet became monotonous. Tensions rose when the supply of sugar cane stalks ran out: when they were stripped of their outer skin and cut into short lengths, the men could enjoy chewing on them for the sweet juice contained in the fibres. Then some of the men became sick with fever, and as success continued to elude them they began to lose interest in their work. Drunkenness became a problem and accidents began to happen: even the camp cook was hurt, when he managed to chop his foot with a meat cleaver.[22]

When letters arrived from the Syndicate in London asking for progress reports, Kitchen had little good news for them. He returned to Georgetown to talk with Conrad about how best to proceed and to take a brief rest from the responsibilities and challenges of life in the bush. Kitchen felt unwell, but he returned to Karacoon, where provisions

---

21   Ibid.
22   Ibid.

continued to run short. To add to his problems, the rain became almost continuous. Kitchen was so ill that it was difficult for him to leave his bed to supervise the mining operations, and Conrad sent an overseer up-river to assist. But rather than helping the mine to run more smoothly, the overseer caused dissension among the men, and Kitchen sent him back to Georgetown.

The mine's fortunes did not improve, so Kitchen reluctantly suspended operations and returned to Georgetown with his men. His doctor suggested that he should go to Barbados, where the cool sea breezes might help him recover, and Kitchen agreed to go. He was suffering from headaches, fever, coughing, shortness of breath and stomach problems: all probably symptoms of typhoid fever. When he arrived in Barbados he returned to the Marine Hotel where he had been a guest as he waited for the steamer which would take him to Georgetown. So he was relatively comfortable – but there was no sign of recovery, and a doctor advised him to move to the house of an elderly lady who was willing to take care of him. He accepted the offer and stayed in Barbados for a month, but then insisted on returning to Georgetown. There, however, as his health continued to decline, his doctor advised him to return to England. He left on the next available mail steamer but 'unhappily, the unfortunate gentleman only lived some six or seven hours after the sailing of the steamer. He was buried at sea [on 23 June, 1888][23] with the usual mournful ceremonies.'[24]

The Karacoon concession was not the only enterprise to fail. Large areas of quartz were located on both the Demerara and Barima rivers, and several companies set up mines to work the outcrops, like Kitchen's investors spending large sums to purchase, transport and install mills to crush the ore. The mills were difficult to maintain in the heat and damp, and were put into operation before the mine was producing sufficient gold-bearing quartz to ensure the mills were used to their full – and economically profitable – capacity. None of the early attempts to mine

---

23 Ibid.
24 'Death of Captain Kitchen, of Germoe.' *The Cornishman*, pp.4–5. (2 August 1888).

quartz outcrops succeeded,[25] but alluvial gold continued to be mined successfully, and there were plenty of men willing to replace those who, like Kitchen, met an early death from tropical disease.

As interest in developing a profitable alluvial or placer mining operation grew, the colonial government considered various options to reduce the time it took to reach the mining areas and to lessen the dangers of the journey. One option was to build a railway which was to run from Bartica up the left bank of the Essequibo, avoiding the rapids, cataracts and falls, and delivering goods and passengers to the smoother waters of the Potaro river. A branch line was also planned, which was to run up the right bank of the Mazaruni river to the Puruni gold fields, connecting with another branch line from the Yuruari valley, which lies on a branch of the Cuyuni river. This ambitious project would have opened up the whole area for mining development, but because of an ongoing boundary dispute with Venezuela the lines were never built.[26] A railway was instead constructed from Wismar on the west bank of the Demerara river, to Rockstone on the east bank of the Essequibo, again avoiding the dangerous river journey above Bartica. The Demerara is calm and navigable, with the width and depth to give access to ocean-going steamers from Georgetown to the terminus at Wismar, a distance of about 65 miles (105 km). With the opening of this line, miners and their equipment and supplies had much easier access to the gold fields, and the town of Bartica began to lose its importance.

As the number of mining operations grew, the colonial government realised the need to employ an inspector of mines to supervise the development of the industry. The man they chose was Josiah Rodda Hosken. He had been born sometime between 1865 and 1867 in Breage, a village about 2½ miles (4 km) from Tresowes, Germoe, the birthplace of Thomas Kitchen. Hosken started his working life as a miner but qualified as a mining engineer in 1887, when he went to work in the United States. On his return to Cornwall he became a

---

25 Harrison, J.B. *The geology of the goldfields of British Guiana.* London: Dulau and Co., 1908, p.6.
26 Allicock, Dmitri. 'Bartica: the gateway to Guyana's interior.' *Explore Guyana*, pp.56, 59 (2015).

The steamer terminus and railway station at Wismar, Demerara river.
Photograph by H.I. Perkins, from: Harrison, J.B. *The geology of the goldfields of British Guiana*. London: Dulau and Co., 1908, p.220.

Freemason, joining the Lodge of the True and Faithful in Helston in 1893.[27] Many Cornish miners, mine agents, mine captains and mining engineers were Freemasons,[28] as membership gave them 'unparalleled access to insider knowledge of the profitable potential of all mines, large and small, throughout the county'.[29]

As the local mining industry began to fail, the Freemasons' role in

---

27 'Originating in its modern form in Scotland at the beginning of the eighteenth century, Freemasonry ... made use of the tools and craft skills of the stone mason to act as an allegorical guide for the moral and spiritual improvement of its members. Organisationally it consisted of a series of mainly locally focused 'lodges', warranted by the Grand Lodges of Free and Accepted Masons of England, Scotland and Ireland ... Their ritual embraced the egalitarian philosophy of the Enlightenment, they were sworn to strict codes of moral conduct and were under an obligation to help other Masons when there was no conflict with their own interests. In all aspects, it was highly 'business friendly'.' Burt, Roger. *Freemasonry and business networking during the Victorian period*. Exeter: University of Exeter, 2005. Accessed 27 August 2016, http://people.exeter.ac.uk/RBurt/exeteronly/HEC2005/EcHRarticle.htm

28 Burt, Roger. *Freemasonry and business networking during the Victorian period*. Exeter: University of Exeter, 2005. Accessed 27 August 2016, http://people.exeter.ac.uk/RBurt/exeteronly/HEC2005/EcHRarticle.htm

29 Ibid.

providing news of employment opportunities expanded to include overseas mines. The number of men seeking membership increased and included 'gold miners' – men returning from foreign gold fields – whose:

> motivation for joining may have been enjoyment of the fraternal support, elevated status, social conviviality or any of the other advantages to membership while at home. However, it is equally likely that they had seen how Masonic membership had facilitated successful economic and social integration in frontier mining districts and sought to achieve that membership, using home town connections, before undertaking further journeys.[30]

Hosken was one of these men. He left for British Guiana from Southampton in June 1895 and probably, like Kitchen, disembarked in Barbados before boarding another steamer bound for Georgetown. Here he took up his duties as inspector of mines, but he did not spend long in the colony. By 13 April 1897 he was back in Redruth, participating in a meeting of the Mining Association and Institute of Cornwall, which was discussing the depression in the Cornish mining industry and proposing remedies for the situation. He is listed in a report of the meeting as 'Josiah Hosken (late Inspector of Mines, British Guiana).'[31] In the same year, perhaps in connection with further employment, he briefly returned to New York, but sailed back to England in February 1898, landing at the port of Liverpool before travelling north to Glasgow, in Scotland. He died there two months later, apparently having contracted an incurable disease during his time in British Guiana.[32]

Investor interest in the British Guiana gold fields continued to grow. In late 1896, it was reported that there were: 'several experts now in the colony, representing syndicates in England, in Germany, and in the States, whose mission is to examine gold mines … and say whether prospects are good enough.'[33]

---

30   Ibid.
31   'Cornish mining: the depression and remedies.' *The Cornishman*, p.3 (15 April 1897).
32   Email from David Gaunt, dated 28 July 2016.
33   'British Guiana: the affairs of the colony.' *Glasgow Herald*, p.8 (15 October 1896).

One of these experts was Mine Captain Frederick Gribble, who, as *The Cornishman* newspaper tersely reported in 1897 'was to take charge of 'a bal in British Guiana'.[34] He had been born in about 1854 or 1855 in Creegbrawse, a hamlet which lies between the villages of Chacewater and Todpool, about 3 miles (5 km) east of the town of Redruth in western Cornwall. Creegbrawse is near one of the most famous mines in the area: Wheal[35] Busy, once known as the Chacewater Mine and owned by the Boscawen family.[36] The other great mine in the Chacewater area was Wheal Jane, which was 2 miles (3 km) south-east of Chacewater. Wheal Jane was chiefly a tin mine and is probably where Gribble and his family worked. Like many Cornish mines, in some years it made a profit and in others a loss. It closed and reopened several times in the later 19th century before it was finally abandoned in 1893.[37]

As Wheal Jane faced an uncertain future, Frederick Gribble and his four brothers left Cornwall for mining opportunities overseas, and their experiences are typical of Cornish families of the period. Albert went out to Cape Town, in South Africa, and died there in 1883. Cyrus became a mine captain at the Vulture Mine near Phoenix, Arizona, in the United States, and was killed by Mexican bandits while transporting gold to Phoenix in 1888. Tobias went to mine silver in southern Peru, and died at the Caylloma Mine in 1891. Elijah emigrated to Australia in 1859 and became the owner of several gold mines around the town of Wandiligong, in the north-east of the state of Victoria.[38] Frederick himself worked in several overseas locations before moving to British Guiana in February 1897, when the *West Briton and Cornwall Advertiser* reported:

Capt. Gribble has had an extensive foreign experience. At one time he was manager of the Callio [sic – El Callao] mine, Venezuela, and

---

34 'Captain Fred Gribble.' *The Cornishman*, p.7 (18 February 1897). The word *bal* is Cornish for 'mine.'
35 The word 'wheal' is often incorrectly said to mean 'mine', but is derived from the Cornish word for 'place of work.'
36 For more about the Boscawen family, see Chapter 3: In Defence of the Empire.
37 *Wheal Jane & West Wheal Jane Mine, Cornwall.* Accessed 17 August 2016, http://www.cornwallinfocus.co.uk/mining/whealjane.php
38 Email from Heather Wilkie, dated 30 June 2016.

he had also been connected with mining enterprises in both America and Australia.[39]

Like Thomas Kitchen and Josiah Rodda Hosken, Frederick Gribble began his voyage to British Guiana from the port of Southampton; he sailed on the *Para* in late January 1897. As Gribble travelled out to British Guiana, gold had been discovered in the Klondike region of the Yukon Territory in north-western Canada, and prospectors were flooding the area. Newspapers of the day reported that while both the Klondike and the British Guiana gold fields were becoming overcrowded and difficult to work, those choosing to prospect in British Guiana had the added disadvantage of coping with an unhealthy climate. The *Aberdeen Journal's* Jamaica correspondent reported from Kingston that:

> British Guiana, though it exported 7000 oz. of gold during the last two weeks of 1897, suffers … from some of the drawbacks which are associated with Klondyke, and others which are not. It is said to be even less healthy for white men than Central Africa.[40]

Frederick Gribble managed to survive the rigours of working in British Guiana, and unlike his brothers he returned home to Creegbrawse. Here he retired to live out the rest of his days with his wife, and here he died just before Christmas in 1918, aged 64.[41]

Many of the dangers faced by miners working in the interior of British Guiana were life-threatening, but there was a lighter side to day-to-day life in the gold fields. Towards the end of 1898, *The Cornishman* reported on the experience of an elderly Cornish miner who had travelled up-river to the gold fields in a steam launch. When night fell, he:

> slung a hammock between two trees on the river-bank. He usually fastened it low, and his weight probably brought it to within three

---

39 'Capt. Frederick Gribble.' *West Briton and Cornwall Advertiser*, p.6 (11 February 1897).
40 'Drawbacks of gold-seeking: no chance for diggers in Guiana.' *Aberdeen Journal*, p.4 (4 February 1898).
41 Email from Heather Wilkie, dated 30 June 2016.

An encampment.
Drawing by Charles Barrington Brown from: Brown, Charles Barrington. *Canoe and camp life in British Guiana*. London: Edward Stanford, 1876, p.205.

feet of the ground at the bottom of the curve. One morning, asked how he had slept, he complained that the frogs had made such a noise underneath his hammock that they had kept him awake. Some natives laughed and looked. There were marks of where a puma had lain. The purr of the puma was the assumed voice of the frogs. The Cornish miner and the puma had kept each other warm.[42]

While they panned for alluvial gold, miners sometimes found small diamonds in their prospecting pans. This attracted little notice until, in 1890, an expedition searching for gold in the upper reaches of the Mazaruni river found small diamonds in some numbers. Subsequently, other expeditions to the area searched specifically for diamonds. Although they did find diamonds in considerable numbers, their size and value were not sufficient to encourage investment until, in 1900, the British Guiana Diamond Syndicate began operations on a 2,000-acre concession along the Putareng creek, a tributary of the Mazaruni.[43] As the syndicate had

---
42 'Naturalists' notebook.' *The Cornishman*, p.2. (3 November 1898).
43 Cattelle, W.R. *The diamond*. New York: John Lane Company, 1911, p.206.

some success, the colonial government made neighbouring areas available for licensing, and when news circulated that the production of diamonds for the year 1900–1901 amounted to 4,981 stones, weighing 740.6 carats, prospectors flooded into the district.[44]

In the early days of diamond mining, the traditional way of working the claims proved to be the most successful. The method was similar to that used to extract alluvial gold. Once a likely source of diamonds was found, the gravel and clay were shovelled into buckets or wheelbarrows and transported to the nearest water source. Here the contents were washed and 'jigged'[45] in sieves until the gravel plus any diamonds were left at the bottom of the sieves. The sieves were then taken to a table and turned sharply upside down. The diamonds, if any, were left on top and could easily be picked out. When the contents of the sieves had been sorted the remaining gravel was taken to a drying table: a sheet of iron under which a fire was kept burning. When the gravel was dry it was taken to another table and searched for any remaining diamonds.[46]

This simple and inexpensive method of diamond mining was introduced to the colony by Cornishman Francis Oats.[47]

Oats had been born in 1848 in the village of Golant, which lies on the west bank of the River Fowey, about 3 miles (4.8 km) up-river from the small south coastal town of Fowey. When Francis was six years old, he and his family moved from Golant to the village of St Just in Penwith which lies about a mile from the coast at the western end of Cornwall. Here he went to the local Wesleyan school. When he had completed his studies, he began working at Balleswidden mine, one of the richest in the St Just district, later moving on to the neighbouring Botallack mine, where the workings, which produced copper, tin and arsenic, extended far inland and out under the sea. Oats continued his education by attending lectures at the Lafrowda Institute in St Just, where he was a gifted student, did

---

44 Harrison, J.B. *The geology of the goldfields of British Guiana*. London: Dulau and Co., 1908, p.7.
45 'Jigging' means slowly turning the sieves around and around while they are under water, pulsating – or jigging – them up and down at the same time.
46 White, Walter Grainge. *Notes and comments on my trip to the diamond fields of British Guiana*. Georgetown: White, 1902, pp.23–24.
47 Ibid., p.24.

well in his examinations, and was employed as a pupil-teacher. In 1865, when only seventeen, he was made curator of the institute. Two years later he was granted £10 by the Cornwall and Devon Miners Association so that he could attend the Paris Exhibition as a working miner. He also received a scholarship to the Royal School of Mines in London, but lack of funds for daily living expenses prevented him from accepting it. In 1871, at the young age of twenty-three, he became a mine captain, and in 1874, looking for fresh opportunities to further his career, he applied to the British Colonial Office for employment overseas. He was appointed as Provincial Engineer for Griqualand West in central South Africa, and was based in the town of Kimberley, the colony's capital. Oats pursued a successful career in Kimberley, and by 1890 he had become a director of the De Beers Consolidated Mining Company.[48]

Although well established as an influential member of the Kimberley community, he liked to periodically return to Cornwall and spend time with his local friends and colleagues while he kept up with developments in the world of mining by regularly reading the newspaper. He was somewhat alarmed when he read an article about the discovery of diamonds in British Guiana: De Beers' policy was to keep the diamond market stable by controlling supply, and if the market was flooded by diamonds from a new source over which De Beers had no control, the price would fall and the economic impact on De Beers would be disastrous. Oats informed the company of his concerns, and it was decided that he should travel to British Guiana to assess developments. In order to disguise the fact that he would be spying on the potential of British Guiana's diamond resources, he writes:

> *I think no Director of De Beers should go in an ostentatious way to the diamond fields, it would lend them an importance they do not deserve; to avoid that I should go somewhere else, to Boliviar [sic – Bolivia] to look at the tin mines there, say, and take British Guiana on route.*[49]

---

48   Ibid., p.42.
49   Ibid., p.43.

As he planned his trip, news of diamond discoveries in Brazil began to surface, and he was asked to add this country to his itinerary. Now aged fifty-three, he was no longer a young man, but in May 1901, accompanied by his eldest son Francis Freathey Oats, he began what would be an exhausting journey.

When they arrived in Georgetown he was eager to reach the diamond fields. Like many before him, he realised the challenges involved in reaching the interior, and notes:

> *We are in the middle of the rainy season, raining more or less every day. [When] the river is up, that is better for the boats, but the worse for us when we have to walk up stream because we shall have to wade as we cannot move out of the river bed – the forests are not like the South African veldt ... However we have come so far, and if there is any chance left to get up there we shall do so but it looks a much nastier undertaking than we expected.*[50]

The two men managed to reach the Mazaruni, and after many days of travel arrived at a concession belonging to Mr Conrad, perhaps the same Mr Conrad of The London Syndicate who had employed Thomas Kitchen. Here, as Oats reports to De Beers:

> *Mr Gilkes is in charge ... I spent eight days going over the concession and other claims and made tests in large numbers to justify the conclusion I came to. Mr. Gilkes discovered diamonds here in 1899 ... We then went two days by boat higher up the river Mazzaruni [sic – Mazaruni], to Mr. Bernard's gold workings, where some diamonds had been found ... He told me all he knew, admitted that in the 12 years of his working here, he had found 30 or 40 diamonds (at the same time one ton of gold). He denied that it was possible for his workers to have missed any diamonds and stated briefly he had no belief whatever that any payable diamond ground exists in the numerous creeks that he works. I believe all this. After this we went up*

---

50   Ibid., p.43.

the Paruni [sic – Puruni] tributary where alluvial washings for gold have been carried on for years past and where diamonds were alleged to be found. On examination I found that statement very mythical.[51]

Father and son then made a trip to the Omai gold mines, steaming up the Demerara river from Georgetown to Wismar and crossing over to Rockstone on the Essequibo by the new Demerara–Essequibo Railway. They continued up the Essequibo to the Potaro Landing by launch, and travelled overland to Omai. Oats' report continues:

Here too, as I found on the Mazzaruni river creeks there were few diamonds. But I was told of a claim not on the landing so we took some pains to visit it. It is called Green Heart and was worked by two negroes called Magin and Budia. But again only in the gold debris some diamonds are found.[52]

At the end of his taxing travels Oats concludes:

There certainly exists a few small diamonds in some of the alluvial on the creeks but so far as the concession goes, or the land outside of a few small creeks ... the ground is not diamondiferous. The diamonds so far found are small ... The place is a most expensive one to work, practically for every man engaged in work another man had to be employed on the river to bring up supplies ... I consider export of diamonds from these parts will be very limited ... I am aware however that some of our Board have the feeling that we should watch things of this kind [but] to my mind I think it is not necessary ... However I can put forward the name of a possible candidate, a Mr. Laurence, barrister-at-law and brother-in-law to the Judge President of Kimberley, who is willing to keep a watching brief for us.[53]

---

51 Ibid., p.43.
52 Ibid., p.44.
53 Ibid., p.44.

Having allayed the fears of De Beers concerning competition from the diamonds of British Guiana, Oats continued on his journey and visited the mines of Bolivia and Brazil. But he contracted malaria during his time in the interior of British Guiana, and would never fully recover the energy of his younger days. Feeling his age, he writes to a friend, one Mr Pickering: 'I think I am getting too old now for these trips, it was very fortunate I took my son with me else I should surely have been left behind somewhere.'[54]

In later life he turned to politics, and was elected to represent Namaqualand in the western part of South Africa, a position he held until 1907. He continued to pay periodic visits to Cornwall, where he built Porthledden, a splendid mansion in a spectacular position overlooking Cape Cornwall, and he bought shares in the mine at nearby Levant and in Wheal Basset near Redruth.[55] In 1908, he became Chairman of De Beers. He died in Port Elizabeth, in the Eastern Cape of South Africa, in 1918, aged 69.

British Guiana, although it never became a competitor for De Beers' South African diamond mines, did develop a diamond mining industry – but as Oats had reported, most of the diamonds produced were, and still

Francis Oats in later life.

---

54   Ibid., p.48.
55   Deacon, Bernard William. *The Cornish family*. Fowey: Cornwall Editions, 2004, pp.100–101.

are, small in size. Gold production, however, continued to grow: Guyana is still a major gold producer, and the mine at Omai is one of the largest gold mines in the world.

If you travel from Georgetown in a westerly direction along the north coast of South America, you arrive at Aruba and its neighbouring islands, Curaçao and Bonaire, which lie close to the coast of Venezuela.

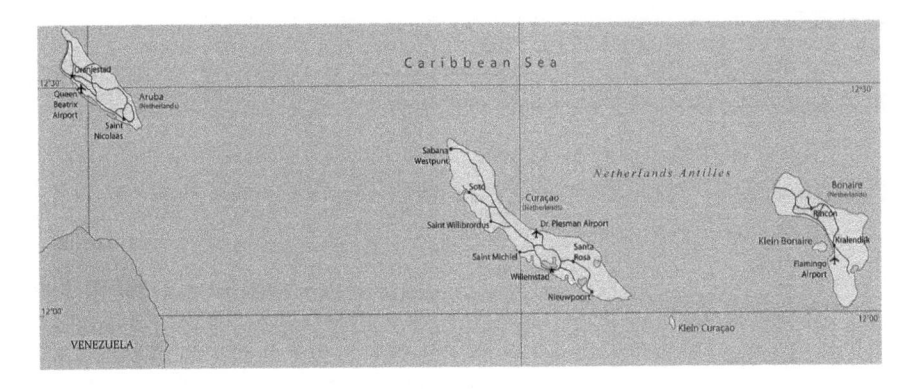

A modern map of the islands of Aruba, Curaçao and Bonaire.

Claimed by Spain in 1499, the islands were taken by the Dutch in 1634 and remained under Dutch control for the remainder of their colonial history. Gold was discovered on Aruba in 1824 – legend has it by a twelve-year-old boy, Willem Rasmijn, as he was herding sheep in Rooi Fluit (Flute Gully), near Lagabai, on the island's north coast. As the gold was alluvial, it was fairly accessible from the surface, and islanders flocked to the site to look for the precious metal. After a few years the Dutch government took control of the situation, declaring the gold-bearing areas of the island out of bounds to casual miners, sending guards to protect the resource, and issuing regulations for the purchase of concessions.

The gold was extracted using fairly primitive methods. Clay was dug from the gullies and allowed to dry in the sun, then broken up and pulverised by hand. The pulverised clay was then placed on large pieces of cloth in the steady Aruban wind which blew away the lighter clay, leaving any pieces of gold behind. Alternatively, the pulverised clay was put in a large trough and rinsed with water so that the heavier gold sank to the bottom.[56] Large gold nuggets were occasionally found, including one weighing about 5 pounds (2.3 kg).[57]

The Dutch government systematically researched the mineral content of the island's soils, eventually leading to the discovery of gold at West Point. This gold, unlike the alluvial gold found in the gullies, was found in veins underground, and had to be extracted from the ore that was brought to the surface. By 1840, miners were having trouble with the inflow of groundwater into the mine, and although the government made recommendations for an examination into the working of the mine and a report was produced, no action was taken.[58]

From time to time unregulated gold mining was reintroduced; then in 1854 a concession to exploit all of Aruba's mineral resources was granted to a Dutch company. But in spite of several years spent exploring various options the company was unable to make a profit, and in 1866 closed down its operations. After several investors had failed to make the concession pay, the concession was bought by the London-based Aruba Island Goldmining Company Ltd.[59] A man with considerable knowledge of both alluvial and ore gold mining was needed to manage the project, and the company selected Mine Captain Benjamin F. Rule as their mining engineer and superintendent of mines.

Rule had been born in about 1827 in Camborne, then the centre of some of the most profitable tin and copper mines in Cornwall. As the Cornish mining industry started to decline and opportunities became available overseas, Rule and his family went to Mexico, where he spent about five years working in the silver mines, probably where two of his brothers worked as well, around the town of Pachuca de Soto, which lies about 56 miles (90 km) from Mexico City. When Rule returned to Cornwall, prospects for employment in the mining sector in Cornwall

---

56 Ross, Helen. *The ruins at Bushiribana, Aruba, circa 1872: a preliminary investigation into Aruba's gold mining history.* Corning: Caribbean Volunteer Expeditions, 1999, pp.2–3. Accessed 17 June 2016, http://ufdc.ufl.edu/AA00012428/00005
57 Hartog, Johan. *Aruba past and present: from the time of the Indians until today.* Oranjestad: D.J. De Wit, 1961, p.142.
58 Ibid., p.142.
59 Ibid., p.144.

showed no signs of improving, so he found work in the copper mines of Belleville, New Jersey, in the United States,[60] where in 1870 he was offered the opportunity to manage the mines on Aruba.

When he arrived on the island he made a methodical survey of the mineral resources, estimated the cost of mining the ore per ton, and in April 1872 reported to the concessionaires that:

> *After a complete examination of the mines then discovered, I found that though an immense amount of work had been done at various times, it was done regardless of regular mining, and apparently only with the view of immediate profits; but no preparation whatever was made for future operations. This method of operations I determined at once to abandon, and to work the mines in a proper manner by sinking shafts, drifting levels, &c. Through want of the necessary capital, my operations were confined to the development of the following lodes, – namely, North Sombrero, Serro Blanco, Sombrero, West Serro Blanco, South Calabasa, Cien Fuegos, Bushiribana, Kadushi, and Urataka. And for want of lumber and pumping machinery, I found it impossible to execute work on these veins to advantage. Notwithstanding these facts, the mines produced nearly 22,000 tons of ore ... The cost of producing that amount of ores, as per pay roll, was 5s. 10d. per ton of 2,000 lbs.*[61]

Rule's report went on to recommend development of an infrastructure that would help ensure the efficient working of the concession, and the company invested money in an expensive construction programme. So that gold could be extracted from the ore before shipment and shipment costs thereby lowered, a gold smelter was built at Bushiribana on the north coast. To facilitate shipment of the gold, a pier – the Waaf de Compania at Forti Abao – was built in the harbour of the main town, Oranjestad. To enable the machinery shipped in to reach the smelter

---
60   Ibid.
61   *Reports on the Island of Aruba (Dutch) West Indies, and its gold ores with a general description of the island.* London: H.W. Foster, 1872, pp.8–9. Accessed 17 June 2016, https://catalog.hathitrust.org/Record/008429423

and the gold to be transported to the shipment point relatively easily, a road was made between the smelter and the harbour.[62] The construction effort quickly ran through the initial share capital of the company, and by 1873 the directors were planning to open more companies and offer more shares so they could purchase the mining machinery they needed. This opportunity was promoted through an optimistically worded article published in the June 1873 issue of *The Engineering and Mining Journal*:

> *Superintendent Rule is employing a force of 159 men at the rate of 14d. per day, and can readily obtain 300 or 400 more at the same rate for nine hours' labour. He represents them to be a very industrious and superior class of laborers. From reports recently made, it appears that the existence of gold-bearing quartz in unexhaustible quantities upon the island is beyond doubt ... Supt. Rule, in his report, states – 'On the whole the Kadushi is looking finely, and I believe that this vein alone, when developed, will be of more value than you have paid for the whole concession.*[63]

As Rule recommended, stamp mills, furnaces, zinc tanks and tram works were purchased and installed,[64] but for reasons unknown, in May 1876, he left Aruba via Curaçao on board the Brig *Curaçao*, bound for New York.[65] Perhaps he foresaw that the company had overreached itself and would not succeed, or perhaps the company felt that he had spent their money too freely on a gold extraction process that proved expensive, and chose to replace him. His brother, William N. Rule, a mining engineer, also spent some time in the Caribbean in the early 1870s, but research has not yet revealed where he worked, and by 1874 he had returned to the United States.[66]

---

62 Hartog, Johan. *Aruba past and present: from the time of the Indians until today*. Oranjestad: D.J. De Wit, 1961, p.144.
63 'The Aruba Island Gold Mining Company.' *The Engineering and Mining Journal*, pp.139–140. (Vol.15, January to June 1873).
64 Ross, Helen. *The ruins at Bushiribana, Aruba circa 1872: a preliminary investigation into Aruba's gold mining history*. Corning: Caribbean Volunteer Expeditions, 1999, p.3. Accessed 17 June. 2016 http://ufdc.ufl.edu/AA00012428/00005
65 Email from Flynn Warmington, in an email dated 29 June 2016.
66 Ibid.

When Benjamin Rule left Aruba he too returned to the United States, settling once again in Belleville, New Jersey.[67] Here he spent his retirement, dying in about 1910 after a life spent, in common with so many 19th-century Cornish miners, travelling the mining world.

In 1879, the Aruba Island Goldmining Company Ltd employed another Cornishman as its superintendent. This was Thomas Bawden, who had been born in the village of St Day in 1822.[68] St Day is in the same mining area as Camborne, the birthplace of Benjamin Rule and near to the Poldice tin and copper mine, where Bawden was first employed.[69] When the copper mining industry began to decline, Bawden, like Rule, went overseas, where he: 'for many years had the management of the Potosi [the great silver and tin mines in Bolivia] and other gold and silver mines in South America'.[70]

Bawden went out to Aruba with his eldest son, who was employed by the company as an assistant engineer. Unfortunately, having survived the rigours of working in South America, Bawden succumbed to yellow fever within three months of his arrival on Aruba. He was fifty-seven years old. His son died from the same disease shortly afterwards. As the *West Briton and Cornwall Advertiser* for 15 May 1879, reported:

> *Tidings of their safe arrival were received by both families at home, but on Sunday last a telegram arrived with the sad news of the father having died of yellow fever, and on Thursday last another telegram was received announcing the death of the son, who had also succumbed to the same disease. Great sympathy is felt for the families for these sad bereavements, as both father and son were much respected and beloved.*[71]

---

67 Ibid.
68 Email from the Biblioteca Nacional Aruba, dated 18 May 2016.
69 'Appointment of a mine agent [Captain Thomas Bawden]' *West Briton and Cornwall Advertiser*, p.8 (15 May 1879).
70 Ibid., p.8.
71 'Sad bereavements [Capt. Thomas Bawden and eldest son].' *West Briton and Cornwall Advertiser*, p.5 (7 August 1879).

Between 1878 and 1880 the Aruba Island Goldmining Company mined 2,938 tons of ore, producing 2,075 ounces of fine gold. In 1880 and 1881 no gold was exported, as the company was increasingly unable to recover the costs of its investment against the payment it received for its gold. In 1881, the company assigned its rights to the Aruba Agency Company Ltd, another group of London-based investors, but mining was not resumed until 1889 and then it was on only a small scale. By the mid-1890s a new process for extracting gold from the ore was introduced at Bushiribana. This used a solution of calcium cyanide and lime, and proved to be more efficient than the smelting system introduced by Benjamin Rule. The downside of the new process was that it required the purchase of new machinery, and its cost was more than the price the company received for the gold. So the Aruba Agency was forced to close down its operations.[72]

In 1899, a new London-based company obtained the concession: the Aruba Gold Concessions Ltd. Cornishman Arthur Francis Hosking, or Hoskin, was appointed as its chief reduction officer, and arrived on Aruba, along with the superintendent, Mr Jennings, on the mail packet schooner *Gouverneur Van Heerdt*.[73] Hosking had been born in 1875[74] and, like Benjamin Rule, was from Camborne. He was a student at the Camborne School of Mines,[75] founded in 1888 to meet the needs of the local mining industry. By the time the school opened, Cornish copper mining had slumped and tin mining was beginning to follow suit, so as Cornish miners such as Hosking sought employment outside of Cornwall, the school began to train specialists for overseas mines. The quality of the training they received gained the school a good reputation the world over, and it continued to flourish.[76] Soon after graduating, Hosking continued his education as a student member of the Institution of Mining and

---

72 Ross, Helen. *The ruins at Bushiribana, Aruba, circa 1872: a preliminary investigation into Aruba's gold mining history*. Corning: Caribbean Volunteer Expeditions, 1999, p.3. Accessed 17 June 2016, http://ufdc.ufl.edu/AA00012428/00005
73 Hartog, Johan. *Aruba past and present: from the time of the Indians until today*. Oranjestad: D.J. De Wit, 1961, p.146.
74 Email from the Biblioteca Nacional Aruba, dated 18 May 2016.
75 'Mining [Death of Mr. Arthur Francis Hosking]'. *The Cornishman*, p.6 (5 February 1948).
76 *Camborne School of Mines: history*. Accessed 20 June 2016, http://emps.exeter.ac.uk/csm/about/

Metallurgy, a research organisation based in London, where he became an associate member.[77] But apparently Aruba Gold Concessions failed to learn from the mistakes of the previous concessionaires. Before ascertaining the quantity of high quality gold-bearing ore available, they invested heavily in new infrastructure. They left the smelter at Bushiribana and built another more modern facility at Balashi, not far from Oranjestad. New mines were opened, including one at Mira Lamar which supplied much of the ore to Balashi. By the turn of the century, the company had installed several furnaces, an ore-crushing mill, various tanks needed for the cyanide refining process, an electrical plant and a railroad.[78] But it was unable to recover the cost of its investment and its works engineer reported that the existing mines were all too small, poor and unreliable to be worked at a profit; he advised the company to give up its concession. The directors took his advice in 1908.[79] As Aruba Gold Concessions began to fail Arthur Hosking left Aruba and travelled the world as a mining expert, retiring to his home town of Camborne where he died, aged 73, in 1948.[80]

In 1908, when Aruba Gold Concessions Ltd ceased operations, a Dutch company, the Aruba Gold Maatsschappij, took over the business, and in the early 20th century produced about 871 lbs (395 kilos) of gold. When the First World War began in 1914, the spare parts and the chemicals needed to process the ore became unavailable, so gold production ceased and the mines closed.[81] Today, the ruins of the mine buildings and smelters at Bushiribana and Balashi can still be found on Aruba, where they have become two of the island's tourist sites.

Cornish miners never went to British Guiana or to Aruba in large numbers, as they did to Cuba. Nor did they usually travel with their

---

77 'Mining [Death of Mr. Arthur Francis Hosking]'. *The Cornishman*, p.6 (5 February 1948).
78 Ross, Helen. *The ruins at Bushiribana, Aruba circa 1872: a preliminary investigation into Aruba's gold mining* history. Corning: Caribbean Volunteer Expeditions, 1999, p.3. Accessed 17 June 2016, http://ufdc.ufl.edu/AA00012428/00005
79 Hartog, Johan. *Aruba past and present: from the time of the Indians until today*. Oranjestad: D.J. De Wit, 1961, p.147.
80 Ibid., p,6.
81 *Historia di Aruba: gold*. Accessed 20 June 2016, http://www.historiadiaruba.aw/index.php?option=com_content&task=view&id=16&lang=en

families, as did some of the miners that went to Virgin Gorda. Those that came were mostly employed as individuals in a supervisory capacity and while these men left little impact on the local culture, their expertise contributed to the development of the local mining industry.

7

Men of God: Methodist Missionaries[1]

It was either Divine Providence or chance that first brought Methodism to the Caribbean. In early 1759, Nathaniel Gilbert, an influential sugar planter from Antigua,[2] invited John Wesley to come and preach at the home of his brother, Francis Gilbert, in London. It had been through the efforts of the two Wesley brothers, John (1703–1791) and his younger brother Charles (1707–1788), that Methodism came into being, and Nathaniel Gilbert had first learnt about their teachings when, suffering from an illness and at a loss as to how to occupy his time, he had happened to read one of John Wesley's pamphlets. It impressed him deeply, and when he was next in London he contacted Wesley, whose preaching moved him to such an extent that not only did he convert to Methodism himself but he also converted two of the enslaved women he had brought with him to England.

When he returned to Antigua, he began to preach to his enslaved workers and with the help of three black women, Sophia Campbell, Mary Alley and Bessie,[3] he began his ministry in Antigua. After Nathaniel died in 1774 his work was continued by his brother, Francis, and when he, because of ill health, returned to England, responsibility for the development of Methodism in Antigua was taken on by Campbell, Alley

---

1 See Appendix 7 for the early history of Methodism and the development of its popularity in Cornwall.
2 Nathaniel Gilbert was also a lawyer and the Speaker of the Antigua House of Assembly.
3 Sophia Campbell and Mary Alley were both free women. Bessie was one of the slaves baptised by Wesley in London.

and Bessie. But then, in 1778, the Methodist lay preacher John Baxter arrived in Antigua. He was a shipwright, employed at the naval dockyard in English Harbour on the south-east coast of Antigua, and as he began preaching to slaves throughout the island, the three women largely relinquished their leadership role.[4]

Baxter's continued efforts to develop the Methodist community on Antigua were bearing fruit, and he succeeded in building a chapel in St John's, the colony's capital, in 1783. In 1786, the Rev. Dr Thomas Coke, one of Wesley's most accomplished disciples, was on his way to Nova Scotia in North America when the ship on which he was travelling was blown off course and badly damaged during a storm. The captain decided he could no longer make landfall in Nova Scotia and set course for the Caribbean, arriving in the harbour of St John's on the morning of Christmas Day, 1786. To Coke's surprise and delight, as he and his companions disembarked and walked up the main street, they met John Baxter on his way to preach in the Methodist chapel. 'Chance had brought the great missionary pioneer to the one Island in the West Indies where the Methodists had already obtained a footing.'[5]

Coke's arrival created a flurry of social activity:[6] he was invited to the houses of the colony's social elite and dined with the Duke of Clarence, the future King William IV, who was visiting the naval dockyard at English Harbour. Coke was offered the post of parish rector in an effort to encourage him to stay, but as he had a larger project in mind he declined. His objective was the establishment of a network of Methodist Societies throughout the British Leeward Islands and beyond, and Antigua was the ideal base to start from. It was the administrative centre for the Leeward Islands, and it was a trading and business centre from which contact could be made with those on neighbouring islands who might have a similar spiritual outlook. Coke decided to investigate the possibilities of implementing his project, and set out on a tour of the islands.

---

4   Information supplied by the Rev. Dr John C. Neal in an email attachment dated 7 July 2016.
5   Hughes, Henry Brackenbury Louis. 'Christian missionary societies in the British West Indies during the Emancipation era.' PhD diss., University of Toronto, 1944, p.155.
6   Ibid., p.156.

Back in London, John Wesley began to align the Methodists more closely with the work of the Society for the Abolition of Slavery, which was established in 1787. In October of that year he wrote to Granville Sharpe, the society's chairman:

Ever since I heard of it first I felt a perfect detestation of the horrid Slave Trade ... Therefore I cannot but do everything in my power to forward the glorious design of your Society. And it must be a comfortable thing to every man of humanity to observe the spirit with which you have hitherto gone on. Indeed, you cannot go on without more than common resolution, considering the opposition you have to encounter, all the opposition which can be made by men who are 'not encumbered with either honor, conscience, or humanity, and will rush on ... through every possible means, to secure their great goddess, Interest.'[7]

A year later, Wesley preached an anti-slavery sermon in Bristol, one of the foremost slave-trading ports in England. Not unexpectedly, it produced violent reactions among his listeners, some of whom were pro-slavery. Wesley wrote in his journal:

The people rushed upon each other with the utmost violence; the benches were broke in pieces, and nine-tenths of the congregation appeared to be struck with the same panic.[8]

Meanwhile, in the Caribbean, Coke had had some success in establishing Methodism in the Leeward Islands, and decided to extend his project to Barbados, which he visited in 1788, 1790 and 1793. Here he met opposition from the sugar planters, who were determined that the Methodists should not minister to their enslaved workers or to the

---

[7] *The Letters of John Wesley: a delightful old age; July 24, 1787, to December 26, 1789.* Accessed 9 June 2016, http://wesley.nnu.edu/john-wesley/the-letters-of-john-wesley/wesleys-letters-1787/

[8] *John Wesley (1703–1791): biography.* Accessed 13 June 2016, http://www.brycchancarey.com/abolition/wesley.htm

growing number of free black people. They firmly believed that this would lead to instability and rebellion. The reaction of the planters in Jamaica, which Coke visited in 1791, 1793, 1794 and 1795, was even more hostile. Here he met with considerable and often violent resentment.[9]

Methodist missionary activity continued under the personal supervision of Coke until 1804, when his work load became so great that he agreed to the assistance of a small committee. As the number of overseas missions continued to grow still further, better coordination and support for their work was required, and in 1818 the General Wesleyan Methodist Missionary Society was established and given the task of managing the foreign missions.[10]

More missionaries were needed to serve the growing number of Caribbean missions. Given the popularity of Methodism in Cornwall and the large numbers of local preachers that ministered to the needs of the Cornish Societies, there were many Cornishmen among the new missionaries. In Cornwall, preachers brought not just spiritual fulfilment but also basic health and education services to local communities, and in the Caribbean they did the same, although there was one aspect of the local community's belief system the missionaries failed to understand. To the Methodists, humanity was sinful and in need of salvation by God – but when slaves or freed slaves were asked to repent of their sins before being saved, it is not surprising if many considered that it was they who had been grievously sinned against and that the sinners who should be repenting were those who had enslaved them.

One of the early Cornish missionaries was William Jenkin (1757–1830). Born in St Keverne, on the Lizard in south-west Cornwall,[11] he came from a poor family, but:

> being ardently desirous of mental improvement, he separated himself from the vanities of youth, and by intense application, which no

---

9 Ibid., pp.157–171.
10 Email from the Rev. Dr John C. Neal, dated 7 July 2016.
11 *Harvest festivals to missions: rough list of Cornish Methodist missionaries.* Unpublished list from Courtney Library pamphlet file.

discouragement could repress, he made considerable progress in various branches of useful learning.[12]

Accepted as a Methodist preacher in 1797 when he was already forty years old, he volunteered to go out to the Caribbean. He was sent to St Christopher but, as he wrote to the Missionary Society when in early March 1799 he finally arrived at his destination, his journey was lengthy and exhausting:

> *We embarked on board a ship at Bristol and put to sea. But after five days beating to windward, we were obliged to bear up again for Bristol, where we waited some time longer for a fair wind. We made two attempts more with out success. But trying a fourth time, and getting some distance from Bristol, a heavy gale of wind came on, which split our foretopsail and obliged us to put into Milford Haven. Having repaired our damages, we set sail again with the intention of going to Cork, and joining the West Indies fleet. But a terrible storm overtook us on the Irish coast ... in consequence of which we were driven onshore at a place called Old Head, off Kinsale ... When the water ebbed the vessel was left almost dry, so we escaped on shore.*[13]

Jenkin's troubles were not yet over. Once ashore, he and his fellow passengers were surrounded by robbers who stole everything they managed to bring with them from the wrecked ship. Fortunately, just as they were beginning to think they would not escape alive from this latest disaster: 'providentially a party of soldiers came to our assistance; and they fired upon the plunderers and killed four of them, which intimidated the rest, and they dispersed'.[14]

Nothing daunted, Jenkin, having partially recovered with the assistance of the local Kinsale Methodists, once more took ship for St Christopher. When he arrived he was favourably impressed by the Methodist Society he found there and looked forward to beginning his ministry, but as he

---

12 Moister, William. *Heralds of salvation: memorial sketches of Wesleyan missionaries.* London: Wesleyan Conference Office, 1878, p.96.
13 Ibid., p.97.
14 Ibid., p.97.

was still unwell after the hardship he had suffered during his voyage he was advised to return to England. Here, having regained his strength, he resumed his work. He was recognised as 'an able Minister of the Gospel'[15] and continued to minister for the next few years, retiring in 1815. He died in May 1830, at the age of 73.

The Rev. William Dixon Goy (1792–1866) was another early Cornish missionary.[16] He entered the Ministry in 1817 and was sent out to Grenada, where he was stationed in the capital, St George's. During his time in St George's he managed both to build a chapel and to develop a good relationship with some of the plantation owners. Some planters refused to let the missionaries preach on their estates, but Goy managed to convince them that the Methodists were a force for stability. In 1820, the Assembly requested the Methodists to extend their ministering to the eastern side of the island where there were large numbers of enslaved workers, asking Goy if he would: 'communicate Christian instruction to a people who previously had no knowledge of Christianity'.[17]

When an additional missionary arrived on Grenada, Goy moved up to Grand Bras Estate. This property lay in St Andrew's Parish, midway along the east coast of the island. The estate belonged to a Mr B. Hewitson, one of the planters who was favourably impressed with Goy's achievements. Pleased that the estate owners were willing to fund the cost of a house and a chapel, Goy wrote to the Missionary Society:

> *I arrived at Grand Bras, the residence of B. Hewitson, Esq., late in the evening, and was kindly received by that gentleman. I am to stay with him a few weeks, until we can fix on an eligible spot on which to build a small*

---

15 Ibid., p.97.
16 *Harvest festivals to missions: rough list of Cornish Methodist missionaries.* Unpublished list from Courtney Library pamphlet file.
17 Jackson, Thomas. *Memoirs of the life and writings of the Rev. Richard Watson: late Secretary to the Wesleyan Methodist Society.* 2nd ed. London: John Mason, 1834, p.308. Accessed 11 June 2016, http://books.googleusercontent.com/books/content?req=AKW5QafM5hShjl svlcJy1gm0zOVrNvyeFZjMb_-roj4BsahMJV4IUhkrpOUTz-HiMI22kt6rlzY1iwfCmSG 3DVpdfI93lEzT45rSVvMFnFr7-Vi-XCIYJ8gA0hgLpRQ5ENlAR9G4XiTUjaoWV8c 3lu2OHa0POWx2vcQ8tYcE8yLHBeNeS-y-so8rCpwsBvGJc7SSzVjBFsdH1T7_9qGS aM_MjDzJ1soe_yxAtiJZhGV6KY09WNes2xx1NHZDSNrXvcNgc6FiErv1S-8ssvLc7i eQP60kY5Nqe31bjI1d0xhkBgxgU5Gp-P4

house. As this is a sickly part of the island, it will be necessary to select a place with care. There are some healthy situations, and we have already decided upon one for our dwelling. Mr. H. and his friends propose erecting a house free of expense to the society. Mr. H. has built a small chapel on his estate for the negroes, and many seem willing to attend. I commenced my labours the day after I arrived, and am now busy arranging my plans. I have taken in five estates; two belonging to the Hon. J. Berkeley, the other three are those of Mr. Hewitson. On these five estates there are more than a thousand negroes. There is also a port and a village (Grenville), two miles distant, where I propose to preach once a fortnight.[18]

After his success in Grenada, Goy was moved by the Missionary Society to Barbados in 1823, and in 1824 moved again, this time to Trinidad.[19] When he returned to England he continued to minister to various communities throughout the country until the late 1850s.[20][21][22] By 1857

---

18 Rose, George Henry. *A letter on the means and importance of converting the slaves in the West Indies to Christianity.* London: John Murray, 1823, p.75. Accessed 11 June 2016, http://books.googleusercontent.com/books/content?req=AKW5QacgDllY3zPRlSgk u54Ah1KRNw1vXoiPkzsCWAD38rBW9gmURuZOrs9rKcHfLdCQbZFPgLdmo i3bsDGxhkuUZu7VeiskTZav92f9qC1aXKb4v5lUgLg8ON-lhVlyvhk6DifCiiIFZy_ VX2hRPH9l0EaJM6hAuPg4eMtnCnQYOWUDlhyvEVhdiU0crRmRQlCf5rnOe_ GMrMDxl2LKZgvOslVoVZKiw02Ssa814i-wyqGs-bM8gi2uG0hWVGB788dgcB7Fky na9c7KyxfK4RlTHwMwTZ0_FgGmg_OIWZZJZpjgFXfGYDQ
19 Wesleyan Methodist Church. *Minutes of the Wesleyan Methodist Conferences from the first …* Vol.5. London: J. Kershaw, 1825, pp.407, 496. Accessed 11 June 2016. http://books.googleusercontent.com/ books/content?req=AKW5QadfHhrkGcNq7IGsUJLcVkLnC5HCq_ nzr9dN87CQD82I3Q8spxIR3F_0SsKRF3veE_bqRPRenUTl0vteskoIX2e2ehfvXprgiF H5X1rrLom9ArhJ-YNcMO-IeJ4fpO3ozpABeIEfoMsIwfiUrispAQCUMO9Qq4xuGdY dPkSIsWrI_lDonH98d8-P45rkw9en-dFSA78_iHw7fpaXvaCOqEA42gGIr3IDlwMesh TicjuM0rqWBe4r8yFwJ0xipYtYlkkzbP6v0QOE-TwuOxwpQRAU2GoofeWWUpSt3g qRL_I_8_iI7Eg
20 Wesleyan Methodist Church. *Minutes of the Wesleyan Conferences from the first …* Vol.6. London: John Mason, 1833. Accessed 11 June 2016, https://archive.org/stream/ minutesseveralc10churgoog#page/n8/mode/2up
21 Wesleyan Methodist Church. *Minutes of the Wesleyan Conferences from the first …* Vol.8. London: John Mason, 1841. Accessed 11 June 2016, https://books.google.com/ books?id=RygRAAAAIAAJ&q=title+page#v=onepage&q=title per cent20page&f=false
22 Wesleyan Methodist Church. *Minutes of the Wesleyan Conferences from the first …* Vol.10. London: John Mason, 1848. Accessed 11 June 2016, https://books.google. co.uk/books?id=mxsRAAAAIAAJ&printsec=frontcover&vq=goy&source=gbs_ge_ summary_r&cad=0#v=onepage&q=goy&f=false

he was Chairman of the Nottingham and Derby District of Methodist Societies[23] and by the early 1860s had moved to the county of Kent. By now, into his seventies and blessed with a strong constitution, he continued to preach at least until the late 1860s.[24] He died in 1866 aged 74, having given a lifetime of service to the Methodist Society.[25]

Unlike Goy, Cornishmen Thomas Truscott (?-1826) and William Oke (1796–1826) were not destined for longevity.[26] Oke was from St Tudy, as were those two early Cornish travellers to the Caribbean, Nicholas Leverton[27] and Captain William Bligh.[28] Oke entered the Ministry in 1821 and was briefly based in his local village – where he was 'loved and esteemed'[29] – before he volunteered for missionary work and was appointed to St Christopher. He arrived on the island in 1822 and ministered to the local community until 1823, when he was moved to Antigua. Here, as on St Christopher, he worked 'with great faithfulness and success',[30] preaching regularly at the Ebenezer Methodist Chapel in St John's. This was not the wooden structure built by John Baxter in 1783, but a much larger and imposing structure, built at a cost of nearly £2,000 in 1815.[31]

Thomas Truscott served in the Caribbean for nearly seven years,

---

23 Wesleyan Methodist Church. *Minutes of the Wesleyan Conferences from the first ...* Vol.13, p.442. London: John Mason, 1859. Accessed 11 June 2016, https://archive.org/stream/minutesseveralc07churgoog#page/n8/mode/2up

24 Wesleyan Methodist Church. *Minutes of the Wesleyan Conferences from the first ...* Vol.14. London: John Mason, 1862. Accessed 11 June 2016, https://books.google.com/books?id=PMEQAAAAIAAJ&pg=PA3-IA4#v=o Harvest festivals to missions: rough list of Cornish Methodist missionaries. Unpublished list from Courtney Library pamphlet file.

25 Information supplied by the Rev. Dr John C. Neal from the Database of Methodist Missionaries maintained by the Rev. Dr Albert Mosley [as yet unpublished] in an email attachment dated 7 July 2016.

26 *Harvest festivals to missions: rough list of Cornish Methodist missionaries.* Unpublished list from Courtney Library pamphlet file.

27 For more about Nicholas Leverton see Chapter 5: Barbados, the Windward Islands and Trinidad.

28 For more about Captain William Bligh, see Chapter 3: In Defence of the Empire.

29 Moister, William. *Heralds of salvation: memorial sketches of Wesleyan missionaries.* London: Wesleyan Conference Office, 1878, p.78.

30 Ibid.

31 Findlay, G.G. and W.W. Holdsworth. *The history of the Wesleyan Methodist Missionary Society.* Vol.2. London: Epworth Press, 1859, p.138.

South-east view of the Ebenezer Methodist Chapel, St John's, Antigua. Artist unknown. About 1815. Courtesy of Caroline Simpson Library and Research Collection, Sydney Living Museums.

ministering on the islands of Dominica, Tortola and St Eustatius[32] before joining William Oke on Antigua.

Methodist missionaries from various parts of the Caribbean met regularly to share experiences and discuss future developments, and in early 1826 Truscott and Oke travelled to St Christopher to participate in the Annual General Meeting of the Methodist Missionaries from the Leeward Islands. After the meeting the two men, along with other missionaries including the Rev. and Mrs Jones and their family, began the return voyage to Antigua. They stopped at Montserrat on the way when:

> *their friends advised them to leave the vessel in which they were, (being a dull sailer,) and go on board the mail-boat Maria, then ready to sail for this island [Antigua]. They did so ... The schooner which they had left arrived here [in Antigua] seasonably, and brought the baggage of the mission family ... Some alarm, after the schooner's arrival, was felt for the safety of the mail-boat; but as the wind was very high, it*

---
32 Ibid., p.77.

was supposed that she had probably lost some of her sails, and put back. On Friday p.m. the 3d [of March] instant, however, word was brought to town, that part of the wreck was seen on the Weymouth [a reef near the entrance to St. John's Harbour] with two persons on it. Two or three boats immediately went down to her, and found it to be the wreck of the mail-boat Maria, and the only survivor of 21 souls was Mrs. Jones, in a state of insensibility. It appears that she had been placed by the Captain (Whitney), between the bow-sprit bitts, where she could not wash away. She was in her night dress only, with her husband's cloak or coat on, and a sailor's cap on her head. The body of Captain Whitney, the only one found, was lying near the wreck. He was buried yesterday ... Mrs. Jones is slowly recovering.[33]

Truscott and his wife, child and servant were on the section of the boat that broke up when the boat struck the reef on 28 February, and were 'thus mercifully saved from that lingering death that was the lot of some of their fellow-sufferers.'[34] Another of the passengers, Daniel Hillier, drowned while trying to swim to the nearest point of land, probably Deep Bay, which is about 1.5 miles (2.7 km) from Weymouth Reef. On 3 March, after the *Maria* had been aground for three days and three nights, Oke decided to take the same course of action and prepared to swim to shore. Although one of the other surviving passengers tried to dissuade him he: 'plunged into the waves; but he had no power to use his hands and was carried away with the current and seen no more.'[35] He was twenty-nine years old.

Not all Cornish Methodist missionaries were as unswervingly committed to the Wesleyan way of life as were Thomas Truscott and William Oke. William Woods Harvey (1798–1864) was born in Penzance, and as a young member of the Methodist Society he volunteered to become an overseas missionary. In 1819, he was sent out

---

33   *The diary of the Reverend William Fidler: January 1827.* Accessed 10 June 2016, http://www.kevinlaurence.net/genealogy/fidlerdiary/1827_January.php
34   Moister, William. *Heralds of salvation: memorial sketches of Wesleyan missionaries.* London: Wesleyan Conference Office, 1878, p.77.
35   Ibid., p.79.

to Cape Henry (now Cap Haitien), on the north coast of Haiti. The early 19th century was an unstable time in post-independent Haiti, when the country was split between two ruling parties: in the north the Kingdom of Haiti led by King Henri Christophe, and in the south the Republic of Haiti led by Jean-Pierre Boyer. After the death of Christophe in 1820, Boyer succeeded in briefly uniting the whole of Hispaniola, but Harvey seems to have had a stressful time trying to minister to the Cape Henry community during those turbulent years; in 1821 he was 'retired from want of health' and returned to Cornwall.[36]

Soon after his return he went up to Queens' College, Cambridge, where in 1828 he earned a BA, and in 1835 an MA. While he was completing his studies, he became involved in a confrontation between the Baptists and the Methodists in and around Truro, writing his contributions to the differences of opinion between the two under the pen-name 'Pindar'. He also edited some of John Wesley's writing about his experiences in Haiti, publishing *Sketches of Hayti* in 1827. During these years his religious thinking gradually aligned itself less with the Methodists and more with the Anglicans. By the time he had completed his MA, he was firmly in the Anglican fold, and in 1839 was made Vicar of Truro. He remained in this post until his retirement in 1860, when he moved to Torquay in Devon and where, in October 1864 he died.[37]

Unlike Harvey, Benjamin Tregaskis (1814–1885) never had a shred of doubt about his commitment to Wesleyan Methodism. Less popular than many of his contemporaries, he was:

---

36 Wesleyan Methodist Church. *Minutes of the Wesleyan Methodist Conferences from the first ...* Vol.5. London: J. Kershaw, 1825, p.27,pp.121, 204. Accessed 11 June 2016, http://books.googleusercontent.com/books/content?req=AKW5QadfHhrkGcNq7IGsUJLcVkLnC5HCq_nzr9dN87CQD82I3Q8spxIR3F_0SsKRF3veE_bqRPRenUTl0vteskoIX2e2ehfvXprgiFH5X1rrLom9ArhJ-YNcMO-IeJ4fpO3ozpABeIEfoMsIwfiUrispAQCUMO9Qq4xuGdYdPkSIsWrI_IDonH98d8-P45rkw9en-dFSA78_iHw7fpaXvaCOqEA42gGIr3IDlwMeshTicjuM0rqWBe4r8yFwJ0xipYtYlkkzbP6v0QOE-TwuOxwpQRAU2GoofeWWUpSt3gqRL_I_8_iI7Eg
37 Stephen, Leslie and Sidney Lee. *Dictionary of national biography*. Vol.25, Harris – Henry I. London: Smith, Elder and Co., 1891, p.81. Accessed 11 June 2016, https://books.google.com/books?id=79XEJJzNaKYC&printsec=frontcover&source=gbs_ge_summary_r&cad=0#v=onepage&q&f=false

a Missionary of forceful character and special usefulness – a strict asserter of discipline, conscientious in every detail and expecting others to be so, endowed, moreover, with an iron frame and a passion for work.[38]

Tregaskis became a missionary for the Antigua Circuit in 1836 and spent over twenty-five years in the Caribbean, moving on from Antigua to St Christopher, Tortola, Nevis, Dominica, Montserrat, Anguilla, St Eustatius, St Martin and Dominica.[39][40][41]

In 1839, he was unexpectedly moved from Tortola to Nevis, replacing John Bell who had died from yellow fever less than a year after starting work on the island, leaving a young wife and baby. Bell had been working on the estates belonging to George Webbe,[42] a sugar planter who was a devout Methodist. Following Emancipation, Webbe built a chapel for his workers and a Sunday school, both of which were run by Methodist missionaries. But almost as soon as he arrived on Nevis, Tregaskis, in turn, fell ill with yellow fever. However, he survived, largely because of his determination and his 'iron frame', but also because of the care he received from Webbe and his wife Sarah. Even the demanding Tregaskis was impressed by the treatment he had received during his sickness, and in October 1839 he wrote to the Missionary Society in London:

As soon as His Honour was made acquainted with the fact of my illness he came to the Mission House and proposed that I should be removed to his residence ... [and] in the cool of the second day of my illness, His Honour came with his easy English-built carriage ... both

---

38 Findlay, G.G., and W.W. Holdsworth. *The history of the Wesleyan Methodist Missionary Society*. Vol.2. London: Epworth Press, 1859, p.348.
39 Ibid., p.348.
40 Wesleyan Methodist Missionary Society. *The Wesleyan juvenile offering: a miscellany of missionary information for young persons*. London: Wesleyan Methodist Missionary Society, 1865, pp.15–16. Accessed 12 June 2016, https://books.google.com/books?id=IF0EAAAAQAAJ&printsec=frontcover#v=onepage&q&f=false
41 Information supplied by the Rev. Dr John C. Neal from the Database of Methodist Missionaries maintained by the Rev. Dr Albert Mosley [as yet unpublished] in an email attachment dated 7 July 2016.
42 For more about George Webbe and his family, see Chapter 1: The British Leeward Islands.

the Judge and His Lady watched over me with all possible solicitude, securing to me the most minute attendance and ministering their own hands to alleviate my condition. My convalescence also, when it began was not at all retarded by the highly interesting and comprehensive conversation with which I was privileged.[43]

Tregaskis was even more impressed with the care the Webbes showed to the widow and son of the deceased Bell. Keeping the Missionary Society up to date with events, he wrote:

You have doubtless heard of the kindness shown to our dear sister Bell also, since the removal of her affectionate husband. I have seen the Judge here working with his own hands, arranging her boxes and otherwise assisting in her behalf. The dear infant is doing well through the kind attention of Mrs. Webbe and the blessing of God.[44]

After returning to England in 1863, Tregaskis was called upon in 1864 to serve as general superintendent of the Wesleyan Methodist Mission in Sierra Leone, West Africa, replacing the acting general superintendent, Charles Knight. But as in the Caribbean, Tregaskis failed to endear himself to his colleagues:

Through his intolerance and militancy, Tregaskis created considerable disharmony within the Church, and treated his African colleagues with such contempt that, fearing a general revolt of the African clergy in Sierra Leone, the London headquarters prevailed upon him to return to Britain on leave in 1874. In that year Charles Knight replaced him as substantive general superintendent, the first African to hold such a position.[45]

---

43 Uppingham Methodist Church. *Mary Drake and the missionary*. Uppingham: Uppingham Methodist Church, nd, np.
44 Ibid.
45 *Knight, Charles c. 1799–1879, Wesleyan Methodist Mission, Sierra Leone.* Accessed 11 June 2016, http://www.dacb.org/stories/sierraleone/knight_charles.html

William Francis Cocks (?–1881) another native of Cornwall,[46] was unfortunately not blessed with Tregaskis' strong constitution. Cocks entered the Ministry and was sent out to St Vincent in 1876. Two years later Emily Hales, his wife-to-be, travelled from her home in St Agnes, Cornwall, to join him. On 22 November 1878 the couple married in the Kingstown Methodist Chapel[47] and, in a house conveniently situated next door to it, settled down to have two children. The Kingstown Chapel was built in 1840, and was considered to be:

> *a commodious and elegant chapel, the front of which is built of polished stone, and the other parts of hewn stone and brick ... It was erected ... at a cost of about 7000 pounds ... and being furnished with galleries, will seat nearly two thousand persons. It is generally well attended by a respectable and intelligent congregation, chiefly of black and coloured persons.*[48]

Cornishman Henry Blewett, captain of the *Roseau*, made some of his many voyages to St Vincent[49] while Cocks and his family were living in Kingstown. As a committed Methodist who regularly attended the Kingstown Chapel, Blewett would have come to know fellow Cornishman Cocks and, especially when his wife, Jane, accompanied him to St Vincent, would have spent time with the Cocks family.

In 1880, Cocks and his family were transferred to Barbados and here, in the July of that year, Cocks and his elder child died from yellow fever.[50] His wife and younger child returned to Cornwall. The newspaper which reported the death of Cocks and his child describes the impact of a yellow fever outbreak on daily life, noting that:

---

46 Courtney Library. *Cornish people overseas from 1840: index compiled from local newspapers.* Truro: Courtney Library, nd.
47 Ibid.
48 Moister, William. *Memorials of missionary labours in Western Africa and the West Indies and at the Cape of Good Hope ...* 3rd ed. London: [Wesleyan Conference Office], 1850, p.324.
49 For more about Henry Blewett, see Chapter 5: Barbados, the British Windward Islands and Trinidad.
50 'Letters from Barbados.' *Royal Gazette: Bermuda Commercial and General Advertiser and Recorder*, p.1. (Vol.57, 23 August 1881).

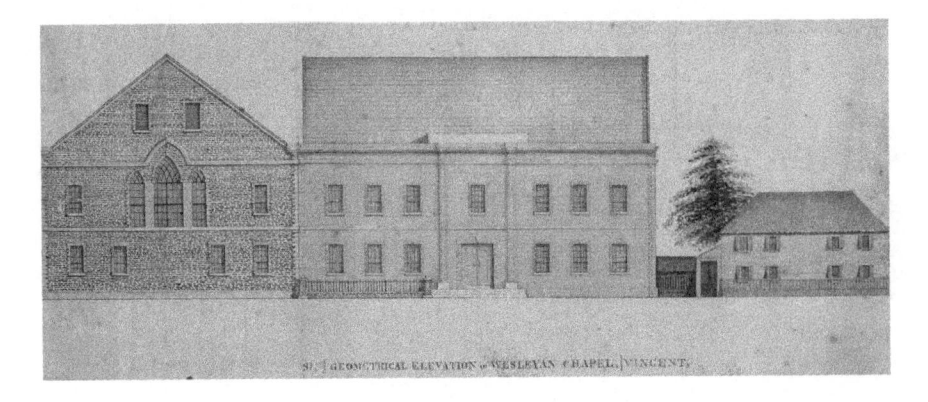

Geometrical elevation of the Wesleyan Chapel, [Kingstown] St Vincent, front [to the left] and east wing [centre, with the Missionary's Residence to the right].
Artist unknown. About 1840. Courtesy of the Caroline Simpson Library and Research Collection, Sydney Living Museums.

There have also been some deaths among the military at the garrison.

The Receptions at Government House had been discontinued until further notice.

The Barbadoes Mutual Life Insurance Society have determined for the present, not to issue policies on the lives of persons of fair complexions (Coloured) owing to the prevalence of yellow fever in the island, under the supposition that such persons are more susceptible of contracting the disease.[51]

Among local Caribbean populations, possession of a lighter skin brought better employment opportunities and social advantages. But the insurance company's decision to stop issuing life insurance policies to those with a fair skin is surely one of the few instances when to be a local person with fairer rather than darker skin was a disadvantage.

James Curtis Brewer (1843–1931) was born in Flushing, near Falmouth. Educated at Falmouth Grammar School, he began his working life as an apprentice to a ship's carpenter, entering the Ministry

---

51 Ibid., p.1.

in 1868.[52] Between 1868 and 1879 he first ministered in Antigua and then in British Guiana.[53] In Antigua he was based in Parham, the town on the north-east coast of the island which had once been its capital.[54] The Chairman and General Superintendent of the Antigua District was the Rev. James T. Hartwell,[55] and while Brewer was in Antigua he met Hartwell's daughter, Hannah. Shortly before he was transferred to British Guiana in 1873, the two married.[56] He first ministered from the chapel at Golden Grove, a village in the area known as Demerara-Mahaica which lies about 16 miles (25.7 km.) east along the coastal road from the capital, Georgetown. Brewer was later transferred to Georgetown itself,[57] where he ministered from a wooden building constructed in the vernacular style of the day in 1821. It was both his chapel and his place of residence.[58]

After ministering in British Guiana, Brewer returned with his family to Helston in Cornwall. He continued to preach as a Wesleyan minister, transferring to Yorkshire, then to Huntingdonshire, and later to Gateshead. Brewer spent his last years in Hitchin, Hertfordshire, where, aged 88, he died in 1940.[59]

Thomas H. Bailey (1850–1917) was born in Gwennap, near to the pit where Wesley had so often preached. Bailey entered the Ministry in 1876 and was appointed to St Bartholomew in that year, moving to St Christopher in 1879. Like the Rev. Cocks, he chose his wife from Cornwall: Annie Whitburn, who was from Bleak House in Devoran, a

---

52 *The Methodist who's who.* London: Charles H. Kelly, 1912, p.37.
53 Ibid.
54 Ibid.
55 Wesleyan Methodist Church. *Minutes of the Wesleyan Conferences from the first ...* Vol.18. London: Wesleyan Conference Office, 1874, pp.73, 315. Accessed 28 June 2016, https://archive.org/details/minutesmethodis00churgoog
56 Wesleyan Methodist Church. *Minutes of the Wesleyan Conferences from the first ...* Vol.19. London: Wesleyan Conference Office, 1877, pp.90, 373. Accessed 28 June 2016, https://archive.org/details/10735743.269.emory.edu
57 Ibid., p.633.
58 Historic Houses Trust. *Pictures [Wesleyan chapels].* Accessed 28 July, http://collection.hht.net.au/firsthhtpictures/resbyfield.jsp?term=chapels&field=SUBJECT&searchtable=CATALOGUE_SEARCH_PICTURES&displayFormat=TABLE
59 Email message from Kate Crombie, dated 28 July 2016.

Wesleyan Chapel and dwelling house, Georgetown, British Guiana. Artist, the Rev. John Mortimer. Date, about 1824. Courtesy of the Caroline Simpson Library and Research Collection, Sydney Living Museums.

village near Falmouth. She sailed out to St Christopher, and in August 1880 they married at the Wesleyan Chapel in Sandy Point.[60]

Many of the Methodist Society members on St Christopher were of an advanced age, and Bailey felt a sense of achievement when he had some success in converting a number of young people on the island. In July 1881, as he reported to the Mission House in London:

> *I addressed the Sunday school, where we have a great number of young men and women, but whom I knew were unconverted. I felt it was a rare opportunity for letting down the net. I addressed them and prayed; but though I was so sanguine, yet there was no sign of a catch ... I made one more appeal, and the tears began to flow, and again we went to prayer ... being strong, robust young people, their cries for mercy were rather boisterous. I tried to quiet them as carefully as possible, though I knew what a relief it was to give vent to strong feelings of repentance ... This was quite an opportune revival for this place; for although it has*

---

60   Courtney Library. *Cornish people overseas from 1840: index compiled from local newspapers.* Truro: Courtney Library, nd.

been remarkable for its zealous, pious members, yet as the old veterans pass away, grave doubts were entertained for the future.[61]

During 1882, Bailey ministered on Anguilla and St Martin, and then in 1883 he and his wife, now with a baby daughter, moved to Montserrat. Unlike most of the Leeward Islands, a predominant number of Montserrat's population was Roman Catholic, descended both from early Irish settlers and from those deported after the failed Monmouth Rebellion. There was competition for souls both between Roman Catholics and Protestants and between the different Protestant denominations. There was also competition from Obeah, a system of belief slaves brought with them from West Africa which uses ritual to ward off misfortune or, less commonly, to cause harm. Obeah was illegal in the colony but was practised secretly, and the Methodists tried hard to persuade the local community away from their belief in its power. In this they were supported by the plantocracy, who resented the influential position Obeah men and women had among their labourers. Until he faced competition from the Anglican clergyman, Bailey made some progress in one village where Obeah was still popular but, as he reported to the Missionary Society:

the town [Anglican] clergyman, an inveterate enemy of Methodism, came on the scene ... and began services and a Sunday School ... For eight months this went on, till suddenly a revival broke out.

After this revival of faith in Methodism, Bailey went on to establish a class of twenty Society members in the village.[62]

The Baileys moved back to Cornwall in 1887 and Bailey first served on the Bodmin Circuit, then transferred to more northerly locations including Leicestershire, Derbyshire, Cheshire, Yorkshire and Lancashire. He died, aged 66, in March 1917.[63]

---

61 Findlay, G.G. and W.W. Holdsworth. *The history of the Wesleyan Methodist Missionary Society*. Vol.2. London: Epworth Press, 1859, p.274.
62 Ibid., p.424.
63 *Old St Keverne news, Cornwall*. Accessed 13 June 2016, http://www.st-keverne.com/History/Misc/West-Briton.php

Bailey's contemporary, Cornishman John Kernick (1853–1921), entered the Ministry in 1875 and went out to Nevis in 1876.[64] In 1879 he was transferred to Antigua, where he was joined by his future wife. Like his fellow missionaries Cock and Bailey, Kernick chose a Cornishwoman, Lizzie Williams, who came from St Agnes, and the couple married in the Methodist Chapel in St John's in October 1879.[65] The family later returned to Cornwall and in 1887 Kernick served with his fellow Cornish missionary, Thomas Bailey, on the Bodmin Circuit.[66]

William Lanyon Bennett (1856–1936) was born in Gwithian,[67] a village on the north coast of Cornwall that sits across the bay from the town of St Ives. His family had been part of the local Methodist Society since Wesley's early visits to Cornwall, and Bennett preached to his first congregation at Helston, near Camelford, at a young age. In 1879, along with his brother Richard, he entered the Ministry.[68] He volunteered to serve as a foreign missionary and was sent to St Christopher in 1880, moving to Antigua in 1882 and to Dominica in 1884.[69] When he returned to England in 1886, he spent most of the next forty-four years ministering to the Methodist Societies in Cornwall, where he is remembered as a good pastor and a faithful friend.[70]

Throughout the Caribbean, just as back in Britain, Methodist missionaries were supported by lay preachers. Some of these came from among the Cornish mine captains who had come to work in the local mines. In Cornish mines, it was the mine captain who was responsible

---

64 Information supplied by the Rev. Dr John C. Neal from the Database of Methodist Missionaries maintained by the Rev. Dr Albert Mosley [as yet unpublished] in an email attachment dated 7 July 2016.
65 Courtney Library. Cornish people overseas from 1840: index compiled from local newspapers. Truro: Courtney Library, nd.
66 *Old St Keverne News, Cornwall*. Accessed 13 June 2016, http://www.st-keverne.com/History/Misc/West-Briton.php
67 *Harvest festivals to missions: rough list of Cornish Methodist missionaries*. Unpublished list from Courtney Library pamphlet file.
68 Information supplied by Rev. Dr John C. Neal from the Database of Methodist Missionaries maintained by the Rev. Dr Albert Mosley [as yet unpublished] in an email attachment dated 7 July 2016.
69 Ibid.
70 Bennett, Dennis Stanley Lanyon. *William Lanyon Bennett, born 1856. His life story*. Unpublished notes, 1982, used with permission of George Waterman, via email message of 16 June 2016.

for both workplace discipline and for providing social leadership among the miners, a position reinforced if he was also a lay preacher in the local Methodist chapel.[71] When a Cornish mine captain came to the Caribbean, he brought with him his traditional responsibility for the spiritual welfare of the men he supervised. One day early in 1853, one such mine captain arrived at the Grateful Hill Methodist chapel in St Catherine's Parish in Jamaica, where he was received by the Rev. William G. Steadman.

We don't know the captain's name, nor the name of the company that employed him, but Steadman was delighted to have an additional preacher, and reported to the Wesleyan Methodist Missionary Society how it had:

> *pleased the 'Lord of the harvest' to 'send forth' a man of faith and prayer from Cornwall, (England,) whose labours as a Local Preacher, &c., promise to be of no small value here. On the first Sabbath after landing, himself and brother (both mining captains) were found in the Lord's house, and the newly-arrived speedily produced his ... credentials as a Local Preacher. As he fills a very responsible situation, and the Company whose agent he is seem to have entrusted to his care the moral and spiritual welfare of the men under him, he is not at liberty, at present, to occupy any other pulpit than Unity, within five miles of which he is located, and where copper mining is commenced.*[72]

Methodist missionaries were committed to the idea that all people were equal in the eyes of God. All could be redeemed, and everyone's life could be improved with education and self-help. The Cornish Methodist missionaries grew up with and ministered to local communities of miners,

---

71 Cornish Mining World Heritage. *Mining bosses and businesses.* Accessed 20 July 2016, https://www.cornish-mining.org.uk/delving-deeper/mining-bosses-and-businesses

72 'Arrival of brethren from Cornwall: mining in Jamaica.' in Wesleyan Methodist Missionary Society. *Missionary notices relating principally to the foreign missions.* London: Wesleyan Methodist Missionary Society, 1853, p.176. Accessed 20 July 2016, https://books.google.com.ag/books?id=bygEAAAAQAAJ&dq=jamaica+copper+mining+history+cornwall&q=arrival+of+brethren+from+cornwall#v=snippet&q=arrival per cent20of per cent20brethren per cent20from per cent20cornwall&f=false

fishermen and agricultural labourers: men and women who felt ignored by both Church and State. The missionaries' experience of working with Cornish communities who felt marginalised by society gave them a special understanding of the skills needed to minister to the slaves and free coloured people of the Caribbean.

8

Gold and Copper: the Mines of Cuba and the Dominican Republic[1]

When James Whitburn arrived in the harbour of Santiago de Cuba in late July 1836 he was pleased at what he saw. 'About 12 o'clock on Thursday,' he writes in his diary:

we came in sight of the Fort at the mouth of the river, beautifully situated. I think it is one of the prettiest in the world ... Went on shore at 4 o'clock in the city of St. Jago [Santiago]. Had one of the best drinks of water I ever had in my life.[2]

An engine mechanic from Gwennap, in the heart of Cornwall's mining country, Whitburn was one of a group of Cornish miners who went to the Spanish colony of Cuba to work at the copper mines of El Cobre.

In the recent Wars of Independence Spain had lost all her American possessions with the exception of Cuba and Puerto Rico, and those two loyal colonies were rewarded by a lifting of the economic restrictions that prevented them from doing business with nations friendly to Spain. This development gave foreigners an opportunity to invest in the islands in general, and in the potential mining sector in Cuba in particular.[3] Of special interest were the copper resources at El Cobre, a long-established

---

1 See Appendix 8 for a background history of Cuba and the Dominican Republic.
2 Whitburn, James. *A Cornish man in Cuba: transcript of a diary of his visit to Cuba 1836–1838*. np: Whitburn, nd, p.2.
3 Waszkis, Helmut. *Mining in the Americas: stories and history*. Cambridge: Woodhead Publishing, 1993, p.17.

Santiago de Cuba, also known as St Jago de Cuba,
sketched from the harbour in 1849.
From the author's collection.

mining community near Santiago de Cuba, where Spain had mined copper since its initial period of the island's settlement in the early 17th century.

One English businessman who went to Santiago de Cuba in the 1830s was John Hardy. His father was a London-based West India merchant who sent son John to Cuba to recover an outstanding mortgage debt on a property near to El Cobre. While Hardy Junior was visiting the mining area he came across some tailings from the copper mine, and sent them for analysis to see if the copper content was sufficient to warrant investing in the development of the mine.[4] The ore proved to be rich in copper, and Hardy lost no time in finding investors – his father included – who were interested in forming a company to restore and work the mines. Once the company was established, Hardy, with the help of local investor Joaquín Arrieta, acquired a licence from the Governor-General of Cuba, Miguel Tacon,[5] to mine at El Cobre for a period of 10 years.[6]

---

4   Turnbull, David. *Travels in the West. Cuba; with notices of Porto Rico and the slave trade.* London: Longman, Orme, Brown, Green and Longmans, 1840, p.10. Accessed 16 November 2016, https://archive.org/details/travelsinwestcu01davigoog
5   Pérez Drago, Ileana. 'El hierro en la arquitectura colonial habanera. Condicionantes formales, técnicas e históricas.' Tomo 1. PhD diss., Universidad Politécnica de Madrid, 2004, p.20.
6   Turnbull, David. *Travels in the West. Cuba; with notices of Porto Rico and the slave trade.* London: Longman, Orme, Brown, Green and Longmans, 1840, pp.11–12. Accessed 16 November 2016, https://archive.org/details/travelsinwestcu01davigoogIbid

The mine began to operate with some success, but further expansion depended on a much larger investment, and in 1835 Hardy formed a new joint-stock company: La Compañía Consolidada de Minas del Cobre (The Cobre Mines Consolidated Company) known locally as La Compañía Consolidada.[7] The new investors were wealthy British men with longstanding experience in the copper industry.[8] Some had Cornish connections: Charles Pascoe Grenfell (1796–1867) and his half-brother Riversdale William Grenfell (1807–1871) were the sons of Pascoe Grenfell (1761–1838), born in Marazion, west Cornwall. As a young man Pascoe Grenfell had joined the company of Welshman Thomas Williams, and had risen to the position of his principal manager. Williams, a mine owner, had also developed a large Swansea-based copper-smelting business in south Wales, and when the Williams family retired from the copper business in 1825, the Grenfell family continued the industry: they set up Pascoe Grenfell & Sons, owning the Middle and Upper Bank Copper Works which smelted copper in the Lower Swansea Valley.[9] A smelter needs a steady supply of high-grade copper ore to operate profitably, and as El Cobre had the potential to supply Pascoe Grenfell & Sons with the product it required,[10] the Grenfells were willing to invest in La Compañía Consolidada. When the company was launched, almost half of the 12,000 shares offered were retained by the Grenfells and other company directors, while the rest were successfully sold at £40 each.

Other investors began to take an interest in the mineral resources of Cuba. In 1836, El Real de Santiago (The Royal Santiago Mining Company) acquired a licence to mine on land adjacent to La Compañía Consolidada. El Real de Santiago, too, had Cornish connections. One

---

7   Evans, Chris. *Slave Wales: The Welsh and Atlantic Slavery, 1660–1850*. Cardiff: University of Wales Press, 2010, p.120.
8   Evans, Chris. *Carabalí and culíes at El Cobre: African slaves and Chinese indentured labourers in the service of Swansea copper*, p.2. Accessed 16 November 2016, https://www.academia.edu/1889345/_Carabal per centC3 per centAD_and_cul per centC3 per centADes_at_El_Cobre_African_slaves_and_Chinese_indentured_labourers_in_the_service_of_Swansea_copper
9   Ibid.
10 Ibid.

of the investors was Michael Williams (1785–1858) whose family had been involved in Cornish mining since the mid-17th century. The Williamses became one of the wealthiest and most influential families in Cornwall and, like the Grenfells – and sometimes in partnership with them – they expanded their business interests to south Wales and to copper smelting. In 1831, they established a smelting works at Morfa, Swansea, and so, like the Grenfells, their interest in El Cobre's copper was based on their need for a steady supply of high-grade copper ore with which to feed the plant.[11] Other Cornish investors included Colin Harvey, Samuel Stephens, Henry L. Stephens and Francis H. Rodd.[12]

Williams and his partners continued to finance the development of El Real de Santiago. In 1836, Williams invested £35,000 in:

> *sending out experienced persons, opening works, in erecting dwellings, stores, dressing-houses and workshops; and in the purchase of cattle, materials and other effects. The workings in some of the mines has been partially commenced and carried on only to the extent requisite to acquire the legal right, and ascertain the course of the lodes.*[13]

By 1838, having shipped 583 tons of high-grade copper ore valued at nearly £11,500, El Real de Santiago decided to increase its investment and was re-launched as a joint-stock company. The existing investors retained about one-third of the 7,000 shares issued, while the remaining two-thirds were offered to subscribers. The investment capital of El Real de Santiago was set at £210,000.[14] Investment poured into El Cobre,

---

11 Ibid.
12 *Williams family*. Accessed 24 November 2016, http://www.gracesguide.co.uk/Williams_Family
13 British Library Board. 'The copper mines of the Royal Santiago Mining Company.' *Gore's Liverpool General Advertiser*, p.1 (29 March 1838). British Newspaper Archive, accessed 26 November 2016, http://www.britishnewspaperarchive.co.uk/
14 Evans, Chris. *Carabalí and culíes at El Cobre: African slaves and Chinese indentured labourers in the service of Swansea copper*, p.4. Accessed 16 November 2016, https://www.academia.edu/1889345/_Carabal per centC3 per centAD_and_cul per centC3 per centADes_at_El_Cobre_African_slaves_and_Chinese_indentured_labourers_in_the_service_of_Swansea_copper

and by 1851 some thirty-one mining companies, most with British and American investors, were mining in the area.[15]

Mines were established in other parts of Cuba at about the same time. Mexican prospectors found copper near Holguín in the north-east of the island, and set up the San Fernando mine and in 1834, the La Buena Isabella and Perseverencia mines opened in the same area. La Buena Isabella employed Cornish miners in 1835, but closed soon after when the owners ran into financial difficulties. By the early 1840s copper had been found at Bayatabo, which lies near to the north coast port town of Nuevitas. The prospector, George Diston, an American from Boston, secured investment from the Boston-based company, John Simmons and Son, and opened the Marion mine. He brought miners from Cornwall, as did the neighbouring Royal Consolidated Mines of San Fernando, and began shipping copper ore to Liverpool. He built a smelter in Baltimore and had plans to ship the ore from the Marion mine to Baltimore for smelting, but by the early 1850s the mine was failing and had to close.

Several copper mines were established at Manicaragua, which lies up in the Escambray Mountains in the southern part of Villa Clara Province; the most important of these mines were San Fernando and Santa Rosa. The mines were owned by the Cuba Mining Company and financed by Thomas B. Smith and Hezekiah Bradford, both Americans, who employed Cornish mine captain, Matthew Staple of Redruth, and nine Cornish miners. The ore was shipped out of the port of Cienfuegos, but operations came to an end in 1844, when the rich copper lode suddenly ran out. The Cornish miners had a difficult time returning home to Cornwall. They were not given the correct leaving papers and were not allowed to leave. Until their documentation was sorted out they had to stay in the prison at Cienfuegos. The San Fernando mine was bought by the San Fernando Mining and Smelting Company, financed by London-based investors, and in 1854 was put under the management of a Cornish mine captain, Jehu Richards. The mine operated until 1868.[16]

---

15 Waszkis, Helmut. *Mining in the Americas: stories and history.* Cambridge: Woodhead Publishing, 1993, p.27.
16 Schwartz, Sharron P. *The Cornish in Latin America: 'Cousin Jack' and the New World.* Wicklow: The Cornubian Press, 2016, pp.83–84.

With capital in place at the mines of El Cobre, a labour force had to be found to mine the copper resources. The recently freed Kings Slaves were a possibility. In 1801, the Kings Slaves of El Cobre were given their freedom by a Spanish Royal Decree that recognised their liberty, guaranteed them against a return to enslavement and established their right to exploit the local resources.[17] Their history as miners at El Cobre went back to the early 17th century, when the Spanish Crown had awarded the right to mine the area to a private contractor who worked the mines using African slave labour. In 1670, when private interest in the development of the mines had declined to the extent that little copper was being produced, Spain took over the mine and the privately-owned enslaved labourers became the property of the Spanish king: 'the King's Slaves'. When the government failed in its efforts to make the mine profitable, El Cobre began to develop its own small surface mining enterprises, producing enough copper to supply the island. Women played an increasing part in the mining community, and the female King's Slaves became the main, and at times the only, producers of copper in Cuba, helping to create a largely self-sufficient settlement that was unique not only in Cuba but throughout the Caribbean.[18] But while the freed Kings Slaves were experienced miners, their expertise was in very small-scale mining using basic tools, and they did not have the modern technical skills required to work in the large mines. Given their long history of working for themselves, they would also have been unwilling to work for a foreign company under close supervision and for a small wage.

So skilled labour had to come from further afield, and La Compañía Consolidada and El Real de Santiago turned to Cornwall, using the Cornish connections of their directors to help them source the men they

---

17 Evans, Chris. *Carabalí and culíes at El Cobre: African slaves and Chinese indentured labourers in the service of Swansea copper,* p.7. Accessed 16 November 2016, https://www.academia.edu/1889345/_Carabal per centC3 per centAD_and_cul per centC3 per centADes_at_El_Cobre_African_slaves_and_Chinese_indentured_labourers_in_the_service_of_Swansea_copper

18 Díaz, María Elena, 'Mining women, royal slaves: copper mining in colonial Cuba, 1670–1780'. In *Mining women: gender in the development of a global industry, 1670 to 2005,* ed. Jaclyn J. Gier-Viskovatoff and Laurie Mercier, pp.21–25. New York: Palgrave Macmillan, 2006.

needed. Paradoxically, as Cornish mines declined following the discovery and exploitation of overseas mines that could be profitably operated at a lower cost than the mines of Cornwall, Cornish miners found new employment in the mines that had put them out of work.

In 1834, La Compañía Consolidada employed Mine Captain William Reynolds of Redruth to manage the reactivation of the mine and present his findings to potential investors.[19] The choice of mine captain was all-important to the success of any mining venture. Usually chosen from among the working miners, a mine captain was selected for his shrewdness, ability and knowledge of mining, and also because he had gained the respect of the miners. He was responsible for their safety and well-being while at work and, particularly if he was a Methodist lay preacher – which mine captains often were – he was in addition responsible for their spiritual well-being. He was an intermediary between management and men, responsible for enforcing sometimes unpopular decisions and policies, and for achieving profitable returns on whatever was being mined – a requirement which meant constant vigilance over every aspect of the mine's working.[20]

Miners and mechanics were needed to develop the mine, and in 1836 the company employed Alfred Jenkin from Redruth to act as their mine agent. Jenkin was employed by the company until 1839, and during those three years he sent 136 miners and mechanics to Cuba, most from the mining areas of Redruth, Camborne and Illogan.[21] From his base at Trewirgie House in Redruth, Jenkin sent out handbills advertising the employment opportunities offered by the company, interviewed possible recruits, arranged for their medical examinations, set out the terms of their contracts, and organised their transport. Young, sober, single men with no spouse and children to support were preferred and, in August 1836, fifteen miners were contracted for £9 a month each, Jenkin noting:

---

19 Ibid., p.4.
20 *The duties of mine agents [captains]*. Accessed 4 June 2016, http://freepages.genealogy.rootsweb.ancestry.com/~staustell/Word_Doc/Life/Duties per cent20of per cent20a per cent20Mine per cent20Agent.htm
21 Payton, Philip. *The Cornish overseas: the history of Cornwall's 'Great Emigration.'* Fowey: Cornwall Editions, 2005, p.114.

'I have selected them from a considerable number of applicants and trust they will give satisfaction to their employers – they are mostly young men.'[22]

Successful applicants were given a Bible, £10 to outfit themselves and a £10 advance on their salary. They sailed from the Cornish ports of Portreath, Hayle and occasionally Falmouth on the copper barques which sailed to and fro across the Bristol Channel between Cornwall and Swansea, taking Welsh coal to the Cornish mine engines and returning with Cornish copper ore for the Swansea smelting works. When the men arrived in Swansea they were provided with board and lodging until they set sail for Santiago de Cuba, a journey of some six weeks.[23]

El Real de Santiago also looked to Cornwall for its skilled labour supply. In 1838, when the company was ready to expand its operations, the directors noted that all its skilled miners came from the county: 'The present establishment consists of one superintendent [Mr James Treweek, born in Gwennap[24]], one head and two sub-mine captains, thirty-eight miners, one head blacksmith, one head carpenter, all from Cornwall.'[25]

Cornish miners were much sought after for their hard-rock mining skills and there was competition from other Cuban mines, including one Thomas B. Smith from the Cuba Mining Company's San Fernando mine at Manicaragua, to employ them. Jenkin informed his employers at La Compañía Consolidada that, even though he could supply their requirements for miners:

There is a gentleman in this town [Redruth] who has declared his object to engage about 50 miners to go to the island of Cuba on behalf of a New York Company styling themselves the Cuba Mining Company –

---

22 Tangye, Michael. 'Emigration: Cornish miners in Cuba 1836–1838.' In *Old Redruth: original studies of the town's history*, ed. Terry Knight, p.22. Redruth: Redruth Old Cornwall Society, 1992.
23 Ibid., p.23.
24 Email from Lesley Trotter, Institute of Cornish Studies PhD student, dated 30 March 2014.
25 British Library Board. 'The copper mines of the Royal Santiago Mining Company.' *Gore's Liverpool General Advertiser*, p.1 (29 March 1838). British Newspaper Archive, accessed 26 November 2016, http://www.britishnewspaperarchive.co.uk/

his name is Smith, an American. I do not find he has mentioned any terms, but I am informed that he picked up a Cornishman in New York and engaged him at £9 per month, board and lodging.[26]

Not only did Cornwall provide the skilled labour force for the Cuba mines, but it also supplied much of the machinery and supplies the mining companies required. Business was brisk, facilitated by the Spanish government's agreement not to impose import duties on machinery sent from Great Britain to Cuba.[27] Jonathan Stephens, from Ashfield near Falmouth, shipped capstan and whim ropes[28] from Penryn. George Arnall of Redruth made and shipped jigging bottoms and riddles.[29] Bickford and Smith shipped barrels of the latest safety fuse from their factory at Tuckingmill, near Camborne. Harvey's Foundry at Hayle supplied the Cornish beam engine for La Compañía Consolidada at a cost of £1,400. This included the 'rods by which the engine draws water from the shaft and the woodwork of the engine house [including the] beams, floors and stairs,'[30] but not the boiler, which was purchased separately. Jonathan Pearce, a mining engineer employed by Harvey's, sailed to Cuba with the engine to supervise its installation in the engine house and stayed on to maintain it in good working order. Pearce was employed on a three-year contract at £180 per year and received free board and lodging.[31] By 1863,

---

26 Tangye, Michael. 'Emigration: Cornish miners in Cuba 1836–1838.' In *Old Redruth: original studies of the town's history*, ed. Terry Knight, p.22. Redruth: Redruth Old Cornwall Society, 1992.
27 Schwartz, Sharron P. *The Cornish in Latin America: 'Cousin Jack' and the New World*. Wicklow: The Cornubian Press, 2016, p.204.
28 A whim is used to haul mining materials to the surface. It works like a windlass, a horse providing the power and a number of pulleys reducing the load. Around the drum is wound a long rope, with a large bucket attached to each end; as an empty bucket is lowered, so a full bucket is raised.
29 Jigging bottoms, or beds, are used to separate particles in the ore, based on their density. The particles are often crushed and sieved before being fed over the jig bed – usually a screen. The particles are then pushed upward by pulsing water so they are suspended within the water. When the water leaves the jig bed the particles again settle on the jig bed but now the denser particles – in this case the ore containing copper – settle at the bottom. The copper ore can then be extracted from the jig and the rest discarded as tailings.
30 Tangye, Michael. 'Emigration: Cornish miners in Cuba 1836–1838.' In *Old Redruth: original studies of the town's history*, ed. Terry Knight, p.25. Redruth: Redruth Old Cornwall Society, 1992.
31 Ibid., p.25.

La Compañía Consolidada had imported eleven steam engines, while El Real de Santiago and the San José and the Cubana Cobrera Mining Company mines had each brought in several additional engines.[32]

When the Cornish miners landed at Santiago de Cuba after their long voyage from Swansea they, like James Whitburn, liked what they first saw of the island although they too felt the unaccustomed tropical heat. The engine mechanic James Whitburn from Gwennap was one of a group of miners who sailed for Cuba in early June 1836, and arriving in Santiago's harbour in late July he wrote in his diary that he was not impressed with the transport arrangements that took them from the harbour to El Cobre:

It is a pretty country but very hot. We started from St. Jago on Monday evening at about 6 o'clock. I had a bad horse and was thrown and had a narrow escape for my life, but through the mercies of God we arrived at Cobre at about 8 o'clock that night.[33]

The Cornishmen must indeed have felt the heat: June through to October is the hottest season of the year in much of the Caribbean, a time when the cooling trade winds scarcely make a breeze. Providing transport for the 12-mile (19 km) journey between the mines and the port at Santiago de Cuba was a challenge for the mining companies of El Cobre. Both the employees and the partly processed copper ore were transported on the backs of horses, mules and – perhaps more surprisingly – camels.[34]

Machinery and supplies made the same laborious trek from the port to the mine. David Turnbull, the British abolitionist and writer, who visited El Real de Santiago in 1838, remarked that the downtrodden horses and mules would survive much better if they:

---

32 Schwartz, Sharron P. *The Cornish in Latin America: 'Cousin Jack' and the New World.* Wicklow: The Cornubian Press, 2016, p.204.
33 Whitburn, James. *A Cornish man in Cuba: transcript of a diary of his visit to Cuba 1836–1838.* np: Whitburn, nd, p.2.
34 Waszkis, Helmut. *Mining in the Americas: stories and history.* Cambridge: Woodhead Publishing, 1993, p.17.

The camels can be seen in the bottom left-hand corner of this 1853 image of El Cobre. May, B. y Ca. Santuario de El Cobre, Santiago de Cuba, taken from the *Mapa Historico Pintoresco Moderno de la Isla De Cuba*.

possessed the prudence or the instinct of the camel, which teaches it to lie down when overloaded, and refuse to proceed until its burden is so reduced to make it compatible with its strength. The poor horse, however, and even the mule, stagger on to the last, under the excessive burdens which are heaped upon them, the average[load of copper ore] not being less than 224 English pounds.[35]

Fortunately for both men and beasts, in 1843 a railway was built between the mines and Santiago de Cuba.[36]

Whitburn's positive impressions did not last long. Like many of the Cornish miners, he was a devout Methodist, and in common with many

---

35 Turnbull, David. *Travels in the West. Cuba; with notices of Porto Rico and the slave trade*. London: Longman, Orme, Brown, Green and Longmans, 1840, p.13. Accessed 16 November 2016, https://archive.org/details/travelsinwestcu01davigoog
36 Waszkis, Helmut. *Mining in the Americas: stories and history*. Cambridge: Woodhead Publishing, 1993, p.17.

of his fellow workmen was horrified by the religious observances of El Cobre's community. In addition to its importance as a copper mining centre, El Cobre was renowned as the Roman Catholic sanctuary of Nuestra Señora de la Caridad del Cobre (Our Lady of Charity of Cobre), the patron saint of Cuba. At El Cobre, as in other parts of Cuba, Roman Catholic beliefs mixed with the beliefs of Afro-Cuban slaves and their descendants, and to many Cubans Our Lady of Charity was – and still is – both Our Lady, Mother of Jesus and Ochún (or Oshún), the Yoruban Mother Goddess.[37] Little wonder, then, that Whitburn was confused by the worship that took place on what was probably the feast day of Our Lady of Guadalupe, patron saint of the Americas. He writes:

> *about a fortnight before Christmas a great number of people attend the church at 4 o'clock in the morning. The Priest also attends. They continue there for an hour or so. The Priest commences with reading something in Latin ... After the Priest had read for sometime I was surprised to hear several rattles break out all at once, with a tremendous noise, while others were blowing into something which made a noise similar to that of a bullock horn [a conch shell?] in England and others shrieking and yelling while the Priest was sanctifying the wine. After repeating this twice or thrice – and I was considering how different from thee oh Happy England – the meeting ended.*[38]

No provision was made for the Methodist miners to worship as they had at home in Cornwall, but they continued to observe Sunday as a day of worship – and even during working hours, if the spirit moved them, they would lay down their tools and together pray, sing hymns and listen to the words of one of the Methodist lay preachers among them.[39] One of these preachers was William Whitburn. His religious activities were

---

37 Díaz, María Elena. *The virgin, the king, and the royal slaves of El Cobre: negotiating freedom in colonial Cuba, 1670–1780*. Stanford: Stanford University Press, 2000, p.1.
38 Whitburn, James. *A Cornish man in Cuba: transcript of a diary of his visit to Cuba 1836–1838.* np: Whitburn, nd, p.3.
39 Tangye, Michael. 'Emigration: Cornish miners in Cuba 1836–1838.' In *Old Redruth: original studies of the town's history*, ed. Terry Knight, p.25. Redruth: Redruth Old Cornwall Society, 1992.

thought to cause so much disruption to the mine's production that the directors wrote to their agent, Alfred Jenkin, to complain. Perhaps Jenkin understood that being able to practise their religion freely helped the miners to work steadily in a culture which was strange to them, and he put in a good word for Whitburn, writing that he hoped they would not be prevented:

> *from meeting together in an orderly manner and at suitable seasons for the purpose of worshipping the Almighty in the manner which may be most in accordance with their views and feelings. I have known Will Whitburn for seven years – his wife was a servant in my family. It may not be amiss for one to say that nearly all such of the laboring class in this part of Cornwall as have any regard for religion, are either members of one or other of the Methodist Societies, or be in the habit of attending their meetings.*[40]

If El Cobre's religious practices were alien to the newly arrived Cornish miners, so was the use of enslaved labour in the mines. David Turnbull, the abolitionist who had remarked on the sensibility of camels, noted with dismay:

> *that the labourers employed were nearly nine hundred in number; but to our great regret we found that nearly half of them were slaves, some the property of the Mining Company, and others hired out, as is not uncustomary, from their owners in the neighbourhood.*[41]

The enslaved in the British Caribbean were emancipated in 1834, but although under the terms of the Anglo-Spanish Treaty of 1817 shipping enslaved people to Cuba was illegal, keeping them was not. The treaty was in any case widely ignored, as following the collapse of the sugar industry on neighbouring Saint-Domingue during the Haitian Revolution, the

---

40 Ibid., pp.25–26.
41 Turnbull, David. *Travels in the West. Cuba; with notices of Porto Rico and the slave trade.* London: Longman, Orme, Brown, Green and Longmans, 1840., pp.8–9. Accessed 16 November 2016, https://archive.org/details/travelsinwestcu01davigoog

Cuban sugar industry was booming and enslaved labour was in great demand.[42] In addition, although the French coffee planters who had fled Haiti for eastern Cuba during and after the Haitian Revolution had brought their enslaved workers with them, once they had established successful coffee plantations in the high sierra surrounding Santiago they needed additional enslaved labour.[43] With enslaved men, women and children being imported for both the sugar and coffee industries, there were plenty of them available for the use of the British mining companies. So John Hardy Junior, who was both a major shareholder in La Compañía Consolidada and the British consul in Santiago, had to choose his words carefully when asked by the British government to investigate and report on the illegal import of enslaved workers and their use by British mining companies. In 1836, his company was employing 422 slaves, but Hardy managed to make the unlikely case that all the enslaved employed in the mines were not imported but were locally born, or they had been brought to Cuba before the trade had been made illegal.[44]

The recently formed British and Foreign Anti-Slavery Society sought legal advice on the possibility of prosecuting British companies who used enslaved labour. British lawyers thought this was not possible: the trafficking of enslaved people was illegal, but they could still be kept and used in countries not under British jurisdiction. The 1843 Act for the More Effectual Suppression of the Slave Trade, known as the Brougham Act, did little to alter the situation, as there was nothing in its provisions that made the hiring of enslaved workers from local owners illegal. The mining companies went ahead and hired the manpower they needed, be thatlabour sourced from enslaved people illegally imported or already resident in Cuba.[45]

---

42 Evans, Chris. 'El Cobre: Cuban ore and the globalization of Swansea copper, 1830–1870.' *Welsh History Review/Cylchgrawn Hanes Cymru*, p.121 (Vol.27, No.1, 2014).
43 Evans, Chris. *Carabalí and culíes at El Cobre: African slaves and Chinese indentured labourers in the service of Swansea copper*, p.8. Accessed 16 November 2016, https://www.academia.edu/1889345/_Carabal per centC3 per centAD_and_cul per centC3 per centADes_at_El_Cobre_African_slaves_and_Chinese_indentured_labourers_in_the_service_of_Swansea_copper
44 Ibid., pp.9–10.
45 Evans, Chris. *The British slaves of Latin America*, pp.1–3. Accessed 12 December 2016, https://www.academia.edu/497596/The_British_slaves_of_Latin_America

The miners from Cornwall were unprepared for the realities of enslaved labour, and James Whitburn writes in his diary:

The flogging of the negroes in this country is most cruel. I have seen them laid on the ground, sometimes tied to a ladder, and at other times held by one man at the foot and another at the head, while another Negro with a whip 10 or 12 ft. long from the end of the stick to the point of the lash, gives the Negro confined 25 blows or I may say, cuts with the aforementioned whip, and, while every blow rattles almost as loud as a gun, I have seen I think from 15 blows out of 25 to make cuts in the flesh from 8 to 12 inches long and open as if done with a knife, while the poor fellow shrieks and twingles[46] as if at the point of death.[47]

In the short term the combination of Cornish mining expertise, Cornish steam technology and increased enslaved labour resulted in increased production and profit for the mine owners. In 1837, La Compañía Consolidada produced 5,969 tonnes of copper ore, in 1839, 13,874 tonnes and in 1841 over 25,000 tonnes.[48] The mines of El Cobre were booming, and an 1871 woodcut, perhaps taken from an earlier image when the mines were flourishing, shows the sanctuary of Nuestra Señora de la Caridad del Cobre barely visible among the mining infrastructure that surrounds it.

While Cornish miners found both enslavement and unfamiliar religious practices difficult to accept, their greatest challenge was in coming to terms with the likelihood that they would catch yellow fever, malaria, cholera or typhoid and not survive the length of their contract. Like the interior of British Guiana, the area around Santiago de Cuba gained a reputation as a destination from which you might not return. James Whitburn notes in his diary entries for August 1836: 'Richard Trestrail died after being confined eight days with fever.'[49] In July 1837 he writes:

---

46 A word used in Cornwall, meaning 'wriggle' or 'writhe'.
47 Whitburn, James. *A Cornish man in Cuba: transcript of a diary of his visit to Cuba 1836–1838.* np: Whitburn, nd, p.4.
48 Evans, Chris. 'El Cobre: Cuban ore and the globalization of Swansea copper, 1830–1870.' *Welsh History Review/Cylchgrawn Hanes Cymru*, p.124 (Vol.27, No.1, 2014).
49 Whitburn, James. *A Cornish man in Cuba: transcript of a diary of his visit to Cuba 1836–1838.* np: Whitburn, nd, p.3.

An 1871 wood engraving of El Cobre copper mines.

Ben Evans died, one of my particular friends, and eight others all in 12 days which caused me almost to despair of ever seeing my native country and friends again, that the Lord applied a word in season, it was this, 'why should a living man complain.' Our working stopped this day.[50]

Of the twenty-four miners who sailed from Portreath in June 1837, eleven were dead within six months: John Clemo, John Harry, William Gribble, William Tangye, Martin Andrew, William Bishop, Jonathan Harry, William Blight and William Carpenter, Jeremiah Hampton and William Curnow. As was the custom, when Curnow died his clothes and watch were sold at public auction and the proceeds sent home to his family in Ludgvan.[51] Whitburn writes:

---

50 Ibid., p.5.
51 Tangye, Michael. 'Emigration: Cornish miners in Cuba 1836–1838.' In *Old Redruth: original studies of the town's history*, ed. Terry Knight, p.24. Redruth: Redruth Old Cornwall Society, 1992.

This day we went round to see the sick. Sunday morning. On entering the House of the men belonging to Mr. Mitchell's establishment I found a man acting as auctioneer selling the clothes of some or all of the dead, while many who appeared like ghosts who ought to be in bed, offering and buying what no person would ever think them likely to wear.[52]

The modest one-storey houses where the miners lived, close to the mines on the edge of town, were of a typically Spanish design: constructed of wood and adobe, painted in bright colours and roofed with tiles.[53] Windows were protected with iron bars and adjustable wooden shutters which could be closed at night, when it rained, or when a hurricane threatened. The only ventilation the houses received was from whatever breeze blew in through the windows where, as the windows had no glass, mosquitoes, including those carrying yellow fever, also entered, especially as the sun went down in the early evening and as it rose again in the morning.

High levels of sickness and death created a financial burden for the mining companies, especially when miners fell ill or died soon after their arrival and so had not repaid any of the costs incurred for their passage. John Hardy Junior, with profit foremost in his mind, began to cut the wages of sick men, and was reluctant to have them shipped back on the copper barques bound for Swansea: it was cheaper to bury a man at El Cobre than pay the cost of the return passage.[54] As the number of deaths rose, it became necessary to make a Protestant cemetery available, so that non-Roman Catholic members of the community could be buried in the proper manner.

Some medically unfit miners did receive permission to make the voyage back via Swansea to Cornwall. La Compañía Consolidada's Agent, Alfred Jenkin, reports on four of the returnees:

---

52 Whitburn, James. *A Cornish man in Cuba: transcript of a diary of his visit to Cuba 1836–1838*. np: Whitburn, nd, p.5.
53 *The Cornish in Latin America: Cobre*. Accessed 8 April 2017, https://projects.exeter.ac.uk/cornishlatin/cobre.htm
54 Schwartz, Sharron P. *The Cornish in Latin America: 'Cousin Jack' and the New World*. Wicklow: The Cornubian Press, 2016, p.122.

James Rule and John Pearce have returned from Cuba with certificates stating they were discharged on account of ill-health and claimed three month's wages from the time they ceased work according to the agreement of employment. I am sorry to hear such a poor account of William Thomas and Edward Simons. Captain James Reynolds says that William Thomas was a fine healthy looking man.[55]

James Whitburn, his young brother-in-law – also called James Whitburn – and Richard Roberts were all returned to Cornwall as medically unfit. On his arrival at Swansea, Whitburn the diarist heard that his brother-in-law had died during the voyage home. He writes:

It was here I got the particulars concerning the death of my dear Boy. He appeared to be quite merry and active the first two or three days and served as Interpreter for some Spanish Ladies bound for St. Domingo. But the weather blowed hard and he got seasick which appeared brought on dysentery. He gradually grew worse ... [and] died on the 14th day after they left St. Jago ... The day following, after the usual ceremonies observed at sea, he was committed to the mighty deep ... I often think of the kind and wishful look of my dear Boy when I was sick, and the attention paid to me by him when I could not talk the language.[56]

Whitburn returned to his wife and children in Devoran, where he recovered his health and went on to live to the age of 84.[57]

As news of the likelihood of sudden death at El Cobre spread throughout the mining districts of Cornwall, Cornishmen began to look for alternative destinations. Jenkin was aware of the problem, and wrote: 'The sickness and deaths which have occurred at Cobre since the

---

55 Tangye, Michael. 'Emigration: Cornish miners in Cuba 1836–1838'. In *Old Redruth: original studies of the town's history*, ed. Terry Knight, p.24. Redruth: Redruth Old Cornwall Society, 1992.
56 Whitburn, James. *A Cornish man in Cuba: transcript of a diary of his visit to Cuba 1836–1838*. np: Whitburn, nd, p.9.
57 Ibid., pp.9–10.

commencement of the present year will, I expect, cause some shyness in the minds of our miners as to going there.'[58]

There were still rich veins of copper to be mined, so La Compañía Consolidada raised its wages to persuade miners to go to El Cobre: they were to be paid not £9 but £12 a month.[59] The high death rate meant that the supply of miners had to be continually replenished, and while Cornish migration to the El Cobre mines was greatest during 1837 and 1838, Cornish miners continued to travel to Cuba until the late 1860s to meet the need of the mining companies for skilled labour. The advertisements placed in local Cornish newspapers were at pains to point out that not all mining locations in Cuba had the same health risks as El Cobre. In January 1842, the *West Briton* carried notice of an employment opportunity for a mining engineer:

> *Wanted to proceed immediately to Habana, in the Island of Cuba, a MINING ENGINEER, competent to superintend the workings of a Copper Mine, situated within eight or ten miles of the city of Habana [La Habana, or Havana], and in one of the most healthy parts of the Island, which, from its elevation and being within reach of the daily sea breeze, is free from the influence of the yellow fever, which has rendered the neighbourhood of St. Jago [Santiago] de Cuba so dreaded.*[60]

Cornish miners were supplemented by miners from Wales. A number of Welsh investors had shares in the mines of El Cobre and knew how to source local miners, who even if they lacked the experience of many of the Cornish miners were less expensive to contract, and if they became sick or died while working were cheaper to replace.

The miners were not alone in facing the health challenges of working at El Cobre. The crews of the copper barques that sailed between Swansea and Santiago de Cuba faced similar risks. In the mid-19th century the

---

58 Tangye, Michael.'Emigration: Cornish miners in Cuba 1836–1838.' In *Old Redruth: original studies of the town's history*, ed. Terry Knight, p.24. Redruth: Redruth Old Cornwall Society, 1992.
59 Ibid., p.24.
60 'Wanted to proceed immediately to Habana ...' *West Briton* (7 January 1842). From the Courtney Library Cornish Newspaper Index.

price of copper was high and Swansea was responsible for smelting over 40 per cent of the world production of copper. The cost of freighting the ore over long distances only became feasible after Britain lowered the import tax on copper ore in the late 1820s,[61] making it profitable for ships to transport ore to Swansea from wherever there was a copper mine: from Cuba, Jamaica, and Virgin Gorda, from Mexico, Colombia, Peru, Chile, Australia and New Zealand. The barques were adapted in Swansea by adding strongly timbered and internally divided bulkheads, which improved the stability of the ore cargo in rolling seas.[62] Profit was all important, and the sea shanty 'Cobre Days' expresses the well-founded belief that shareholders' profit came before the health of mine employees:

> Oh the *Hecla* is a good old barque on the Swansea–Cuba run,
> She brings copper ore from Cobre, every trip 400 tons,
> For the cargo on our latest trip, there's a bitter price to pay,
> Oh don't let us have to face more Cobre days.
> (Chorus)
> Cobre days, oh Cobre days,
> Cobre days, oh Cobre days,
> Oh don't let us have to face more Cobre days.
> We anchored off the Mumbles, and we knew that it was bad,
> We'd lost three men in the tropics, and a fourth was raving mad,
> But the Cobre men said 'Bring her in, we've shareholders to pay'
> So the scene was set for deadly Cobre days.
> (Chorus)
> So we tied up at the Cobre wharf under hot blue sunny skies,
> The men swarmed all around her, and so did all the flies,
> But working hot and thirsty seemed to sap our strength away,
> As we staggered through those weary Cobre days.
> (Chorus)
> And soon the folk were shivering, despite the sticky heat,

---

61 Evans, Chris and Olivia Saunders. 'Copper ore: an unlikely global commodity.' *Commodity Histories*. Accessed 20 May 2014. http://www.commodityhistories.org/research/copper-ore-unlikely-global-commodity
62 Email from Chris Evans, 3 November 2014.

> The sorters and the grinders, the patrolman on his beat,
> They sickened and they perished, turning yellow as they lay,
> Oh don't let us have to face more Cobre days.
> (Chorus)
> And you who give the orders, you who count up all the costs,
> Can you enter in your ledgers all the lives that have been lost?
> When you make your next decision, when you've had your final say,
> Will we have to face another Cobre day?
> (Chorus) [63]

In addition to the high death rate, during the 1840s several other factors began to impact negatively on the El Cobre mining companies profit margins.

One was the passage of several particularly strong hurricanes, including those of September 1842, October 1844 and October 1846. Cuba has long suffered from the passage of frequent hurricanes, which typically hit the island towards the end of the June-to-November hurricane season. In the 19th century there was no meteorological service to provide advance warning of an impending hurricane, so mining companies would have been unable to make any preparations to prevent, or at least minimise, the storm damage caused by the flooding and destruction of the mining infrastructure, and the disruption it caused to the mining operations and the shipment of ore.[64]

Another factor was an increase in unrest amongst the enslaved and a greater demand for freedom, which was supported by a growing abolitionist movement.[65] Anticipating the end of enslavement, some planters began to hire Chinese indentured labourers, a practice that the El Cobre mines would also introduce. In theory, indentured labourers, largely from southern China, were supposed to sign contracts of their

---

63 'Cobre Days'. Accessed 9 December 2016, http://www.shanty.org.uk/pdfbox/andy_mckay/CobreDays.pdf.
64 Pérez, Louis A. *Winds of Change: Hurricanes and the Transformation of Nineteenth-Century Cuba*. Chapel Hill, University of North Carolina Press, 2001, p.17.
65 *Cuba and the slave trade*. Accessed 8 December 2016, http://www.tracesofthetrade.org/guides-and-materials/historical/cuba-and-the-slave-trade

own free will, and on completion of their contract term to have their return passage paid. But in practice, they were often abducted, forced to sign a contract, and not allowed to return to their place of origin.[66]

A third was the growing strength of the movement for Cuban independence from Spain. Unrest was expressed in several uprisings of popular feeling. One of the most significant was the 1843–1844 Conspiración de La Escalera (the Ladder Conspiracy) which took its name from the torture method used on captured conspirators, during which they were tied to a ladder and whipped until they either confessed or died. Not just free blacks and slaves but also white intellectuals and professionals took part in the conspiracy, which was put down with brutal repression: about 300 died from torture, 78 were executed, more than 600 were imprisoned, and over 400 were expelled from the island. Unrest continued throughout the 1850s and into the 1860s, as local planters and business owners demanded social and economic reform from the Spanish government.

There was unrest among the Cornish miners, too, at El Cobre. In 1843, a number of them went on strike for better wages. They were arrested, and when they were released some of them became violently drunk, fighting and causing disruption in the community. Mine managers who until then had preferred to employ young single men with no family responsibilities began to reason that miners who came with their families might lead a more stable existence and be a more reliable source of skilled labour. So married men were encouraged to come, and despite the health risks of working at El Cobre, some of the Cornish employees began to bring their wives and children to the island. Senior employees, such as James Treweek at El Real de Santiago, having brought wife and family to Cuba were given relatively comfortable accommodation, and Treweek added two daughters to his family during their stay.[67] Having

---

66 Evans, Chris. *Carabalí and culies at El Cobre: African slaves and Chinese indentured labourers in the service of Swansea copper.* Accessed 16 November 2016, https://www.academia.edu/1889345/_Carabal per centC3 per centAD_and_cul per centC3 per centADes_at_El_Cobre_African_slaves_and_Chinese_indentured_labourers_in_the_service_of_Swansea_copper

67 Based on information provided by Lesley Trotter, Institute of Cornish Studies PhD student, in an attachment to an email dated 30 March 2014.

worked in South America and Jamaica, the mine agent John Holman arrived in Cuba with his wife and family in 1835, where his wife gave birth to a daughter and a son. Similarly, Richard May, a master blacksmith born in the village of Tregony, near Truro, took his wife to Cuba, where his first three children were born.[68] Despite the challenges, many Cornish miners managed to live as a family in Cuba, supported by Cornishwomen capable of accompanying their husbands wherever they found a job, bearing their children, and bringing those children up in an unfamiliar environment.

The stability of the skilled work force might have improved, but by the late 1840s the mining companies were facing a more serious challenge than labour unrest: the international price of copper, which began to fall. It was no longer economical to ship copper ore across the ocean to Swansea, and the mines began to operate at a loss. At El Real de Santiago, the mine began working at a loss in 1848,[69] and following the collapse of the mine's engine shaft the company was unable to continue. The mine closed in 1858.[70] La Compañía Consolidada continued to function, but in 1865, as copper prices continued to fall ever lower, the company operated at a serious loss for the first time. In addition, after a long period of drought the Cobre river began to dry up. The river ran through the mining area, and its water was essential both for the ore-dressing operations and to provide steam for the Cornish engines. There were also bitter disagreements between La Compañía Consolidada and the owners of the railway that ran from the mines to the port at Santiago de Cuba.[71]

Meanwhile, the Independence movement continued to gain strength.

---

68 Ibid.
69 Piggot, Aaron Snowden. *The chemistry and metallurgy of copper including a description of the principal copper mines of the United States and other countries*. Philadelphia: Lindsay and Blakiston, 1858, p.215. Accessed 10 December 2016, https://play.google.com/books/reader?id=d5ZEAAAAIAAJ&printsec=frontcover&output=reader&hl=en&pg=GBS.PA30.
70 Evans, Chris. *Carabalí and culíes at El Cobre: African slaves and Chinese indentured labourers in the service of Swansea copper*, p.17. Accessed 16 November 2016, https://www.academia.edu/1889345/_Carabal per centC3 per centAD_and_cul per centC3 per centADes_at_El_Cobre_African_slaves_and_Chinese_indentured_labourers_in_the_service_of_Swansea_copper
71 Waszkis, Helmut. *Mining in the Americas: stories and history*. Cambridge: Woodhead Publishing, 1993, p.17.

In May 1865, the Cuban elite made specific demands of their colonial masters: tariff reform, Cuban representation in Parliament, judicial equality with Spaniards, and full enforcement of the banning of the trade in enslaved people. Spain's response was to attempt to repress all attempts at liberal reform and increase the tax on local planters and businesses. This caused widespread discontent, especially among the powerful plantation and estate owners in eastern Cuba. It was here that Cuba began, in 1868, to fight for its independence in earnest, led by Carlos Manuel de Céspedes, a wealthy plantation owner from Bayamo, a city about 60 miles (97 km) from El Cobre. The Cornish engineer Edward Hodge noted that the El Cobre mine workers and their families were constantly finding themselves caught in the fighting between the Spanish and Independentista forces. When the monthly payroll for the mines arrived in the port of Santiago it was a target for the Independentistas, and it became a nightmare to move the money from the port to the accounting office. Mine officials resorted to transporting the money in hidden money belts. Matters deteriorated further when the five bridges that carried the railway from the port to the mines were destroyed.[72] La Compañía Consolidada, already operating at a loss, and unable to cope with the continuing fall in copper prices, did not survive the dislocation brought by the outbreak of the war. The mine ceased operation in 1869.[73]

The first war between the Independentistas and Spain lasted for ten years, disrupting not only the operations of the remaining mining companies but the economy of the island in general. After heavy fighting and loss of life, the war ended in failure for the Independentistas.[74] So among some of the Independentistas there was a growing interest in inviting the United States to intervene. But their second attempt to fight

---

72 Schwartz, Sharron P. *The Cornish in Latin America: 'Cousin Jack' and the New World.* Wicklow: The Cornubian Press, 2016, pp.114–115.
73 Evans, Chris. *Carabalí and culies at El Cobre: African slaves and Chinese indentured labourers in the service of Swansea copper*, p.18. Accessed 16 November 2016, https://www.academia.edu/1889345/_Carabal per centC3 per centAD_and_cul per centC3 per centADes_at_El_Cobre_African_slaves_and_Chinese_indentured_labourers_in_the_service_of_Swansea_copper
74 *History of the Cuban liberation wars.* Accessed 10 December 2016, http://www.cubagenweb.org/mil/war-hist.htm

for independence, the 1879–1880 Guerra Chiquita, or Small War, also ended in defeat. The third attempt became, after the intervention of the United States, the Spanish–American War; this gave Cuba independence, but only after Cuba had signed the Platt Amendment with the United States. This stipulated seven conditions for the withdrawal of United States troops remaining in Cuba, one of which allowed the United States to intervene unilaterally in Cuban affairs. United States investment in Cuba subsequently increased which, in the mining sector, favoured the development of United States-owned mines. In 1903, La Compañía Consolidada reopened as an American company.[75]

While most of the Cornish employees left Cuba after the closure of El Real de Santiago and La Compañía Consolidada, there were some who, despite the challenges, decided to make Cuba their home. John Harvey, a mining engineer born in Redruth in about 1820, is an example. He married Jane Kemp, also from Redruth, and in 1855 the family moved to El Cobre, where John worked as resident agent for La Compañía Consolidada. Having spent some years in Cuba, the couple converted to Roman Catholicism, re-baptising into the Roman Catholic faith their seven children who had been born in England. An eighth child, Carlos de la Caridad, was born at El Cobre in 1861. As the sons grew to working age, they joined their father at La Compañía Consolidada. After the death of his first wife, John Harvey married Dolores Guerra y Toledo, a widow who had previously married a Mr Husband, also once employed at the El Cobre mines.[76] The family remained in Cuba. John Harvey's daughter Jane married Edward Hodge at El Cobre, and their children were born there. John Harvey's son Alberto married Juana Guerra y Toledo (possibly related to his step-mother) in El Cobre, and their children, too, were born there. Alberto Harvey's daughter, Isabel Juana de la Caridad Harvey y Guerra, later married Luis del Castillo y Jimenez in Santiago de Cuba, where the family settled.

After its reopening in 1903, El Cobre continued to operate for almost

---

75 Waszkis, Helmut. *Mining in the Americas: stories and history.* Cambridge: Woodhead Publishing, 1993, p.17.
76 Was this perhaps the Edward Husband who was contracted by Colonel Heneken to report on the copper ores of El Platanito in the Dominican Republic?

100 years, but it never flourished as it had in the middle of the 19th century, when Cornish investors and Cornish skilled labour did so much to develop its potential. El Cobre finally closed in 2001, and although in recent years there have been government plans to reopen the mine, or to develop it as a tourist attraction, at the time of writing it remains closed.

In the mid-1850s, as the mines of El Cobre were beginning to face these challenges, there was a renewed interest in mining the mineral resources of the Dominican Republic on the neighbouring island of Hispaniola. Colonel T.S. Heneken, an Englishman who for some years had lived in Pontón[77] near the old mining area around the town of Concepción de La Vega, spearheaded the surveying efforts. Heneken was a geologist and a Fellow of the Geological Society of London,[78] and it was to this well-respected organisation that he presented his findings in 1854.[79] Like his near-contemporary, Charles Barrington Brown, who had completed a geological survey of British Guiana, Heneken was sufficiently encouraged by his findings to invest in the potential of the country's mineral resources. He contracted two Cornish mine captains, John Pooley and Thomas Husband, to report on the copper lodes of El Platanito estate.[80] Pooley and Husband supported Colonel Heneken's findings, which were backed up by: 'the reports of Professor Ansted and of Don Manuel Fernandez de Castro, Inspector General of the Cuba Mines, commissioned by the Spanish government.'[81]

The Spanish government was involved in the surveying, as by 1863 the Dominican Republic was once again in Spanish possession. The Spanish government reports were in turn supported by:

> *those eminent mining authorities, Mr. Josiah H. Hitchins [from Devon], Mr. Adam Murray, Mr. Ivan Hopkins, and Captain*

---

77 Ibid., p.3.
78 *Quarterly Journal of the Geological Society of London.* (Vol.10, 1854). Accessed 21 September 2016, https://babel.hathitrust.org/cgi/pt?id=mdp.39015006918091;view=1up;seq=8
79 Ibid., p.vii, p.xlix.
80 British Library Board. 'Copper mines in Santo Domingo.' *Dundee People's Journal*, p.3 (5 September 1863). British Newspaper Archive, accessed 21 September 2016. http://www.britishnewspaperarchive.co.uk/
81 Ibid., p.3.

Sampson Vivian [a Cornishman from St Austell] – the two latter having had extensive copper-mining experience in the western hemisphere, tropical as well as northern.[82]

A sample of the copper ores 'from the eight copper lodes and their feeders at El Platanito,'[83] was sent for analysis to a smelting company in Swansea, and met with approval. Based on the positive analysis and earlier report, the Platano Mining Company (Limited) was formed and shares floated: 'to purchase the freehold estate of El Platinito [sic] and realise its mineral wealth.'[84] John Pooley functioned as the mine's captain for a short period: his memorial in Ludgvan Parish Church notes that he was 'sometimes Captain of the Coobre [sic] mine in Santo Domingo'[85] before his death in 1864.[86] In spite of the widespread optimism that a profitable mining business could be established, the Platano enterprise was short-lived.

Colonel Heneken continued in his efforts to develop copper mining in the Dominican Republic but, perhaps because he was trying to encourage new investment at a time when the international price of copper was already falling, he failed. When in 1871 the United States Senate was considering the Dominican Republic's request for the United States to take over possession of the country, the Vermont Senator, Justin C. Morell, urged caution on taking an optimistic view of the potential for the United States to develop a profitable mining business in the country. He thought it proper to state:

---

82 British Library Board. 'Copper mines in Santo Domingo.' *Manchester Courier and Lancashire General Advertiser*, p.5 (5 September 1863). British Newspaper Archive, accessed 21 September 2016. http://www.britishnewspaperarchive.co.uk/
83 British Library Board. 'Copper mines in Santo Domingo.' *Dundee People's Journal*, p.3 (5 September 1863). British Newspaper Archive, accessed 21 September 2016. http://www.britishnewspaperarchive.co.uk/
84 Ibid., p.3.
85 The El Cobre copper mine is in Cuba, not the Dominican Republic. Captain Pooley does not appear to have worked in Cuba, but, as the word 'cobre' is Spanish for copper, perhaps this just means that he worked 'in a copper mine' in the Dominican Republic.
86 Cornwall Online Parish Clerks. *The parish of Ludgven*. Accessed 20 September 2016, http://www.cornwall-opc.org/Par_new/l_m/ludgven.php

[as] a warning to such as may be tempted to embark capital in Dominican mining enterprises ...that Mr. Heneken, an English gentleman who resided in this country for more than thirty years, was constantly engaged in visiting all parts of the island ... but it proved to be labor lost. He died about five years ago, impoverished and disappointed.[87]

The Cornish contribution to the development of copper mining in the Dominican Republic was, compared with Cuba, short-lived and at an individual level. Mining would not contribute substantially to the local economy until the latter part of the 20th century, when nickel, gold, silver, bauxite, amber, salt and gypsum all became important mineral resources.

---

87   Morrill, Justin S. *Annexation of Santo Domingo. Speech ... delivered in the Senate of the United States, April 7, 1871*. Washington, DC, F. and J. Rives and George A. Bailey, 1871. Accessed 21 September 2016, https://books.google.com.agbooks?id=zAvSwFPK kckC&dq=speech+justin+s+morrill+santo+domingo+1871&source=gbs_navlinks_s

9

Copper and Guano: the Mines of Virgin Gorda and Sombrero[1]

When Peter J. Minvielle arrived at the south-eastern tip of the small island of Virgin Gorda and stood on the windblown and desolate point now called Coppermine Point he was not impressed by what he saw. Barbados-born and accustomed to the relatively more sophisticated delights of that island, in 1835[2] he had been employed as resident mine agent by the Virgin Gorda Mining Company, a syndicate of English investors led by John Whitley, a senior partner in the Liverpool law firm of John Whitley & Co. Minvielle's task was to clear and develop the area the company planned to develop, which comprised 190 acres of freehold land, about 800 acres of leased land and some old mine workings.

The point had a long mining heritage. In 1493, when Christopher Columbus anchored off the point, he noticed the copper staining the low cliffs facing the sea and recognised it as the outcrop of a copper lode. It had first been mined by the island's Amerindian inhabitants,[3] then by early Spanish colonisers and in the early 18th century by an unknown group of miners,[4] possibly Dutch.

---

1 See Appendix 9 for the background history of Virgin Gorda.
2 Briggs, Lin and Simon Chapman. 'Scenes of Copper Point mine.' *Cornish Mining*, p.18 (Winter 2013).
3 Heritage Tourism Consulting for National Parks Trust. *Management plan [for] Copper Mine Point, Virgin Gorda, British Virgin Islands*, p.4. Road Town: National Parks Trust, December 1995.
4 Birchall, Frank and Margaret Birchall. 'The Virgin Gorda copper mine, British Virgin Islands.' *Journal of the Trevithick Society*, p.23. (No.20, 1993).

When Minvielle had finished preparing the site, he reported to the company on the derelict appearance of the area:

> *the mine hadn't been worked [for] 105 years previous to my getting this Company into operation ... [and as the] Steam Engine was not known in former days the old mines must have been routed [flooded?] by water ... we now had to begin the work from the Surface of the Earth and go through all the old mine workings, it took up a considerable time.*[5]

With the site ready, the company began to search for a workable lode. In 1838 a first shaft was sunk[6] and revealed considerable resources of copper ore. Prospects for operating the mine at a profit looked promising, so in early 1840 Minvielle travelled to England: 'for the purpose of procuring a few English miners, a steam engine and other necessary apparatus.'[7]

Map of Virgin Gorda.
Courtesy of Ultimate BVI.

---

5   Letter of P.J. Minvielle to Julius Price, 30 April 1847, St Thomas, Virgin Islands. Baring Archive. HC5 5.13.1 1847.
6   Birchall, Frank and Margaret Birchall. 'The Virgin Gorda copper mine, British Virgin Islands.' *Journal of the Trevithick Society*, p.23 (No.20, 1993).
7   Burt, R. 'Virgin Gorda copper mine 1839–1862.' *Industrial Archaeology Review*, p.56 (Vol.6 Issue 1, 1981).

He purchased a second-hand steam engine which had been manufactured four years earlier by the Cornish-owned Perran Foundry at Perranarworthal, near Falmouth.[8] During the 19th century, Perran Foundry was a vibrant business which employed hundreds of Cornishmen, shipping its engines to mines throughout the United Kingdom and beyond.[9] The steam engine was the workhorse of any deep mining enterprise, used to pump water from the mine, raise the copper ore up the shafts and power the ore-dressing machinery. To produce the steam that would drive the engine, Minvielle also purchased a second-hand Cornish boiler of the type invented in 1815 by the Cornish engineer Richard Trevithick.[10]

While Minvielle was recruiting miners and sourcing mining machinery, John Whitley began negotiations with the Board of Customs and Excise in London. He wanted them to allow the company to ship directly in and out of Virgin Gorda without having to go to the added expense of having to trans-ship via Tortola. As the company was willing to meet the expense of establishing the position of a superintendent of Customs and Excise based in Virgin Gorda, the Customs and Excise in London was happy to oblige.

The miners employed by Minvielle came from the St Austell mining area of Cornwall: 'some 31 men and 5 women'.[11] The local St Austell economy had long been dependent on the extraction of tin, copper and china clay – but by 1840, although the copper and china clay mines were still operating at a profit, tin mining was already in decline. The recruits for Virgin Gorda may have been out-of-work tin miners, or men and women willing to travel to the Caribbean to take advantage of the better wages that the Virgin Gorda Mining Company offered. The mine captain was Joel Hitchins, who had been recruited from the Fowey Consols[12]

---

8   Briggs, Lin, and Simon Chapman. 'Scenes of Copper Point Mine.' *Cornish Mining*, p.18 (Winter 2013).
9   Richards, Bob. 'Perran foundry'. *My Cornwall*, p.80 (April/May 2011).
10 *Letter of P.J. Minvielle to Julius Price*, 22 April 1847, St Thomas, Virgin Islands. Baring Archive. HC5 5.13.1 1847.
11 Birchall, Frank, and Margaret Birchall. 'The Virgin Gorda copper mine, British Virgin Islands.' *Journal of the Trevithick Society*, p.23 (No.20, 1993).
12 'Consols' is the abbreviated form of 'Consolidated'.

Copper Mine, one of the deepest, richest and most important copper mines in Cornwall, which lies in the parish of Tywardreath, about 3 miles (5 km) inland from the south-coast town of Fowey.[13] In 1822, the mine employed 1,680 people.[14] It was only a few miles from St Austell, and Captain Hitchins may well have been familiar with some of the miners he would manage on Virgin Gorda.

When the Cornish miners arrived on Virgin Gorda they moved into the cottages which had been built for them to the north of the mining operations. The coastal location of the mine and its buildings would have reminded them of the coastal mines back in Cornwall: the Levant and Geevor Mines along the coast near St Just in Penwith, the Crowns Mine near Botallack, Wheal Trewavas and Wheal Prosper near Porthleven, and Wheal Coates near Chapel Porth.

In addition to the Cornish miners, the company employed a number of Virgin Islanders: '55 labourers, 13 masons and carpenters, 64 women, boys and girls',[15] thus helping to ease the island's unemployment problem.

On his return to the Virgin Islands, Peter Minvielle petitioned the local Council and Assembly for permission to cut a road from the mine to the harbour at Spanish Town.[16] The company needed to ship out its ore, and ship in provisions, construction materials, the mine workers' wages, and the coal to power the steam engine. Some of the shipments would arrive on the copper barques from Swansea, and some from the nearby island of St Thomas. By August 1840 the Council and Assembly had drawn up and passed the necessary legislation. But having now facilitated the development of the Mining Company, the Council and Assembly members turned their attention to the possibility of taxing any profit that the company might make. Unsurprisingly, the very next piece of

---

13 Briggs, Lin, and Simon Chapman. 'Scenes of Copper Point mine.' *Cornish Mining*, p.18 (Winter 2013).
14 *Fowey Consols*. Accessed 2 October 2014. http://www.gracesguide.co.uk/Fowey_Consols_Copper_Mine
15 Birchall, Frank, and Margaret Birchall. 'The Virgin Gorda copper mine, British Virgin Islands.' *Journal of the Trevithick Society*, p.23 (No.20, 1993).
16 National Archives of the UK. Public Record Office. *Virgin Islands. Minutes of the Legislative Council and Assembly 1828–1841*. CO 316/4.

legislation passed was: 'An Act to impose a duty on the exportation [of] Metallic Ore and Metal Produced in these Islands'.[17]

With labour, mining equipment and road approval in place, mining began. The local labourers, masons and carpenters developed and maintained the mine site, while the Cornish miners extracted the ore. Both the Cornishwomen and the local women and children were employed as surface workers – and, as was the custom in Cornwall, their job was to break down the ore by hand using special hammers. They first broke the ore into manageable lumps, then broke the lumps into gravel-sized pieces – so waste matter could be picked out and discarded – and they finally crushed the gravel into small grains.

A miner's day on Virgin Gorda was similar to that of mine workers in Cornwall during the mid-1800s. In the early morning:

> *the scene becomes animated ... men, women, and children of all ages begin to creep out from the cottages. On their arrival, the women and children whose duty it is to dress or clean the ore, repair to the rough sheds under which they work, while the men, having stripped and put on their underground clothes (which are coarse flannel dresses) ... one after another descend the ... mine. As soon as they have all disappeared, a most remarkable stillness prevails – scarcely a human being is to be seen. The tall chimneys of the steam-engines [the Virgin Gorda mine had only one steam engine] emit no smoke; and nothing is in motion but the great 'bobs' or levers of these gigantic machines, which, slowly rising and falling, exert their power, either to lift the water or produce from the mine, or to stamp the ores.*[18]

Underground, the miners worked for six or seven hours in dark and damp conditions:

> *There is no light in a mine but that afforded by the candles of the workmen; while the universal presence of water soaking through the*

---

17 Ibid.
18 Watson, Joseph Yelloly. *A compendium of British mining*, p.12–13. London: Watson, 1843.

crevices of the gallery, and intermixing with the dust and rubbish, keep up a constant succession of dirty puddles, rendering it no very pleasant affair going underground. Each miner has a candle, which is stuck close by him against the wall of his gallery, by means of a piece of clay. [At the end of the working day the miners leave the shaft] hot-dirty-and jaded; each with the remainder of his bunch of candles hanging at the bottom of his flannel garb. [The men then] repair to the engine house, where they generally leave their underground clothes to dry, wash themselves in the warm water of the engine-pool, and put on their clothes ... By this time the maidens and little boys have also washed their faces, and the whole party migrate ... to their respective homes.[19]

Sunday was free from mine work, and religious observance was an important part of the day. Many Cornish miners were Methodists, and as Methodism was well established in the Virgin Islands and there was a Methodist chapel in Spanish Town,[20] these miners, unlike their compatriots on Roman Catholic Cuba, would have felt comfortable worshipping with the local community.

Work at the mine was going well, and in September 1840 the stipendiary magistrate for the Virgin Islands could report:

At Virgin Gorda, the arrangement of the mining operations is highly satisfactory. The work is conducted with great regularity and energy; several Cornish miners (some of them married men with their wives) have arrived; native labourers and tradesmen find employment on advantageous terms, and a stimulus has been given to the industry of the inhabitants of these islands which cannot fail to produce the happiest results.[21]

---

19 Ibid.
20 Email from Peter and Verna Moll, 23 November 2014.
21 Burt, R. 'Virgin Gorda copper mine 1839–1862.' *Industrial Archaeology Review*, p.57 (Vol.6 Issue 1, 1981).

Early visitors to the mine included the Quakers George Truman, John Jackson and Thomas Longstreth, who visited the Caribbean between 1840 and 1841. Their visit came not long after Emancipation, and they noted that although:

> this visit was altogether of a religious character, and was not undertaken with any view to elicit information as to the results of Emancipation in the British Islands... [But to] be present among a people just released from bondage, and not to ascertain some facts, or make some enquiries as to their well-being, would exhibit much indifference to their situation.[22]

Having begun their research on Tortola, they enthusiastically set forth from Road Town to Virgin Gorda on 15 December 1840:

> Having been furnished with an excellent barge by our kind friend T.B., the Methodist missionary, we employed four athletic oarsmen and left Roads Town [sic] early this morning for Spanish Town, or Virgin Gorda, an Island about twenty miles distant.[23]

They went to Virgin Gorda to hold a meeting with some of the inhabitants and continue their fact-finding, but finding that the planned meeting would not be until the evening they changed their plan and first went to see the copper mine:

> The island having but poor soil, and droughts frequently occurring, the coloured people had become discouraged, and almost entirely neglected cultivation. Instead of advancing through the medium of freedom into a higher rank of civilization, they continued where slavery left them. Through the exertions of the manager [Joel Hitchins] of the copper mines this condition of things has been improved. Needing assistants, he called these people around him,

---

22 Truman, G., John Jackson and Thomas Bedford Longstreth. *Narrative of a visit to the West Indies in 1840 and 1841*, p.3. Philadelphia: Merrihew and Thompson, 1844.
23 Ibid. p.32.

offering them a compensation for their labour greater than they had been accustomed to receive.[24]

From their narrative, we also learn the name of one of the local carpenters working at the mine: Charles O'Neal:

Charles O'Neal, a young colored man, gave us much information in respect of the condition of the people. During our stay upon the island he provided for us the best his house could afford, without reward – desiring no other than our prayers for his preservation. The remembrance of Charles, and his careful attentions, will remain with us when far separated from him.[25]

The mining company had access to several veins of copper, but the miners were working Whitley's Lode, named for the company's major shareholder. The lode was located to the east of the site and had three vertical shafts, two of which were used only for ventilation. It was found that the deeper the shaft was sunk the more the ore improved: 'In the lowest level, the lode South, is three feet wide and will produce Ore worth about 50 Pounds Sterling per Fathom – The North end, although not so rich, is in an improving state.'[26] As the shaft went deeper, the company could report that: 'the lode was 3–4 ft. big with a great deal of strong, native copper.'[27]

In the first year of production 20 tons of concentrated ore were prepared and assayed as containing between 25 per cent and 50 per cent copper: a high percentage. In the following year 90 tons of concentrate were prepared.[28] *The Royal Cornwall Gazette* reported that between June 1841 and June 1842, 146 tons of concentrate were sold at a value of £2,346 17s 6d [17 shillings and 6 pence]. (A ton was listed, as was

---

24 Ibid. p.33.
25 Ibid. p.33.
26 *Prospectus of the New Virgin Gorda Mining Company*, 1845. Baring Archive. HC5 5.13.1.
27 Earle, Kenneth Wilson. *Geological survey of the Windward and Leeward Islands: interim report on the Virgin Gorda copper mine*, p.2. Washington DC: US Government Printing Office, June 1921.
28 Ibid, p.2.

the custom, at 21 cwt [hundredweight] rather than 20 cwt, to allow for weight loss in transit.[29]) In 1842, 154 tons of concentrate sold for £2,694 5s 0d, this shipment having between 18⅞ and 23¾ per cent pure copper – quite a reduction in copper content from the first year of production.[30]

As the mine was developing satisfactorily the company was ready to invest in building the 3 miles (5 km) of road from the mine to Spanish Town. When the road was completed, the Virgin Gorda ore was shipped from the harbour at Spanish Town. Freight costs were high and in the mid-19th century, even after Britain had lowered the import tax and when copper was selling for a good price, the percentage of pure copper in the prepared ore had to be high to offset the freight cost. Peter Minvielle lamented that in addition to the burden of paying export tax on the ore: 'Freights ... ran away with a vast deal of money.'[31]

With the mine producing, shipping and selling high quality ore, the President of the Virgin Islands had no hesitation in reporting to the Governor of the Leeward Islands, based in Antigua,[32] that:

A new channel of industry for the inhabitants and a fresh source of benefit to the colony has been opened in this enterprise which may be regarded as giving fair promise for the future prospects of these islands.[33]

In early March 1842, the Virgin Islands Council and Assembly even agreed to exempt the Cornish miners from jury service in the local courts so that they could focus on the business of raising ore.[34] Then, unexpectedly, on 20 March 1842, work at the mine abruptly ceased. Minvielle writes that

---

29 'Produce and returns of English and foreign mines.' *Royal Cornwall Gazette*, 5 August 1842.
30 *Prospectus of the New Virgin Gorda Mining Company, 1845.* Baring Archive. HC5 5.13.1.
31 *Letter of P.J. Minvielle to Julius Price*, 22 April 1847, St Thomas, Virgin Islands. Baring Archive. HC5 5.13.1 1847.
32 Administered locally by a president, the Virgin Islands were part of the Leeward Islands grouping, administered by a governor based in Antigua.
33 Burt, R. 'Virgin Gorda copper mine 1839–1862.' *Industrial Archaeology Review*, p.58 (Vol.6 Issue 1, 1981).
34 National Archives of the UK. Public Record Office. Virgin Islands. *Minutes of the Legislative Council and Assembly 1842–1844.* CO 316/5.

the investors ran out of money,[35] and the Birchalls (1993) note that when the mine closed the accounts showed that the production of ore had so far only covered a third of the working costs.[36] Burt (1981), on the other hand, is of the view that Minvielle had a disagreement with the governor and that this was the cause of the closure. The governor accused Minvielle of speaking contemptuously about some part of the Virgin Islands legislation,[37] probably in relation to the legislation that taxed the exports of the Virgin Gorda Mining Company. But it seems unlikely that such a disagreement would lead to the closing of a business that supported the local economy through the employment of large numbers of Virgin Islanders, the payment of taxes and the purchase of local supplies.

Mine Captain Joel Hitchins returned to his family in Mount Charles on the outskirts of St Austell.[38] All the Cornish miners and their families left Virgin Gorda, too. Remarkably, given the high mortality in less healthy parts of the Caribbean, as Peter Minvielle reports: 'I had only one death in three years and that was an infant of about six weeks of age, sickly from birth.'[39] Joel Hitchins would not stay in Cornwall long: by 1849 he was employed by a British mining company, the Imperial Brazilian Mining Association, to manage their Gongo and Bananal gold mines in Minas Gerais, Brazil. He died in about 1852, possibly in Brazil.[40]

The mine remained the property of John Whitely, who moved to St Thomas where he established a law firm under the name of Whitely, Suárez and Co. In 1845, he attempted to reopen the mine by forming a new company, to be called the New Virgin Gorda Mining Company. A prospectus was produced describing the opportunities to be derived

---

35 Letter of P.J. Minvielle to Julius Price, 22 April 1847, St Thomas, Virgin Islands. Baring Archive. HC5 5.13.1 1847.
36 Birchall, Frank, and Margaret Birchall. 'The Virgin Gorda copper mine, British Virgin Islands.' *Journal of the Trevithick Society*, p.25 (No.20, 1993).
37 Burt, R. 'Virgin Gorda copper mine 1839–1862.' *Industrial Archaeology Review*, p.58 (Vol.6 Issue 1, 1981).
38 The National Archives of the UK. Public Record Office. *Census Returns 1841*. HO 107/146/4.
39 Letter of P.J. Minvielle to Julius Price, 22 April 1847, St Thomas, Virgin Islands. Baring Archive. HC5 5.13.1 1847.
40 *Joel Hitchens*. Accessed 5 October 2014, http://www.gracesguide.co.uk/Joel_Hitchens.

from investing in the enterprise,[41] but insufficient shares were sold and the company was not established. Local business interests were still keen to encourage investment in the mine, however, and in 1847 St Thomas businessman Julius Price (apparently no relation of the Price family of Penzance and Jamaica) contacted Peter Minvielle, now also living in St Thomas, to ask him his opinion on the feasibility of reopening the mine. Minvielle replied:

> *I now give you some idea of the Virgin Gorda Mines ... For three years I was the Agent, that is to say from the day the Mines commenced work until they closed, a considerable sum of money has been expended, I presume upwards of £40,000 ... just as the mine was likely to turn a profit the funds of the Company gave out. I sent to Swansea about 200 tons ore, some very rich, but the average of the whole was about 18 3/4 per cent. I am very confident if a new company could be formed they would do well as the Engine is a fine one, but a new boiler is required, it had been in use before we had it and the salt water corroded it very quick. The place is one of the most healthy in the West Indies.*[42]

Price had been contacted by Thomas Baring, a leading British merchant banker and senior partner in Baring Brothers & Co, for information about the mine, samples of the ore, and the possibility of finding local investors. Baring Brothers was beginning to focus its attention on the business opportunities available in the Americas, and had recently invested in the Royal Mail Steam Packet Company (RMSPC) that had superseded the sailing ships of the Falmouth packet service. Price sent Baring copper ore samples as requested and, enclosing Minvielle's letter, advised that:

> *having lately stablished myself in a General Line of Business at this Port I had the opportunity to enquire about the Virgin Islands Copper Mine. Mr. Whitely the principal owner resides here and I had seen him on this subject. The Company expended about 200,000 Dollars*

---

41 Prospectus of the New Virgin Gorda Mining Company, 1845. Baring Archive. HC5 5.13.1.
42 Letter of P.J. Minvielle to Julius Price, 22 April 1847, St Thomas, Virgin Islands. Baring Archive. HC5 5.13.1 1847.

[£40,000] *but having no more cash to work the mine just when the property began to return the money ... I have taken leave to bring this to your kind notice and shall feel greatly obliged you would bring it to the notice of some merchant speculating in mines.*

It is Mr. Whitely's wish to sell the mines etc ... The Mine is certainly valuable and the ore gets much richer by increasing in depth. Captain John [sic] Hitchins at St. Austell in Cornwall was of the Mines and he is able to give you the best information.[43]

Nothing more was heard from Baring, who had presumably decided to invest elsewhere, and there is no further correspondence from Peter Minvielle concerning the mine. Minvielle later moved to Ponce on the southern coast of Puerto Rico, where he became a consular agent for the United States. He died in Ponce in September 1873.[44]

The next attempt to reopen the Virgin Gorda Mine was in early 1852, when the Royal West India Mining Company was formed. In its enthusiasm to sell shares the company advertised its intent to mine:

copper, silver, gold, quicksilver, platina, tin, molybdenum and other metals and minerals in the West Indies, where they are now known to exist, especially silver and copper, which have been procured in considerable quantities at the British Island of Virgin Gorda. A few private gentlemen have recently expended a large sum of money on this lofty volcanic island, in opening and partially working a valuable copper mine ... constructing buildings, erecting steam machinery, and acquiring freehold and leasehold mining land which they have agreed to assign upon very advantageous terms: making their remuneration, in fact, contingent upon the future prosperous state and profitable development of the mines transferred to the Company.[45]

---

43 Letter of Julius Price to Thomas Baring, 30 April 1847, St Thomas Virgin Islands. Baring Archive. HC5.5.13.1 1847.
44 Martinez-Fernandez, Luis. *Protestantism and political conflict in the nineteenth-century Hispanic Caribbean*, pp.92 and 99. Piscataway: Rutgers University Press, 2002.
45 British Library Board. 'Royal West India Mining Company.' *Morning Post* (Saturday 28 February 1852). British Newspaper Archive, accessed 30 September 2014. http://www.britishnewspaperarchive.co.uk/ .

Its promotional efforts were dishonest: the highest point of Virgin Gorda is only 1,370 ft (420 m) above sea level – hardly 'lofty' – and silver had never been 'procured in considerable quantities' on the island. Nevertheless, a year later the company received its Royal Charter and was optimistically reporting: 'The first works undertaken will be in connection with certain copper mines in the island of Virgin Gorda.'[46] Despite its efforts, however, the company was unable to attract sufficient investment to reopen the mine and there were no further developments.

It was not until 1859 that a group of shareholders calling themselves the Virgin Gorda Mine Adventure showed interest in reactivating the mine. Some of the earlier investors had maintained their interest. One of these – a Mr Orred, of the Liverpool agents North & Orred – was listed in the 1865 prospectus of the New Virgin Gorda Mining Company. Another, a Mr Robert Lowe, was one of the directors of the 1852 Royal West India Mining Company. Both appear on the list of the shareholders of the new company.[47] The major shareholder was John Taylor, of the firm John Taylor & Sons, an established and well-respected civil engineering firm with considerable experience in the development of mines in Cornwall and elsewhere.

The President of the Virgin Islands from 1859–1861 was Thomas Price,[48] son of Cornishman Rose Price[49] who owned sugar plantations in Jamaica. The previous president had demitted office in 1857, but Thomas Price, although he left England early in 1857, did not take up his post until 1859. Perhaps on his way to the Virgin Islands he had visited what was left of the family holdings in Jamaica. In any case, his departure from Southampton had nearly been delayed because of an altercation about lodging charges. To save expenses he and his family stayed at the lodging house of one Mr Arnold rather than in a hotel, perhaps an indication

---

46 British Library Board. 'Royal West India Mining Company.' *Royal Cornwall Gazette* (Friday 14 January 1853). British Newspaper Archive, accessed 3 October 2014. http://www.britishnewspaperarchive.co.uk/ .
47 Birchall, Frank, and Margaret Birchall. 'The Virgin Gorda copper mine, British Virgin Islands.' *Journal of the Trevithick Society*, p.25 (No.20, 1993).
48 For more on Thomas Price, see Chapter 1: The British Leeward Islands, and Chapter 2: Jamaica and the Cayman Islands.
49 For more on Rose Price, see Chapter 2: Jamaica and the Cayman Islands.

of the shortage of funds available in the Price family coffers. The family stayed for three nights, and Price expected: 'to pay for certain rooms, for himself, wife and four children, £2 10s., that sum including cooking, attendance, lights & etc ... instead of which he was charged the frightful sum of £16.'[50] When Price disputed the bill, eventually offering to pay £12, Arnold demanded £14, and when this was not forthcoming confiscated his guest's luggage. The matter reached the Southampton Magistrate's Court, where Arnold was told that it was illegal to confiscate Price's luggage in lieu of payment of his bill. Nevertheless, eager not to miss the steamship *Plata* as she left for the Caribbean:

> *It appears that Mr. Price paid the £14 after all – the fact being, according to Mr. Arnold's statement, that he had so many continuous visitors that nearly twelve people were continuously having refreshments.*[51]

Once settled on Tortola, President Price soon became aware of the possible reopening of the Virgin Gorda Mine, and in February 1859 he reported to Governor Hamilton in Antigua:

> *I am informed from a perfectly reliable private source, the mines at Virgin Gorda are again to be opened by a small body of adventurers from England, with ample means at their disposal.*
>
> *The partial success of the first body of adventurers 17 or 18 years since – the favourable reports sent I believe by the Government at a later date*[52] *and perhaps the encouragement afforded by an opinion that the undertaking might be resumed without the necessity of an extravagant outlay, but with a fair prospect of a speedy return of, probably, considerable value seems to have combined to induce this new effort for the development of our resources.*[53]

---

50 'High charges at lodgings – detention of luggage illegal [Thomas Price].' *Hampshire Advertiser*, p.6. (21 February 1857).
51 Ibid., p.6.
52 Burt notes that Lieutenant G.B.A. Lawrence and J. Parsons conducted a survey of the Virgin Islands between 1848 and 1852. Burt, R. 'Virgin Gorda copper mine 1839–1862.' *Industrial Archaeology Review*, p.62 (Vol.6 Issue 1, 1981).
53 Burt, R. 'Virgin Gorda copper mine 1839–1862.' *Industrial Archaeology Review*, p.58 (Vol.6 Issue 1, 1981).

The Council and Assembly acted on the president's optimism that the mine would lead to the 'development of our resources', by passing legislation to waive: 'for a limited time the tonnage and package duty in favour of vessels importing articles for the Virgin Gorda Mining company'.[54]

Governor Hamilton reported to the Board of Trade and Plantations in London that:

> *Importation of materials and requisites, has induced the present enactment, to encourage as much as possible the enterprise, by reducing the expenditure for tonnage or package duty on vessels bringing certain articles for the Company.*
>
> *Vessels importing building materials, lumber, machinery, coal, draught livestock, or labourers for the bona fide use in working the mines at Virgin Gorda, are exempt from payment of tonnage or package duty, such exemption to continue until the first shipment of ore by the Company from the said mines.*[55]

Plans were made to put the mine back into production and were quickly implemented. The mine captain was H. Clemes, a Cornishman lately returned from the Fort Bowen Mine Company in Veraguas, Panama, where he had surveyed the potential of the Panamanian mine to produce profitable quantities of gold.[56] (Was this perhaps the same Captain Clemes who had earlier managed the Silver Hill copper mine for the Port Royal and St Andrew's Copper Mining Company?)[57] A Cornish boilermaker and an assistant were recruited, along with an engineer, a carpenter, a blacksmith, a doctor and four miners. Machinery for the mine, including engine parts, belt wheels and iron pipe, was shipped out. Provisions, candles, beds and bedding, medicines, roofing material, and roofing slate for the cottages were sent as well.[58]

---

54 Ibid., p.58.
55 Ibid., p.58.
56 British Library Board. 'Mines.' *London Daily News* (Monday 20 April 1857). British Newspaper Archive, accessed 4 October 2014. http://www.britishnewspaperarchive.co.uk/
57 See Chapter 2: Jamaica and the Cayman Islands for more on Captain Clemes.
58 Birchall, Frank, and Margaret Birchall. 'The Virgin Gorda copper mine, British Virgin Islands.' *Journal of the Trevithick Society*, p.26 (No.20, 1993).

Captain Clemes and his men travelled out to Virgin Gorda via St Thomas on one of the Royal Mail Steam Packet Company ships. The miners were contract workers, employed for an initial period of two years. While travelling to and from Virgin Gorda, they were paid at a rate of £5 per month, and while working at the mine £9 per month. By comparison, the monthly wage of a miner in Cornwall at about the same time was on average between £2 and £3 a month: good reason to leave Cornwall for Virgin Gorda.[59] In November 1859, four additional Cornish miners were employed: Thomas Kempe, William Pope, T. Hooper and W. Hooper. In February 1860, with work proceeding well, a bonus was given to the miners and to the engineer, carpenter and blacksmith. Mine offices were built. A powder magazine and a large rainwater catchment area leading into a sunken cistern were constructed. The boiler and the steam engine were repaired.

As it had been during the 1839–42 working of the mine, the copper ore extracted was still high grade, and by June 1860 the company was ready to sink a new shaft to over 240 feet (73 m), and to invest in a mill to crush the ore. Three additional miners joined the workforce: T. Merrett, T. Jose and J. Chynoweth. During 1860, the company shipped 150 tons of copper ore, valued at £3,000, to Swansea, and President Price was happy to report to Governor Hamilton in Antigua:

> *New energies have been developed and new sources of industry opened and brought into action by the operations of the Virgin Gorda Mining Company and although the speculators in their works must be supposed to have had their own interests primarily in view, we will not withhold from them an acknowledgement of the beneficial results likely to accrue to the Colony from their exertions, nor deny them the credit due to their energy. The helping hand held out to them at the outset of their undertaking by your remission on duties on vessels importing supplies for the use of the Company, and lately by the very modest impost on their exportations is another evidence of your liberal appreciation of works of enterprise tending to develop the resources of*

---

59 Watson, Joseph Yelloly. *A compendium of British mining*, p.6. London: Watson, 1843.

the Colony and to promote the industry and further the advancement of its people.[60]

In addition to the Cornish mine captain and miners there were now 150 local men, women and children employed at the mine: the future of the Virgin Gorda Mine Adventure looked secure.

During the life of the Virgin Gorda Mining Company, the Council and Assembly had been eager to impose a tax on the company's ore exports, thinking that the monies raised by the tax would improve the financial stability of the colony. But the tax burden was one of the major reasons that the company failed. Yet, as the Council and the Assembly continued to search for a means to improve the colony's finances, they again relied on increasing the export tax on copper. Legislation now required the company to pay 2s 6d [2 shillings and 6 pence] duty on each ton of copper ore it exported during its first year of mining. At this rate, it could still make a profit – but on completion of the first year of ore extraction, the export duty was increased to 5 shillings per ton. To make matters worse, the percentage of copper in the ore it was mining began to drop. In March 1861, the 147 tons of ore shipped was mostly assayed at about 12 per cent: 71 tons at 11⅞ per cent, 69 tons at 12⅝ per cent and 7 tons at 40 ½ per cent. But then the price of pure copper began to fall: between January 1860 and June 1862 the market price fell from £120 sterling to £93, a drop of over 20 per cent.[61]

The Virgin Gorda Mine Adventure was in trouble, but the Council and Assembly were not sympathetic to its partners' request for a reduction in the export duty. So John Taylor[62] wasted no time in writing directly to Britain's Secretary of State for the Colonies, Henry Pelham-Clinton, the Duke of Newcastle, to plead for a reduction of the export duty to 1 shilling per ton of copper ore, and to protest against:

---

60 Burt, R. 'Virgin Gorda copper mine 1839–1862.' *Industrial Archaeology Review*, p.59 (Vol.6 Issue 1, 1981).
61 Ibid., p,62.
62 Burt notes that the letter was most probably written by John Taylor Junior, the eldest son of the firm, as John Taylor Senior, though still alive, was old and infirm. Burt, R. 'Virgin Gorda copper mine 1839–1862.' *Industrial Archaeology Review*, p.62 (Vol.6 Issue 1, 1981).

the unwise and very short sighted policy of burdening such an enterprise with so heavy an impost and which under present circumstances may lead to an abandonment of the works to the heavy loss of our memorialists and the great disadvantage of the numerous class of persons now benefitted by such expenditure.[63]

The Duke of Newcastle replied that Mr Taylor must petition the local Council and Assembly, as it was they who had passed the relevant legislation. The petition was not successful, and the duty remained at 5 shillings per ton. The company continued to extract and ship ore and in 1861 it produced a total of 721 tons, valued at £10,120. But the quality of the ore continued to drop, now yielding only about 10 per cent pure copper, with the ore now selling at only about £10 per ton. Although the company continued to extract and ship ore during the early months of 1862, at this price it could not pay the 5 shillings per ton export duty and operate at a profit.

On 12 April 1862, Isidor Dyett, who had replaced Thomas Price as President of the Virgin Islands, wrote in surprise to Governor Hamilton:

I learn from a verbal communication made to me a few days ago by Mr. Clemes, the Manager of the Virgin Gorda mines, that the mining company are about to suspend their works at that place.[64]

Dyett did not, perhaps, recall that John Taylor had mentioned the possibility of closure in his correspondence with the Duke of Newcastle, or had neglected to study the correspondence in sufficient detail. Captain Clemes proved to be correct. The company could no longer continue to operate at a loss, and closed the mine. The mine workings were dismantled, and the steam engine was taken to pieces so that the parts could be shipped to England. President James Robert Longden, who had replaced President Dyett, visited the mine and reported to the governor:

---

63 Burt, R. 'Virgin Gorda copper mine 1839–1862.' *Industrial Archaeology Review*, p.60 (Vol.6 Issue 1, 1981).
64 Burt, R. 'Virgin Gorda copper mine 1839–1862.' *Industrial Archaeology Review*, p.61 (Vol.6 Issue 1, 1981).

> *Captain Clemes showed me a specimen of the black oxide of copper which had yielded 60 per cent of metal and was worth about £60 a ton, of this only a very small quantity was obtained. Captain Clemes states that, in his opinion, there are few veins more continuous than those of Virgin Gorda, although the quality of the ores varies greatly, and that besides the vein now abandoned, there are others on the island which might be more profitably worked if undertaken by a company able to command the necessary capital.*[65]

President Longden went on to report on the high expenses of working the mine:

> *The actual working expenses of the mines are very considerable, and although the proprietors held the property free of any royalties from the Crown, yet the export duty of 5s. a ton was felt as a heavy charge on the depreciated value of the ore. Had the ore realized on an average £30 or even £25 a ton the tax would have been small, but under the actual circumstances, I have reason to doubt not only whether the proprietors will reap any profits, but whether they will not sustain a loss, from their speculation. Other taxes too pressed heavily on the enterprise, such as the House Tax which was assessed at £5 a year, on the blacksmith's and carpenter's shops. If at any future time the mines of Virgin Gorda should be reopened, it would seem expedient that the local legislature should rather offer every encouragement and trust to the general increased prosperity of the Colony for the improvement of the revenues, than by heavy direct taxation to exact a small immediate sum and at the same time discourage the investment of capital.*[66]

Captain Clemes, the contracted miners and the other employees from Cornwall returned home.[67] The local Virgin Gorda population, having

---

65   Ibid., p.61.
66   Ibid., p.61.
67   The records of John Taylor & Co. were unfortunately destroyed during the Second World War, so we do not know whether all the miners returned to Cornwall or if, as the story goes, some remained in the islands.

lost their main source of employment, had little choice but to return to earning their living through subsistence farming, fishing and charcoal production. The other option was to leave Virgin Gorda. The local Methodist Church reported that the closure of the mine had caused a drop in the number of its members and in its income.[68]

By November 1862, the mining machinery and materials had been shipped back to Liverpool, where they were advertised for auction:

> *All the valuable MACHINERY and MATERIALS just received from the Virgin Gorda Mines, West Indies, consigned to Messrs. John Taylor and Sons for immediate sale, comprising several parts of a 36 inch condensing steam engine, an 18 inch crushing mill, nearly new, pitwork mining tools, railway iron, water and air pipes, chain, rope, blocks, winch etc. and various other useful mining effects in excellent condition.*[69]

Not all the steam engine parts arrived in Liverpool. At Taylor's Bay, just to the north of Coppermine Point, the broken engine beam still lies in the sand, where it had been transported to await trans-shipment. The beam is still clearly marked 'Perran Foundry 1836'. Since the failure of the Virgin Gorda Mine Adventure, potential investors have shown intermittent interest in reopening the mine, but commercial copper mining has never resumed on the island. In 2003, Coppermine Point became a British Virgin Islands National Park, and in January 2017 a visitor centre, which provides interpretive displays of the area's history, was opened.

The islet of Sombrero lies about 40 miles (64 km) from Virgin Gorda, and nearly east of it. Only 0.9 miles (1.4 km) long, and 0.25 miles (0.40 km) wide, Sombrero was the place where the Cornish seaman Robert Jeffery had been marooned in December 1807,[70] and after his rescue it

---

68 Blackman, Francis. *Methodism: 200 years in British Virgin Islands*, p.46. Road Town: Methodist Church in the British Virgin Islands, 1989.
69 British Library Board. 'To Proprietors of Mines, Collieries, etc.' *Liverpool Daily Post* (Saturday 22 November 1862). British Newspaper Archive, accessed 3 October 2014. http://www.britishnewspaperarchive.co.uk/ .
70 See Chapter 3: In Defence of the Empire, for Robert Jeffery's story.

remained uninhabited for nearly 50 years. In 1825, a British geological survey team found on the islet large deposits of guano, a fertiliser derived from bird excrement, but the British government made no move to mine the resource. But then, in 1856, under the United States Guano Act of that year, two men from Boston claimed Sombrero, formed the Sombrero Company, and began to mine the phosphate. Four years later, they had developed an infrastructure that included a railway, several quarries and housing for about 200 workers, who mostly came from the British and Danish Virgin Islands and Anguilla. There were also twelve managers and a superintendent. Food and various supplies came from the nearby island of St Martin, brought to Sombrero by the company schooner.

Britain, belatedly realising the value of the resource it had ignored, sought to reclaim the island. The United States Guano Act stated that any United States citizen who discovered guano on an uninhabited island could ask for government support should third parties dispute their activities but, after some diplomatic negotiations between the two countries, settlement was made in Britain's favour. For a fee of £1,000 per year Britain awarded the Sombrero Company a licence to extract the guano for the following twenty-one years. After shipping over 100,000 tons of guano from Sombrero, the company ran into financial trouble and was liquidated in 1871. The enterprise was then bought by the banker Emile Erlanger, who established the New Sombrero Phosphate Company. The superintendent he employed was a Cornish mine captain, Thomas Corfield.[71]

Corfield had been born in the village of St Day, near Redruth, in 1844. He had probably begun his working life as a miner, because when he moved to Llanidloes, in central Wales, he became a mine captain. He then took up the offer of work on Sombrero, a very different kind of mine, probably sailing to Sombrero via St Thomas on one of the Royal Mail Steam Packet Company ships. With him came his wife and their eldest daughter.[72]

On Sombrero, Captain Corfield's responsibilities included managing the workforce, ensuring that the mined guano provided profitable returns, and overseeing the maintenance of the infrastructure developed by the

---

71 *The Corfields and their relations*. Accessed 11 March 2015, http://www.corfield.port5.com/web/10.htm .
72 Ibid.

Sombrero Island in 1865 from the *Illustrated London News*. Courtesy of the Antiqua Print Gallery / Alamy Stock Photo.

Sombrero Company, so that the guano could be transported to where it was loaded onto the lighters which took it out to the ships waiting offshore. He lived in the superintendent's house, a wooden one-storey house constructed near the middle of the island, around which were the living quarters of the company's technicians, storekeepers and workers. After several vessels had run aground on the nearby Horseshoe Reef – including in 1859 the Royal Mail Steam Packet Company's *Paramatta* – a lighthouse was erected on the island. This was initially maintained by the mining company.[73]

While Corfield settled into the superintendent's house, his wife spent much of her time on St Martin and on St Christopher, where her children were born. Corfield's wife and children most likely preferred to live away from the superintendent's house, where life was made difficult by the noise from the blasting operations that were used to break up the phosphate, plus the continual dust from the mining operation and the lack of social life.[74] Thomas Corfield died on St Martin in 1885 aged 41, leaving his wife and young family to return to Llanidloes. The New Sombrero Phosphate Company continued its operations on the island until 1890, by which time the guano resources in Sombrero were so scarce and difficult to access that their extraction was no longer viable.

Sombrero is now part of the British Overseas Territory of Anguilla, and since its lighthouse was automated in 1992 has remained uninhabited. In recent years the island has been recognised as a valuable habitat for wildlife, including seabirds, lizards and geckos, and has started to develop as an eco-tourism destination. It has been designated an Important Bird Area (IBA) by Birdlife International and the Government of Anguilla has declared the island and its surrounding waters a Nature Reserve Marine Park. In 2018, the island was designated as Wetland of International Importance under the Ramsar Convention[75] site designation.[76]

---

73 *Sombrero: part of Anguilla's cultural heritage.* Accessed 7 April 2017, http://web.archive.org/web/20071006203854/http://sombrero.ai/island.htm .
74 'Sombrero Island.' *Caribbean Beach News*, pp.7–8 (June 2012). Accessed 11 March 2015, http://www.caribbeanbeachnews.com/CBN4WEB.pdf .
75 The Ramsar Convention, also known as the Convention on Wetlands, is so-called because it was adopted in the Iranian city of Ramsar.
76 *Sombrero – Anguilla's first Ramsar site designated.* Accessed 19 July 2018, https://www.ukotcf.org.uk/news/sombrero-designation .

Appendices

Appendix 1

Background History of the British Leeward Islands

The British Leewards comprise the group of islands that start east of Puerto Rico and reach as far south as Dominica, while the islands from Dominica down to Trinidad are known as the Windward Islands.

Over time there have been changes in the membership of each group. Dominica was once part of the Leeward Islands, but is now included in the Windward Islands group and at one period all the islands between Puerto Rico and Martinique were considered part of the Leewards.

The names 'Leeward' and 'Windward' were given to the islands in the days of sailing ships, whose movements were governed by the direction of the wind. Across the Caribbean island chain, as today, the prevailing winds blow from east to west, so the islands to the north and west of the chain were reached by sailing downwind – to leeward – from the more easterly ones, while the islands to the south and east of the chain were reached by sailing upwind, or to windward, from the more westerly ones. Appropriately, in an age when European powers fought to exploit and trade in Caribbean resources, these winds – and for that matter, the prevailing winds in the tropics worldwide – were named the Trade Winds.

Home to various groups of indigenous people, the Leeward Islands' first contact with Europeans came in 1493 with the second voyage of Christopher Columbus. The islands had all been given meaningful names by their early settlers, but Columbus, sailing on behalf of Spain, gave

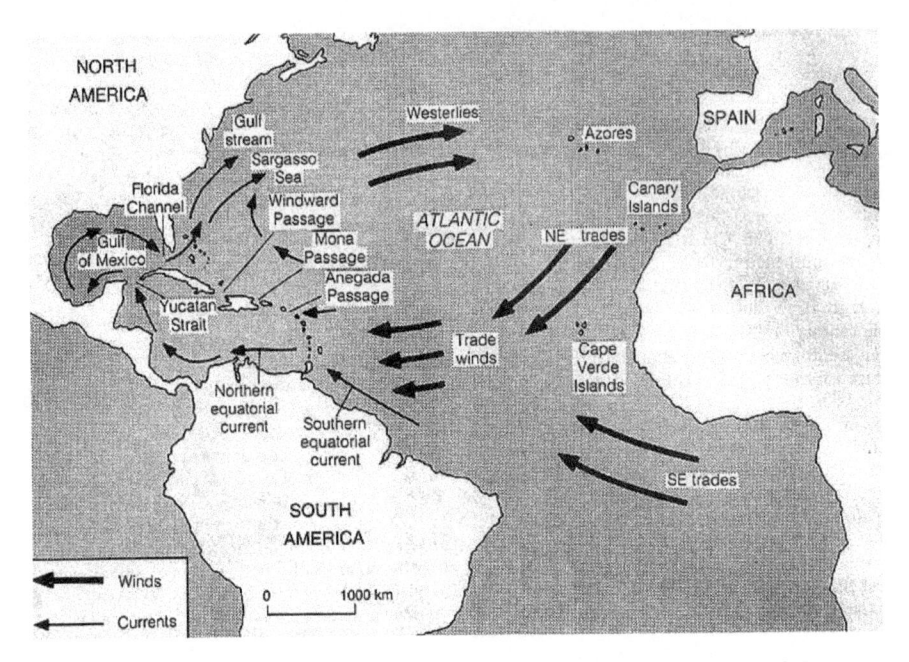

The prevailing Trade Winds from *Institutionalized Piracy and the Development of the Jamaica sloop, 1630–1743*.
Scientific figure on ResearchGate. Accessed 26 July 2018, https://www.researchgate.net/Ships-sailing-into-and-from-the-Caribbean-region-utilized-a-reliable-system-of-water_fig3_35458399

them Spanish names.[1] It was the first step in the colonisation of the Caribbean by European powers for: 'to give something a name is one way of appropriating it for oneself'.[2]

Passing by the island named Waitukubuli ('Tall is her Body') for its mountainous terrain he renamed it Domenica, choosing the name because he sighted it on a Sunday. It is now spelt Dominica. The island of Wadadli (Land of Fish Oil – perhaps because the island was a good source of this resource), he renamed after the Virgin Mary as Santa Maria de la Antigua, and it is now simply Antigua. Liamugua (Fertile Land), became San Cristóbal after St Christopher, his own patron saint, and is now

---

1   Society for Caribbean Linguistics. *Names and pronunciations*. Accessed 8 December 2015, http://www.scl-online.net/FAQS/caribbean.htm
2   San Miguel, Pedro L. 'Historical visions of the Caribbean: from imperial perspectives to subaltern resistances'. *Revista Brasileira do Caribe*, p25. (Vol.1, Number 2, 2001). English translation by Jane Ramirez. Accessed 7 December 2015, https://www.academia.edu/17426181/San_Miguel_Pedro_L.-Historical_Visions_of_the_Caribbean

generally known by the abbreviated name of St Kitts. The neighbouring island of Oualie (Land of Beautiful Water) he called Nuestra Senora de las Nieves (Our Lady of the Snows) because of the white clouds that usually cover the top of its volcanic peak; it is now called Nevis. Another nearby island, once called Alliougana (Land of the Prickly Bush) he named Santa Maria de Montserrat (Our Lady of Montserrat). The serrated shape of the island's mountains reminded him of Montserrat in Spain where there is a shrine to the Blessed Virgin of the Monastery of Montserrat. It is now known simply as Montserrat. As he moved further west he began to sail through a large number of small islands, and these he named Santa Ursula y las Once Mil Virgines (Saint Ursula and her Eleven Thousand Virgins). These are now known as the Virgin Islands.

Spain was the first European nation to colonise the larger Caribbean islands, including Santiago (later Jamaica), Hispaniola, Cuba, Puerto Rico, and Trinidad, but the Spanish established no permanent settlements in the Leeward Islands and by the early 17th century England and France had begun to take an interest in colonising the area.

St Christopher was the first of the Leewards to be settled by the British, when Sir Thomas Warner, having failed to establish a colony on the Guiana coast of South America, sailed up through the islands of the Lesser Antilles and decided that St Christopher, with its fertile soil and abundant fresh water, was ideal. He landed on the island in 1622, then left for England to gather men and resources, returning to St Christopher in 1624. In 1625, the French Captain Pierre Belain d'Esnambuc was privateering in the area when his vessel was attacked by the Spanish. He found refuge on St Christopher, liked what he saw, and decided that he, like the British, would establish a colony there. As Warner needed assistance in fighting the indigenous population, and also because Spain was then the common enemy of England and France, he allowed the French to settle on part of the island. The local community increased their efforts to defend their island against the invading Europeans, sending to Dominica for reinforcements but by 1626 the English and French colonisers had succeeded in almost annihilating the local population. The few that remained were deported to Dominica.

Both France and England began expanding their colonial presence to neighbouring islands: the French to Martinique, Guadeloupe, St Martin and Saint Barthélemy; the English to Nevis, Antigua, Montserrat and Anguilla, and in 1672 they took control of the Dutch-owned Virgin Islands. The Dutch had settled on some of the Virgin Islands in the early 17th century: on Tortola, Anegada, Virgin Gorda and, along with some English and French colonists, on part of St Croix. The Dutch later took over other islands in the Leeward group, including Saba, Sint Maarten, and Sint Eustatius. Denmark also made her presence felt, moving into the uninhabited island of Saint Thomas in 1672, and St John in 1675. In 1733, Denmark purchased Saint Croix from the French West India Company which, after Spain had briefly taken the island from England in 1650, took it from Spain in 1651.

The British Leeward Islands were initially governed from Barbados, but given the distance between Barbados and the Leewards this was not a practical form of administration. So in 1667, England gave in to the demands of the Leewards for separate government and established the Leeward Caribee Island Government, which was administered from Antigua.

As alliances between the European powers changed and France and England became enemies, fighting over the islands of the Caribbean increased and islands changed hands. St Christopher and Nevis were captured by France but in 1713, at the end of the War of Spanish Succession, reverted to England. Conflict continued throughout much of the 18th century and islands changed allegiance with confusing rapidity.

The Leeward Islands economy was initially based on the growing and trading of tobacco, sea island cotton, spices, indigo and arrowroot – crops that needed a regular supply of labour if they were to be grown profitably. In the earlier part of the 17th century this labour was provided by indentured men and women, recruited by individual merchants or ships masters and sold to the settler for about 500 lbs of tobacco per labourer.[3]

---

3   Dyde, Brian. *Out of the crowded vagueness: a history of the islands of St Kitts, Nevis and Anguilla*. Oxford: Macmillan Education, 2005, p.52.

There was no shortage of those willing to provide their labour and give up their freedom for a period of between three and ten years to serve a named settler in one of the colonies. In exchange for labour the settler agreed to pay the labourer's passage, to maintain them for the duration of their contract, and on completion of the contract to supply them with £10 in cash, or with land or tobacco worth an equivalent amount. In later years, as sugar became a major crop, sugar was also used as a means of payment.[4]

---

[4] Button, Andrea. *The trade in white labour in 17th century Bristol*. Accessed 10 October 2015, http:humanities.uwe.ac.uk/bhr/Main/white_labour/servants.htm

Appendix 2

Indentured Cornishmen who Sailed from Plymouth to St Christopher in 1634

Sailed aboard the *Robert Bonaventure*, leaving Plymouth in February 1634: 21 husbandmen:

Name	Age	Place of origin in Cornwall
John Badland	22	North Hill
Michel Bowden	27	Helston
Christopher Carter	45	St Gilt (St Giles?)
William Clarke	20	Truro
William Curke	24	Menheniot
Nicholas Dabbin	40	St Stephens
William Dunn	16	Truro
Rawleigh Edye	15	Bodmin
Thomas Frethye	24	Perranuthnoe
John Liddicott	22	St Columb
Ellin Nancarro	20	Penryn
Anthony Pearse	15	St Breock
Thomas Pollard	23	Gwinear
Henry Rensby	28	St Stephens
Martin Rooby	23	Gwinear
Henry Thomas	15	Luxulian [sic]

APPENDIX 2

John Thomas	26	St Issey
Edward Tremineere	18	Helston
Robert Treneighan	34	Helston
William Wade	33	Bodmin
Anthony Webb	20	Launceston

Sailed aboard the *Margaret* later in 1634: 20 husbandmen:

Name	Age	Place of origin in Cornwall
William Badcocke	20	St Hilary
Thomas Borinthon	22	Helston
Walter Burlacy	22	Ludgven
Anthony Burrowes	20	Jacobstow
John Duston	26	St Columb
Samuel Forgine?	26	Wallen Lizard
George Griffen	18	Marazion
John Martin	18	St Ives
Simon Martin	18	St Ives
Thomas Martin	24	Cardinham
George Matthew	23	Ludgven
John Merry	28	Withiel
John Newdon	28	St Ewe
Robert Pavie	29	Marazion
Francis Pedlar	28	St Breock
Robert Pedlar	22	St Breock
Samuell Purefoy	13	St Ives
Nicholas Waterman	15	Marazion
William Wiett	17	Marazion
Richard Williams	30	St Columb

Appendix 3

Background History of Jamaica and the Cayman Islands

Jamaica is the third largest island in the Caribbean after Cuba and Hispaniola, and lies about 90 miles (145 km) south of Cuba and 119 miles (191 km) west of Hispaniola: the island now shared by Haiti and the Dominican Republic. Jamaica was first named Xaymaca (Land of Wood and Water) by the indigenous people who settled there, but when Christopher Columbus landed on the island in May 1494 and claimed it for Spain, he named it Santiago, a word derived from the Spanish word for saint, *santo*, combined with 'Yago', an old Spanish form of James, Spain's patron saint. Unusually, this attempt to rename the island was unsuccessful and the indigenous name continued in use until after the English gained possession, when the island came to be known as Jamaica.

Spanish settlers came fifteen years later led by their governor, Juan de Esquivel. They settled on the north coast in an area now known as St Ann's Bay, which they named Sevilla la Nueva (New Seville). In 1534, they moved south to Villa de la Vega (Town on the Plain) which became the centre of government and trade and was later renamed St Jago de la Vega (St James on the Plain). In their efforts to find the large quantities of gold they believed existed on the island, the Spanish settlers, as elsewhere in their empire, enslaved the indigenous population, most of whom died either from overwork or from the diseases introduced by the colonisers. It is thought that small amounts of gold may have been found in some of the rivers:

The Rio Minho had been searched for gold in the days of the Spaniards, and the basins that had been constructed for washing the sand were to be traced near Longville estate, in Clarendon [Parish].[5]

If gold was not forthcoming, copper was available and was mined from about 1598, its presence reflected in Spanish names such as the Rio Cobre (Copper River) that flows through St Catherine Parish.[6]

Spain lost interest in the island when it failed to produce large quantities of gold, and paid little attention to its development, using it only as a supply base for their ships as they sailed south to colonise the mineral-rich lands of Central and South America.[7]

In Villa de la Vega, disagreements between church authorities and the governor grew, and lack of support from Spain undermined the governor's authority. At the same time, as Spain continued to ignore the need to develop the colony's defence capability, attacks from pirates became more frequent. In 1655, the island's poor state of readiness against attack provided an opportunity for Oliver Cromwell's armed forces, led by General Robert Venables and Admiral William Penn. After they failed to take Spain's fort at Santo Domingo on the island of Hispaniola they were unwilling to return to England and face Cromwell's wrath at their defeat, so they decided to attack Jamaica. The English force soon overwhelmed the small number of Spanish troops and claimed Jamaica for England.

In the early days of their occupation the English were hard put to defend the island against attempts by the Spanish to reclaim the territory. Part of the solution was to fortify the cay, named Cayo de Carena, which had been used by the Spanish as a place to clean and refit their ships. The cay was situated on the south coast near St Jago de la Vega, and as the English recognised the area's strategic importance in defending the island from the threat of recapture by the Spanish, they set about

---

5   Gardner, William James. *A history of Jamaica from its discovery by Christopher Columbus to the present time; including an account of its trade and agriculture* ... London: Elliot Stock, 1873, p.162.
6   Jamaica Information Service. *Mining in Jamaica*. Kingston: Jamaica Information Service, nd.
7   *Jamaican History*. Accessed 17 January 2016, http://jis.gov.jm/information/jamaican-history/

building fortifications, completing Fort Cromwell in less than two years.[8] A settlement grew up around the fort which, after the restoration of the English monarchy under Charles II, was named Port Royal. There were insufficient numbers of soldiers to defend Port Royal, so its governor came up with a novel if risky solution: he invited the group of pirates known as the Brethren of the Coast to come and make the town their home. The Brethren were settled on the island of Tortuga off the north-west coast of Hispaniola – present-day Haiti – when the Spanish, eager to rid their colony of such a bunch of lawless individuals, drove them off. After their expulsion the Brethren had no love for Spain and so were happy to oblige Port Royal's governor by concentrating their attacks on Spanish shipping. They later became privateers, sailing against Spanish, French and Dutch ships under letters of marque issued by the Governor of Jamaica.

Spain never recaptured Jamaica, losing the Battle of Ocho Rios in 1657 and the Battle of Rio Nuevo in 1658. The remaining Spanish settlers briefly continued to put up some resistance to the English but, having failed, left the island for neighbouring Cuba in 1660. Those enslaved members of the population that did not accompany their masters to Cuba moved into the mountainous interior of Jamaica, where they joined with the few remaining members of the indigenous population and continued to harass the English. They were known as maroons, coming from the Spanish word *cimarrón* meaning 'fugitive' or 'runaway'.[9] After England gained formal possession of Jamaica from Spain through the 1670 Treaty of Madrid, Port Royal served as the island's capital, but after the 1692 earthquake put an end to the legendary wild lifestyle of its occupants it was replaced by St Jago de la Vega.

Northwest of Jamaica and south of Cuba lie the Cayman Islands, which comprise three small islands: Grand Cayman, Cayman Brac and Little Cayman, with a total land area of 102 square miles (264 square km). Although the islands were not permanently settled, it is thought that indigenous people visited the islands to harvest their marine life.

---

8   *The Underwater City of Port Royal.* Accessed 17 January 2016, http://whc.unesco.org/en/tentativelists/5430/
9   Metcalf, George, for the Royal Commonwealth Society. *Royal government and political conflict in Jamaica, 172 where he9-1783.* London: Longmans, 1965, pp.3-4.

They were sighted by Christopher Columbus in May 1503 during his fourth voyage, when his ship was blown off course westward, toward 'two very small and low islands, full of tortoises [turtles], as was all the sea all about, insomuch that they looked like little rocks, for which reason these islands were called Las Tortugas'.[10] The two islands were Cayman Brac and Little Cayman. A 1523 map, which shows all three Islands, gave them the name Lagartos, meaning 'large lizards', but by 1530 the name Caymanas was being used. This is derived from the Amerindian word for marine crocodiles, many of which, along with the turtles, lived on the islands. This name, or a variant, has been the name of the islands ever since.[11] An early English visitor was Sir Francis Drake who, during his 1585–86 voyage confirmed the presence of caymans: 'great serpents called Caymanas, like large lizards, which are edible'.[12] The islands' abundant turtle supply made them a popular port of call for ships wanting meat for their crews, a practice which eventually depleted the local resource.

---

10 *Cayman Islands history*. Accessed 9 May 2017, https://web.archive.org/web/20081012073753/http://www.gocayman.ky/history.html
11 Ibid.
12 Ibid.

Appendix 4

Major Military Conflicts that Impacted the Caribbean During the 18th and 19th Centuries

Throughout much of the 18th century European nations focused their attention on fighting for power, dominance and territory in wars that often spread to their possessions in the Caribbean. Spain, Great Britain, France, the Dutch Republic and Denmark fought to keep the colonies on which so much of their economic prosperity depended, and tried to prevent them from trading with any colony other than the 'Mother Country' they belonged to.[13] The main conflicts are listed here:

The **War of the Spanish Succession** (1701–1714), was brought about by the death in 1700 of the childless Charles II, King of Spain. Charles had named Philip, Duke of Anjou and grandson of the French king, Louis XIV, as his successor. But the resulting possible unification of France and Spain would have altered the balance of power in Europe, so this caused those opposed to Philip – England, Holland, the Holy Roman Empire, the Dutch Republic, Portugal and the Duchy of Savoy – to declare war against France and Spain.

The War of Jenkins' Ear (1739–1742) was part of a larger conflict: the **War of the Austrian Succession** (1740–1748). This war again involved most of the European powers, who fought over the eligibility of the Austrian Archduchess, Maria Theresa, daughter of the Holy

---

13   The country from which the people of a colony or former colony derive their origin.

Roman Emperor Charles VI, to rule over the Hapsburg lands. The War of Jenkins' Ear was fought between Britain and Spain, and arose from longstanding antagonism between the two countries because of British trading activities in the Spanish Caribbean in contravention of the Treaty of Utrecht. This treaty had ended the War of Spanish Succession in 1713 and had given Britain a thirty-year contract to supply unlimited slaves and supply 500 tons of trade goods to the Spanish colonies. But British ships were trading far more than the 500-ton allowance, and Spain's coast guard vessels began to board British ships and confiscate their cargoes. Open hostilities broke out after the alleged sinking of several British merchant ships by Spanish privateers and the suspension of the slave supply contract. The unusual name comes from an incident when the brig *Rebecca*, bound for London with a cargo of sugar from Jamaica and captained by one Robert Jenkins, was boarded by a Spanish coast guard vessel. In the fighting that followed, Jenkins' ear was severed.

In the **Seven Years' War** (1754–1763), France and Spain fought against Britain. The war affected Europe, North America, Central America and the Caribbean – the latter becoming an important theatre of war as the opposing powers struggled to retain their lucrative sugar colonies. When France and Spain were defeated they agreed in the Treaty of Paris to give up all of Canada, then known as New France, rather than the sugar islands of Guadeloupe and Martinique. Britain seized Havana toward the end of the war but traded the city for all of Florida. In addition, France ceded the islands of Grenada and Dominica to Britain. The islands of Tobago and St Vincent, which had been declared neutral and to be left to the indigenous population, came under British supervision.

The **American Revolutionary War** (1775–1783) saw the American colonies reject the British monarchy, defeat the British forces, and found the United States of America. In 1778, the French entered the war in support of the United States, and later the Spanish and the Dutch entered the conflict as French allies. The Caribbean again became a focus of conflict as the European powers fought to retain their respective possessions. France lost St Lucia to Britain early in the war but then captured the islands of Dominica, Grenada, Saint Vincent, Montserrat, Tobago, St Kitts and the Turks and Caicos. Dutch possessions were first taken by Britain, but later recaptured by France and restored to the Dutch Republic. At the Battle of the Saintes, small islands south of Guadeloupe, the British Admiral Rodney defeated the French fleet, frustrating the hopes of France and Spain to take the important sugar island of Jamaica. At the end of the American Revolutionary War, all the British islands that had been captured by the French, except for Tobago, were returned to Britain.

The **French Revolutionary Wars** (1792–1802) were a series of military conflicts that developed after the French Revolution. Fighting began within Europe between the French First Republic and several European powers, but the conflict spread as the ambitions of the republic grew. In December 1801, the French sent an expedition to the French Caribbean colony of Saint-Domingue to put down the revolution that had started there in 1791, but the blockade by the British fleet made the sending of reinforcements impossible and the expedition failed. The revolution on Saint Domingue ultimately succeeded, and in 1804 the French colony became the Republic of Haiti.

The 1802 Treaty of Amiens, signed between the British and the French, is generally considered to be the point of transition from the French Revolutionary Wars to the **Napoleonic Wars** (1803–1815). The Napoleonic Wars were fought by the French Empire, led by Emperor Napoleon I, against various coalitions of other European powers. Napoleon planned to invade Britain, but first had to defeat the British navy, or at least move its ships away from the English Channel. He developed a complex plan to distract the British by threatening its possessions in the Caribbean. This failed when a Franco-Spanish fleet under Admiral Villeneuve turned back after an indecisive action off Cape Finisterre. Villeneuve was then blockaded in Cadiz, and when he broke through the blockade was chased by the British fleet to the Caribbean and back to Cape Trafalgar off the south-west coast of Spain. Here, in 1805, the Franco-Spanish fleet was caught by the British and overwhelmingly defeated at the Battle of Trafalgar.

APPENDIX 4

War in the Caribbean did not, however, end with the Battle of Trafalgar, and fighting continued between the European powers and, in 1898, the Spanish-American War ended Spanish control of the Caribbean islands of Cuba and Puerto Rico.

Appendix 5

Background History of Barbados, the British Windward Islands and Trinidad

Barbados is the most eastern of the Caribbean islands. Named Ichirouganaim (Island with White Teeth, because of its reefs) by its first Amerindian settlers, it was sighted in the early 16th century by both the Portuguese explorer Pedro a Campos and by the Spanish, who landed on it in 1518. It could have been either the Portuguese or the Spanish who gave the island the name of Barbudos (meaning Bearded Ones in both languages) possibly because of the bearded appearance of the aerial roots of the local strangler fig trees. As there appeared to be no mineral resources Spain was not interested in settling on the island, but made frequent slave-raiding missions onto it from its other colonies. This led to the total destruction of the indigenous population, who either were captured and taken away or fled to nearby mountainous islands, where it was easier to defend themselves against the invading Europeans.[14] The first English ship to arrive on Barbados landed under the command of Captain John Powell in 1625. He claimed Barbados for King James I, just three years after Sir Thomas Warner had claimed St Christopher as the first Caribbean possession for England. Captain Powell returned to Barbados in 1627, founding a settlement on the west coast of the island that was named Jamestown (today known as Holetown).

---

14 *Barbados: history*. Accessed 16 May 2016, http://thecommonwealth.org/our-member-countries/barbados/history

APPENDIX 5

The Windward Island of St Lucia lies south of Martinique and north-east of St Vincent. The Amerindians who first inhabited the island called it Iouanalao, Hewanarau, or Hewanorra ('There where, there are Iguanas') and it is claimed that a group of French sailors were the first to call it Sainte Alousie in about 1502. Subsequent French and Spanish spellings include Sainte Alpouzie, Santa Lucia, Saint Luzia and Sancta Lucia. First settled by the Dutch in about 1600, the island changed hands between the English and the French over the next 200 years, while the local population made strenuous efforts to defend their territory.[15]

Further south in the chain of islands is the island of St Vincent, which lies east of Barbados. Called Hairoun (Land of the Blessed) by its early inhabitants it, like St Lucia, was fought over by the French and the British and fiercely defended by the Garinagu, or Garifuna, people of mixed Amerindian and African heritage. Hairoun, along with the small islands of the northern Grenadines that lie to the south of St Vincent, was their home.

To the south of St Vincent lies the island of Grenada. It was named Camarhogne by its Amerindian population, but when Christopher Columbus passed by the island in 1498 he named it Concepcion. It is said that passing Spanish sailors renamed it after Granada, the beautiful city in the southern Spanish region of Andalucia, because it reminded them of it. When France took the island, nearly exterminating the indigenous population in the process, the name was adapted to La Grenade and in 1763, when the island was ceded to Britain, the name was adapted again, this time to Grenada (pronounced GrenAYda). Grenada briefly returned once more to France before becoming a British colony in 1783.[16]

Tobago lies south-east of Grenada and north-east of the island of Trinidad and was sighted by Columbus during his third voyage in 1498. The Amerindian inhabitants of the island gave it a name not dissimilar to the name it bears today: Tavacco, the local name for the pipe in which they smoked their tobacco. The first European settlers were Dutch; they were

---

15   *St Lucia: history.* Accessed 16 May 2016, http://thecommonwealth.org/our-member-countries/saint-lucia/history
16   *Grenada: history.* Accessed 16 May 2016, http://thecommonwealth.org/our-member-countries/grenada/history

followed by the French, and then by the Duchy of Courland (present-day Latvia). France and Britain then fought over the island until it was ceded to Britain in 1763, even so, they continued to fight for it until it was returned to Britain in 1814. Tobago changed hands during its colonial history more than any other island in the Caribbean.[17]

After Britain gained possession of Tobago in 1763, development of the island focused on the creation of an economy based on the large-scale production of crops for export to foreign markets.[18] Sugar was the major crop, but cotton and indigo were also produced. Tobago's sugar cultivation began late in comparison to the other Caribbean sugar islands, and its sugar production didn't peak until the early 19th century. This was partly because during the era of sailing ships the island was valued not so much for its agricultural potential as for its strategic importance: except for Barbados, Tobago is the most easterly of the Caribbean islands, enabling ships, both merchant and military, to catch the prevailing easterly trade winds from the coast and sail the island chain at will. Ships from other islands had a much harder time reaching Tobago, needing to sail into the wind to get there. As the importance of the sugar islands increased, so did the importance of Tobago as a strategic possession: no European country with Caribbean colonies wanted Tobago to belong to a rival power.[19] Other reasons for the late agricultural development of Tobago include the availability of land on other islands and the relatively mountainous topography of Tobago that made much of the island unsuitable for sugar cultivation. Tobago's first capital was George Town, situated on the south coast of the island and overlooking Barbados Bay. Scarborough, also on the south coast but further to the west, later became the capital.

The island of Trinidad lies just off the coast of north-eastern Venezuela and about 81 miles (130 km) south of Grenada It was first named Iere, or Kairi (both variations of the word meaning 'island') by its early Amerindian inhabitants, but Columbus renamed it La Trinidad in 1498, as he had

---

17 Trinidad and Tobago: history. Accessed 22 May 2016, thecommonwealth.org/our-member-countries/trinidad-and-tobago/history
18 Clement, Christopher Ohm. 'Landscapes and plantations on Tobago: a regional perspective.' PhD diss., University of Florida, 1995, p.10.
19 Ibid, pp.35–36.

vowed to name after the Holy Trinity the first land he saw during his third voyage. There was no Spanish settlement on the island until 1592, and as there were no valuable metals to mine, its development proceeded slowly. The few Spanish colonists who established themselves on Trinidad grew some tobacco and cacao, and fought off spasmodic raids by the English, Dutch and French settlers from neighbouring islands. To increase development, under the 1783 Royal Decree, or Cedula, the Spanish government offered generous land and tax incentives to Roman Catholics from other Caribbean islands who were willing to move to Trinidad. The events of the French Revolution had led to a growing instability among the plantocracy of the French islands in the Caribbean, especially on Haiti, so many French Roman Catholic planters were eager to come to Trinidad and take advantage of the new opportunities being offered by Spain.[20]

By 1797, when the island surrendered to a British expedition, Trinidad was established as a sugar economy. The island became a British Crown colony in 1802 when it found itself in the unusual position of being a British possession with a population that was largely French-speaking which was administered under laws that remained Spanish. Sugar had exhausted the soil on some of the older British possessions in the eastern Caribbean, and planters looking for new and undeveloped land on which to plant sugar began to arrive. Trinidad had plenty to offer. After Emancipation, Trinidad was still relatively underpopulated and, with a still-growing sugar economy, needed a large supply of labour. Between about 1845 and the early 20th century that need was met, as in British Guiana, by the importation of indentured labourers. A total of about 150,000 arrived during the period, mostly from the British colony of India, with some from China and Madeira. They came on contract, on completion of which they were in theory free to return home or buy plots of land. But in practice, they worked long hours in appalling conditions and often became debt peons, compelled to renew their contract because they were unable to pay off their debt to the estate at the end of their indenture.

---

20   *Trinidad and Tobago: history*. Accessed 22 May 2016, thecommonwealth.org/our-member-countries/trinidad-and-tobago/history

Appendix 6

Background History of British Guiana and Aruba

The colony of British Guiana which, after gaining independence from Britain in 1966, became Guyana, lies on the coast of the north-eastern mainland of South America. Bordered by the Atlantic Ocean to the north, it is today bordered by Brazil to the south and south-west, Suriname to the east, and Venezuela to the west. The whole of the north-eastern part of the continent was first inhabited by various groups of Amerindians, including the Arawak, Akawaio, Arecuna, Carib, Macushi, Patamona, Warrau, Wapisiana, and Wai. As their land was crossed by many rivers, creeks, rapids and waterfalls, they called the region Guiana, a name which probably comes from the Arawak words *Wai Ana* which mean 'Land of Many Waters.'[21]

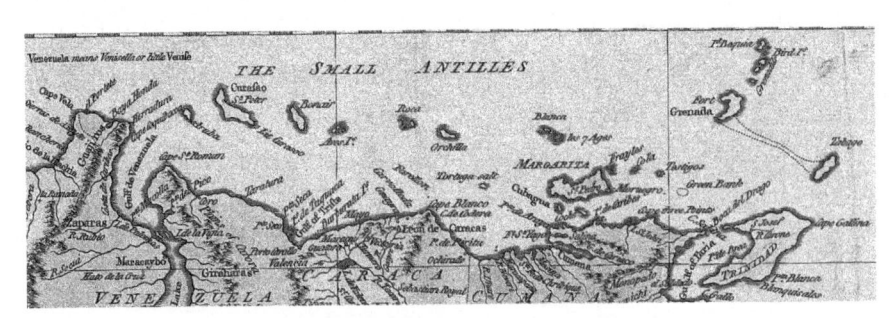

Part of: A map of the Dutch settlements of Surinam, Demerary, Issequibo, Berbices, and the islands of Curassoa, Aruba, Bonaire, &c., with the French colony of Cayenne, and the adjacent Spanish countries, taken from a map executed under the patronage of the Court of France.
Engraved by John Lodge. Published by John Bew in 1781.

---

21   *History of Guyana*. Accessed 1 August 2016, http://www.guyanesepride.com/about/

APPENDIX 6

Guiana is thought to have been sighted in about 1499 by either the Spaniard, Alonso de Ojeda, or by his co-voyagers, Amerigo Vespucci and Juan de la Cosa. Spain claimed the area, but took little interest in its exploration or settlement. Almost a century later, in 1595, the area was visited by English explorers under the leadership of Sir Walter Raleigh (about 1552–1618). Raleigh was born in Devon, not Cornwall, but in 1585, Queen Elizabeth I appointed him Lord Warden of the Devon and Cornwall Stannaries.[22] This gave him executive authority over the Stannary Parliaments and Stannary Courts of the two counties, which were responsible for the legislative and legal administration of the tin mining industry. He was also made Lord Lieutenant of Cornwall and Vice-Admiral of Devon and Cornwall.[23] The year before his first voyage to Guiana, Raleigh read a Spanish account of the legendary golden city of El Dorado, which was supposedly in the Guiana region, and enthusiastically set out in search of its riches. He succeeded in exploring many miles of the interior of Guiana and although he failed to find El Dorado, on his return to England he made exaggerated claims about his discoveries in a book entitled *The Discoverie of the Large, Rich, and Bewtiful Empyre of Guiana*,[24] which became one of the bestsellers of the day.

In 1603, soon after the death of Queen Elizabeth, Raleigh's fortunes changed: he was arrested and charged with treason for his involvement in a plot against Elizabeth's successor, King James I. He remained in prison until 1617, when he was pardoned and given permission to lead another expedition to Guiana. England was currently at peace with Spain, and Raleigh received the king's pardon on condition that he avoided any hostility against England's erstwhile enemy. During the expedition, a detachment of Raleigh's men attacked a Spanish outpost on the Orinoco River, and on Raleigh's return to England, the furious Spanish ambassador demanded the explorer's execution. King James acceded to the ambassador's demands, and Raleigh was beheaded on 29 October 1618.[25]

22　The English word 'stannary' is derived from the Latin word 'stannum', meaning 'tin'.
23　*Walter Raleigh (c.1552–1618)*. Accessed 1 August 2016, http://www.bbc.co.uk/history/historic_figures/raleigh_walter.shtml
24　*Sir Walter Raleigh (1554–1618): The Discovery of Guiana, 1595*. Accessed 1 August 2016, http://sourcebooks.fordham.edu/mod/1595raleigh-guiana.asp
25　*Walter Raleigh (c.1552–1618)*. Accessed 1 August 2016, http://www.bbc.co.uk/history/historic_figures/raleigh_walter.shtml

The Dutch were the first Europeans to settle Guiana. They became independent from Spain in the late 16th century and, as the Dutch Republic, soon emerged as a major commercial power, trading with the English and French colonies in the Caribbean. In the early 17th century, a party of Dutch colonists sailed into the estuary of the mighty Essequibo River, which at its mouth is more than 20 miles (32 km) wide. They explored the Essequibo up as far as the Mazaruni River, and on a small island at the confluence of the Mazaruni with the Cuyuni River they built a trading post defended by a fort. The fort was initially named Fort Ter Hoogen after one of the colonists, but because of its position, which gave the settlers a good view of all who travelled up and down the rivers, it became known as Kyk-over-Al, Dutch for 'See over All'.[26]

In 1621, the Dutch Republic established the Dutch West India Company, a private trading company, giving it the responsibility both of managing Dutch possessions in the region and of making war against the colonies of Spain and Portugal. The company was given complete control over the Dutch colony of Essequibo, and in 1627 established a second colony to the west, along the Berbice River. In 1650, the colony of Surinam, to the east of the Corentyne River and bordering Berbice, was settled by the English under a grant from the English king, Charles II. The settlers were led by Lord Willoughby, then Governor of Barbados. And here, at Willoughby's invitation, Cornishman Nicholas Leverton briefly ministered to the Surinamers' spiritual needs.[27] Meanwhile, the French were attempting to settle the area to the east of Surinam, which would become known as French Guiana. The colony of Demerara, situated along the Demerara River between the colonies of Essequibo and Berbice, was settled by the Dutch in 1741.[28]

---

26 Ishmael, Odeen. *The Guyana story: from earliest times to Independence.* Georgetown: Guyanese Online, 2005. Accessed 4 August 2016, https://guyaneseonline.wordpress.com/2011/11/23/history-the-guyana-story-dr-odeen-ishmael/

27 For more about Nicholas Leverton, see Chapter 5: Barbados, the Windward Islands and Trinidad.

28 Ishmael, Odeen. *The Guyana story: from earliest times to Independence.* Georgetown: Guyanese Online, 2005. Accessed 4 August 2016, https://guyaneseonline.wordpress.com/2011/11/23/history-the-guyana-story-dr-odeen-ishmael/

APPENDIX 6

The first of the colonists to take an interest in the potential of the mineral resources of Guiana was Laurens Storm van's Gravesande. In 1738, he arrived in the Dutch colony of Essequibo as secretary to the governor. He became Governor of Essequibo in 1743, and later became Governor of both Essequibo and Berbice. Although his main focus was the development of plantations along the coast and beside the main rivers, he also encouraged prospecting for gold and silver, although by the time he retired in 1772 little progress had been made in the discovery of valuable mineral resources.[29]

As competition between the European powers for Caribbean possessions increased, Essequibo, Demerara and Berbice, and Surinam and French Guiana repeatedly changed hands between Dutch, French and British colonisers. In 1814, at the end of the Napoleonic Wars, the colonies of Essequibo, Demerara and Berbice were ceded to Britain, which in 1831 united them as British Guiana. Britain now began to pay attention to the potential of the colony's mineral resources, but because in the early days of settlement colonial boundaries had not been properly demarcated, as mineral exploration got under way, disputes arose with neighbouring Venezuela and Surinam, which were, like Britain, both starting to establish mines.[30][31]

About 900 miles (1,450 km) west of Georgetown along the north coast of South America is the island of Aruba, which lies in the southern Caribbean Sea, 18 miles (29 km) north of the coast of present Venezuela. Its neighbouring islands are Curaçao and Bonaire, both to the east of Aruba. It is a small island, only 20 miles (32km) long from its north-western to its south-eastern end, and 6 miles (10 km) across at its widest point; but during the 19th century, although it did not possess the mineral riches of Guiana, it was mined for its gold.

Like Guiana, Aruba was first inhabited by Amerindians, who called it Ora-oubao (Shell Island) or Oirubae (Companion of Curaçao). The island was thought to have been sighted in about 1499 by Alonso de Ojeda, as

---

[29] Josiah, Barbara P. *Migration, mining, and the African diaspora: Guyana in the nineteenth and twentieth centuries.* New York: Palgrave Macmillan, 2011, p.10.

[30] Harvard Law School. Human Rights Program. International Human Rights Clinic. *All that glitters: gold mining in Guyana – the failure of government oversights and the human rights of Amerindian communities.* Cambridge: Harvard Law School, 2007, p.2.

[31] To this day, Venezuela considers the area of Guyana west of the Essequibo to be rightly theirs.

he and his fellow explorers sailed westwards along the coast from Guiana. Somewhat unimaginatively, Ojeda named the group of small islands Las Islas Adyacentes a la Costa Firma (literally, 'the Islands Lying off the Firm Shore'). In 1501, Ojeda was appointed factor (royal representative) of the islands as part of a royal decree issued by the Catholic monarchs of Spain, Ferdinand and Isabella. Quantities of logwood, or dyewood[32] were found on Aruba and exported back to Spain, but no precious metals were discovered, and as the island was flat and dry and given to long periods of drought, it was not thought suitable for agriculture. In 1513, Diego Columbus,[33] governor of Spain's possessions in the Caribbean, decreed the islands to be 'islas inútiles' (useless islands), and two years later traders succeeded in capturing nearly the whole indigenous population of Aruba and the nearby islands. The traders took them north to the Spanish colony of Hispaniola, where they were sold into enslavement, to replace the local labour force which had been decimated both by the introduction of European diseases, to which they had no resistance, and by the harsh treatment they received from the Spanish settlers.[34]

Some of these enslaved people were later repatriated to Aruba to harvest the remaining logwood. They were sent by Juan Martín de Ampués who, in about 1526, was made Governor of Curaçao, Aruba and Bonaire. He sent cattle to run free on the island and as they multiplied rapidly they became a ready source of hides. As only small numbers of Amerindians migrated across from the South American mainland to join the islanders the population grew slowly, but with the exception of small scale cattle and horse breeding ventures there was little development.[35]

Dutch West India Company ships stopped at the island from time to time. They initially came in search of logwood and for the salt needed to develop their herring industry, but it did not take them long to realise that Spain had left her southern Caribbean islands – those 'useless islands' – largely

---

32 A hard tropical wood, also known as Brazilwood or Fustic, from which red colouring matter is extracted for use in the manufacture of luxury textiles such as velvet.
33 Eldest son of Christopher Columbus.
34 Hartog, Johan. *Aruba past and present: from the time of the Indians until today*. Oranjestad: D.J. De Wit, 1961, pp.28–31.
35 Ibid., pp.28–31.

undefended. By 1636, the company took Aruba, Curaçao and Bonaire on behalf of the Dutch Republic, when Aruba and Bonaire became dependencies of Curaçao. On Aruba the Dutch began to improve the management and production of both the cattle- and horse-breeding enterprises. A cattle ranch was soon supplying meat to feed the people of Curaçao, and the horses produced by the breeding station improved in quality and grew in number, enabling Aruba to provide the Dutch with the horses they needed as they fought against Spain on the South American mainland. These were still relatively small enterprises. The local Amerindian labour was sufficient to look after the cattle and horses and, although enslaved people from Africa were starting to be imported to Hispaniola and other Caribbean colonies, none were brought to Aruba. The island continued as the company's private estate, only to be settled with the permission of the director.[36]

The company began to take an interest in the local mineral resources. In 1725, in an effort to widen the development possibilities on Aruba and the neighbouring islands, it sent Paulus Printz from Amsterdam to conduct an analysis of soil samples on Curaçao, Bonaire and Aruba. He found a small amount of gold on Aruba, but not in sufficient quantities to make investment in mining a worthwhile risk, and after spending three years on the island he returned to Amsterdam.[37]

In 1754, the Dutch West India Company decided to open Aruba to settlers. The majority came from Curaçao and Bonaire, which had a mixed European population comprising not only Dutch and Spanish, but Belgians, Germans, Italians, French and English. When the settlers arrived, they brought with them enslaved people from Africa and began to develop small plantations, mostly for the breeding of sheep and goats. The horse-breeding station continued to expand its business, and the exportation of horses to Cuba and Jamaica became one of the island's most important sources of income.[38]

---

36   Aruba. National Archaeological Museum. *The first inhabitants of Aruba*. Accessed 17 June 2016, http://www-namaruba.org/_media/first-inhabitants.pdf

37   Hartog, Johan. *Aruba past and present: from the time of the Indians until today*. Oranjestad: D.J. De Wit, 1961, p.62.

38   Aruba. National Archaeological Museum. *The first inhabitants of Aruba*. Accessed 17 June 2016, http://www-namaruba.org/_media/first-inhabitants.pdf

From the end of the 18th into the beginning of the 19th century, Aruba, like many other islands in the Caribbean, went through a period of instability. While the impact of the French Revolution and its ideas apparently went largely unnoticed, there were other events that caused disruption to the steady pace of island life. The Dutch West India Company went bankrupt in 1792 and the company's possessions were taken over by the Dutch state. In 1799, Britain took possession of Aruba. But the island was suffering from a long period of drought, and food became short as the drought continued into the following year. In 1802, the Peace of Amiens gave Aruba back to the Dutch, but in 1805 Aruba was returned to Britain. France then tried to take the island, but the attempt failed and in 1814, with the end of the Napoleonic Wars, Aruba returned to Dutch control. The island was able to start to repair its damaged infrastructure and rebuild its neglected livestock and horse-breeding enterprises.[39] Aruba seemed destined to return to a life based on animal husbandry – but in 1824 gold was discovered.

---

39   Ibid.

Appendix 7

The Early History of Methodism and the Development of its Popularity in Cornwall

Methodism came into being through the efforts of the two Wesley brothers, John (1703–1791) and his younger brother Charles (1707–1788). They were born in Epworth, Lincolnshire, where their father was rector of the local parish church. They came from a large family where money was short but education was important, and both John and Charles continued their studies at Oxford University. Here, along with a number of their student friends, they founded the Holy Club, which met weekly for methodical religious study. Fellow students mocked the club, and because of the focus on disciplined spirituality called them 'Methodists'. John Wesley took this as a compliment, and the members of the Holy Club were known as Methodists from then on.[40]

John Wesley was ordained in the Anglican Church in 1728 and initially sought reform from within the Church. His message was simple: redemption was available to all, and anyone with sufficient faith could be saved. The movement was dominated by Wesley, who determined its structure and defined its doctrine. He built up a network, or Connexion, of travelling preachers and groups of like-minded people known as Societies, who were bound together by their shared beliefs and their

---

40 Methodist Church in the Caribbean and the Americas. *Our history and heritage*. Accessed 6 June 2016, http://www.mccalive.org/our_church.php?mid=9

loyalty to Wesley. Ordained preachers and the lay preachers appointed by Wesley met with him at an annual conference, when they were assigned to the Methodist Societies established in different areas of Britain. The preachers travelled around their 'Circuit' of Methodist Societies, visiting each society on a regular basis.[41]

As Methodism developed it drew increasing criticism from the Anglican Church, whose bishops disapproved of Wesley's freelance preaching activities, and whose local incumbents resented Methodist preachers who came uninvited to their parishes. Meanwhile, among the Methodists, calls for greater independence from the Anglican Church became more frequent. There was no formal separation between Anglicans and Methodists during Wesley's lifetime, but after his death in 1791 there was a gradual disengagement from Anglicanism as Methodism evolved into a movement with a distinctive organisation and ethos. Responsibility for the development of Methodism rested with the conference, which comprised 100 elected preachers and acted under the guidance of an annually elected president. Differences of opinion on theology, church government and mission strategy resulted in the establishment of several different Methodist groups over the next sixty years, most of which later re-united.[42]

In his effort to spread his message, Wesley travelled widely throughout England, Scotland and Wales. He first went to Cornwall in 1743 and frequently returned there to preach, most famously in a hollow among old mine workings at Gwennap Pit, near Redruth. During the 18th and early 19th centuries, Gwennap was in the centre of Cornwall's greatest copper mining district, and one of the most densely populated areas of the county,[43] so Wesley could always be sure that a large crowd would gather to listen to his words. After his death, in honour of his work in Cornwall local people excavated the pit into a regular oval and added tiers

---

41 Ibid.
42 Ibid. In 1907, the Bible Christians, United Methodist Free Churches and the Methodist Connection reunited as the United Methodist Church. In 1932, the Wesleyan Methodist Church, primitive Methodist Church and United Methodist Church amalgamated.
43 *Gwennap–Chacewater mining district*. Accessed 13 June 2016, https://web.archive.org/web/20090414074307/http://www.cornish-mining.org.uk/sites/gwennap.htm

of turf seats, creating a gathering place which remained in use for many years.[44]

In Cornwall, many of the travelling lay preachers were from the county, a good number of them women who spoke the local dialect and were comfortable interacting with groups of Cornish men and women wherever they found them, be it in a cottage, a barn, or a field – an approach to spreading the Word that Anglican vicars, tied to their respective churches, could never emulate. The Methodist preachers brought comfort, hope and a sense of security to members of the mining, fishing and agricultural communities living in uncertain times. This was especially true in the mining areas, where miners faced physical danger every day they went to work, and their jobs were often subject to sudden changes in the global mineral market changes that could mean a sudden increase in employment opportunities but could lead just as rapidly to job losses.[45] Strong believers in self-improvement, the Methodists provided healthcare and literacy training to local communities, helping the people to achieve a better standard of living – something that the Anglican Church seemed to show no interest in doing.[46]

As the popularity of Methodism in Cornwall grew, chapels began to appear. By 1785, over 30 per cent of Cornish parishes had an active Methodist Society. By 1815, this had risen to 83 per cent, and when the Religious Census of 1851 was completed, it showed that more churchgoers attended a Methodist chapel in Cornwall than anywhere else in Britain.[47]

John Wesley once wrote to his friend John Hervey, who had been a member of the Oxford Holy Club: 'I look upon all the world as my parish; thus far I mean, that in whatever part of it I am I judge it meet, right,

---

[44] *Gwennap pit.* Accessed 13 June 2016, https://web.archive.org/web/20090612113705/http://www.cornish-mining.org.uk/sites/gwnnppt.htm
[45] Deacon, Bernard. *The causes of Methodist growth.* Accessed 6 June 2016, https://bernarddeacon.wordpress.com/cornish-methodism-or-methodism-in-cornwall/the-causes-of-methodist-growth/
[46] *John Wesley and the Methodist movement.* Accessed 6 June 2016, http://www.cornwalls.co.uk/history/people/john_wesley.htm
[47] Deacon, Bernard. *Cornish Methodism or Methodism in Cornwall?* Accessed 6 June 2016, https://bernarddeacon.wordpress.com/cornish-methodism-or-methodism-in-cornwall/

and my bounden duty to declare, unto all that are willing to hear, the glad tidings of salvation.'[48] This missionary spirit naturally led to the early development of missions overseas. Indeed: 'There was never any need to inject into the Methodist body a missionary spirit. For Methodism, from its inception, <u>was</u> a missionary movement. This was its *raison d'être*.'[49]

As a young man, Wesley visited North America, including the southern state of Georgia, where he encountered enslaved people for the first time. The experience gave him a strong dislike of enslavement and he was keen to focus his early overseas missionary work on colonies where the enslaved made up a major part of the local population. He later wrote a tract entitled *Thoughts upon slavery*,[50] in which he attacked the trade in enslaved people with considerable passion, proposing a boycott of slave-produced Caribbean sugar and rum.[51]

But it was the Moravians,[52] not the Methodists, which was the first denomination to make a serious attempt at mission work among the enslaved population of the Caribbean, when in 1732 a group of German Moravians arrived on the then Danish island of St Thomas. A small group of Moravians later settled in London, where they attracted a lot of attention: 'For … the London Moravians provided both a stimulus and an example: they helped to make the evangelically-minded who contacted them mission-conscious.'[53] John Wesley was among those 'evangelically-minded' who met, and was greatly impressed by, the Moravians and their work, and they greatly influenced his thinking on how best to establish the Methodist overseas mission programme.

---

48 [Letter] to *James Hervey, March 20, 1739*. Accessed 10 July 2016, http://wesley.nnu.edu/john-wesley/the-letters-of-john-wesley/wesleys-letters-1739#Four
49 Hughes, Henry Brackenbury Louis. 'Christian missionary societies in the British West Indies during the Emancipation era.' PhD diss., University of Toronto, 1944, p.151.
50 Wesley, John. *Thoughts upon slavery*. London: John Cruikshank, 1778. Accessed 13 June 2016, http://docsouth.unc.edu/church/wesley/wesley.html
51 *John Wesley (1703–1791): The Methodist Minister*. Accessed 13 June 2016, http://abolition.e2bn.org/people_32.html
52 The movement that became the Moravian Church was started in the late 14th century in Moravia, now part of the Czech Republic, by a group of people who objected to some of the practices of the Roman Catholic Church and wanted to return the Church to the simpler practices of early Christianity.
53 Hughes, Henry Brackenbury Louis. 'Christian missionary societies in the British West Indies during the Emancipation era.' PhD diss., University of Toronto, 1944, p.151.

Appendix 8

Background History of Cuba and the Dominican Republic

Cuba, with an area of 42,800 square miles (110,860 square km), is the largest island in the Caribbean. Located in the northern part of the region, its closest neighbours are Hispaniola to the east, the Bahamas and Florida to the north, Mexico to the west, and Jamaica and the Cayman Islands to the south. Named Cubanascnan, or Cubanacan, by its indigenous population, it was renamed Isla Juana, after Spain's Crown Prince Juan, by Columbus during his 1492 voyage. But use of the indigenous name continued, although it was gradually abbreviated until it took the form we know today: Cuba.[54] Columbus returned to Cuba in 1494, when he explored the island's south coast, but although some superficial exploration for gold deposits took place, Cuba did not appear to possess potential for gold production and there was no immediate settlement. Instead, from about 1506, regular expeditions were sent from Hispaniola to Cuba to capture its indigenous population. Transported back to Hispaniola, the captives were used as slave labour in the local gold mines.[55]

It was not until 1511 that Diego Velázquez de Cuéllar, along with some 300 soldiers, was sent from Hispaniola to settle Cuba.[56] He met

---

54 Wilkinson, Jerry. *History of Cuba.* Accessed 11 November 2016, http://www.keyshistory.org/cuba.html
55 Waszkis, Helmut. *Mining in the Americas: stories and history.* Cambridge: Woodhead Publishing, 1993, p.16.
56 Velázquez' treasurer was Hernán Cortés, who would soon subdue the Aztec Empire and claim Mexico for Spain.

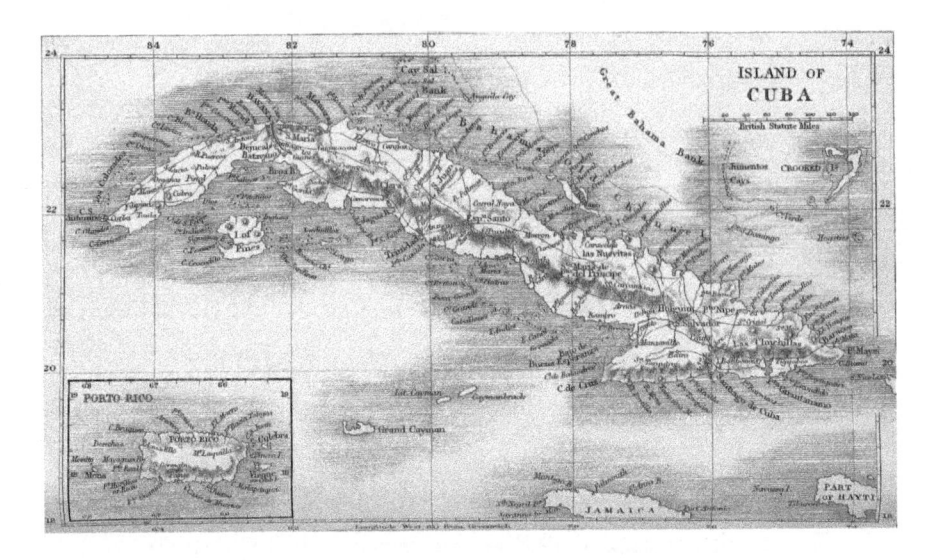

Map of the Island of Cuba. Turnbull, David. *Travels in the West. Cuba; with notices of Porto Rico and the slave trade*. London: Longman, Orme, Brown, Green and Longmans, 1840, p.24.

fierce resistance from the local population, led by Hatuey, Hispaniola's head cacique or chief, who after fighting against the Spaniards on his home territory, crossed over to Cuba with a party of his warriors to warn the local people what to expect from Velázquez. But Hatuey's efforts failed, and he was eventually captured and condemned to be burned at the stake. Before he was put to death a priest demanded that he become a Christian so he could go to Heaven and not to Hell. In response to the priest's question, Hatuey asked: 'And the Spaniards, where do they go?' The priest answered: 'If they are baptized, of course they shall go to Heaven like all good Christians.' To which Hatuey replied: 'If the Spaniards will go to Heaven, then I certainly do not wish to go there! So, do not baptize me, I'd rather go to Hell!'[57]

Velázquez was appointed Governor of Cuba and established a small number of settlements throughout the island. One of these was Nuestra Señora de la Asunción de Baracoa, situated on the coast near the north-

---

57 *Hatuey: The Forgotten Haitian Cacique*. Accessed 11 November 2016, http://haitianarawak.com/documents/essays/hatuey.php

eastern tip of the island. It was founded in 1511 and became Cuba's first capital. Then Santiago de Cuba, founded on the south-east coast in 1514, became the capital in 1522. San Cristóbal de la Habana was also established in 1514. Initially built on the south coast, in 1519 the settlement was moved to a site on the north-west coast which had a natural deep-water harbour, a location which was both favourable to the development of trade and commerce, and easy to defend. The settlement grew to become the city of La Habana (Havana) and replaced Santiago as Cuba's capital in 1607. The new capital developed into a major centre for the development of Spanish colonial power in the region: the base from which conquistadors left to colonise Central and South America, and the port where the Spanish treasure ships gathered before sailing home in convoy to Spain.

During these early years of Spanish settlement, further attempts at mineral exploration were made, and expeditions ventured into the interior of the island. Some gold was found in a few of Cuba's rivers, and placer mines were set up to exploit whatever resources were found, but the quantity of gold recovered was relatively small and the mines did not develop into major enterprises. Focus changed from gold to copper with the discovery of rich copper veins in the east of the island, about 12½ miles (20 km) north-west of Santiago de Cuba. The quantity and quality of the copper produced from the ore encouraged investment, and the Spanish Crown awarded the mining rights to a private contractor which worked the mines using enslaved labour from Africa. The mining settlement was first called Santiago del Prado, but over time it came to be known simply as El Cobre – 'cobre' being the Spanish word for copper. By 1545, the quantity of copper ore mined at El Cobre made it economically viable to build a smelter to process the ore.[58] The copper it produced was used in the local manufacture of the large copper pans used to refine sugar and to meet the needs of the Spanish army in Cuba, in neighbouring Hispaniola and in other Spanish possessions in the Caribbean.

Throughout the first half of the 17th century the mines of El Cobre operated at a profit, but as the years passed the various contractors

---

58 Waszkis, Helmut. *Mining in the Americas: stories and history*. Cambridge: Woodhead Publishing, 1993, p.16.

lost interest in managing the business. The Spanish government found it difficult to find new investors willing to develop the site to its full potential, and to meet their Caribbean requirements began importing copper from their Mexican and Peruvian colonies.[59] El Cobre's copper production continued to decline, and in 1670 the Spanish Crown decided to confiscate the property, at which point the enslaved people owned by the private contractor became the property of the Spanish king: they were now entitled to be called the 'King's Slaves'.

Efforts to reactivate the mine under government control failed, and El Cobre slowly began to develop into a quasi-independent community largely comprised of King's Slaves and free coloured people. The only administrative control came from the eastern region's governor, who resided some miles away in Santiago de Cuba and, as nothing was done to reinstate the direct supervision that had been in place when the mine was managed by private contractors, the community began to develop its own surface mining enterprises. They mined the ore and smelted it in small quantities, producing enough copper to supply the domestic market.[60]

As the 18th century drew to a close the desire for social and economic reform within the Spanish Empire began to make an impact. There was a growing interest in Enlightenment philosophy, favouring concepts such as reason, liberty and scientific method over religion, monarchy and hereditary aristocracy. The examples of the American, French and Haitian Revolutions provided practical examples of what could be achieved by applying the principles of Enlightened thought, and encouraged the desire for change.[61] In response, Spain attempted to enforce stricter controls. The practice of appointing *peninsulares* (Spanish-born Spaniards) to royal offices was reintroduced, leaving *criollos* (Spaniards born in Spanish possessions) under-represented in the decision-making process. Trade

---

59 Ibid., p.16.
60 Díaz, María Elena. 'Mining women, royal slaves: copper mining in colonial Cuba, 1670–1780.' In *Mining women: gender in the development of a global industry, 1670 to 2005*, edited by Jaclyn J. Gier-Viskovatoff and Laurie Mercier, pp.21–25. New York: Palgrave Macmillan, 2006.
61 Minster, Christopher. *Latin America: Causes of Independence*. Accessed 14 November 2016, http://latinamericanhistory.about.com/od/19thcenturylatinamerica/a/09independencewhy.htm

restrictions aimed at protecting Spain's economy prohibited trading outside the Spanish Empire and prevented the development of local manufacturing and industrial enterprises. As the collapse of the Bourbon dynasty in Spain left a weakened Spanish Crown, tensions in the Spanish American colonies erupted into open revolt. The Independence Movement, led by such men as José de San Martín and Simón Bolívar, fought hard against Spanish domination, and by 1830, all the Spanish American colonies except for Puerto Rico and Cuba had gained their independence.

To the east of Cuba lies the neighbouring island of Hispaniola, now shared by the Dominican Republic and Haiti. It is the second-largest island in the Caribbean, with an area of 29,418 square miles (76,192 square km). Other neighbouring islands include Puerto Rico to the east and Jamaica to the south-west. Hispaniola was first settled by indigenous people from South and Central America, and was known by various names including Quisqueya, or Kiskeya (meaning 'Mother of the Earth'), Haití and Bohío. Christopher Columbus landed on the island in late 1492 and renamed it la Isla Española (the Spanish Island), a name that was later anglicised to become Hispaniola.[62]

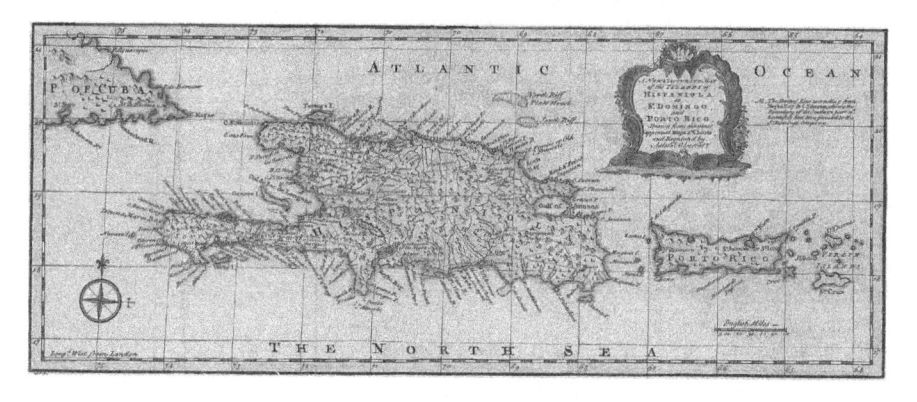

A New and Accurate Map of the Islands of Hispaniola or St Domingo, and Porto Rico, by Emanuel Bowen. Published by William Innys, 1747.

---

62 Guitar, Lynne. *History of the Dominican Republic*. Accessed 19 September 2016, http://www.hispaniola.com/dominican_republic/info/history.php

As Columbus reported that Hispaniola had rich gold deposits, Spanish colonisation began soon after his visit: 1,300 settlers arrived from Spain with their governor, Christopher's brother, Bartolomeo Columbus. Bartolomeo founded the settlement of Nueva Isabella, on the north coast of the island, a location which gave the settlers easy access to the gold resources of the Cibao Valley. The valley proved to have substantial alluvial gold deposits, and as mining increased a new settlement was established within the valley. This was Concepción de La Vega, which soon developed into a thriving town, only to be destroyed by an earthquake in 1562. The town was then relocated to a site on the banks of the Camú River and its name shortened to La Vega. In 1496, after the discovery of gold in the south of the island, Bartolomeo founded the settlement of Santo Domingo, which grew to become an important population centre, the oldest European city in the Americas.[63] In about 1505, the mining settlement of Pueblo Viejo de Cotuí, near to Santo Domingo, was established and, like Concepción de La Vega, became an important gold-mining centre, until it too was levelled by the 1562 earthquake.[64]

To extract the gold, the Spanish settlers first enslaved the indigenous population, forcing them to pan for gold under appalling conditions. When the local population had been decimated through famine, the cruelties of forced labour and the introduction of diseases to which they had no immunity, the settlers imported labour from other Spanish colonies in the Caribbean, including nearby Cuba, and Aruba and its neighbouring islands far to the south.[65] By the early 16th century, as forced local migration failed to satisfy requirements, the labour force was supplemented by the importation of enslaved people from Africa. By 1515, the alluvial placer mines of Hispaniola were becoming exhausted, gold production fell, and the local economy began to contract. In response, as

---

63 Ibid.
64 Barrios, Enrique. *Then and now: 500 years of mining history in the Dominican Republic: evaluating potential impacts on culture and areas of historical significance is now common practice in new mine developments.* Accessed 21 September 2016, http://barrickbeyondborders.com/mining/2013/11/then-now-500-years-of-mining-history-in-the-dominican-republic/
65 For more information about Aruba, see Chapter 6: Gold and Diamonds: the Mines of British Guiana and Aruba.

news spread of Hernán Cortés' conquest of Mexico, many of the Spanish settlers left Hispaniola for Mexico and the promise of its rich silver deposits. Those remaining turned to raising livestock to make a living, supplying pigs, cattle and leather to the Spanish ships as they headed to richer colonies on the mainland of South and Central America.[66]

As rival European powers began to take notice of the potential of the Caribbean as a source of mineral and agricultural wealth, particularly in the production of sugar, they showed an increased interest in dislodging Spain from her Caribbean possessions. To provide some protection from invasion, the Spanish Crown ordered the inhabitants of Hispaniola to move close to the main settlement of Santo Domingo, leaving large areas of the island deserted. Pirates soon took advantage of the sudden availability of undefended land. They moved in to establish bases on the north and west coasts and on the small island of Tortuga, which lies off the north-west coast of Hispaniola near to what is now Cap-Haïtien. Tortuga became the home port for a growing number of pirates of all nationalities, and from here they set off to plunder the Spanish treasure ships as they sailed back to Spain, fully laden with silver and gold from Central and South America. The French also took advantage of Spain's depopulation of large parts of the island, successfully establishing small settlements in the west of Hispaniola until, in 1665, French colonisation of the western part of the island was officially recognised. The new colony was given the name Saint-Domingue and in 1697, Spain formally ceded the western third of the island to France under the terms of the Treaty of Ryswick. The two-thirds of Hispaniola that remained in Spain's possession became known as Santo Domingo.

Saint-Domingue quickly came to overshadow Santo Domingo in both wealth and population, and over the next century became one of the Caribbean's wealthiest colonies, its economy based on sugar cane production.[67] In 1791, inspired in part by events taking place during the French Revolution, a major revolt of the enslaved erupted in Saint-Domingue, leading to the growth of an independence movement which,

---

66 Guitar, Lynne. *History of the Dominican Republic*. Accessed 19 September 2016, http://www.hispaniola.com/dominican_republic/info/history.php
67 Ibid.

in 1804, established the Republic of Haiti, the first independent nation in the Caribbean. Spain had ceded Santo Domingo to France in 1795, so Haiti initially comprised the whole of Hispaniola. Over the next few decades, Santo Domingo changed hands between Haiti and Spain several times until, in 1844, it became the independent state of the Dominican Republic, with Santo Domingo the name of its capital city.[68]

The Dominican Republic faced many challenges as it sought to establish itself as an independent state, and there were multiple outbreaks of civil unrest as political parties fought for control. In 1861, in an effort to establish some stability and make economic progress, Spain was invited to reclaim its former colony. In 1865, after this intervention failed, the country reverted to its independent status, only to invite the United States to take over a few years later. This request was turned down by the United States Congress and Senate.[69]

During the later 19th century, the economy of the Dominican Republic shifted from livestock production to the felling and export of precious woods, and the production of tobacco and coffee.[70] There was also a renewed interest in mining, with focus on copper deposits.

---

68 Ibid.
69 Some years later, in an effort to expand their influence and power in the Dominican Republic, the United States used the First World War as an excuse to bring in the US. Marines, supposedly to protect the country against Germany. From 1916 the US forces occupied the Dominican Republic for eight years.
70 Guitar, Lynne. *History of the Dominican Republic*. Accessed 19 September 2016, http://www.hispaniola.com/dominican_republic/info/history.php

Appendix 9

Background History of Virgin Gorda

The island of Virgin Gorda is part of the Virgin Islands archipelago, a group of small islands that lie in the north-eastern part of the Caribbean between the Atlantic Ocean and the Caribbean Sea. The Virgin Islands are about 50 miles (80.5 km.) east of Puerto Rico and today comprise two groups of islands, the United States Virgin Islands (USVI) and the British Virgin Islands (BVI).

The islands were first settled by Amerindians, then in 1493 they were sighted by Christopher Columbus during his second voyage to the

The Virgin Islands today.
Courtesy of the Library of the University of Texas, Austin.

Americas. Amazed by the large number of islands and the unspoilt nature of their beauty, he named them Santa Ursula y las Once Mil Virgines (Saint Ursula and her Eleven Thousand Virgins) after the legend of St Ursula who, with her following of virgins, was martyred for her faith. He anchored off the south-east point of one of the islands he passed, now known as Coppermine Point, and reportedly named this island Virgen Gorda (Fat Virgin) because the topography reminded him of a voluptuous woman lying on her side. Perhaps he had been too long at sea.

The Spanish colonists soon settled on neighbouring Puerto Rico, but although they were interested in the copper resources they did not extend their settlements to Virgin Gorda. In an effort to keep the Spanish away and to defend their land and its resources, the local population on Virgin Gorda began to send groups of fighting men to raid Puerto Rico, and in 1514 succeeded in burning down the settlement of Caparra, Puerto Rico's first colonial capital. The Spanish governor, Juan Ponce de Leon, was quick to retaliate, sending Captain Juan Gil with a force of 60 soldiers against the enemy stronghold on Virgin Gorda. When the Spaniards landed, they fought hard and totally defeated the island's defenders. The few that remained alive managed to escape to neighbouring islands. With local opposition at an end, Ponce de Leon began to investigate the island's potential for copper mining. The results of his investigations were positive and led to the establishment of a small Spanish settlement of copper miners. There is little information about this early Spanish enterprise, but the main centre of population on Virgin Gorda is still known as Spanish Town, and for a time the island became an official landfall for the two annual *flotas de Indias* (Spanish treasure fleets) when they sailed from Spain to the Spanish colonies in the Americas.

After the Spanish miners left Virgin Gorda it seems to have remained uninhabited, although in the early 17th century the Dutch established a settlement on neighbouring Tortola. The Dutch considered the Virgin Islands of important strategic value because they were situated about halfway between Surinam, the Dutch colony on the north-east coast of South America, and New Amsterdam, the most important Dutch settlement in North America, now New York City. As a result of the negotiations that followed the third Anglo-Dutch War (1672–1674) the English obtained sovereignty of the Virgin Islands, and Spanish Town became the capital of the Virgin Island chain. It remained the capital until 1742, when Road Town on Tortola took over the role.[71]

It is thought that the Virgin Gorda mine was reactivated in the early 18th century, and that the miners were possibly Dutch, although there is no evidence to say who they were, or where they were from.[72] After they left in around 1737, the island remained without a permanent population until a group of English planters from the nearby island of Anguilla established an agricultural settlement there. Hindered by poor soil and lack of rainfall, the settlement was slow to develop. The small economy was initially based on cotton and indigo, and later on sugar which was grown with enslaved labour. Sugar production failed, however, to develop into a profitable concern and by 1815 had been discontinued. Following the failure of the sugar industry unemployment grew, workers left to find employment elsewhere and slaves were either transferred to plantations on other islands, purchased their freedom, or were manumitted by their owners.

In 1834, the British government legislation for the emancipation of the the enslaved came into effect, but in the British Virgin Islands full freedom was only given in 1838, after the former enslaved had served an 'apprenticeship'. During this period, they were expected to remain on the plantation where they had been enslaved and to provide their former masters with forty-five hours of unpaid labour per week. Once free, some continued to work on the local plantations while others turned to subsistence farming, supplemented by fishing and charcoal production. Plantation owners looking for a new economic opportunity began to take an interest in the potential for mining the island's copper resources.[73] They reasoned that the development of a mine would provide much-needed

---

71 Email from Peter and Verna Moll, 23 November 2014.
72 Birchall, Frank, and Margaret Birchall. 'The Virgin Gorda copper mine, British Virgin Islands'. *Journal of the Trevithick Society*, p.23. (No.20, 1993).
73 Island Resources Foundation for the British Virgin Islands. Conservation and Fisheries Department. *An environmental profile of the island of Virgin Gorda, British Virgin Islands*, p.26. Red Hook, St Thomas, 2012.

local employment and give the plantations an opportunity to supply the mines with many of the products – from mules to vegetables – that they might require. The local planters lobbied influential British-based absentee planters and merchants to encourage interested individuals to invest in the development of a Virgin Gorda copper mine, and their efforts soon bore fruit: the Virgin Gorda Mining Company re-opened the mine. The first shaft was sunk in 1838 but operations ceased in 1842. In 1859, the Virgin Gorda Mine Adventure took over the mine, working the site until 1862. The ruins of its buildings are now open to visitors, its Cornish beam engine notable as the oldest in the world.

Bibliography

Allen, Robert C. *The British Industrial Revolution in Global Perspective*. Cambridge: Cambridge University Press, 2009.

Alleyne, Warren. *Caribbean Pirates*. London: Macmillan Caribbean, 1986.

Allicock, Dmitri. 'Bartica: The Gateway To Guyana's Interior.' *Explore Guyana*, Pp.56, 59 (2015).

Allicock, Dmitri. *The Demerara Essequibo Railway (Der)*. Accessed 14 August, 2016, Https://Guyanathenandnow.wordpress.com/2011/11/06/The-Demerara-Essequibo-Railway-Der/

Allsopp, Richard. *Dictionary of Caribbean English Usage*. Kingston: University Of The West Indies Press, 2003, P.450.

Anim-Addo, Anyaa. 'Steaming Between the Islands: Nineteenth-Century Maritime Networks and the Caribbean Archipelago.' *Island Studies Journal*, pp.25–38 (Vol.8, No.1, 2013)

Anim-Addo, Anyaa. '"A Wretched and Slave-Like Mode of Labor": Slavery, Emancipation, and the Royal Mail Steam Packet Company's Coaling Stations.' *Historical Geography*, pp.65–84 (Vol.39, 2011)

Antigua and the Antiguans: a Full Account of the Colony and its Inhabitants from the Time of the Caribs to the Present Day interspersed with Anecdotes and Legends. 2 vols. St. John's: Antiguan Publishing Trust, 1980. Work attributed to a Mrs. Flannigan or Lanaghan, first published in 1844.

Appleby, Sue. The Hammers of Towan: A Nineteenth-Century Cornish Farming Family. 2nd ed. Kibworth Beauchamp, 2021.

Archibald, Douglas. *Tobago: "Melancholy Isle"*. Vol.1, 1498–1771. Port-of-Spain: Westindiana Ltd. 1987.

Archibald, Douglas. *Tobago: "Melancholy Isle".* Vol.2, 1770–1814. St. Augustine: University of the West Indies School of Continuing Studies, 1995.

Archibald, Douglas. *Tobago: "Melancholy Isle".* Vol.3, 1807-1898. Port-of-Spain: Westindiana Ltd., 2003.

Archives Wales. *Glamorgan Archives Mathew Family of St. Kew, Cornwall, and the Caribbean Islands Papers.* Accessed 12 October, 2015, http://www.archiveswales.org.uk/anw/get_collection.php?inst_id=33&coll_id=2289&expand=

Aruba. National Archaeological Museum. *The First Inhabitants of Aruba.* Accessed 17 June, 2016, http://www-namaruba.org/_media/first-inhabitants.pdf

Ashie-Nikoi, Edwina. "Beating the Pen on the Drum: a Socio-Cultural History Of Carriacou, Grenada, 1750-1920." PhD diss., New York University, 2007.

Barbados: history. Accessed 16 May, 2016, http://thecommonwealth.org/our-member-countries/barbados/history

Bardudaful History. Accessed 10 January, 2016, http://barbudaful.net/barbudaful-history.html

Baring Archive. HC5 5.13.1 1847 30 Apr, St. Thomas Island (Virgin Islands): *P.J. Minveille to Julius Price; Julius Price to Thomas Baring. The Virgin Gorda Copper Mine; with a Printed Prospectus, 1845, of The New Virgin Gorda Mining Company Formed to Work the Mine.*

Baring-Gould, S. *Cornish Characters and Strange Events.* London: Bodley Head, 1909.

Barrios, Enrique. *Then and Now: 500 Years of Mining History in the Dominican Republic: Evaluating Potential Impacts on Culture and Areas of Historical Significance is Now Common Practice in New Mine Developments.* Accessed 21 September, 2016, http://barrickbeyondborders.com/mining/2013/11/then-now-500-years-of-mining-history-in-the-dominican-republic/

Beckles, Hilary McD. *White Servitude and Black Slavery in Barbados 1627–1715.* Knoxville: University of Tennessee Press, 1989.

Bennett, Dennis Stanley Lanyon. *William Lanyon Bennett, born 1856. His Life Story.* Unpublished notes, 1982.

'Bethell Codrington, Christopher (1764–1843), of Dodington, nr. Chipping Sodbury, Glos.' *The History of Parliament: British Political, Social and Local History.* Accessed 10 January, 2016, http://www.historyofparliamentonline.org/volume/1790-1820/member/bethell-codrington-christopher-1764-1843

Birch, Chris. *The Milk Jug was a Goat: Two Families, Two Caribbean Islands 1635-1987.* Cambridge: Pegasus Publishers, 2008.

Birchall, Frank and Margaret Birchall. 'The Virgin Gorda Copper Mine, British Virgin Islands.' *Journal of the Trevithick Society*, pp.23-34 (No.20, 1993)

Blackman, Francis. *Methodism: 200 Years in the British Virgin Islands.* Road Town: Methodist Church in the British Virgin Islands, 1989.

Blewett, Roy. *The Price and Rose Price Family Tree.* Penzance: Blewett, January 2013.

Brandow, James C. *Omitted Chapters from Hotten's Original Lists of Persons of Quality… and Others who Went from Great Britain to the American Plantations 1600–1700: Census Returns, Parish Registers, and Militia Rolls from the Barbados Census of 1679/80.* Baltimore: Genealogical Publishing Co., 1982.

Brereton, Bridget. 'Post-emancipation Protest in the Caribbean: the "Belmanna Riots" in Tobago, 1876.' *Caribbean Quarterly*, pp.110–123 (Vol. 30, No. 3/4 September-December, 1984).

Briggs, Lin and Simon Chapman. 'Scenes of Copper Point Mine.' *Cornish Mining*, pp.18-20 (Winter 2013).

British Armed Forces and National Service. *The Duke of Cornwall's Light Infantry.* Accessed March 14, 2015, http://www.britisharmedforces.org/li_pages/regiments/dcli/duke_index.htm

British Library Board. 'An Elderly Cornish Miner in British Guiana.' *The Cornishman*, p.2 (3 November, 1898). British Newspaper Archive, accessed September 9, 2016. http://www.britishnewspaperarchive.co.uk/

British Library Board. 'Appointment of a Mine Agent [Captain Thomas Bawden].' *West Briton and Cornwall Advertiser*, p.8 (15 May, 1879). British Newspaper Archive, accessed September 11, 2016. http://www.britishnewspaperarchive.co.uk/

British Library Board. 'British Guiana: the Affairs of the Colony.' *Glasgow Herald*, p.8 (15 October, 1896). British Newspaper Archive accessed September 11, 2016. http://www.britishnewspaperarchive.co.uk/

British Library Board. 'Capt. Frank Oats as a Diamond Miner.' *The Cornishman*, p.4 (22 August, 1901). British Newspaper Archive, accessed September 9, 2016. http://www.britishnewspaperarchive.co.uk/

British Library Board. 'Capt. Frederick Gribble.' *West Briton and Cornwall Advertiser*, p.6 (11 February, 1897). British Newspaper Archive, accessed September 11, 2016. http://www.britishnewspaperarchive.co.uk/

British Library Board. 'Captain Fred Gribble.' *The Cornishman*, p.7 (18 February, 1897). British Newspaper Archive, accessed September 7, 2016. http://www.britishnewspaperarchive.co.uk/

British Library Board. 'Copper Mines in Santo Domingo.' *Dundee People's Journal*, p.3 (5 September, 1863). British Newspaper Archive accessed September 21, 2016. http://www.britishnewspaperarchive.co.uk/

British Library Board. 'Copper Mines in Santo Domingo.' *Manchester Courier and Lancashire General Advertiser*, p.5 (5 September, 1863). British Newspaper Archive, accessed September 21, 2016. http://www.britishnewspaperarchive.co.uk/

British Library Board. 'Cornish Mining: the Depression and Remedies.' *The Cornishman*, p.3. (15 April, 1897). British Newspaper Archive, accessed September 7, 2016. http://www.britishnewspaperarchive.co.uk/

British Library Board. 'Death of Captain Kitchen, of Germoe.' *The Cornishman*, pp.4-5. (2 August, 1888). British Newspaper Archive, accessed September 7, 2016. http://www.britishnewspaperarchive.co.uk/

British Library Board. 'Drawbacks of Gold-seeking: No Chance for Diggers in Guiana.' *Aberdeen Journal*, p.4. (4 February, 1898). British Newspaper Archive, accessed September 7, 2016. http://www.britishnewspaperarchive.co.uk/

British Library Board. 'Foreign Intelligence.' *Norfolk News*, p.2 (30 July 1853). British Newspaper Archive, accessed October 10, 2014. http://www.britishnewspaperarchive.co.uk/

British Library Board. 'Gold in South America.' *The Cornishman*, p.6 (3 July, 1879). British Newspaper Archive, accessed September 7, 2016. http://www.britishnewspaperarchive.co.uk/

British Library Board. 'High Charges at Lodgings – Detention of Luggage Illegal [Thomas Price].' *Hampshire Advertiser*, p.6. (21 February, 1857). British Newspaper Archive accessed August 10, 2016. http://www.britishnewspaperarchive.co.uk/

British Library Board. 'Mines.' *London Daily News* (Monday 20 April, 1857). British Newspaper Archive, accessed October 4, 2014. http://www.britishnewspaperarchive.co.uk/

British Library Board. 'Mining [Death of Mr. Arthur Francis Hosking].' *The Cornishman*, p.6 (5 February, 1948). British Newspaper Archive, accessed September 7, 2016. http://www.britishnewspaperarchive.co.uk/

British Library Board. 'Mining Intelligence.' *Royal Cornwall Gazette*, p.7 (14 January, 1853). British Newspaper Archive, accessed September 9, 2016. http://www.britishnewspaperarchive.co.uk/

British Library Board. 'Mr. William Henry Dunkin.' *The Cornish Telegraph*, p.4 (6 November, 1901). British Newspaper Archive, accessed July 15, 2016. http://www.britishnewspaperarchive.co.uk/

British Library Board. 'Naturalists' Notebook.' *The Cornishman*, p.2. (3 November, 1898). British Newspaper Archive, accessed August 7, 2016. http://www.britishnewspaperarchive.co.uk/

British Library Board. 'Penzance Men Drowned in America.' *The Cornish Telegraph*, p.5 (14 July, 1887). British Newspaper Archive, accessed September 9, 2016. http://www.britishnewspaperarchive.co.uk/

British Library Board. 'Port Royal and St. Andrew's Copper Mining Company.' *London Daily News*, p.7 (13 March, 1855). British Newspaper Archive, accessed July 20, 2016. http://www.britishnewspaperarchive.co.uk/

British Library Board. 'Port Royal and St. Andrew's Copper Mining Company.' *London Daily News*, p.3 (28 February, 1856). British Newspaper Archive, accessed July 20, 2016. http://www.britishnewspaperarchive.co.uk/

British Library Board. 'Port Royal and St. Andrew's Copper Mining Company.' *London Daily News*, (24 August, 1855). British Newspaper Archive, accessed July 20, 2016. http://www.britishnewspaperarchive.co.uk/

British Library Board. 'Produce and Returns of English and Foreign Mines.' *Royal Cornwall Gazette*, 5 August 1842.

British Library Board. 'Royal West India Mining Company.' *Morning Post* (Saturday 28 February, 1852). British Newspaper Archive, accessed September 30, 2014. http://www.britishnewspaperarchive.co.uk/

British Library Board. 'Royal West India Mining Company.' *Royal Cornwall Gazette* (Friday 14 January, 1853). British Newspaper Archive, accessed October 3, 2014. http://www.britishnewspaperarchive.co.uk/

British Library Board. 'Sad Bereavements. [Capt. Thomas Bawden and Eldest Son].' *West Briton and Cornwall Advertiser*, p.5 (7 August, 1879). British Newspaper Archive accessed September 7, 2016. http://www.britishnewspaperarchive.co.uk/

British Library Board. 'The Copper Mines of the Royal Santiago Mining Company.' *Gore's Liverpool General Advertiser*, p.1 (29 March 1838). British Newspaper Archive accessed November 26, 2016, http://www.britishnewspaperarchive.co.uk/

The British Library Board. 'The Government Contract for 100,000 Gallons of Rum for the Navy.' *Morning Post*, p.4 (21 December, 1849). British Newspaper Archive, accessed September 11, 2016. http://www.britishnewspaperarchive.co.uk/

British Library Board. 'To Proprietors of Mines, Collieries, etc.' *Liverpool Daily Post* (Saturday 22 November 1862). British Newspaper Archive, accessed October 3, 2014. http://www.britishnewspaperarchive.co.uk/

British Library Board. 'Two Penzance Men Drowned.' *The Cornishman*, p.4 (14 July, 1887). British Newspaper Archive, accessed September 11, 2016. http://www.britishnewspaperarchive.co.uk/

British Library. *Trelawny Letters*.
Typescript from National Library of Jamaica file on Edward Trelawny.

British Virgin Islands. Town and Country Planning Department. *Tourism Potential of*

Copper Mine Point, Virgin Gorda, British Virgin Islands. Draft. Ed. Road Town: Office of the Chief Minister, [1999?]

Britnor, L.E. *History of the Sailing Packets of the West Indies.* np: British West Indies Study Circle, 1973.

Buchanan, J.E. "The Colleton Family and the Early History of South Carolina and Barbados: 1646-1775." PhD diss., University of Edinburgh, 1989.

Buckingham, James Silk. *Autobiography of James Silk Buckingham; Including his Voyages, Travels, Adventures, Speculations, Successes and Failures...*Vol.1. London: Longman, Brown, Green, and Longmans, 1855.

Buckley-Mathew, George Benvenuto. *Buckley-Mathew Collection.* Accessed 13 October 2015, http://library.missouri.edu/specialcollections/buckley-mathew-george-benvenuto-buckley-mathew-collection/

Bulmer-Thomas, Victor. *The Economic History of the Caribbean Since the Napoleonic Wars.* Cambridge: Cambridge University Press, 2012.

Burdon, Katherine Janet. *A Handbook of St. Kitts-Nevis: a Presidency of the Leeward Islands Colony.* London: West India Committee, 1920.

Burke, Gill, "The Cornish Diaspora of the Nineteenth Century," in *International Labour Migration: Historical Perspectives*, edited by Shula Marks and Peter Richardson. (Hounslow: Maurice Temple Smith for The Institute of Commonwealth Studies, 1984), pp.57–75.

Burnard, Trevor. *Mastery, Tyranny and Desire: Thomas Thistlewood and his Slaves in the Anglo-Jamaican World.* Kingston: University of the West Indies Press, 2004.

Burt, R. 'Virgin Gorda Copper Mine 1839-1862.' *Industrial Archaeology Review*, pp.56–62 (Vol.6 Issue 1, 1981)

Burt, Roger. *Freemasonry and Business Networking During the Victorian Period.* Exeter: University of Exeter, 2005. Accessed 27 August, 2016, http://people.exeter.ac.uk/RBurt/exeteronly/HEC2005/EcHRarticle.htm

Button, Andrea. *The Trade in White Labour in 17th century Bristol.* Accessed October

10, 2015, http:humanities,uwe.ac.uk/bhr/Main/white_labour/servants.htm

Byres, John. *Plan of the Island of Tobago, Laid Down by Actual Survey Under the Direction of the Honourable the Commissioners for the Sale of Lands in the Ceded Islands.* London: Robert Wilkinson, 1794.

Byron, E. *Some Nevis Families.* Charlestown: Byron, nd.

Byron, Margaret. *Post-war Caribbean Migration to Britain: the Unfinished Cycle.* Aldershot: Avebury, 1994.

Calendar of State Papers Colonial, America and West Indies. Accessed throughout 2016, http://www.british-history.ac.uk/cal-state-papers/colonial/america-west-indies/

Camborne School of Mines: History. Accessed 20 June, 2016, http://emps.exeter.ac.uk/csm/about/

Campbell, P.F. 'Richard Ligon.' *Journal of the Barbados Museum and Historical Society,* pp.215–238. (Vol.37, 1985).

Cattelle, W.R. *The Diamond.* New York: John Lane Company, 1911.

Cavanaugh, Jake. *The Cause of the Morant Bay Rebellion: 1865.* Accessed 26 January, 2016, http://scholar.library.miami.edu/emancipation/jamaica4.htm

Cayman Islands History. Accessed May 9, 2017, https://web.archive.org/web/20081012073753/http://www.gocayman.ky/history.html

'Cayman Islands Search for Relatives of their Cornish forefathers.' *Daily Telegraph* (6 April, 2017). Accessed May 9, 2017, http://www.telegraph.co.uk/news/2017/04/06/cayman-islands-search-relatives-cornish-forefathers/

Charles Barrington Brown, Assoc., R.S.M., F.G.S. Accessed 15 August, 2016, http://journals.cambridge.org/actiondisplayFulltext?type=1&fid=5114932&jid=GEO&volumeId=4&issueId=05&aid=5114928

Charles Webbe. Kew: National Archives, nd.Prerogative Court of Canterbury and Related Probate Jurisdictions: Will Registers; Class: PROB 11; Piece: 1916.

Chilvers, Allan. *The Berties of Grimsthorpe Castle*. Bloomington: AuthorHouse, 2010.

Clement, Christopher Ohm. "Landscapes and Plantations on Tobago: a Regional Perspective." PhD diss., University of Florida, 1995.

Cobre Days. Accessed 9 December 2016, http://www.shanty.org.uk/pdfbox/andy_mckay/CobreDays.pdf

Colchester, Marcus, Jean La Rose and Kid James. *Mining and Amerindians in Guyana: Final Report of the APA/NSI Project on 'Exploring Indigenous Perspective on Consultation and Engagement Within the Mining Sector in Latin America and the Caribbean.'* Ottawa: North-South Institute, 2002.

Coleridge, Henry Nelson. *Six Months in the West Indies in 1825*. London: John Murray, 1826.

Colli, Claudia for British Virgin Islands Tourist Board. *Welcome to our British Virgin Islands: a Cultural and Historical Tour of the British Virgin Islands*. Road Town: Colli, 1983.

Cooper, Cliff. 'Barbados Connection.' *Cornwall Family History Society Journal*, p.7. (No.79, March 1996).

'Copper Mining in Jamaica.' *The Civil Engineer and Architects Journal*. (June 1841). Accessed 10 June, 2016, http://steampunkhistoryofjamaica.weebly.com/--copper.html

Cornwall OPC Database. Accessed throughout 2015, http://www.cornwall-opc-database.org/

Cornwall Online Parish Clerks. *Mylor: Some Memorial Inscriptions*. Accessed 7 December, 2015, http://www.cornwall-opc.org/Par_new/l_m/pdfs/mylor_mis.pdf Transcribed from LDS Film 476219 by Shirley Cattermole

Cornwall Online Parish Clerks. *The Parish of Ludgven*. Accessed 20 September, 2016, http://www.cornwall-opc.org/Par_new/l_m/ludgven.php

Cornish Mining World Heritage. *Religion*. Accessed 6 June, 2016, https://www.cornish-mining.org.uk/delving-deeper/religion

'Correspondence Between Sir C.B. Codrington and T.F. Buxton Esq. on the Subject of Slavery.' *The Anti-Slavery Reporter*, pp.301–302. (Vol.5, no.2, Nov.15, 1832)

Couch, Jonathan. *The History of Polperro: Fishing Town on the South Coast of Cornwall, Being a Description of the Place, its People, Their Manners, Customs, Modes of Industry, &C.* Polperro: Simpkin, Marshall And Co., 1871.

Courtney Library. *Cornish People Overseas From 1840: Index compiled from Local Newspapers.* Truro: Courtney Library, Nd.

Craig-James, Susan E. *The Changing Society of Tobago, 1838–1938: A Fractured Whole.* vol.1, 1838-1900. Arima: Cornerstone Press Ltd., 2008.

Craton, Michael And James Walvin. *A Jamaican Plantation: The History of Worthy Park, 1670-1970.* Toronto: University of Toronto Press, 1970.

Cuba and the Slave Trade. Accessed 8 December 2016, Http://Www.tracesofthetrade.org/Guides-And-Materials/Historical/Cuba-And-The-Slave-Trade/

Cundall, Frank. 'Governors of Jamaica in the 18[Th] Century: XIX Sir William Trelawny.' *Daily Gleaner*, np (7 December, 1929)

Cundall, Frank. *The Governors of Jamaica in the Seventeenth Century.* London: West India Committee, 1936. Accessed 21 May 2016, Http://Ufdc.Ufl.edu//Uf00074120/00001

Curry-Machado, Jonathan. *Cuban Sugar Industry: Transnational Networks and Engineering Migrants in Mid-nineteenth Century Cuba.* New York: Palgrave Macmillan, 2011.

Dalton, Charles. 'Soldiering In The West Indies in the Days of Queen Anne.' *Journal Of The Royal United Service Institution*, pp.66-75. (Vol.42, Issue 1, 1898).

Daniel, Wakely. *In Pursuit of Sovereignty.* Bridgetown: Cranlake Publishing, 2001.

Davy, John. 'A Discourse [on Agriculture]' *[Minutes of the Meetings of the] Agricultural Society Of Barbados*, Pp.288–304 (1847)

Davy, John. 'On the Mineral Water of the Baths of Nevis, In The West Indies; in a Letter Addressed To Prof. Jameson.' *Edinburgh New Philosophical Journal*, Pp.1–6 (Vol.xliii, April/October 1847)

Deacon, Bernard William. *Cornish Methodism or Methodism in Cornwall?* Accessed 6 June, 2016, https://bernarddeacon.wordpress.com/cornish-methodism-or-methodism-in-cornwall/

Deacon, Bernard William. *The Causes of Methodist Growth.* Accessed 6 June, 2016, https://bernarddeacon.wordpress.com/cornish-methodism-or-methodism-in-cornwall/the-causes-of-methodist-growth/

Deacon, Bernard William. *The Cornish Family.* Fowey: Cornwall Editions, 2004.

Deacon, Bernard William. 'The Reformulation of Territorial Identity: Cornwall in the Late Eighteenth and Nineteenth Centuries.' PhD diss., Open University, 2001.

Derriman, James. *Killigarth: Three Centuries of a Cornish Manor.* Morden: Derriman, 1994.

Derriman, James. *Marooned: the True Story of Cornishman Robert Jeffery.* 2nd ed. Clifton-Upon-Teme: Polperro Heritage Press, 2006.

Destiny: Hart of Heritage. Accessed 11 September, 2016, http://www.lemonhartrum.com/pathway.html

Devonian Foundation. *Index to the Codrington Family Papers.* Calgary, Devonian Foundation, May 1988.

Díaz, María Elena, 'Mining Women, Royal Slaves: Copper mining in colonial Cuba, 1670-1780.' In *Mining Women: Gender in the Development of a Global Industry, 1670 to 2005*, edited by Jaclyn J. Gier-Viskovatoff and Laurie Mercier, pp.21-39. New York: Palgrave Macmillan, 2006.

Díaz, María Elena. *The Virgin, the King, and the Royal Slaves of El Cobre: Negotiating Freedom in colonial Cuba, 1670–1780.* Stanford: Stanford University Press, 2000.

Dictionary of National Biography. Supplement, vol.2. London: Smith, Elder and Co., 1901.

Digital Archaeological Archive of Comparative Slavery. Accessed October, 2015, http://www.daacs.org

Dunn, Richard S. *Sugar and Slaves: the Rise of the Planter Class in the English West Indies 1624-1713*. Chapel Hill: University of North Carolina Press, 1972.

Dyde, Brian. *Out of the Crowded Vagueness: a History of the Islands of St. Kitts, Nevis and Anguilla*. Oxford: Macmillan Education, 2005.

Earle, Kenneth Wilson. *Geological Survey of the Windward and Leeward Islands: Interim Report on the Virgin Gorda Copper Mine*. Washington DC: US Government Printing Office, June 1921.

English Settlers in Barbados, 1637–1800. Accessed May 2016, http://interactive.ancestry.com/1123/wills_ii-0338/54497?backurl=http%3a%2f%2fsearch.ancestry.com%2fcgi-bin%2fsse.dll%3fgst%3d-6&ssrc=&backlabel=ReturnSearchResults#?imageId=wills_ii-0358

European Magazine, and London Review. (Volume 53, 1808). Accessed 21 January 2015, https://books.google.com.ag/books?id=6McPAAAAQAAJ&q=%22the+european+magazine+and+london+review%22+volume+53&dq=%22the+european+magazine+and+london+review%22+volume+53&hl=en&sa=X&ei=1-S_VP2VH4jlgwSUnIPACA&ved=0CCAQ6AEwAQ

Evans, Chris. *Carabalí and Culíes at El Cobre: African Slaves and Chinese Indentured Labourers in the Service of Swansea Copper*. Accessed November 16, 2016, https://www.academia.edu/1889345/_Carabal%C3%AD_and_cul%C3%ADes_at_El_Cobre_African_slaves_and_Chinese_indentured_labourers_in_the_service_of_Swansea_copper

Evans, Chris. 'El Cobre: Cuban Ore and the Globalization of Swansea Copper, 1830-1870.' *Welsh History Review/Cylchgrawn Hanes Cymru*, pp.112–131 (Vol.27, No.1, 2014).

Evans, Chris. *Slave Wales: The Welsh and Atlantic Slavery, 1660–1850*. Cardiff: University of Wales Press, 2010.

Evans, Chris. *The British Slaves of Latin America*. Accessed 12 December, 2016, https://www.academia.edu/497596/The_British_slaves_of_Latin_America

Evans, Chris and Olivia Saunders. 'Copper Ore: an Unlikely Global Commodity.' *Commodity Histories*. Accessed 20 May 2014, http://www.commodityhistories.org/research/copper-ore-unlikely-global-commodity

Family and Estate Papers of the Mathew Family of St. Kew, Cornwall and of the Caribbean Islands. Accessed throughout May 2016, http://discovery.nationalarchives.gov.uk/download/GB%200214%20DMW

Farrugia, Jean and Tony Gammons. *Carrying the British Mails: Five Centuries of Postal Transport by Land, Sea and Air*. London: National Postal Museum, 1980.

Findlay, G.G. and W.W. Holdsworth. *The History of the Wesleyan Methodist Missionary Society*. Vol.2. London: Epworth Press, 1859.

Fitzpatrick, Scott M. 'The Pre-Columbian Caribbean: Colonization, Population Dispersal, and Island Adaptations.' *PaleoAmerica*, pp.305–331. (Vol.1, No.4, 2015). Accessed 7 December 2015, https://www.academia.edu/17866053/The_Pre-Columbian_Caribbean_Colonization_Population_Dispersal_and_Island_Adaptations

Fort Mathew. Accessed 19 May 2016, http://www.forts.org/fort_mathew/index.html

Fowey Consols. Accessed 2 October 2014, http://www.gracesguide.co.uk/Fowey_Consols_Copper_Mine

Fox Family. Accessed 24 November, 2016, http://www.gracesguide.co.uk/Fox_Family

Galenson, David W. *Traders, Planters and Slaves: Market Behavior in Early English America*. Cambridge: Cambridge University Press, 2002.

Gardner, William James. *A History of Jamaica from its Discovery by Christopher Columbus to the Present Time; including an Account of its Trade and Agriculture…* London: Elliot Stock, 1873.

George, Gwyneth. 'Hinterland Development: the Railway Discussion of the early Twentieth Century.' *Stabroek News*, (5 May, 2011). Accessed 14 August, 2016, http://www.stabroeknews.com/2011/features/history-this-week/05/05/hinterland-development-the-railway-discussion-of-the-early-twentieth-century/

Gill, Crispin. *The Great Cornish Families: a History of the People and their Houses*. Tiverton: Cornwall Books, 1995.

Goldsmith, R.F.K. *The Duke of Cornwall's Light Infantry: the 32nd and 46th Regiments of Foot*. London: Leo Cooper, 1970.

Gordon, Joyce. *Nevis: Queen of the Caribees*. 5th ed. Oxford: Macmillan Education, 2005.

Granville (Grenville), Bevil (1665–1706). Accessed 15 May 2016, http://www.historyofparliamentonline.org/volume/1660-1690/member/granville-(grenville)-bevil-1665-1706

Grenada: History. Accessed 16 May 2016, http://thecommonwealth.org/our-member-countries/grenada/history

Grenfell Family History. Accessed 18 November, 2016, http://www.grenfellhistory.co.uk/index.php

Guitar, Lynne. *History of the Dominican Republic*. Accessed 19 September, 2016, http://www.hispaniola.com/dominican_republic/info/history.php

Gwennap-Chacewater Mining District. Accessed 13 June, 2016, https://web.archive.org/web/20090414074307/http://www.cornish-mining.org.uk/sites/gwennap.htm

Gwennap Pit. Accessed 13 June, 2016, https://web.archive.org/web/20090612113705/http://www.cornish-mining.org.uk/sites/gwnnppt.htm

Hall, Catherine, Keith McClelland, Nick Draper, Kate Donington and Rachel Lang. *Legacies of British Slave Ownership*. Cambridge: Cambridge University Press, 2014.

Harrison, J.B. *The Geology of the Goldfields of British Guiana*. London: Dulau and Co., 1908.

Hartog, Johan. *Aruba Past and Present: From the Time of the Indians Until Today*. Oranjestad: D.J. De Wit, 1961.

Harvard Law School. Human Rights Program. International Human Rights Clinic. *All that Glitters: Gold Mining in Guyana – the Failure of Government Oversights and the Human Rights of Amerindian Communities*. Cambridge: Harvard Law School, 2007.

Harvest Festivals to Missions: Rough List of Cornish Methodist Missionaries. Unpublished list from Courtney Library pamphlet file.

BIBLIOGRAPHY

Hatuey: The Forgotten Haitian Cacique. Accessed 11 November, 2016, http://haitianarawak.com/documents/essays/hatuey.php

Havana (La Habana). Accessed 13 November, 2016, http://www.statesmansyearbook.com/resources/Havana.html

Henry Lowry. Accessed 18 July, 2016, http://www.haine.org.uk/haine-web/mariamartin.htm

Heritage Tourism Consulting for National Parks Trust. *Management plan [for] Copper Mine Point* 2 December 1995.

Heuman, Gad. "Post-emancipation Resistance in the Caribbean: An Overview." In *Small Islands, Large Questions: Society, Culture and Resistance in the Post-emancipation Caribbean*, edited by Karen Fog Olwig, 124-133. New York: Routledge, 2014.

Higman, B.W. *Plantation Jamaica 1750–1850: Capital and Control in a Colonial Economy.* Kingston: University of the West Indies Press, 2005.

Higman, B.W. *Proslavery Priest: The Atlantic World of John Lindsay, 1729-1788.* Kingston: University of the West Indies Press, 2011.

Higman, B.W. and B.J. Hudson. *Jamaican Place Names.* Kingston: University of the West Indies Press, May 2009. Kindle edition, accessed 22 January, 2016, amazon.com/Jamaican-Place-Names-B-Higman/dp/9766402175/ref=sr_1_2?s=books&ie=UTF8&qid=1453502221&sr=1-2&keywords=jamaica+place+names

Historia di Aruba: Gold. Accessed 20 June, 2016, http://www.historiadiaruba.aw/index.php?option=com_content&task=view&id=16&lang=en

Historic Basseterre: Buckley's Estate. Accessed 12 October, 2015, http://www.historicbasseterre.com/hs_summation.asp?HSID=19

Historic Houses Trust. *Pictures [Wesleyan chapels].* Accessed 28 July, http://collection.hht.net.au/firsthhtpictures/resbyfield.jsp?term=chapels&field=SUBJECT&searchtable=CATALOGUE_SEARCHPICTURES&displayFormat=TABLE*History of Guyana.* Accessed 1 August, 2016, http://www.guyanesepride.com/about/

History of the Cuban Liberation Wars. Accessed 10 December 2016, http://www.cubagenweb.org/mil/war-hist.htm

Hotten, John Camden. *The Original List of Persons of Quality: Emigrants, Religious Exiles, Political Rebels. Serving Men Sold for a Term of Years, Apprentices, Children Stolen, Maidens Pressed, and Others. Who went from Great Britain to the American plantations, 1600-1700.* New York: Empire State Book Company, 1874. Kindle edition. Accessed 21 May 2016.

Hughes, Henry Brackenbury Louis. "Christian Missionary Societies in the British West Indies during the Emancipation era." PhD diss., University of Toronto, 1944.

Ishmael, Odeen. *The Guyana Story: From Earliest Times to Independence.* Georgetown: Guyanese Online, 2005. Accessed 4 August, 2016, https://guyaneseonline.wordpress.com/2011/11/23/history-the-guyana-story-dr-odeen-ishmael/

Island Resources Foundation for the British Virgin Islands. Conservation and Fisheries Department. *An Environmental Profile of the Island of Virgin Gorda, British Virgin Islands.* Red Hook, St. Thomas, 2012.

Jackson, Thomas. *Memoirs of the Life and Writings of the Rev. Richard Watson: Late Secretary to the Wesleyan Methodist Society.* 2nd ed. London: John Mason, 1834. Accessed 11 June, 2016, http://books.googleusercontent.com/books/content?req=AKW5Qaf M5hShjlsvlcJy1gm0zOVrNvyeFZjMb_-roj4BsahMJV4IUhkrpOUTz-HiMI22kt6 rlzY1iwfCmSG3DVpdfI93lEzT45rSVvMFnFr7-Vi-XCIYJ8gA0hgLpRQ5ENlAR-9G4XiTUjaoWV8c3lu2OHa0POWx2vcQ8tYcE8yLHBeNeS-y-so8rCpwsBvGJc7S SzVjBFsdH1T7_9qGSaM_MjDzJ1soe_yxAtiJZhGV6KY09WNes2xx1NHZDSN rXvcNgc6FiErv1S-8ssvLc7ieQP60kY5Nqe31bjI1d0xhkBgxgU5Gp-P4

Jacobs, Curtis. *The Fedons of Grenada, 1763–1814.* Accessed, 14 June, 2016, http://www.open.uwi.edu/sites/default/files/bnccde/grenada/conference/papers/Jacobsc.html

Jamaica Information Service. *Mining in Jamaica.* Kingston: Jamaica Information Service, nd.

'Jamaica's Mineral deposits.' *Sunday Gleaner*, p.16. (25 October, 1973).

Jamaican History. Accessed 17 January, 2016, http://jis.gov.jm/information/jamaican-history/

James Silk Buckingham. Accessed 30 May, 2016, http://spenserians.cath.vt.edu/BiographyRecord.php?action=GET&bioid=4462

Jeffery, Robert. *A Marrative of the Life Sufferings and Deliverance of R. Jeffery, who was put on the Desolate Rock of Sombrero, Dec 13, 1807, with portrait.* London. Jeffery, 1811.

Jenkin, Alfred. *Letterbook 1836–38.* Redruth: Jenkin, nd.

Joel Hitchens. Accessed 5 October, 2014, http://www.gracesguide.co.uk/Joel_Hitchens

John Wesley and the Methodist Movement. Accessed 6 June, 2016, http://www.cornwalls.co.uk/history/people/john_wesley.htm

John Wesley (1703–1791): Biography. Accessed 13 June, 2016, http://www.brycchancarey.com/abolition/wesley.htm

John Wesley (1703–1791): The Methodist Minister. Accessed 13 June, 2016, http://abolition.e2bn.org/people_32.html

Johnson, Charles."Of Captain Anstis, and his Crew," in *A General History of the Pyrates: From their First Rise and Settlement in the Island of Providence to the Present Time.* London: T. Warner, at the Black-Boy in Pater-Noster-Row, 1724.
Amazon Kindle edition – no pagination. Charles Johnson is thought to be a pseudonym of either the author Daniel Defoe, or the printer and journalist Nathaniel Mist.

Johnson, Howard and Karl Watson. *The White Minority in the Caribbean.* Kingston: Ian Randle, 1998.

Josiah, Barbara P. *Migration, Mining, and the African Diaspora: Guyana in the Nineteenth and Twentieth centuries.* New York: Palgrave Macmillan, 2011.

Julian Fedon. Accessed 19 May 2016, http://culture.gd/index.php/aunty-tek-spiceword-festival-gallery/16-hry/228-julien-fedon

Kendall, James (1647–1708). Accessed 15 May 2016, http://www historyofparliamentonline.org/volume/1690-1715/member kendalljames-1647–1708

Kendall, Thomas (1609–66). Accessed 15 May 2016, http://www.historyofparliamentonline.org/volume/1660-1690/member/kendall-thomas-1609-66#family-relations

Kendal Plantation. Shilstone Memorial Library, Barbados Museum & Historical Society vertical file.

Kingdon, Mavis and Sue Dibble. *The Binding Stone: Memories of St. Tudy 1900-2000*. St. Tudy: St. Tudy Women's Institute, [2000].

Kingsley, Charles. *At Last: a Christmas in the West Indies*. London: Macmillan, 1872. Accessed 28 November, 2016, https://archive.org/details/atlastachristma02kinggoog

Knight, Charles c.1799–1879, Wesleyan Methodist Mission, Sierra Leone. Accessed 11 June, 2016, http://www.dacb.org/stories/sierraleone/knight_charles.html

Lake, Hazel. *Sugar Planters in Little Parndon*. Harlow: Lake, 2002.

Laurence, Kenneth Ormiston. *Tobago in Wartime: 1793-1815*. The Press, University of the West Indies, 1995.

Legacies of British Slave Ownership. Accessed throughout 2015, https://www.ucl.ac.uk/lbs/

Leith, Claire. 'A South American Adventure with Francis Oats and his Son Francis Freathy Oats in 1901.' *Journal of the Royal Institution of Cornwall*, pp.41-49. (New Series II, Vol. II, Part 3, 1996).

Lemon Hart: a Real Rum Story. Accessed 11 September, 2016, http://thedabbler.co.uk/2011/02/lemon-hart-a-real-rum-story/

[Letter] to James Hervey, *March 20, 1739*. Accessed 10 July, 2016, http://wesley.nnu.edu/john-wesley/the-letters-of-john-wesley/wesleys-letters-1739#Four

'Letters from Barbados.' *Royal Gazette: Bermuda Commercial and General Advertiser and Recorder*, p.1. (Vol.57, 23 August, 1881)

Ligon, Richard and Karen Ordahl Kupperman. *The True and Exact History of the Island of Barbados*. Cambridge: Hackett Publishing, 2011.

Long, Edward. *The History of Jamaica: Or, General Survey of the Ancient and Modern State of that Island, with Reflections on Its Situation, Settlements, Inhabitants, Climate, Products, Commerce, Laws, and Government.* Cambridge: Cambridge University Press, 2010.

Luttrell, Narcissus. *A Brief Historical Relation of State Affairs from September 1678 to April 1714.* 6 vols. Oxford: University Press, 1857. Accessed 15 May 2016, https://catalog.hathitrust.org/Record/011539870

Mackay, David. 'Banks, Bligh and the Breadfruit.' *New Zealand Journal of History*, pp.61-77. (Vol.8, Issue 1, April 1974).

Mackay, Ruddock and Michael Duffy. *Hawke, Nelson and British Naval Leadership, 1749-1805.* Woodbridge: Boydell Press, 2009.

Marsden, Philip. *The Levelling Sea: the Story of a Cornish Haven and the Age of Sail.* London: Harper Press, 2012.

Martinez-Fernandez, Luis. *Protestantism and Political Conflict in the Nineteenth-century Hispanic Caribbean.* Piscataway: Rutgers University Press, 2002.

Mason, Jane. *The Mount People.* Redruth: Dyllansow Truran, 1990.

Mazzullo, Ricki. 'The Copper Mine: History in the Making.' *The Welcome*, pp.11-14 (Vol.19, No.2, February/March 1990).

Metcalf, George for the Royal Commonwealth Society. *Royal Government and Political Conflict in Jamaica, 1729-1783.* London: Longmans, 1965.

Methodist Church in the Caribbean and the Americas. *Our History and Heritage.* Accessed 6 June, 2016, http://www.mccalive.org/our_church.php?mid=9

Minster, Christopher. *Latin America: Causes of Independence.* Accessed November 14, 2016, http://latinamericanhistory.about.com/od/19thcenturylatinamerica/a/09independencewhy.htm

Moister, William. *Heralds of Salvation: Memorial Sketches of Wesleyan Missionaries.* London: Wesleyan Conference Office, 1878.

Moister, William. *Memorials of Missionary Labours in Western Africa and the West Indies and at the Cape of Good Hope...* 3rd. Ed. London: [Wesleyan Conference Office], 1850.

Moore, Brian L., B.W. Higman, Carl Campbell and Patrick Bryan. *Slavery, Freedom and Gender*. Kingston: University of the West Indies Press, 2001.

Morgan, Claire. *Governors of Jamaica: Edward and William Trelawny*. Redruth: Cornish Studies Library, nd.

Morgan, Kenneth. *Materials on the History of Jamaica in the Edward Long Papers Held at the British Library*. London: Brunel University, 2006.

Morrill, Justin S. *Annexation of Santo Domingo. Speech... Delivered in the Senate of the United States, April 7, 1871*. Washington, DC, F. and J. Rives and George A. Bailey, 1871. Accessed 21 September, 2016, https://books.google.com.ag/books?id=zAvSwFPKkckC&dq=speech+justin+s+morrill+santo+domingo+1871&source=gbs_navlinks_s

Mudd, David. *The Falmouth Packets*. Bodmin: Bossiney Books, 1984.

Murray, Roy James. "'The Man That Says Slaves be Quite Happy in Slavery... is Either Ignorant or a Lying Person...' An Account of Slavery in the Marginal Colonies of the British West Indies." PhD diss., University of Glasgow, 2001.

Nardin, Jean-Claude. *La Mise en Valeur de L'ile de Tobago (1763–1783)*. Paris: Mouton, 1969.

National Parks Trust. *The Copper Mine National Park*. Road Town: National Parks Trust, nd.

National Parks Trust and British Virgin Islands. Conservation and Fisheries Department. *British Virgin Islands Protected Areas System Plan 2007–2017*. Road Town, National Parks Trust [2007?].

Neumann-Holzschuh, Ingrid and Schneider, Edgar Werner. *Degrees of Restructuring in Creole Languages*. Amsterdam: John Benjamins Publishing, 2000.

Nevis Historical and Conservation Society. *Nevis Genealogies*. Charlestown: Nevis Historical and Conservation Society, nd.

Nicholson, Desmond V. *The Codrington Papers: Their History and Content*. St. John's: Antigua Archaeological Society, September 1981.

Norway, Arthur H. *History of the Post Office Packet Service Between the Years 1793-1815 Compiled from Records, chiefly official*. London: Macmillan, 1895.

O'Byrne, William R. *A Naval Biographical Dictionary: Comprising the Life and Services of Every Living Officer in Her Majesty's Navy, from the Rank of Admiral of the Fleet to that of Lieutenant, Inclusive*. Vol.1. London: John Murray, 1849.

O'Connor, Mike. *Cornish Folk Tales*. Stroud: The History Press, 2010.

O'Shaughnessy, Andrew Jackson. *An Empire Divided: The American Revolution and the British Caribbean*. Philadelphia: University of Pennsylvania Press, 2000.

O'Toole, Laurence. *The Cornish Captain's Tale: Rear Admiral Sir Richard Spry*. Redruth: Dyllansow Truran, 1986.

Old St. Keverne News, Cornwall. Accessed 13 June, 2016, http://www.st-keverne.com/History/Misc/West-Briton.php

Oliver, Vere Langford. *Caribbeana: Being Miscellaneous Papers Relating to the History, Genealogy, Topography, and Antiquities of the British West Indies*. London: Mitchell, Hughes and Clarke, 1910.

Oliver, Vere Langford. *The History of the Island of Antigua: One of the Leeward Caribees in the West Indies, from the First Settlement in 1635 to the Present Time*. Vol.2. London: Mitchell and Hughes, 1896.

Oliver, Vere Langford. *The History of the Island of Antigua: One of the Leeward Caribees in the West Indies, From the First Settlement in 1635 to the Present Time*. Vol.3. London: Mitchell and Hughes, 1899.

Olwig, Karen Fog. *Global Culture, Island Identity: Continuity and Change in the Afro-Caribbean Community of Nevis*. London: Routledge, 1993.

Olwig, Karen Fog. *Small Islands, Large Questions: Society, Culture and Resistance in the Post-emancipation Caribbean*. London: Frank Cass, 1995.

O'Neil, Mervyn J. *An Analytical History of Tobago*. Scarborough: O'Neil, 2015.

Osler, Edward. *The Life of Admiral Viscount Exmouth*. London: Smith, Elder and Co., 1835.

Paquette, Robert L. and Stanley L. Engerman. *The Lesser Antilles in the Age of European Expansion*. Gainesville, University Press of Florida, 1996.

Pares, Richard. *A West-India Fortune*. London: Longmans, Green and Co., 1950.

Parker, Matthew. *The Sugar Barons*. London: Windmill Books, 2012.

Parkinson, C. Northcote. *Edward Pellew, Viscount Exmouth, Admiral of the Red*. London: Methuen, 1934. Accessed February 28, 2015, http://www.pellew.com/Exmouth/Exmouth%20003/Cover%20Page.htm

Parsons, Jack and Nora Parsons. *Cornish Fisherboy to Master Mariner: The Life of Henry Blewett 1836-1891. Part One 1836–1861: Mousehole Boyhood and Early Days at Sea*. Bournemouth: Bournemouth Local Studies Publications, 1993.

Parsons, Jack and Nora Parsons. *Cornish Fisherboy to Master Mariner: The Life of Henry Blewett 1836-1891. Part Two 1861–1866: Mate and Master Mariner*. Bournemouth: Bournemouth Local Studies Publications, 1993.

Parsons, Jack and Nora Parsons. *Cornish Fisherboy to Master Mariner: The Life of Henry Blewett 1836–1891. Part Three 1866–1881: Roseau Days*. Bournemouth: Bournemouth Local Studies Publications, 1994.

Pathway to Legend. Accessed 9 September 2016, http://www.lemonhartrum.com/rum-always.html#visioneer

Pawlyn, Tony. *The Falmouth Packets 1689–1851*. Truro, Truran Books, 2003.

Payton, Philip. *Cornwall: A History*. 2nd edn. Fowey: Cornwall Editions, 2004.

Payton, Philip. *The Cornish Overseas: The History of Cornwall's 'Great Emigration.'* Fowey: Cornwall Editions, 2005.

Peirce, Richard. *Pirates of Devon and Cornwall*. Bude: Shark Cornwall, 2010.
Pencarrow House. Accessed 21 May 2016, http://www.pencarrow.co.uk/house

Penrose, John. *Lives of Sir Charles Vinicombe Penrose and Captain James Trevenen.* London: John Murray, 1850.

Pérez, Louis A. *Winds of Change: Hurricanes and the Transformation of Nineteenth-Century Cuba.* Chapel Hill, University of North Carolina Press, 2001.

Pérez del Castillo, Guillermo. 'The Harvey family in El Cobre.' *Revisita Cuban Genealogical Society,* pp.2–6 (Vol.15, January 2006). Accessed 11 December 2016, http://www.cubagenweb.org/Revista%20v15-N1.pdf

Pérez Drago, Ileana. "El Hierro en la Arquitectura Colonial Habanera. Condicionantes Formales, Técnicas e Históricas." Tomo 1. PhD diss., Universidad Politécnica de Madrid, 2004.

Perkins, H.J. *Notes on British Guiana and its Gold Industry.* 2nd ed. London: British Library, 2011. First published 1876.

Philbrick, M.E. 'The Falmouth Packet Service [Part 1].' *Postal History: The Bulletin of the Postal History Society,* pp.14–20 (No.207, 1978).

Philbrick, M.E. 'The Falmouth Packet Service [Part 2]' *Postal History: The Bulletin of the Postal History Society,* pp.9–10 (No.209, 1979)

Philbrick, M.E. *The Packet Captains of Flushing, Cornwall: A Survey of the History of the Post Office Packet Captains Known to have Lived in the Village of Flushing 1689-1815.* Truro, Philbrick, 1982.

Phillips, David. *La Magdalena: The Story of Tobago, 1498–1898.* New York: iUniverse, 2004.

Pickering, Vernon W. *A Concise History of the British Virgin Islands: From the Amerindians to 1986,* Cambridge: Cambridge University Press. New York, Falcon Publications International, 1987.

Pickering, Vernon W. *The Early History of the British Virgin Islands.* 2nd Ed. New York: Falcon Publications International, 1997.

Pickersgill, Fay. *Jamaica's Fascinating Falmouth.* Kingston: Pickersgill, 2013.

Piggot, Aaron Snowden. *The Chemistry and Metallurgy of Copper Including a Description of the Principal Copper Mines of the United States and Other Countries*. Philadelphia: Lindsay and Blakiston, 1858. Accessed 10 December 2016, https://play.google.com/books/reader?id=d5ZEAAAAIAAJ&printsec=frontcover&output=reader&hl=en&pg=GBS.PA30

Price, George. *Jamaica and the Colonial Office: Who Caused the Crisis?* London: Sampson Low and Son, and Marstone, 1866.

Price, Rose. *Pledges on Colonial Slavery, to Candidates for Seats in Parliament, Rightly Considered*. Penzance: Price, 1832.

Quarterly Journal of the Geological Society of London. (Vol 10, 1854). Accessed 21 September, 2016, https://babel.hathitrust.org/cgi/pt?id=mdp.39015006918091;view=1up;seq=8

Rabbi Abraham Hart. Accessed 10 September, 2016, http://www.farhi.org/wc117/wc117_320.htm

Rea, Robert R. 'The Naval Career of John Eliot, Governor of West Florida.' *The Florida Historical Quarterly*, pp.451–467 (Vol.57, No.4, April 1979).

Rees, Edward. *Sir Rose Price*. Unpublished typed manuscript in the Morrab Library. MOR/RE/26-38.

Reports on the Island of Aruba (Dutch) West Indies, and its Gold Ores with a General Description of the Island. London: H.W. Foster, 1872. Accessed 17 June, 2016, https://catalog.hathitrust.org/Record/008429423

Rev. Nicholas Leverton 1610-1662: Life and Death of a Non Conformist. Accessed 1 June, 2016, http://www.nickleverton.com/life-and-death-story.html

Richards, Bob. 'Perran Foundry.' *My Cornwall*, pp.80–81 (April/May 2011)

Robley Genealogy. Accessed 23 May 2016, http://www.robley.org.uk/

Rogers, John Jope. *Opie and his Works: Being a Catalogue of 760 Pictures by John Opie, R.A. Preceded by a Biographical Sketch*. London: Paul and Dominic Colnaghi, 1878.

Romantic Circles. *Tobin, James Webbe (1767–1814)*. Accessed 9 December 2015, https://www.rc.umd.edu/node/59426

Rose, George Henry. *A Letter on the Means and Importance of Converting the Slaves in the West Indies to Christianity*. London: John Murray, 1823. Accessed 11 June, 2016, http://books.googleusercontent.com/books/content?req=AKW5Qacg DllY3zPRlSgku54Ah1KRNw1vXoiPkzsCWAD38rBW9gmURuZOrs9r KcHfLdCQbZFPgLdmoi3bsDGxhkuUZu7VeiskTZav92f9qC1aXKb4v5 lUgLg8ON-lhVlyvhk6DifCiiIFZy_VX2hRPH9l0EaJM6hAuPg4e MtnCnQYOWUDlhyvEVhdiU0crRmRQlCf5rnOe_GMrMDx I2LKZgvOslVoVZKiw02Ssa814i-wyqGs-bM8gi2uG0hWVGB788dgcB7Fky na9c7KyxfK4RlTHwMwTZ0_FgGmg_OIWZZJZpjgFXfGYDQ

Ross, Helen. *The Ruins at Bushiribana, Aruba Circa 1872: A Preliminary Investigation into Aruba's Gold Mining History*. Corning: Caribbean Volunteer Expeditions, 1999. Accessed 17 June. 2016, http://ufdc.ufl.edu/AA00012428/00005

Roth, Cecil. *The Rise of Provincial Jewry: The Early Communities, Section 5 (Oxford to Yarmouth)*. Accessed 10 September, 2016, http://www.jewishgen.org/JCR-uk/susser/provincialjewry/oxfyarm.htm#penzance

Roughley, Thomas. *The Jamaica Planter's Guide or, a System for Planting and Managing a Sugar Estate or Other Plantations in that Island, and Throughout the British West Indies in General*. London: Longman, Hurst, Rees, Orme and Brown, 1823. Accessed May 15, 2015, https://books.google.com.ag/books/about/The_Jamaica_planter_s_guide_or_A_system.html?id=bOIMAAAAYAAJ&hl=en

Rubinstein, William D., Michael Jolles and Hilary L. Rubinstein. *The Palgrave Dictionary of Anglo-Jewish History*. Basingstoke: Palgrave Macmillan, 2011.

Sacks, David Harris. *The Widening Gate: Bristol and the Atlantic Economy, 1450-1700*. Berkeley: University of California Press, 1992. Accessed May 15, 2015, http://publishing.cdlib.org/ucpressebooks/view?docId=ft3f59n8d1&brand=

San Miguel, Pedro L. 'Historical Visions of the Caribbean: From Imperial Perspectives to Subaltern Resistances.' *Revista Brasileira do Caribe*, p.36. (Vol.1, Number 2, 2001). English translation by Jane Ramirez. Accessed 7 December 2015, https://www.academia.edu/17426181/San_Miguel_Pedro_L.-Historical_Visions_of_the_Caribbean

Salusbury-Trelawny of Trelawne, John Barry. *The Trelawny Family*. Hythe: Trelawny, nd.

Sanders, Joanne McRee. *Barbados Records: Wills and Administrations Volume II, 1681-1700*. Baltimore: Clearfield, 2011.

Satchell, Veront. *Jamaica*. Accessed 22 January 2016, http://www.hartford-hwp.com/archives/43/130.html

Schaw, Janet. *Journal of a Lady of Quality; being the Narrative of a Journey from Scotland to the West Indies, North Carolina and Portugal, in the years 1774 to 1776*. Edited by Evangeline Walker Andrew in collaboration with Charles McLain Andrews. New Haven: University of Yale Press, 1921.

Schwartz, Sharron P. *The Cornish in Latin America: 'Cousin Jack' and the New World*. Wicklow: The Cornubian Press, 2016.

Schwartz, Sharron P. 'The Great Cornish migration.' *My Cornwall*, pp.20–25. (February/March 2012)

Senior, Olive. *Dying to Better Themselves: West Indians and the Building of the Panama Canal*. Kingston: University of the West Indies Press, 2014.

Sir George Buckley Mathew. Accessed 12 October, 2015, http://www.findagrave.com/cgi-bin fg.cgi?page=gr&GRid=134230305&ref=acom

Sir Walter Raleigh (1554–1618): The Discovery of Guiana, 1595. Accessed 1 August, 2016, http://sourcebooks.fordham.edu/mod/1595raleigh-guiana.asp

Smelt, Maurice. *101 Cornish Lives*. Penzance: Alison Hodge, 2006.

Smith, S.D. *Slavery, Family, and Gentry Capitalism in the British Atlantic: the World of the Lascelles, 1648-1834*. Cambridge: Cambridge University Press, 2006.

Smith, Raymond T. *The Matrifocal Family: Power, Pluralism and Politics*. New York: Routledge, 2014.

Snell, Lawrence S. *A Short History of the Duke of Cornwall's Light Infantry 1702-1945*. Aldershot: Gale and Polden, 1945.

Sombrero: Part of Anguilla's Cultural Heritage. Accessed April 7, 2017, http://web.archive.org/web/20071006203854/http://sombrero.ai/island.htm

Sombrero – Anguilla's First Ramsar Site Designated. Accessed 19 July 2018, https://www.ukotcf.org.uk/news/sombrero-designation .

'Sombrero Island.' *Caribbean Beach News*, pp. 7-8 (June 2012). Accessed March 11, 2015, http://www.caribbeanbeachnews.com/CBN4WEB.pdf

Some Folk Songs of Guyana: Itaname. Accessed 7 August, 2016, http://silvertorch.com/folksongs-of-guyana.html#Itaname

Sparrow, Elizabeth. *The Prices of Penzance: The Influence of 18th Century Jamaican Sugar Plantation Owners on West Cornwall.* Penzance: Penzance Library, 1985.

'Spry, Sir Richard (1715-1775).' *Dictionary of National Biography*, pp.432-433 (Vol.53 1898). Accessed 6 February 2015, https://ia601607us.archive.org/34/items/DictionaryOfNationalBiographyVolume53/DictionaryOfNationalBiographyVolume53.pdf

St. Johnstone, Reginald. *The French Invasions of St. Kitts-Nevis.* Basseterre: Brimstone Hill Restoration Fund, nd.

St. Keverne Local History Society. *Jonathan Trelawny.* Accessed 23 January, 2016, http://www.st-keverne.com/History/Misc/Trelawney.php

St. Lucia: History. Accessed 16 May 2016, http://thecommonwealth.org/our-member-countries/saint-lucia/history

St. Michael Caerhays. Accessed 20 May 2016, http://www.genuki.org.uk/big/eng/Cornwall/StMichaelCaerhays/

St. Vincent and the Grenadines: History. Accessed 16 May 2016, http://thecommonwealth.org/our-member-countries/st-vincent-and-grenadines/history

Stephen, Leslie and Sidney Lee. *Dictionary of National Biography.* Vol.25, Harris–Henry I. London: Smith, Elder and Co., 1891. Accessed 11 June, 2016, https://books.google.com/books?id=79XEJJzNaKYC&printsec=frontcover&source=gbs_ge_summary_r&cad=0#v=onepage&q&f=false

Stewart, William. *Admirals of the World: A Biographical Dictionary, 1500 to the present.* Jefferson: McFarland, 2009.

Stoute, Edward. 'Kendal Plantation.' *Barbados News*, np. (15 March 1964).

Sutherland, Gaulbert. 'Mahdia.' *Stabroek News*. (1 September, 2013). Accessed 11 August, 2016, http://www.stabroeknews.com/2013/features/sunday/beyond-gt/09/01/mahdia/

Swiney, G.C. *Historical Records of the (32nd) Cornwall Light Infantry Now the 1st Battalion Duke of Cornwall's L.I. from the Formation of the Regiment in 1702 to 1892.* London: Simpkin, Marshall, Hamilton, Kent and Company, 1893. Accessed March 14, 2015, https://play.google.com/books/reader?printsec=frontcover&output=reader&id=Hob4Cs7dqNoC&pg=GBS.PR3

Tam, Laird. *Hester the Slave*. np: Tam, 1 December 2010. Accessed 10 December, 2015, https://www.youtube.com/watch?v=htplEYHtXMc

Tangye, Michael. 'Emigration: Cornish Miners in Cuba 1836-1838.' In Redruth Old Cornwall Society, *Old Redruth: Original Studies of the Town's History*, edited by Terry Knight, pp.22-26. Redruth: Redruth Old Cornwall Society, 1992.

Tennant, Robert. *British Guiana and its Resources*. London: G. Philip, 1895. Accessed 31 July, 2016, http://hdl.handle.net/2027/cool.ark:/13968/t6vx0z19w

'The Aruba Island Gold Mining Company.' *The Engineering and Mining Journal*, pp.139-140. (Vol.15, January to June, 1873)

The Corfields and their Relations. Accessed March 11, 2015, http://www.corfield.port5.com/web/10.htm

The Cornish in Latin America: Cobre. Accessed April 8, 2017, https://projects.exeter.ac.uk/cornishlatin/cobre.htm

The Diary of the Reverend William Fidler: January 1827. Accessed 10 June, 2016, http://www.kevinlaurence.net/genealogy/fidlerdiary/1827_January.php

The Duties of Mine Agents. Accessed 4 June, 2016, http://freepages.genealogy.rootsweb.ancestry.com/~staustell/Word_Doc/Life/Duties%20of%20a%20Mine%20Agent.htm

The Gentleman's Magazine, Vol.192. London: John Bowyer Nicholls and Son, 1852.

The Gold Rush: Dominican Republic 2015. Accessed 21 September, 2016, https://www.thebusinessyear.com/dominican-republic-2015/the-gold-rush/focus

The Letters of John James Esq.: A Collection of Letters Written by the Estate Manager of Barbuda and Clare Hall, Antigua 1804–1826. Accessed January 2016, http://johnjamesesq.blogspot.ca/

The Letters of John Wesley: A Delightful Old Age; July 24, 1787, to December 26, 1789. Accessed 9 June 2016, http://wesley.nnu.edu/john-wesley/the-letters-of-john-wesley/wesleys-letters-1787/

The Life of Nicholas Leverton. Accessed 1 June, 2016, http://wesley.nnu.edu/john-wesley/christian-library/a-christian-library-volume-15/the-lives-of-jospeh-woodward-nicholos-leverton-sir-nathanael-barnardiston-and-samuel-fairclough/

The Life, Times and Influences of Captain Stephen Hutchens of Paul, near Penzance, Cornwall. Accessed 21 July, 2016, http://freepages.family.rootsweb.ancestry.com/~treevecwll/hutchens.htm.

The Methodist Who's Who. London: Charles H. Kelly, 1912.

The Moravians and John Wesley. Accessed 9 June, 2016, http://www.christianitytoday.com/history/issues/issue-1/moravians-and-john-wesley.html

The National Archives of the UK. Public Record Office. *Census Returns 1841*. HO 107/146/4

The National Archives of the UK. Public Record Office. *Census Returns 1851*. HO 107/169/7

The National Archives of the UK. Public Record Office. *High Court of Admiralty: Prize Court: Registers of Declarations for Letters of Marque*. HCA 26/6/123

The National Archives of the UK. Public Record Office. Virgin Islands. *Minutes of the Legislative Council and Assembly 1828-1841*. CO 316/4.

The National Archives of the UK. Public Record Office. Virgin Islands. *Minutes of the Legislative Council and Assembly 1842–1844*. CO 316/5.

The National Archives of the UK. Public Record Office. *Will of Edward Mathew Esquire, General in His Majesty's Army*. PROB 11/1437.

The Packet Surgeon's Journals: Voyage 7. Accessed 4 July, 2016, http://87.106.22.33/index.php?/packet_surgeons_journals_voyage_7/

The Underwater City of Port Royal. Accessed 17 January, 2016, http://whc.unesco.org/en/tentativelists/5430/

Thomas, Clive. *Too Big to Fail: A Scoping Study of the Small and Medium Scale Gold and Diamond Mining Industry in Guyana*. df. Ed. Turkeyen: University of Guyana, 2009. Accessed 31 July, 2016, http://guyanaminers.com/document/too-big-fail-scoping-study-small-and-medium-scale-gold-and-diamond-mining-industry-guyana

Thomas Kitchen: A Cornish Mining Adventure in British Guiana. Accessed 31 July, 2016, http://www.cornishreunited.com/thomas-kitchen-a-cornish-mining-venture-in-british-guiana/

Treffry of Place. Accessed 11 July, 2016, http://discovery.nationalarchives.gov.uk/details/rd/4449c2c8-6a65-424b-9d83-b6def4cb6d07

Trereife Manor House. Accessed 21 January, 2016, http://trereifepark.co.uk/the-house/

Trinidad and Tobago. Office of the Prime Minister. *Tobago Hurricane of 1847*. Port-of-Spain: Office of the Prime Minister, 1966.

Trinidad and Tobago: History. Accessed 22 May 2016, thecommonwealth.org/our-member-countries/trinidad-and-tobago/history

Truman, G., John Jackson and Thomas Bedford Longstreth. *Narrative of a Visit to the West Indies in 1840 and 1841*. Philadelphia: Merrihew and Thompson, 1844.

Turnbull, David. *Travels in the West. Cuba; with Notices of Porto Rico and the Slave Trade*. London: Longman, Orme, Brown, Green and Longmans, 1840. Accessed 16 November, 2016, https://archive.org/details/travelsinwestcu01davigoog

Tweedy, Margaret T. 'A History of Barbuda under the Codringtons 1738–1833.' PhD diss., University of Birmingham, 1981.

Uppingham Methodist Church. *Mary Drake and the Missionary*. Uppingham: Uppingham Methodist Church, nd.

Vendryes, Harry E. *An Old Jamaican Mining Venture*. Transcript of broadcast made over Radio ZQ1 in Jamaica on 1 May, 1946.

Virtual Jamestown: Registers of Servants Sent to Foreign Plantations; Bristol Registers 1654-1686. Accessed May, 2015, http://www.virtualjamestown.org/indentures/about_indentures.html#Bristol

Walter Raleigh (c.1552 – 1618). Accessed 1 August, 2016, http://www.bbc.co.uk/history/historic_figures/raleigh_walter.shtml

'Wanted to Proceed Immediately to Habana…' *West Briton* (7 January, 1842). From the Courtney Library Cornish Newspaper Index.

'The Aruba Island Gold Mining Company.' *The Engineering and Mining Journal*, pp.139-140. (Vol.15, January to June, 1873).

Ward, Geoffrey. *Nowhere is Perfect: British Naval Centres on the Leeward Islands Station during the Eighteenth Century*. Accessed March 6, 2015, http://fieldresearchcentre.weebly.com/uploads/1/8/0/7/18079819/ward_2011.pdf

Wareham, Thomas. *The Frigate Captains of the Royal Navy, 1793–1815*. PhD thesis, University of Exeter, May 1999.

Warwick, Peter. *Trafalgar: Tales From the Front Line*. Newton Abott: David and Charles, 2011.

Watson, Joseph Yelloly. *A Compendium of British Mining, with Statistical Notices of the Principal Mines in Cornwall; to Which is Added, the History and Uses of Metals and a Glossary of the Terms and Usages of Mining*. London: Watson, 1843.

Watters, David R. 'Historical Documentation and Archaeological Investigation of Codrington Castle, Barbuda, West Indies.' *Annals of Carnegie Museum*, pp.229–288 (Vol.66, No.3, August 1977).

Watters, David R. 'Observations on the Historic Sites and Archaeology of Barbuda.' *Journal of Archaeology and Anthropology*, pp.125-156 (Vol 3, No.2, 1980).

Watts, David. *The West Indies: Patterns of Development, Culture and Environmental Change since 1492*. Cambridge: Cambridge University Press, 1987.

Waszkis, Helmut. *Mining in the Americas: Stories and History*. Cambridge: Woodhead Publishing, 1993.

Webbe, George. 'Estimated Position of the Great Comet of 1844-5.' *Monthly Notices of the Royal Astronomical Society*, (Vol. 6, p.206). Accessed 9 December, 2015, http://articles.adsabs.harvard.edu/full/seri/MNRAS/0006//0000206.000.html

Wesley, John. *Thoughts upon slavery*. London: John Crukshank, 1778. Accessed 13 June, 2–16, http://docsouth.unc.edu/church/wesley/wesley.html

Wesleyan Methodist Church. *Minutes of Several Conversations at the One Hundred and Fortieth Annual Conference of the People called Methodists...* London: Wesleyan-Methodist Book-Room, 1883. Accessed 11 June, 2016, https://books.google.com/books?id=y7oQAAAAIAAJ&q=william+l.+bennett#v=snippet&q=william%20l.%20bennett&f=false

Wesleyan Methodist Church. *Minutes of the Wesleyan Methodist Conferences from the first...* Vol.5. London: J. Kershaw, 1825. Accessed 11 June, 2016, http://books.googleusercontent.com/books/content?req=AKW5QadfHhrkGc
Nq7IGsUJLcVkLnC5HCq_nzr9dN87CQD82I3Q8spxIR3F_0SsKRF3veE_bqRP
RenUTl0vteskoIX2e2ehfvXprgiFH5X1rrLom9ArhJ-YNcMO-IeJ4fpO3ozpABeI
EfoMsIwfiUrispAQCUMO9Qq4xuGdYdPkSIsWrI_lDonH98d8-
P45rkw9en-dFSA78_iHw7fpaXvaCOqEA42gGIr3IDlwMeshTicju
M0rqWBe4r8yFwJ0xipYtYlkkzbP6v0QOE-TwuOxwpQRAU2Goofe
WWUpSt3gqRL_I_8_iI7Eg

Wesleyan Methodist Church. *Minutes of the Wesleyan Conferences From the First...* Vol.6. London: John Mason, 1833. Accessed 11 June, 2016, https://archive.org/stream/minutesseveralc10churgoog#page/n8/mode/2up

Wesleyan Methodist Church. *Minutes of the Wesleyan Conferences From the First...* Vol.8. London: John Mason, 1841. Accessed 11 June, 2016, https://books.google.com/books?id=RygRAAAAIAAJ&q=title+page#v=onepage&q=title%20page&f=false

Wesleyan Methodist Church. *Minutes of the Wesleyan Conferences From the First…* Vol.10. London: John Mason, 1848. Accessed 11 June, 2016, https://books.google.co.uk/books?id=mxsRAAAAIAAJ&printsec=frontcover&vq=goy&source=gbs_ge_summary_r&cad=0#v=onepage&q=goy&f=false

Wesleyan Methodist Church. *Minutes of the Wesleyan Conferences From the First…* Vol.13. London: John Mason, 1859. Accessed 11 June, 2016, https://archive.org/stream/minutesseveralc07churgoog#page/n8/mode/2up

Wesleyan Methodist Church. *Minutes of the Wesleyan Conferences From the First…* Vol.14. London: John Mason, 1862. Accessed 11 June, 2016, https://books.google.com/books?id=PMEQAAAAIAAJ&pg=PA3-IA4#v=onepage&q=goy&f=false

Wesleyan Methodist Church. *Minutes of the Wesleyan Conferences From the First…* Vol.18. London: Wesleyan Conference Office, 1874. Accessed 28 June, 2016, https://archive.org/details/minutesmethodis00churgoog

Wesleyan Methodist Church. *Minutes of the Wesleyan Conferences from the first…* Vol.19. London: Wesleyan Conference Office, 1877. Accessed 28 June, 2016, https://archive.org/details/10735743.269.emory.edu

Wesleyan Methodist Missionary Society. *The Wesleyan Juvenile Offering: A Miscellany of Missionary Information for Young Persons.* London: Wesleyan Methodist Missionary Society, 1865. Accessed 12 June, 2016, https://books.google.com/books?id=IF0EAAAAQAAJ&printsec=frontcover#v=onepage&q&f=false

West India Docks (1803–1980). Accessed 30 May, 2016, http://www.portcities.org.uk/london/server/show/ConFactFile.83/West-India-Docks.html

Westley, Megan. 'A Global Service: The Former Glory of Falmouth's Packet Ships.' *My Cornwall*, pp.48–53 (February/March 2014)

What is Placer Gold Mining? Accessed 6 August, 2016, www.nps.gov/yuch/learn/historyculture/placer-mining.htm

Wheal Jane & West Wheal Jane Mine, Cornwall. Accessed 17 August, 2016, http://www.cornwallinfocus.co.uk/mining/whealjane.php

Whitburn, James. *A Cornish Man in Cuba: Transcript of a Diary of his Visit to Cuba 1836-1838*. np: Whitburn, nd.

White, Walter Grainge. *Notes and Comments on My Trip to the Diamond Fields of British Guiana*. Georgetown: White, 1902.

Wilkins, Frances. *Bittersweet: A Story of Four Jamaican Plantations*. Kidderminster: Wyre Forest Press, 2007.

Wilkinson, Jerry. *History of Cuba*. Accessed 11 November, 2016, http://www.keyshistory.org/cuba.html 1773).

Williams, Abigail and Kate O'Connor. *Who is Aphra Behn?* Accessed 11 July, 2016, http://writersinspire.org/content/who-aphra-behn

Williams, Thomas (1737–1802), of Llanidan, Anglesey and Temple House, Berks. Accessed 17 November, 2016, http://www.historyofparliamentonline.org/volume/1790-1820/member/williams-thomas-1737-1802

Williams Family. Accessed 24 November, 2016, http://www.gracesguide.co.uk/Williams_Family

Williamson, James. *Voyage 7: Notes of a Voyage to Buenos Ayres and Back. Sailed 19th November 1830 – returned 9th June 1831*. Accessed 28 November, 2016, http://maritimeviews.nmmc.co.uk/index.php?/packet_surgeons_journals/voyage_7/

Woodbury, George. *The Great Days of Piracy*. London: Elek, 1954.

Woodcock, Henry Iles. *A History of Tobago*. Port-of-Spain: Columbus Publishers, 1976. From an 1866 manuscript.

Yates, Geoffrey S. *Rose Hall: Death of a Legend*. Accessed 21 January, 2016, http://www.jamaicanfamilysearch.com/Samples2/mpalmer.htm

Zacek, Natalie A. *Settler Society in the English Leeward Islands, 1670–1776*. Cambridge: Cambridge University Press, 2015.

Index

Abercrombie, Ralph, 100
Alley, Mary, 184-185
American Revolutionary War, 86, 89, 112, 138, 139, 271
American War of Independence *see* American Revolutionary War
Andrew, Martin, 220
Anguilla, 12, 201, 253, 255, 262, 299
Anstis, Thomas, 67-68
Antigua, 4, 12, 13, 22-31, 116, 184-185, 191-193, 199, 202, 260
Antigua *see also* Barbuda
Aruba, 61, 176-183, 281-284
Aruba Agency Company Ltd., 181
Aruba Gold Concessions Ltd., 181-182
Aruba Gold Maatsschappij, 182
Aruba Island Goldmining Company Ltd., 177-181
Austin, Anne, 141
Austin, James, 141
Austin, Jane, 141

Babb, John, 132
Bahamas, 67
Bailey, Annie, 199
Bailey, Thomas H., 199-201
Banks, Joseph, 78
Barbados, 22, 127-128, 186, 190, 197-198, 262, 274
Barbot, James, 15
Barbuda, 12, 22, 24-31

Barbuda *see also* Antigua
Baring, Thomas, 243-244
Bath Botanical Gardens, 79-80
Bawden (family name – Cayman Islands) *see* Bodden
Bawden, Thomas, 66
Baxter, John, 185
Bay of Honduras, 67
Belize *see* British Honduras, 152
Bell, John, 18-19, 195
Bell, Mary, 18-19, 195-196
Belmanna Riots, 145
Bennett, William Lanyon, 202
Bermuda, 131
Bertie, Jane, Lady, 12, 141
Bessie (slave belonging to Nathaniel Gilbert), 184-185
Bishop, William, 220
Blewett, Henry, 151-155
Bligh, William, 77-81
Blight, William, 220
Bodden (family name), 66
Bodden, Isaac, 66
Boscawen, Edward, 71-73
Boscawen, Hugh, 71
Boscawen, William Glanville, 44, 73
Brammer, Elizabeth Williams, 46
Brammer, John, 46
Breadfruit, 78-81
Brewer, Hannah, 199
Brewer, James Curtis, 198-199

British Guiana, 152-153, 155, 156-176, 199
British Guiana Diamond Syndicate, 170
British Guiana Gold Company, 156
British Honduras, 152
British Leeward Islands, 1-32, 185, 186, 259-263
British Leeward Islands *see also* Anguilla, Antigua, Barbuda, British Virgin Islands, Montserrat, Nevis, St Christopher
British Virgin Islands, 12, 299
British Virgin Islands *see also* Tortola, Virgin Gorda, Virgin Islands
British Windward Islands, 275
British Windward Islands *see also* Grenada, St. Lucia, St. Vincent, Tobago, Windward Islands
Brown, Charles Barrington, 161, 230
Browne, Jeremiah, 6-7
Buckingham, James Silk, 146-150
Buckley, Jenett, 11
Buckley, William, 9, 11
Burrell, Thomas, 65
Burt, Louisa Pym, 6
Burt, William Mathew, 8
Burt, William Pym, 6-7
Byam, George, 9
Byam, Mary, 9

Campbell, Sophia, 184-185
Carolina Corps, 138-139
Carpenter, William, 220
Carter, Christopher, 1,2
Carthew, James, 90-91
Case, Robert, 16, 17
Castillo y Jimenez, Luis, 229
Cayman Islands, 66-68, 268-269
Christopher, James, 1

Chynoweth, J., 248
Clemes (mine captain), 61, 63
Clemes, H. (also a mine captain, possibly the same person as the Clemes mentioned above), 247-248, 250-251
Clemo, John, 220
Cobre Days (sea shanty), 224-225
Cobre mines, 63, 104, 205-209, 210-230
Cobre Mines Consolidated Company *see* Compañía Consolidada de Minas del Cobre
Cochrane, Alexander, 95, 114, 151
Cocks, Emily, 197
Cocks, William Francis, 197
Codrington, Christopher, 22-31
Codrington, Christopher Bethel, 22
Coke, Thomas, 185, 186-187
Colbrook, Charles, 58
Cole, Christopher, 87-89
Cole, Francis, 87
Cole, Humphrey, 86-87
Cole, John, 87
Colleton, Peter, 134, 135
Colleton, Thomas, 134
Colleton, Walker, 134, 135
Columbus, Bartolomeo, 293, 294
Columbus, Christopher, 233, 259, 266, 269, 275, 276-277, 289, 293, 297-298
Columbus, Diego, 282
Compañía Consolidada de Minas del Cobre, 207, 208, 210, 211-212, 213-214, 219, 221-222, 223, 227-228, 229
Cook, James, 78
Coomy (slave belonging to Matthew Mills), 15
Copper mining, 60-66, 205-232, 233-

252, 267, 290-291, 298, 299-300
Corfield, Thomas, 253, 255
Cornwall Regiment of Foot, 99-100
Cosa, Juan de la, 279
Cotes, Thomas, 76
Cribbe, John, 15
Cromwell, Oliver, 3, 267
Cuba, 61, 63, 205-230
Cuba Mining Company, 209
Cuban independence movement, 226, 227-229
Curaçao, 68
Curnow, William, 220

Dabbin, Nicholas, 2
Dale, Charles, 51
Danish Virgin Islands, 253
Danish Virgin Islands see also St Thomas
Davis, Howell, 67
Davy, John, 100-102
Davy, Humphrey, 18, 100
De Beers Consolidated Mining Company, 172-175
Diamond mining, 170-176
Dominica, 12, 31-32, 153, 202, 260, 261
Dominican Republic, 230-232, 296
Drake, Francis, 269
Duckworth, John Thomas, 88
Duke of Cornwall's Light Infantry, 98
Dummer, Edmund, 75, 104, 106
Dutch West India Company, 280, 282-283, 284
Dyett, Isidor, 250

Earle, William, 14
Edmunds, Sarah, 34
El Cobre mines see Cobre mines
El Real de Santiago see Real de Santiago

Edye, Rawleigh, 1
Ellis, Robert, 51
Eliot, John, 75-77
Evans, Ben, 220

Falmouth Packet Service, 103-126
Fédon, Julien, 140-141
Fédon Rebellion, 140-141
First West India Regiment, 139
Flowers, John, 67
Forrest, Arthur, 76
Fortesque, Mary, 137
Fortesque, William, 137
Fox, Edward, 98
Freemasons, 166-167
French Revolutionary Wars, 86, 87, 89, 99, 272

Garnier, Margaret, 5
Gashry, Francis, 38
Gil, Juan, 298
Gilbert, Francis, 184
Gilbert, Nathaniel, 184
Godolphin, Sidney, 104, 105
Gold mining, 156-170, 176-183, 266-267, 283, 284, 289, 291, 294
Gordon, James, 7
Goy, William Dixon, 189-191
Granville, Bevil, 135-136
Grasse-Rouville, Francois-Joseph-Paul de, Compte de Grasse, 87
Greatheed, John, 6
Grenada, 137-141, 189-190, 275
Grenfell, Charles Pascoe, 207
Grenfell, Pascoe, 207
Grenfell, Riversdale William, 207
Grenville, Richard, 135
Gribble, Cyrus, 168
Gribble, Elijah, 168

Gribble, Frederick, 168-169
Gribble, Tobias, 168
Gribble, William, 220
Guano mining, 253-255
Guerra y Toledo, Delores, 229
Guerra y Toledo, Juana, 229
Guyana *see* British Guiana

Haiti, 194
Hales, Emily, 197
Hamilton, Ker Baillie, 246, 247, 248, 250, 251
Hampton, Jeremiah, 220
Hardy, John, 206-207, 218, 221
Harris, Richard, 67
Harry, John, 220
Harry, Jonathan, 220
Hart, Abraham, 47-48
Hart, Ezekiel Lazarus, 48
Hart, Lemon (Asher Laman ben Eleazer), 48-49
Hartwell, Hannah, 199
Hartwell, James T., 199
Harvey, Alberto, 229
Harvey, Carlos de la Caridad, 229
Harvey, Colin, 208
Harvey, Jane, 229
Harvey, John, 229
Harvey, William Woods, 193-194
Harvey y Guerra, Isabel Juana, 229
Harvey's Foundry, 213
Hatuey (head cacique of Hispaniola), 290
Heneken, T.S., 230-232
Herbert, Joseph, 7
Hill, Anne, 5
Hill, Thomas, 5
Hispaniola, 293
Hitchins, Joel, 236, 242, 244

Hodge, Edward, 228, 229
Hodge, Jane, 229
Hollow, Richard, 65
Holman, John, 227
Hood, Samuel, 87
Hooper, T., 248
Hooper, W., 248
Hosier, Francis, 71
Hosken, Josiah Rodda, 165-167
Hosking, Arthur Francis, 181-182
Hudson, Thomas, 70
Hurricanes, 144-145, 225
Husband, Thomas, 230
Hutchens, Stephen, 69-71

Indentured labour, 1-3, 14, 132-133, 153, 225-226, 262-263, 264-265, 277
Itaname (folk song), 160-161

Jackson, John, 239
Jamaica, 33-66, 68, 69, 187, 266-268
Jamaica Copper Mining Company, 63-64
Jamaica Station, 69-70, 71, 76, 80, 81, 86, 87, 90
James, Anthony, 99-100
James, John (the Elder), 23
James, John (the Younger), 23-31.
James, Elizabeth, 24, 30
Jeffery, Robert, 93-97, 252
Jenkin, Alfred, 211-212, 217, 221-223
Jessup, Edward, 7
Jewell, James, 156-160
John Simmons and Son, 209
Jose, T., 248

Kemp, Jane, 229
Kemp, John, 65

Kempe, Thomas, 248
Kendall, James (the Elder), 133-135
Kendall, James (the Younger), 134
Kendall, John, 133
Kendall, Thomas, 132-133
Kernick, John, 209
Kernick, Lizzie, 209
King, Benjamin, 7
Kings Slaves of El Cobre, 210, 292
Kitchen, Thomas, 161-164
Knowles, Charles, 38, 39

La Compañía Consolidada de Minas del Cobre *see* Compañía Consolidada de Minas del Cobre
Laing, Malcolm, 45, 50
Lake, Warwick, 94-96
Lambart, Elizabeth, 52, 54
Lanaghan, Mrs, 4, 30-31, 116
Lawrence, George Bennett, 92
Lawrence, William, 65
Leeward Islands, 262
Leeward Islands *see also* British Leeward Islands
Leeward Islands Station, 69, 88, 91, 94
Leverton, Nicholas, 127-132, 280
London Syndicate, 161-164
Long, Charles, 60-61
Long, Edward, 43-44
Longden, James Robert, 250-251
Longstreth, Thomas, 239
Lowry, Henry, 61-63

MacQueen, James, 121
Madron, John, 152
Maroons, 37, 268
Martin, John, 65
Mathew, Abednego (about 1633-1681), 3-4

Mathew, Abednego (1724-1795), 10-12
Mathew, Daniel (I), 9-12, 141-144
Mathew, Daniel (II), 10
Mathew, Edward, 12, 138-141
Mathew, George, 10, 143
Mathew, George Benvenuto Buckley, 12-13, 145
Mathew, William (I), 4-5,
Mathew, William (II), 5-9
Mathew, William (III), 8
Mathew, William (IV), 8
May, Richard, 227
Maynard, Josiah Webbe, 18
Maynard, William, 14
Mckenley, John, 15
Merrett, T., 248
Methodism, 18-19, 184-204, 211, 216-217, 238, 252, 285-288
Methodist missionaries, 18-19, 184-204
Mills, Matthew, 14-15
Minvielle, Peter, 233, 234, 235, 236, 241-242, 243-244
Mitchell, Richard, 34
Modyford, Thomas, 66, 132
Monmouth Rebellion, 3, 134
Montserrat, 12, 16, 20-22, 201, 260
Morant Bay Rebellion, 57-58
Moravians, 288

Nankervis, James, 65
Napoleonic Wars, 86, 93, 113, 120, 272, 281, 284
Nelson, Horatio, 82, 101
Nevis, 12, 14-20, 101, 202, 260
New Sombrero Phosphate Company, 253, 255
New Virgin Gorda Mining Company, 242-243
Nichols, Edwin, 156-160

Nicholls, Frank, 35
Nicholls, Thomas, 65
Nisbet, Walter, 14

O'Neal, Charles, 240
Oats, Francis, 171-175
Oats, Francis Freathey, 173-175
Obeah, 201
Ojeda, Alonso de, 279, 282
Oke, William, 191-193
Opie, John, 42, 45

Parson, Edward (I), 20
Parson, Edward (II), 20
Parson, Edward (III), 20, 21, 22
Parson, George Webbe, 17, 22
Parson, Grace, 20
Parson, Mary, 20
Parson, William Woodley, 22
Pascoe, John, 113
Pearce, John, 222
Pearce, Jonathan, 213
Pearse, Anthony, 1, 2
Pedlar, Francis, 2
Pedlar, Robert, 2
Pelham-Clinton, Henry, 5th Duke of Newcastle, 249, 250
Pellew, Edward, 81-86
Pellew, Fleetwood, 83
Pellew, Israel, 81-82
Pellew, Pownoll, 83-86
Pellew Island, 85-86
Pengelly, William, 51
Penn, William, 33, 267
Penrose, Charles Vinicombe (the Elder), 89
Penrose, Charles Vinicombe (the Younger), 89
Perflit, John, 132

Perran Foundry, 233, 252
Perryman, William, 14
Peter (slave belonging to Mr. Halburd), 15
Pinney, Charles, 16, 17
Pinney, John, 16
Pinney, John Frederick, 22
Pirates, 67-68, 268, 295
Platano Mining Company, 231
Pollard, Thomas, 2
Ponce de Leon, Juan, 298
Pooley, John, 230, 231
Pope, William, 248
Pork-knockers, 158
Port Royal and St. Andrew's Copper Mining Company, 61, 65
Powell, John, 274
Price, Anna, 31-32
Price, Charles (I), 34-35
Price, Charles (II), 35-39, 42-45, 46
Price, Charles (III), 45-46, 52
Price, Charles Dutton, 54
Price, Charles Godolphin, 46, 49
Price, Eleanor, 51
Price, Elizabeth (daughter of Rose Price), 51
Price, Elizabeth (wife of Francis Price), 34
Price, Elizabeth (wife of John Price II), 36, 49-55
Price, Elizabeth (wife of Rose Price), 52, 54
Price, Francis, (patriarch of the family), 33-34, 66
Price, Francis (son of Rose Price), 54
Price, George, 55-59
Price, John (I), 35-36
Price, John (II), 36, 45, 46-47
Price, John (III), 51, 54, 55

Price, Julius, 243
Price, Lizette, 51
Price, Margery, 46
Price, Rose (son of Charles Price II), 45
Price, Rose (son of John Price II), 31, 49-55
Price, Rose Lambert, 54
Price, Sarah, 34
Price, Thomas, 31-32, 54, 55, 56, 245-247, 248-249, 250
Price, Thomas Rose, 35-36
Prideaux, Nicholas, 134
Prinz, Paulus, 283
Providence Island, 129-130
Puerto Rico, 298
Purfroy, Samuell, 1, 2

Raleigh, Walter, 279
Real de Santiago, 207, 208, 210, 212, 214-215, 226, 227, 229
Redonda, 12
Remee, Katherine, Baroness van Lamput, 5
Reyner, Anbitt, 131
Reynolds, Barrington, 86
Reynolds, James, 222
Reynolds, Robert Carthew (the Elder) 86,
Reynolds, Robert Carthew (the Younger), 86
Reynolds, William, 211
Rich, Robert, Earl of Warwick, 128, 129, 130
Richards, Jehu, 209
Richards, Robert, 51
Roberts, Bartholomew, 67
Roberts, Richard, 222
Rodd, Francis H., 208
Rodney, George, 87

Rogers, William, 113-115
Rooby, Martin, 2
Rose, Elizabeth, 34
Royal Consolidated Mines of San Fernando, 209
Royal Mail Steam Packet Company, 122-126, 243, 248, 253, 255
Royal Mines Company, 60
Royal Santiago Mining Company *see* Real de Santiago
Royal West India Mining Company, 244-245
Rule, Benjamin F., 177-180
Rule, James, 222
Rule, William N., 179

St Bartholomew, 199
St Christopher, 1-13, 77, 130, 188-189, 191, 199-201, 202, 255, 259-260, 261
St Kitts *see* St Christopher
St Lucia, 27
St Martin, 201, 253, 255
St Thomas, 123-125, 236, 242, 248, 253, 288
St Vincent, 153-155, 197, 275
St Vincent Botanic Gardens, 79-80
San Fernando Mining and Smelting Company, 209
Scruttons, 151-155
Seven Years' War, 76, 77, 86, 107, 137, 271
Seymour, Hugh, 87-88, 89
Simons, Edward, 222
Slave compensation, 16-18, 22
Slavery, 4, 8-9, 15, 18, 20-21, 29-30, 50, 51, 53, 123-125, 141-142, 143, 148-149, 186, 210, 217-219, 225-226, 274, 282, 288, 289, 292, 294, 299

Smith, Anne, 5
Smith, Thomas, 50, 52
Smith, Penelope, 9
Smith, Daniel, 5
Sombrero Company, 253
Sombrero Island, 95-97, 252-255
South Devon Regiment of Foot, 99
Spanish-American War, 102, 229, 273
Sparrow, Susannah, 4
Spry, Richard, 73-75
Staple, Mathew, 209
Steadman, William G., 203
Stephens, Henry L., 208
Stephens, Samuel, 208
Stephens, Thomas, 132
Storm van's Gravesande, Laurens, 281
Sue River Copper and General Mining Company, 65
Surinam, 139, 280, 281
Suriname see Surinam

Tangye, William, 220
Tayler, Christopher, 34
Taylor, John, 245, 249, 250
Thomas, Richard Darton, 91-92
Thomas, William, 222
Tirriby, Arthur, 132
Tobago, 10, 67-68, 128-129, 141-145, 275-276
Tobin, James Webbe, 18
Tortola, 8, 13, 32
Tortuga, 268, 295
Trade winds, 259-260
Trafalgar Campaign, 82, 272-273
Tregaskis, Benjamin, 19, 194-196
Trelawny, Edward, 36-38
Trelawny, Jonathan, 36
Trelawny, Laetitia, 41
Trelawny, William, 39-41

Trestrail, Richard, 219
Trevanion, Nathaniell, 136-137
Trevithick, Richard, 235
Treweek, James, 212, 226
Trigge, Thomas, 87
Trinidad, 143, 146-149, 151, 155, 190, 276-277
Truman, George, 239
Truscott, Thomas, 191-193
Truscott, William, 65
Turnbull, David, 214-215, 217
United States Virgin Islands, 297
United States Virgin Islands see also Danish Virgin Islands, St, Thomas

Velázquez de Cuéllar, Diego, 289, 290
Venables, Robert, 33, 267
Vernon, Edward, 71
Vespucci, Amerigo, 279
Vinicombe, John, 49-50
Virgin Gorda, 32, 61, 233-252, 297-300
Virgin Gorda Mine Adventure, 32, 245, 246-252, 300
Virgin Gorda Mining Company, 233-236, 242, 300
Virgin Islands, 238, 260, 297, 299
Virgin Islands see also British Virgin Islands, Danish Virgin Islands, St Thomas, Tortola, United States Virgin Islands, Virgin Gorda
Vivian, Sampson, 230-231

Wager, Charles, 70
War of Jenkin's Ear, 71, 270
War of Spanish Succession, 103, 106, 262, 270
War of the Austrian Succession, 270
Warner, Thomas, 261, 274
Webbe, Charles, 17

Webbe, George (known as the Honourable), 18-20
Webbe, George (the Elder), 18
Webbe, George (the Younger), 16-17
Webbe, Joseph, 14-15
Webbe, Josiah, 14
Webbe, Sarah, 19
Wesley, Charles, 184, 285
Wesley, John, 184, 186, 285-288
West India Docks, 146
Whitbread, Samuel, 96
Whitburn, Annie, 199
Whitburn, James (the diarist), 205, 214, 215, 219-222
Whitburn, James (brother-in-law to the diarist James Whitburn), 222
Whitburn, William, 216
White, Walter Grainge, 159

Whitley, John, 233, 240, 242, 243-244
Williams, Lizzie, 202
Williams, Michael, 208
Williams, Thomas, 207
Willoughby, Francis, 5th Baron Willoughby of Parham, 132, 280
Windward Islands, 137, 259
Windward Islands *see also* British Windward Islands, Dominica, Grenada, St Lucia, Tobago, St Vincent
Wolcot, John, 41-42, 44-45
Woodley, Bridget, 20
Woodley, Hester, 20-21
Woodley, Jane, 20
Woodley, John Lewis, 20
Wyke, George, 20